The White Generals

An Account of the White Movement
and the Russian Civil War

Richard Luckett

Routledge & Kegan Paul
London and New York

First published in 1971
This edition first published in 1987 by
Routledge & Kegan Paul Ltd
11 New Fetter Lane, London EC4P 4EE

Published in the USA by
Routledge & Kegan Paul Inc.
in association with Methuen Inc.
29 West 35th Street, New York, NY 10001

Printed in Great Britain
by T. J. Press (Padstow) Ltd
Padstow, Cornwall

ISBN 0–7102–1298–4

To my parents

Contents

CONTENTS

1920: Failure

Maps

The maps are drawn by John Flower

Preface

This book is an informal history of the Russian Civil War. Such a work may need a word of explanation. 1967 saw the fiftieth anniversary of the foundation of the Soviet State. Throughout the Western world appeared books and articles inspired by this occasion. Yet there was barely a mention of the Civil War or of the fate of those Russians who opposed the Bolshevik dictatorship.

It was in the belief that the omission was serious that I began to write this book. The two comprehensive works on the subject, George Stewart's *The White Armies of Russia* and Volume II of W. H. Chamberlin's *The Russian Revolution* were hard to obtain; furthermore, I disagreed with Stewart over matters of fact and I found Chamberlin's political views unacceptable.

Such condemnation was hasty and unjudged. Some of my objections remain, notably those that relate to Chamberlin's politics, but my admiration for both books has been increased by practical experience of the difficulties of imposing any coherence on the history of the war.

An elaborate apparatus would be presumptuous. To explain why I have preferred one source to another, or why I have taken certain statements by unreliable witnesses at their face value, would require a work of an entirely different nature. I am aware that, at several points, I am in sharp disagreement with many writers who have achieved a measure of popular acceptance. For similar reasons, I have passed over these disagreements in silence.

But I cannot similarly ignore those authorities to whom I am positively indebted, notably Dr George Katkov, Mr David Footman, Professor Richard Ullman and Colonel Peter Fleming, without whose work I could not have contemplated this book. Needless to say, they are in no sense responsible for my opinions. This book would be amply justified if it prompted the reader to pass on to theirs.

I am grateful, for prompt answers to queries and the provision of photostats, to the Librarians and staff of: the Hoover Institute,

Stanford (Wrangel Papers); the Columbia University Archive
(Denikin Papers); the University of Helsinki; the University of
Stockholm; the Cambridge University Library; the British
Museum and the Library of the War Office. In particular I must
acknowledge the assistance and patience of Lieutenant-Colonel G.
A. Shepperd and his staff at the Central Library, R.M.A. Sandhurst.

To M. Georges Chavasse I am indebted for the loan of a transcript of the Chatilov memoirs and for an analysis of discrepancies
between General Denikin's source-material and his published re-
collections. M. Chavasse has also been kind enough to provide me
with information about White material at present in Brussels.

To Father Paul Volkonsky I owe first-hand reminiscences of
Denikin at Taganrog and Wrangel in the Crimea. Mr Alexis
Voeykov kindly lent me copies of typescripts circulated in the
Stavka at Omsk which have helped me to assess the characters
of Lebedev and Gajda. The late Field-Marshal Lord Alexander
of Tunis was good enough to discuss at length the difficulties
experienced by British officers in the Baltic States.

It would be invidious to list here all those White officers who
have helped me come to the conclusions outlined in the present
account. Two I must mention, Mr Paul Denisov and Mr Alexander Lopukin. I have often disagreed with them, never without
profit.

I should also acknowledge the part played by my pupils at the
Royal Military Academy, Sandhurst – on whom some of this book
was inflicted in the form of lectures – in determining its final form.

Major C. J. D. Haswell gave me valuable encouragement in
the early stages. Miss Tamara Paulson made extensive translation from Polish and Czech, as well as providing assistance with
material in Russian. Miss Sue Limb typed much of the manu-
script.

I am also grateful, for suggestions and for the loan of materials,
to Mr A. H. le Q. Clayton, Mr D. C. Damant, Mr A. J. M.
Wheatcroft, Mr Charles Ressine and Mrs Alexander de la Haie.

All dates are New Style.

St Petersburg is referred to as St Petersburg throughout.

Transliteration is, I hope, consistently inconsistent.

Cambridge, 1970   R. L.

xi

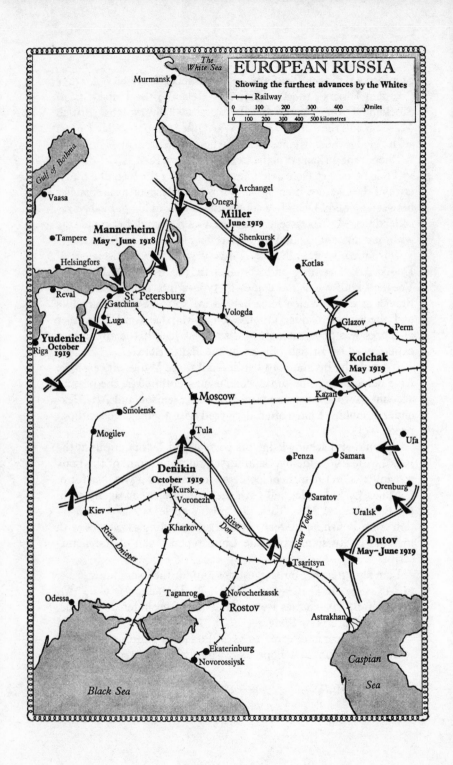

EUROPEAN RUSSIA

Showing the furthest advances by the Whites

Railway

0   100   200   300   400   500 miles
0 100 200 300 400 500 kilometres

The White Sea

Gulf of Bothnia

Murmansk

Archangel
Onega
Miller
June 1919
Shenkursk
Kotlas

Vaasa

Mannerheim
May – June 1918

Tampere

Helsingfors

Reval

St Petersburg
Gatchina
Luga

Vologda

Glazov
Perm

Kolchak
May 1919

Yudenich
October
1919

Riga

Smolensk

Mogilev

Moscow

Kazan

Ufa

Tula

Penza   Samara

Denikin
October 1919

Kursk
Voronezh

Saratov

Orenburg

Kiev

Kharkov

River Don

River Volga

Uralsk

Dutov
May – June 1919

River Dnieper

Tsaritsyn

Odessa

Taganrog

Novocherkassk

Rostov

Astrakhan

Caspian
Sea

Ekaterinburg

Novorossiysk

Black Sea

PROLOGUE

The First White General

As the summer of 1917 drew on it became apparent to many Russians that the abdication of the Emperor Nicholas II had done nothing to resolve the country's most pressing problems. There were few who openly wished for the restoration of the Tsar, but there were many who were eager to see the end of the Provisional Government, which had come into being after the abdication. The Provisional Government had failed to preserve law and order within the Russian Empire, and it was widely held to be responsible for the desperate situation of the Russian armies facing the forces of the Central Powers. Internal services had deteriorated, mob violence was a commonplace and in the army itself many units were in a state of perpetual mutiny.

Foremost amongst those who looked to the downfall of the Provisional Government were the Bolsheviks. Since their object was to seize power, they formulated their plans with as much care and precision as the circumstances of revolution allowed. They were not a large party – in August 1917 they numbered about 20,000. Nevertheless, because they had a clear aim and few scruples about methods of attaining it, they constituted a formidable force.

There were many other Russians who dearly wished to see an end to Kerensky's régime, but who were unwilling to contemplate a course of action so unscrupulous as that proposed by the Bolsheviks. Many liberals and conservatives foresaw disaster – in which category they included a Bolshevik dictatorship – if the Provisional Government remained in power. It was amongst these people, and in these circumstances, that the hope began to be expressed that Russia might yet be saved by a 'White General'.

By this phrase they meant a man who, whether as dictator or Prime Minister, might maintain order at home and lead the

Russian armies to victory against the forces of the Austro-German invaders. But the phrase itself had a definite reference to one man who, in the thirty-five years since his death, had become a firm part of Russian historical myth. That man was General M. D. Skobelev.

In Russia General Skobelev was officially remembered as one of the architects of the victory at Plevna, as the officer who had conceived and led a fantastic winter march across the Balkans to Adrianople in the Turkish War of 1877, and as a commander whose successful campaigns had done much to expand the Russian Empire in central Asia. In Moscow he was commemorated by a famous statue.

Unofficially Skobelev had acquired some of the attributes of a folk-hero. It was said of him that 'he rode to battle clad in white, decked with orders, scented and curled, like a bridegroom to a wedding, his eyes gleaming with delight, his voice tremulous with joyous excitement'.[1]

Born in 1843, he was the youngest general in the Imperial Army, a paragon of energy and valour. His troops did not admire him simply because he was fearless in battle. He was known to be the friend of the common soldier and he was widely regarded as the enemy of the more reactionary elements amongst the staff. He used his pay – of which as a rich man he had no need – to improve the lot of his soldiers. He insisted that no soldier should be exposed to a danger that the officers would not also face. Before important actions he briefed his N.C.O.s in person.

His appeal was not only to the soldier. A man of considerable learning who fostered intellectual pursuits, he had many friends amongst the intelligentsia. His outspoken comments on the censorship and his defence of the freedom of the press earned him the approbation of the liberals. At the same time he was able to arouse intense enthusiasm amongst the conservatives, for he embraced with fervour the higher chauvinism of the pan-Slavist cause. It was known that he criticised the court and his fellow generals, but his personal loyalty to the Tsar was never in doubt.

---

[1] Brayley Hodgetts, in the introduction to his translation of Nemirovich-Danchenko's *Personal Reminiscences of General Skobeleff*, p. x.

To his admirers he became a symbol of all that they regarded as being best in Russia; after his early death in 1882 he was held to be the man who could have saved it from everything that was wrong.

No White General came forward to save Russia at the end of the First World War. But, belated and amorphous, a White Movement did emerge. It was headed by General Kornilov, General Denikin, Admiral Kolchak, General Mannerheim, and General Wrangel – military men who embodied, or tried to embody, aspects of the Skobelev myth. The prolonged and bloody Civil War that these men were to wage lasted from 1917 until late 1920. (In certain areas it continued into 1921.) Too often it has been regarded as a mere epilogue of the ten days during which the Bolsheviks succeeded in concentrating the control of St Petersburg, Moscow, and the pale of European Russia in their own hands. This is only true in the most restricted sense; the war did not, clearly, achieve the Whites' object, but it has conditioned attitudes that we now take for granted. For the Soviet leaders it was a devastating and a formative experience. It influenced the development of their army, their foreign policy, and the structure of the party itself; it also acted as a catalyst on their internal struggle for power. In the spring of 1919, the Soviets were so hard pressed that Lenin was of the opinion that, unless the Urals could be reconquered before the onset of winter, the destruction of the Revolution was inevitable.[1] For much of the Civil War more territory was held by the Whites than by the Soviets, territory that included many of Russia's sources of natural wealth. Only in 1920 was the existence of the Soviet State secured.

Within the Soviet Union, the Civil War is held to be of the greatest historical importance. Yet there is a curious attitude, prevalent amongst Soviet historians, that the Civil War is not for export. This is probably because, whilst it left an irremediable mark on the Russian people, many of whom gave their lives for the Soviet cause in the course of it, its circumstances do not wholly reflect that view of the Soviet State which adherents of the U.S.S.R. are anxious to disseminate abroad. For the Civil

---

[1] Lenin, *Sochineniya*, XXXV, p. 330.

War was to demonstrate that amongst the 'broad masses' of the Russian people there were a great number who were inexplicably unaware of the part that Marx and Lenin had determined they should play in the revolutionary struggle.

The salient point about the White Movement is that it failed. This does not make it any the less valuable to ask why or how. One of the main reasons was that it was never unified, militarily or politically; thus, attempts to study it as a unified phenomenon have tended to get tied down in an analysis of the discrepancies between the various White governments and of their conflicting aims. This is a retrospective reading of the events, and a misleading one.

The common denominator of the different governments is that they were led by generals, and that the governmental apparatus, such as it was, represented a rationalisation of military dictatorships – the shapes of which were determined by the stresses between the actualities of battle and the political fantasy life that obtained behind each front. The significant factors, in each instance, were the generals: it is to the personalities of the generals and their manner of leadership that we must look if we are to understand the war. We also have to examine the army, the environment that conditioned the leaders' attitudes and outlook. In so doing we come full circle, for the behaviour of the army was a decisive factor in the two Russian revolutions of 1917.

1917

The Origins of the Counter-Revolution

That horse whose rider fears to jump will fall,
Riflemen miss if orders sound unsure;
They only are secure who seem secure;
    Who lose their voice, lose all.

Kingsley Amis. The Masters

We are watching an unprecedented spectacle:
revolution coming from above and not from below.

The Grand Duke Alexander Mikhailovich

I

The Imperial Russian Army
before 1917

Nineteenth-century Russia, it has been said, most closely re-sembled not a country, but a vast military academy. In garrisons and outposts over the vastness of the Romanov Empire the relationship of officers and men mirrored the paternalistic struc-ture of the State as a whole. The military and civil spheres were never entirely distinct or entirely independent. The connection between them was dangerously close. A failure in one was im-mediately reflected in the other. Herzen, describing Tsardom, was able to say: 'It is a military and civil dictatorship with far more resemblance to the Caesarism of Rome than to a feudal monarchy.'[1] Parvus-Helphand, the Marxist theorist who was later to master-mind the German attempts to foment revolution in Russia during the First World War, called the Russian state 'an Asian absolutism buttressed by a European type of army'.[2]

The geographical and racial complex of the Russian Empire was, indeed, largely a military affair. The governors of many of the border provinces were serving officers; most of the successes of the army in the latter half of the nineteenth century were achieved in campaigns against the tribes of the Caucasus, Turkestan and the Mongol borderlands. Skobelev himself had enhanced his reputation in this kind of operation. Once con-quered, the native tribes were only too willing to be taken into the Russian army, and showed for their new officers a loyalty and devotion long since out of fashion.

By the turn of the century the circumstances that brought forth the Caesarism diagnosed by Herzen finally began to change. The

[1] Herzen, *Sobrannye Sochineniya*, XII, p. 363. I owe the allusion, to-gether with several of the ideas expressed in this chapter, to John Bayley, *Tolstoy and the Novel*.
[2] Quoted Deutscher, *The Prophet Armed*, p. 105.

Younghusband expedition to Tibet, the various agreements over
China, and the course of events in the Near East limited the
policy of expansion on which Caesarism largely depended. Performance, too, had declined. In general, the reputation of the
Russian army was in excess of its actual achievements. Wars
against Asian tribes served admirably for training, but they were
no demonstration of the army's behaviour in the face of Western
armies and Western technology. In the Crimea the Russians
fought with great bravery but, having lost Sevastopol, they were
compelled to acknowledge defeat. The Turkish War of 1877 was
maladministered and clumsily directed; the eventual victory at
Plevna was accomplished only as a result of the help given Russia
by the Roumanians. Nor had the morale of the country as a whole
been satisfactory to the authorities: the popular enthusiasm engendered by the declaration of war rapidly waned when reverses
were encountered. The outcome of the final attempt at expansion
eastwards, the Russo-Japanese War of 1904, was entirely disastrous.

The most immediate consequence of the unprecedented series
of defeats in the Russo-Japanese War was an outbreak of rioting,
mutiny, strikes and terrorism that threatened to destroy the whole
fabric of the Russian autocracy. The Potemkin mutiny, the
Odessa Revolt, the assassination of Shuvalov (military governor
of Moscow), occurred within a few weeks. Infinitely more damaging, though less spectacular, was a series of strikes affecting all
the main industries. In the turmoil, the conclusion of a remarkably concessive peace treaty with Japan passed almost unnoticed.
The significance of military failure was more apparent in the
chaos of St Petersburg than in the minimal adjustments to the
Far Eastern frontiers that were the outcome of the treaty. Subject nationalities in the Romanov Empire, notably the Poles,
showed signs of serious unrest. The Trans-Siberian Railway became entirely disorganised and there were mutinies by troops
returning along it. Various towns en route were proclaimed republics. Towards the end of October all the main Russian cities
were paralysed by a general strike. In December open revolt
broke out in Moscow, but by then the authorities had begun to
regain control: the rising was ruthlessly suppressed.

For the causes of the Revolution of 1905 we must look further than the failure of Russian arms against Japan. Nevertheless, this failure was the agent that hastened and catalysed the process of revolt. The Emperor regained control of the country, mainly as a result of the work of his future Prime Minister, the former railway official Witte. The concessions offered to the liberals were mostly nominal, and many of the promises made to the disaffected elements in the State were never fulfilled. Yet a pattern had been established – not, perhaps, so obvious a pattern as that suggested by Lenin, when he subsequently remarked that 1905 was the dress-rehearsal for 1917 – but one which was none the less to be intensely relevant to 1917.

The break-down of the Tsarist autocracy in the First World War was accentuated and accelerated by the failures of the Imperial armies; but the ultimate collapse of those armies was made inevitable by the disintegration of the civil power. The Civil War was fought amongst, and with, the military and political débris of a world war. This is why an understanding of the Russian army of 1914 is vital to an understanding of the war.

The Imperial High Command was never particularly knowledgeable about its own army. Constant attempts were made by the General Staff to find out how many men they had in the field. They never did find out. The people who had to know were the foreign military attachés, and the outbreak of hostilities in 1914 was the signal for a desperate series of messages between the Allied governments and their attachés about the real capabilities of the Russian army. The reports drawn up by Major-General Alfred Knox, British representative in St Petersburg, provide us with an informed and penetrating view of the state of affairs. They are very different, in tone and content, from the despatches penned by the various Western newsmen attached to the armies deploying towards Russia's western frontiers, on whom the phrase 'The Russian Steam-Roller' exercised an almost hypnotic effect, although they knew very well that it was a cliché and a misleading one too. Of course, the sheer size of the Imperial Army was something to wonder at. Before it mobilised, on 18 July 1914, it was 1,423,000 strong. This was only a start; reservists were called up from the first day of mobilisation, and the process was carried out in an efficient and organised manner. By the end of 1914 Russia had 6,553,000 men under arms. Six and a half million men is an enormous number by any standards, but their effectiveness is dependent on their motivation, equipment and leadership.

It was a conscript army. Before 1874 it had been a professional army, dependent largely on compulsory and arbitrary recruitment amongst the serfs; anyone luckless enough to be chosen would have had to serve at least twenty years. Alexander II's emancipation of the serfs destroyed the social foundations of this system; his Conscription Law of 1874 underpinned the Imperial Army of 1914. Modifications had been made to it in 1912, but they were of no real significance. The law effectively established military service for all classes of the population. A few exceptions were made for nationalities either newly subject to Russia, or of dubious loyalty: in 1914 the former category included some Turkestan and Far Eastern peoples; the latter category was represented by the Finns. Ninety per cent of the total male population was liable for military service. They would be called up at twenty-one, serve three or four years on the active list, depending on their branch or department, and then remain on the reserve list for thirteen or fifteen years – again, depending on the nature of their original service.

It would be naïve to suppose that, in the case of war, anything remotely approaching ninety per cent of the males in Russia liable and of an age for service could have been mobilised. Vital industries, agriculture and other essential occupations would clearly consume considerable manpower. How many were required to keep the economy of the country going was a question that had barely been considered by the government. The absence of figures encouraged Allied governments to the wildest flights of optimism and the Russian High Command was equally prone to fantasy in this respect. The men who, as it turned out, had to be left performing these key functions were grossly neglected by a government that wished to imagine them at the front. The subsequent loss in political stability was disastrous.

The country had, in fact, succeeded in overmobilising. An army of half the size – say three million men – could have been better equipped, trained and led. Even given that the staff had to provide for the manning of a front line over seven hundred

6

miles long,[1] there was still no profitable way of deploying six million men. To a large extent they had been caught by their own propaganda: the mystique of numbers so influenced public opinion that a smaller mobilisation was, in the brief but intoxicating patriotic euphoria of August 1914, unacceptable.

The majority of those who actually went to the front served in the chief component of the steamroller – the infantry. They went because the Law of 1874 declared that 'the defence of the throne and the country is the sacred duty of every Russian subject'. They joined up in their hundreds of thousands when war was declared. Their enthusiasm was genuine, their bravery unquestioned. They died in their hundreds of thousands, and increasingly they failed to understand.

What sapped their spirit and compromised their morale was the failure of supplies. They were not given adequate artillery support – because there were insufficient shells. They were not reinforced – because the reinforcements could not be equipped. On a number of occasions, when reinforcements were requested with particular urgency, men arrived at vital and threatened sectors of the front without rifles. The failures at the front were often simply extensions of failures at the rear – failures of nascent industrial Russia, failures of the politicians who could not understand the priorities of war in the twentieth century. No one at the front could possibly remain oblivious of this; the expression 'rear' became synonymous with government and Tsar, and if men were sent to the front unarmed, then it became reasonable to believe in, for example, the treason of the Empress. There is nothing astonishing about it; the astonishing thing is that men fought loyally and bravely for so long.

Rifles were the main need, and pre-mobilisation estimates of the number required fell short by at least seventy-five per cent. There was no remedy. Despite purchases from abroad, a crash production schedule, and the establishment of new factories, the need was never satisfied. By the end of November 1914 the armies were at least 70,000 rifles short, and the situation continued to deteriorate. In 1915 General Knox estimated that

---

[1] The figure of nine hundred miles, often given, includes the front line of the Roumanian army and various areas not fully manned.

in the whole Russian army, with a front extending from the Baltic to the Roumanian border, there were only 650,000 rifles. A rifle was in the nature of an heirloom; having been moved up to the front, a recruit waited for someone to be killed and then succeeded to his weapon.

Another shortage, less apparent but more insidious than that of rifles, was of trained personnel. The total number of standing regiments, composed of long-service recruits, was very small; basically, it comprised the Imperial bodyguard and related guards regiments. Most of these standing regiments were cavalry. The Imperial Army attempted to operate a cadre system; that is, each regiment would be expanded with reservists on mobilisation. But reservists had had their annual six weeks' refresher training cut to nothing: it was an easy way for the Ministry of War to economise.

Cadre systems are, above all, dependent on the efficiency of the N.C.O.s; it is the non-commissioned officer who is closest to the men; he is the inculcator of discipline and the mainstay of morale. The Imperial Army's N.C.O.s were all soldiers of high quality, and they were, in general, of exemplary loyalty. After November 1917, despite Trotsky's efforts to recruit them for the Reds, they rallied in large numbers to the White standards. Those few who joined the Bolshevist forces almost invariably rose to high rank, the most remarkable example being Marshal Budenny, a former sergeant. But the number of N.C.O.s in the Russian army was pathetically small, and the lack of N.C.O.s seriously damaged the viability of the cadre system. The percentage ratio of N.C.O.s to men was, in the Russian army, a third of that in the German army.

The shortage of munitions and trained men did not only affect the infantry. Since the Napoleonic wars, the artillery had been considered one of the finest branches of the Russian army, and Russian artillery officers had for a long time been influential in the development of gunnery. Even in 1914 they could claim to lead the field in certain aspects of the science. Yet they were desperately short of weapons and ammunition, stock-piles of shells were virtually non-existent, plans for reorganisation and designs for new, large-calibre guns remained as projects and nothing more. Artillery support, machine-guns, observation bal-

loons, airships and planes, were all in desperately short supply.
Not only this, but Russian technological expertise was being
diverted abroad, some of it to Germany.

The one arm on which the Ministry of War was able to save
money without a consequent failure of efficiency was the cavalry.
Here the Tsar of all the Russians was in a position analogous to
that of a Roman Caesar; he could call, for his cavalry, on the
great horse tribes of the Cossacks.[1] One of the reasons why the
conscription laws for the Cossacks differed from those for the
rest of the Russian nationalities was that they applied, in this
instance, to a people whose business was war. Since the sixteenth
century the Cossack Hosts had provided a bulwark against the
Ottoman peoples who threatened Russia along the enormous exposed distances of her southern borders. The Cossacks had always maintained a distinctive way of life, and a measure of internal
autonomy. As cavalrymen they were excellent; born riders and
having remarkable powers of endurance. To a large extent they
were officered by Cossacks, and the ethnic loyalty implicit in the
regimental structure was one factor in the high level of their
morale.

For field service the Cossacks wore grey or green uniforms;
care was taken to preserve, in their uniforms, traces of their
tribal identity. They were allowed certain pieces of special equipment – silver-mounted bandoliers and belts, sabre furniture and
decorated horse trappings; these were the personal property of
the men. The fact serves to emphasise the difference between the
Cossack and the average infantryman; the former was often a
landowner on a small scale, and a spirit of independence was
deliberately fostered in him by his training. It was one reason why
the Cossacks were, with important reservations, inclined to favour
the White cause in the Civil War. Their fighting spirit should not,
however, obscure the fact that they were lacking in some other
requisite military virtues. If they felt that their independence was
threatened they would mutiny, and when they did so their regimental loyalty meant that they mutinied en masse. The chances

---

[1] It must be noted, however, that not all cavalry were Cossacks. There
were many line cavalry regiments recruited in European Russia and the
Baltic States.

of such a mutiny were, on the face of it, small. The loyalty of the Cossacks was taken for granted. They were the troops who were used as a last resort in outbreaks of civil disorder; they would ride down demonstrators, break up strike meetings, charge mutinying or retreating infantrymen; they had a culture of their own, a contempt for city dwellers, and a sense, nurtured by successive governments, that their own interests lay with those of the Tsar. But when, in the chaos of 1917, they were inadequately supplied, their horses lacked fodder, their orders were confused and contradictory, some of them did mutiny.

The other main Cossack defect was that, though admirable in their conduct of small-scale operations, they had little understanding of broader aims, and were, in their own way, as uneducated as the infantrymen. The lack of education extended to many of the Cossack officers. The consequences of this were particularly noticeable in the Russo-Japanese War. Cossacks failed to report back the results of their scouting missions, lost despatches that they were supposed to be carrying, and added considerably to the sum total of chaos for which the war is remarkable. After the war an attempt was made to improve the training of Cossack officers. In general terms it may be said that those Cossack officers and officers of Cossack origin who went through the requisite training schools were very good – General Kornilov was, as we shall see, an outstanding example – whereas those who were untrained, or untrainable, occupied a position much the same as that of a senior warrant officer in the infantry.

Cavalry was by no means the anachronism in the Russia of 1914 that it had proved to be in France. The Russian frontiers were too extensive to be defended by any system of static fortifications; the Russian army had to be prepared for a war of movement, and cavalry provided the only possible solution. The cavalrymen were given a basic, though not extensive, training in procedures – such as 'dismount and fire' – that were adapted to modern conditions. Their main weapons were still the sword and lance, the latter being much heavier than those in vogue in the Western European armies.

The nature of the fighting in 1914-17 meant that the cavalry were not used as much as the infantry. This did not, of itself, make them any more loyal – disaffection began at the rear. But it did mean that they were still more or less united as regiments, and that discipline tended to be better in consequence. Their importance in the Civil War cannot be overestimated, since the relatively small size of the armies involved, in comparison with the enormous extent of the territory, meant that cavalry were of the first importance. Many of the most effective leaders on both sides were cavalrymen. In this respect, at least, the Russian and American Civil Wars have a certain similarity.

In short, the Russian Army of 1914, from the wreckage of which the White Generals tried to forge a fighting force, was compounded of contradictions. It was vast and ill-equipped, but by no means so large as most people supposed. It was raised by a process of universal conscription, which implies a measure of democratisation, yet the men who served in it were the illiterate products of a rigid autocracy. The cadre system was so badly developed as to be farcical. The result was a bizarre mixture of the modernist and the traditional.

The Russian soldier was brave, but lethargic. The enthusiasm with which the crowds greeted the Tsar's appearance at the Winter Palace when war was declared quickly evaporated; so did the enthusiasm of the troops, yet they fought on. But their mood changed. In 1915, signs of laxity became obvious: despite the theoretical illegality of vodka since the Tsar had forbidden it at the outbreak of the war, by 1916 drunkenness was as bad as it had ever been. The justification for the ban had ceased to be apparent; the soldiers no longer saw any reason to desist from drinking.

Desertion became increasingly common; armed mobs of soldiers terrorised doctors into giving them sick leave and the requisite passes. Despite this process of demoralisation, the soldiers at the front did not become any the less brave, the line was manned through both revolutions, and many Russian soldiers remained under arms from 1914 until 1920. The armies of the Western Allies were at breaking-point in 1918. It is as well to consider this before generalising about the fighting qualities of the Russian soldier.

The officers of the Russian army had one thing in common; they were educated. Their education may not have been of a particularly high order, but it marked the dividing-line between officer and man more than anything else. Anyone with an education was virtually certain to get a posting as a subaltern. The fact that mobilisation revealed a drastic shortage of junior officers made this process inevitable. Birth, particularly as war went on, became of less and less significance. There were, in the Russian regular army, a considerable number of officers of peasant parentage – amongst the Cossacks, as we have already noted, but also in the regiments of the line. By 1916 seventy per cent of those training as officers were of peasant origin, twenty-six of bourgeois or artisan parents, and only four per cent from the nobility.

There is an entirely erroneous, but very commonplace, assumption that in 1914 Russia was suffering from a glut of officers. This is far from the truth. Of the three thousand generals extant, a great number were on the retired list and others were 'honorary' generals whose promotion was the reward for services in non-military fields. In fact, in July 1914 the army was short of 3,000 officers required for its peace-time establishment alone. The situation was not improved by the provision in the Conscription Law for a special category of volunteers, aimed at potential officers, who only had to serve one year – a quite inadequate time for officer training. Nor were the follow-up periods in each subsequent year of an adequate length. In consequence many of the officers who reached the army during the mobilisation period were hopelessly ignorant of their jobs.

The regular officers formed a substantial social grouping in pre-revolutionary Russia. Since in Imperial Russia the educated classes were a small fraction of the nation as a whole, regular officers naturally formed a considerable percentage of the socially acceptable classes. Within these classes they were, consciously, a caste, though not from any arrogance of birth. Rather, because the number of officers needed was large, and the recruiting base amongst the educated classes insufficient, a fair number of places at the military academies went to promising children of poor parents. As a result, the caste consciousness of the army was partly a defence mechanism, preserving those of humble origin from social stigma in society as a whole, and offering social acceptance within the army in return for the observation of a code of honour.

We should not, however, make the mistake of presuming the army to be entirely democratic. The Imperial Guard occupied a position of prestige in the force as a whole, and noble birth was a qualifying factor for its officers. Certain of the non-Cossack cavalry regiments necessarily demanded of their officers a private income, without which the expenses of uniforms and quarters could not be borne. But there was within the officer caste a greater degree of social latitude than has been generally supposed. One effect of this was to make the officers of obscure origin far more jealous of their privileges of position than those who were born to them. This probably accounts for the large number of White officers who originally came from the category under discussion, and it also goes some way to explaining the bitterness of so many left-wing attacks on the 'officer caste'.

In 1914 the regular army still represented the only possible career for many educated Russians. It has always been, in any country, a profession largely populated by those who cannot think of anything else to do – a somewhat passive form of motivation but, in a peace-time army, preferable in many ways to ardent enthusiasm. The problem is that it is not so acceptable an attitude in war. The quietist acceptance of the great military womb by many Russian regulars created an atmosphere in which the kind of abuses so prevalent in the field of organisation and supplies could continue for a long time unchecked. Moreover, in an autocracy of the Russian variety, inaction was easily regarded as a virtue. Another major generic failing of the Russian regular officer, closely related to this attitude, was his tendency to indulge in almost Saltykovian flights of bureaucracy. The infatuation with red tape covered a deep unwillingness, amongst many officers, to accept responsibility or to act independently. It remains, today, perhaps the most common failing of officers in the Red Army.

Tsardom was not a grinding despotism; it was not even very efficient in repressing its critics. It relied, for its continued existence, on a series of negatives, in particular on the lack of a viable alternative and the fear of a mass outbreak of anarchy amongst the illiterate. Enthusiasm, in whatever direction it tended, was treated with suspicion, even though it might arguably have strengthened the government. Thus, young Turks amongst the army officers were not acceptable to the government. There was, too, in the army's desire to keep itself to itself, to have its own courts of honour and its own social conventions, a certain latent isolationism, and this isolationism prevented the army from stating its needs unequivocally. When war broke out one by-product of this feeling, the tendency of fellow officers to rally round indifferent commanders and preserve them from dismissal, was to have the most unfortunate results. Criticism within the army was often outspoken and bitter, but it did not mean that criticism from outside was acceptable. As a consequence, though attempts were made to institute a 'hire and fire' principle for army commanders, it never really worked, and incompetent officers continued in important positions long after their inadequacies were revealed. The group loyalty of the officer corps also exacerbated the prevalent tendency to blame failure on the 'rear', the government. In the majority of cases this was no doubt justified; when it was not it only added to the atmosphere of suspicion and treachery.

A Russian aspiring to be an officer in the Imperial Army achieved a regular commission after attendance at a military cadet school; for a commission in the Imperial Guard it was necessary to attend the Nikolaevsky Cavalry School. The education at a military cadet school was general, within a framework of military discipline and procedure; the Nikolaevsky Cavalry School was a specialist institution concentrating on military training. Many of the various St Petersburg and Moscow high schools were neo-military in their methods and provided the necessary background for a young officer. It is worth emphasising the nature of the ethical training inculcated at these institutions, particularly as such training is particularly vulnerable to sarcasm and incredulity. The Russian officer was educated to put a high value on duty, loyalty and the attributes of what would have been called, in the England of the period, a Christian Gentleman. This is, of course, paradoxical. He was also being trained to kill. It would not be difficult, either, to equate duty and loyalty with self-interest. However, for most of the officers serving in 1914 these concepts would have been perfectly real and meaningful. Duty and loyalty were the assumptions on which an army was run; Christianity provided some kind of rationale for the form of government under which they lived, and it was a definite influence on their moral outlook. We may question the validity of these beliefs, but we must accept the sincerity with which they were held by many Russian officers. They were to influence their behaviour in the critical year of 1917, when, in terms of *Realpolitik*, these beliefs were to prove debilitating.

The military abilities of these regular officers obviously varied according to the nature of the individual. In so far as it is possible to make broad pronouncements, their degree of military skill can be said to be unremarkable. This was largely the responsibility of the Ministry of War, which curtailed the essential manœuvres and training in the interests of economy. There were provisions for the further training of officers – gunnery schools and a General Staff College – but promotion was by seniority on the Army List and did not necessarily favour the best qualified. The High Command was always subject to the whims of the autocrat, the best instance of this factor at work being the replacement of the Grand Duke Nicholas Nikolaevich as Commander-in-Chief.

The circumstances of the Grand Duke's birth should not be allowed to obscure the fact that he was a soldier of real ability. In the words of General Knox: 'though destined by birth to great wealth and high position, he devoted himself to the scientific study of his chosen profession of arms. His active career showed that he possessed the qualities of a real leader of men.' Of imposing presence, over six feet four inches tall, he became an almost legendary figure, and the common soldiers transferred to him much of that personal allegiance that they were not able to give to the physically unimpressive and retiring Nicholas II. The Grand Duke had the charisma that the Emperor lacked, and enjoyed a popularity admitted to even by Bolshevik commentators. His abilities as a strategist are difficult to estimate, the more so since he was replaced in August 1915, when the position in Poland had deteriorated and the Russian armies were in retreat. He seems to have had a firm grasp of the realities of the situation and to have reacted swiftly and intelligently to it; at the time of his dismissal he had just succeeded in restoring some kind of stability to the front.

As it was, the Emperor decided to replace the Grand Duke by taking over command of the forces in the field personally, and he made this decision in the face of almost unanimous opposition from his Council of Ministers. It was a decision based on misinformation, and taken at a time of general panic. Though Nicholas made General Alekseev, a staff officer with a high professional reputation, his Chief-of-Staff and – by implication – the effective commander, he had still performed an action that seemed to many to have served no useful purpose and to have decreased public confidence in the army's leadership. The Grand Duke had been regarded by the soldiers as a bulwark against the allegedly German sympathies of the Empress Alexandra Feodorovna; now he had been dismissed, presumably because of the Empress. It seemed the only possible explanation.

It had been the Emperor's intention to identify himself with his army in their time of need. He was, characteristically, unaware that this service was best performed for him through the person of the man whom he had dismissed. The only man unmoved by the whole business was the Grand Duke, who accepted his dismissal and subsequent appointment as Viceroy of the Caucasus with his customary stoicism and loyalty. Once he had gone the succession of defeats continued, and the popularity of the Emperor declined abruptly.

The Russian regular officers shared many of the attitudes of their colleagues in the other armies of Europe. Politically they were inactive, defining their position mainly in negatives: they disliked anarchy and leftism, but many of them also distrusted wealth, when it was not a function of the ownership of land. Potentially, they were a power in the state, but they were unaware of this; their whole training reflected the tacit agreements that conditioned so much of Tsarism. These agreements had been most precisely formulated by the historian Karamzin in a book[1] published in 1811. He held that the Tsar was an absolute monarch, but that he was, of necessity, influenced by Christian morality and respect for the privileges of the landowning classes. This agreement, in Karamzin's view, constituted the foundation of the Russian state. By extension a similar agreement could be

---

[1] Karamzin, *Memoir on the Old and New Russia.*

advanced in the case of army officers. Many of them were from the landowning classes. All of them received a measure of absolute power in return for their observance of the absolute power of the Tsar. This implicit bargain was the foundation of their loyalty, and after the December conspiracy of 1825, which was largely the work of officers of the Guard, no serious threat to the government emanated from the army. When officers did complain about the condition of Russia, they generally employed the formula that 'the Tsar was badly advised'. The formula was convenient, but little more. In practice their loyalty was considerable, though at times, as we shall see, they were unsure where their loyalties lay.

The reservist officers were generally inadequately trained. Contemptuously known as 'summer lieutenants' their brief appearances at manœuvres – always assuming that there were any – in over-new uniforms were resented by the regulars. They formed an insignificant category, since, if they had any initiative, they either anticipated their call-up and joined as volunteers at the declaration of war or evaded conscription entirely, which was easy enough for anyone of education. (A wide variety of reserved occupations existed within the civil service, yet few existed in industry: the exemptions exactly reversed the terms of the real requirements.) Most reservist officers joined up as volunteers, and the flow of volunteer officers continued until 1917. The influence of patriotism on the intelligentsia was strong, though many of the new recruits held political views that would have been abhorrent to the more conservative of the regular officers. They forgot these differences in the face of what they considered to be an overriding consideration.

The war divided the left-wing intelligentsia; but the political effect was far more basic than that. It has been analysed by N. N. Golovin:

For an educated Russian to avoid being sent to the trenches was not a matter of great difficulty; therefore, only those served at the front who not only professed the idea that the defense of the country was their duty, but also carried it into practice. A certain social selection was taking place, in which the lukewarm 'patriots' settled down in the rear, while men of high character filled the officers' posts. The Revolution, as it demoralised the rank and file, at the same time strengthened the determination of the officers' corps, and caused a sharp split between the soldiery and their leaders.[1]

The process, as described by Golovin, extended beyond the officer corps. Total casualties by the end of the summer campaign of 1917 numbered five and a half million. Casualties amongst officers were, on average, greater than amongst the men, and indicate that the morale of the corps was comparatively higher, particularly towards the end of the war. But the enormous numbers of casualties amongst the men must equally have meant that a potential source of loyalist forces was severely diminished.

The remnants of the Imperial Army provided the nucleus of both Bolshevik and White forces. The polarisation was accomplished by the events of 1917. It has been a natural tendency of historians to focus on the figures of Lenin and Trotsky, on the local events of the ten days during which the Bolshevik takeover was accomplished in St Petersburg. If we are to understand the Civil War, which was the decisive factor in the real struggle for power – a struggle of which the October Revolution was only the dramatised prelude – then we must look further back, to the part played by the army, the generals and the General Staff in the abdication of Nicholas II. The circumstances of this, and of the subsequent Kornilov 'revolt', were to be the kindling of the White movement.

---

[1] Golovin, *The Russian Army in the World War*, pp. 100-101.

II

The Abdication

Throughout the summer of 1915 the Imperial Russian Army had been in retreat. It was forced back through Poland, and several times it was nearly cut in two by the impetus of the German attack. Eventually a stable front line was formed, its purpose being defined by General Mikhail Vasilievich Alekseev as the 'safeguarding of St Petersburg, the nerve-centre of Russia'.[1] In August of that year the Emperor had taken over as Commander-in-Chief, with Alekseev as his Chief-of-Staff; in September they set up their General Headquarters at Mogilev, a provincial capital four hundred miles south-west of St Petersburg. There G.H.Q. remained until after the abdication of Nicholas II.

Nicholas was only intermittently in residence at Mogilev. The continuity was provided by Alekseev – who was, for all practical purposes, the commander of the army. Alekseev is an enigmatic figure. The son of a private soldier, he was commissioned after attendance at a cadet school. He fought in the Turkish War of 1877. Later he joined the staff, and for a time taught military history at the General Staff Academy. In the Russo-Japanese War he served as Quartermaster-General, and in early 1915 he had command of the armies that received the brunt of the German counter-attack through Poland.

Alekseev was far from commanding in manner. He spoke slowly, and softly to the point of being inaudible; but he inspired confidence. He got through an enormous amount of work daily, though he seemed unable or unwilling to deputise. His relations with Nicholas were good, even after he had incurred the displeasure of the Empress by telling her that he would not tolerate the presence of Rasputin at G.H.Q.

In his approach to his job Alekseev was, in the best sense,

---

[1] Hanbury-Williams, *The Emperor Nicholas II as I Knew Him*, p. 47.

professional. He was also loyal to his Emperor. But he was to discover that the two attitudes were not necessarily reconcilable. For even in Mogilev the disaffection that troubled St Petersburg was more than a theoretical issue. The aspect that particularly concerned Alekseev was the attitude to be adopted towards the Voluntary Organisations, for on them the army had largely come to depend for many of its most urgent needs in the field of supplies.

The function of the Voluntary Organisations had become so vital that Prince Lvov, who chaired their main committee, was able, in 1916, to claim that the government was superfluous; the country could be run by the organisations he controlled. That this was not so was to be effectively proved by Lvov's disastrous term of office as first premier of the Provisional Government, but before the event the claim seemed credible. Prince Lvov's statement also indicates with ample clarity the political nature of the Voluntary Organisations. They had come into being when the liberalising reforms of 1864 had made provision for the *zemstvos* which approximated to rural and urban district councils. These had expanded their original functions and during the Russo-Japanese War had rendered great services through their work for the sick and wounded. In 1914 they provided hospital trains, medical equipment and clothing. Soon they had set up what amounted to regional co-operatives, providing the troops with necessities of all kinds. By 1915 they had even taken over a large part of the munitions industry.

The political affiliation of the leaders of these organisations was clearly of paramount importance, and few of the leaders were men who were likely to be satisfied with the very limited powers that they were allowed by the autocracy. They were all, at least in their own terminology, liberals; and all of them were aware of the major part they were playing in the country's war effort, and of the contrastingly limited nature of their personal powers. They were aware, too, that they were on sufferance; they had no guarantee that they would not be discarded as soon as the war was over. Their utility ended, any hopes that they might have of effecting their political aims would be finished also.

It is often argued that the February/March Revolution of 1917 was spontaneous, a sudden and unanimous expression of popular discontent with the Tsarist régime, presumably triggered by an outbreak of mass telepathy. It was, of course, nothing of the kind, though it was certainly not a rising master-minded by any one person or party. It was a sequence of events, some related and others not, that was furthered by the failure or inability of the government to respond, and specifically by the apparent inertia of the military. Running through the sequence of rioting, lock-outs and mutiny is the unifying theme of a planned coup d'état that had not, when events in St Petersburg precipitated the revolution, come to fruition.

Such was the climate of the times that this coup d'état was a talking point for a great many people, though only a few of these had any active part in its preparation. Indeed, there may have been more than one plan, and more than one group, directed at creating a situation in which a coup might be effected. It was generally agreed that the main aim was to achieve the abdication of Nicholas II. It was also agreed that any government formed after that was certain to include various prominent members of the Voluntary Organisations and the Duma. Beyond that, nothing was certain. The man who actually got nearest to carrying out a coup, Guchkov, was a monarchist. Several of those who were anxiously waiting to exploit such a coup were republicans. There was a limited concurrence of interest and opinion: just enough to make the plot a reality.

Guchkov was a member of the Duma, conservative in his sympathies, who had made a speciality of military affairs. By temperament he was an adventurer. He had fought a number of duels, often on dubious grounds. He was also inclined to be anti-British and had taken part in the South African War on the Boer side. In 1914 he announced that his loyalty to Russia took precedence over his former sentiments – which indeed, could be seen as having been an aspect of his patriotism. He was completely unscrupulous, and used his knowledge of defence matters for attacks on the autocracy. These attacks took the form of newspaper articles that were in many ways more acceptable to the liberals than to his own party; Guchkov was soon to be found in the liberal St Petersburg salons. It was largely as a result of the contacts thus established that he became chairman of that section of the Voluntary Organisations which dealt with war industries. As chairman he had considerable executive power, and excellent contacts amongst officers of all ranks. This did not inhibit him in his pursuit of his political ambitions; rather, it seems to have been a means to an end.

One aspect of his unscrupulousness was a predilection for the distribution of copies of other people's private correspondence, usually on a large scale. He is believed to have done this with some letters written by the Empress and the Grand Duchesses to Rasputin. He certainly did it with various letters relating to Rennenkampf's contribution to the Russian defeat at Tannenberg. Finally, he used the method to ensure the mass distribution, through the Voluntary Organisations, of a letter that he himself had written in August 1916 to General Alekseev.

This letter is ostensibly about the order for a consignment of rifles from Britain, an order that had eventually been cancelled by the Deputy Minister of War. In fact, it becomes a bitter attack on the entire Tsarist cabinet, its basic theme being that:

> When you think that this government is headed by Stuermer . . . who has an established reputation as one who, if not actually a traitor, is prepared to commit treason . . . you will understand why so deadly an anxiety for the fate of our Motherland has gripped public opinion and popular feeling.[1]

The letter, in its circulated form, may only have been addressed to Alekseev as a literary device, a device that gave it a great and more incisive relevance. The question that was naturally asked, when copies of it began to reach cabinet circles, and eventually the Emperor and Empress, was whether the original of the letter had ever been sent to Alekseev privately and, if so, why he had not informed the Emperor. The letter seemed to imply that there was actually a correspondence, beyond this one isolated instance, between Guchkov and the Chief-of-Staff. Nicholas is known to have questioned Alekseev about the letter and to have warned him that he could not continue such a correspondence.

It seems that Alekseev denied to the Emperor his contacts with Guchkov. Exactly what he said we do not know, but it is clear that he was in an impossible situation. If he severed his connections with the leaders of the Voluntary Organisations he would jeopardise both the war effort and the régime; yet his

---

[1] Golovin, *Voenne usiliya*, II, pp. 167-8.

loyalty to the Emperor demanded that he should not continue
in a relationship which could be construed as treasonable. Whether
or not Alekseev received a copy of this particular letter is irrelevant; he was undoubtedly in communication with Guchkov, who
was now attempting to compromise him by the publication of the
letter. Any denials Alekseev might make, however much they
proved to be justified, would be liable to misinterpretation. A
rift would be created between Emperor and Chief-of-Staff, and
this was undoubtedly what Guchkov wished to achieve.

Ideally he hoped to put Alekseev in a firm alignment with the
leaders of the Voluntary Organisations and the plotters in the
Duma. This he did not succeed in doing. The effect of Guchkov's
intrigues was, in practice, to isolate Alekseev from both groups.
Though the Chief-of-Staff still officially enjoyed the Emperor's
confidence, their relations could never be the same; on the other
hand Alekseev was not prepared to throw in his lot with the conspirators. Consequently Guchkov had to rely on another general,
Krymov, as his main contact amongst the higher ranks of the
army.

Officers of lesser rank were far more accessible, particularly in
St Petersburg. Those attached to the reserve battalions of the
Guards still stationed in the capital continued to enjoy their pre-
war social importance. War-time conditions and the absence of
most officers at the front meant that members of the Duma were
coming increasingly to dominate social functions. Meanwhile, the
unhealthy moral atmosphere and prevalence of rumour and
calumny in some of the most lustrous of aristocratic circles gave
increased relevance to the political arguments advanced by the
liberals. Thus Guchkov gained a number of adherents amongst
the junior officers of regiments stationed in St Petersburg and,
largely because of the Russian system of separate messing for
senior and junior officers, he was able to ensure that certain of
these units would come over to him intact. This division of messes
deserves notice. It not only contributed to a lack of understanding
between senior and junior officers, but also allowed subversive
elements such as Guchkov a freedom of speech that they could
never have enjoyed had senior officers been present.

Guchkov's plan for a coup was intended to go into operation in
March 1917. A group of selected officers, including several of

high rank, would divert the Imperial train on one of its frequent trips between St Petersburg and Mogilev, and then compel the Emperor to abdicate. A constitutional monarchy would be announced, with the Grand Duke Michael, Nicholas's brother, as Emperor, and Rodzyanko, President of the Duma, as Prime Minister. Or so at least one faction of the conspirators hoped. The plan was destined never to come into operation; it was forestalled by the first Revolution of 1917. Yet certain elements of it exercised a decisive influence on the course that the revolution was to take.

In November 1916 General Alekseev left his quarters in Government House at Mogilev for the Crimea. He had been in bad health for some time. The Emperor had become concerned for him, and just when Nicholas had come to the decision that he must be given some leave, Alekseev collapsed. The doctors could find nothing seriously wrong. They considered that the best cure would be a change of air and a complete rest from the burdens of command. Alekseev's wife, who had joined him at Mogilev when he first became ill, accompanied him to Sevastopol. General Gurko took over as acting Chief-of-Staff.

It was natural to assume, particularly in view of Alekseev's reluctance to deputise, that his illness was the consequence of overwork. But in various respects this interpretation is inadequate: Alekseev had faced worse military crises in the past, and he had overcome them despite conditions of acute physical discomfort. His collapse, moreover, shows all the signs of being a nervous breakdown. This breakdown is hardly typical of the man. He shared some of the Emperor's equanimity in the face of disaster and, like Nicholas, seldom lost his temper or gave evidence of great emotion. By far the most likely explanation is that his health failed as the result of the strain consequent on the situation in which he was placed by Guchkov, Rodzyanko, and the other proponents of a coup as the key to Russian victory.[1] Alekseev's job was to win the war; his loyalty was to the Emperor as the head, and also the metaphoric embodiment, of the Russian state. In the fetid political atmosphere of 1916 every opportunity had

---

[1] See Katkov, *Russia 1917: The February Revolution*, p. 186.

been taken by the opposition parties to distinguish between loyalty to the Emperor and loyalty to the state; some of the criticisms that underlay this distinction were justified, others were not; some were based on truth, others on untruth. Men better versed than Alekseev in the internal situation of Russia were unable to distinguish which was which; but the issue of veracity had become, by late 1916, beside the point. Alekseev had to deal with the actual and threatened actions of men who were no longer interested in discussion of their motivation, and as effective commander of the Russian forces he was faced with an external problem that gave no cause for optimism. At regular intervals he saw the Emperor; at irregular but as frequent intervals he had to deal with representatives of the Duma and the Voluntary Organisations. It was becoming increasingly evident that at some point he would have to align himself and this, in as much as it involved premeditation, he was incapable of doing. The only answer to his dilemma, and that a temporary one, was psychosomatic: the eventual expression of his doubts was his breakdown.

There was to be no real alleviation of his situation when he reached Sevastopol. Whilst he was there he was visited by emissaries of the various groups involved in plans for a coup, who told him openly what they were plotting. They were anxious both to gauge his reaction, and to learn what effect he thought a revolution would be likely to have on the front line. Alekseev replied that the consequences could only be harmful to the army, and strongly urged that the country should not be committed to a course of action that, in his opinion, would rapidly prove disastrous.

Meanwhile, a related approach was being made to the Grand Duke Nicholas, now Viceroy of the Caucasus and nominal C-in-C Caucasian front. (The effective commander was General Nicholas Yudenich.) During a reception that he gave in his palace at Tiflis on New Year's Day 1917 the Grand Duke was asked for an audience by the mayor of the city. The mayor, A. I. Khatisov, acting on behalf of liberal leaders in the Duma and the Voluntary Organisations, told the Grand Duke that a coup was under consideration, that it was intended to ensure the abdication of the Emperor, and that it was proposed to replace him with the Grand Duke. After considerable deliberation the Grand Duke declined to take any part in the plot, arguing that the reactions of the army and of the peasants were likely to be adverse. It is noteworthy, however, that the Grand Duke is not reported to have dissented from the opinion that the removal of the Emperor was, in many respects, to be desired; nor is he on record as having informed the Emperor of the conspiracy.

The plotters received a more encouraging response from General Brusilov (C-in-C South-western Front) and General Ruzsky (C-in-C Northern Front). General Brusilov, so it was said, had expressed the situation with a clarity that the liberals could only applaud: 'If I must choose between the Emperor and Russia, I march for Russia.' The question was whether he had to make the choice, whether the situation as it existed demanded that the choice be made. Brusilov, the hero of the successful offensive of 1916, seemed to imply that it did. The dilemma that he succeeded in stating and resolving in one sentence was one that Alekseev and the Grand Duke wished, but would not be able, to avoid.

The Tsar must have suspected something of what was going on. The strength of the opposition to him and its ubiquity were demonstrated dramatically enough by the murder of Rasputin on the night of 30/31 December 1916.

Public opinion, alerted to the possibility of the murder, was openly jubilant at its accomplishment, and this jubilation necessarily constituted a defiance of the Emperor and Empress. Rasputin's murder in no way assisted the monarchy. Its effect was to emphasise its defects and accelerate its fall.

The jubilation that greeted Rasputin's death was softened into relief in the immediate vicinity of the Emperor. Even so, it revealed to him the frailty of so many loyal protestations and oaths of service. It must have increased his sense of isolation and even of abandonment. This feeling of solitariness, together with his conviction of his own moral rectitude, is the key to his behaviour in the critical two months that followed. For Nicholas, holding power that he did not ask or, perhaps, wish to hold, was always intensely suspicious of those who aspired to wield such power themselves – not because he felt his own position threatened, but because he conceived their motives to be venal. To him the notion of a constitutional government was inseparable from the reality of men whom he considered to be self-seeking and incompetent: men such as 'that fat Rodzyanko', as he described the President of the Duma.

After the murder of Rasputin it was remarked that the Emperor always looked ill. Paléologue, the French Ambassador, who saw Nicholas on 7 January, noted his intense and anxious condition and reflected that this

> . . . confirmed the idea in circulation for some months that the Emperor already felt that he was being swept away by destiny, had already lost all faith in his mission and in all that he did, had abdicated in spirit, resigned himself to imminent catastrophe, and was awaiting martyrdom.[1]

Kerensky, in one of his historical works,[2] even goes so far as to suggest that the Emperor was hypnotised and hints that this was achieved through the agency of the Empress. There is not a shred of evidence to support this view, and if there were any truth in it, it would almost certainly have come out in the course of the various enquiries put on foot by the Provisional Government. Paléologue's interpretation, allowing for a hint of *arrière pensèe*, seems much nearer the mark.

Nicholas II was in a position somewhat like that of Alekseev – also a sick man. But, whilst the situation in which Alekseev found himself admitted of an eventual resolution, there could be no such consolation for Nicholas. There is no reason for us to assume that the Emperor was a particularly stupid or unseeing monarch, or that he was unaware of what was going on around him: a great deal of information was available to him from one source and another, and he could not fail to take notice of it. His failure lay in the realm of action, and this failure is perfectly explicable. He had, at his father's deathbed wish, dedicated himself to the preservation of the autocracy. He was not prepared to grant a constitutional monarchy of any kind. Yet he could not, in war-time, strike at Guchkov, Rodzyanko and Prince Lvov, for precisely the same reason that Alekseev was unable to sever his connections with them: the war effort was too dependent on the

---

[1] Paléologue, *La Russie des Tsars pendant la Grande Guerre*. III, p. 149.
[2] Kerensky and Bulygin, *The Murder of the Romanovs*, pp. 57-65. See, in particular, the innuendoes on page 64.

Voluntary Organisations. Nicholas did attempt, through the police, to disrupt the various unions that were uneasily co-operating with the Voluntary Organisations. The consequences were muffled by the revolution, but the reaction was bitter and damaging. He could not rely on the higher aristocracy and the Grand Dukes, as the Rasputin affair had demonstrated. Similarly, the Rasputin affair had revealed (through the involvement of Purishkevich and Vassily Maklakov) the disaffection of right-wing elements in the Duma; it had also, indirectly, still further damaged the reputation of the police – though this, in the Emperor's eyes, was already tarnished. His final resort, so long as he was unwilling to make concessions, was the army; and the army was suspect, as his interview with Alekseev had shown. It was, in any case, fighting a war in circumstances that were never less than ominous.

In late February 1917 Alekseev returned to duty at Mogilev from his convalescence in Sevastopol. He was still far from well, and remained subject to feverish fits throughout the critical weeks that followed. His return was necessary if he was to direct the planned spring offensive himself. He was not at all happy about the dispositions drawn up in his absence by General Gurko. One of his first actions was to request the presence of the Emperor at G.H.Q.

Quite why Alekseev asked Nicholas to come to Mogilev has never been made clear. The telegram does not survive, and it is possible that there was nothing particularly urgent about it; what is certain is that Nicholas responded at once. Some have seen the telegram as a part of Guchkov's plot for a coup, but there is no evidence to suggest that this is so. It seems more probable that Alekseev wanted Nicholas formally to approve the new plans for the spring offensive and that Nicholas, anxious to escape the claustrophobic atmosphere at Tsarkoe Selo, was pleased for an opportunity of moving to the more congenial headquarters at Mogilev.

The situation in St Petersburg was in many ways inauspicious. On 23 February Rodzyanko had sent his last 'loyal report' to the Emperor. It contained ominous warnings of revolution: 'the country would rise in defence of its legitimate rights', if a constitution was not granted. The report embodied thinly veiled blackmail. The Emperor would have been the first person to realise this, and his reaction would undoubtedly have been to ignore the document. A meeting between Rodzyanko and the Emperor had been arranged for 13 March. By going to Mogilev Nicholas II avoided a confrontation to which we know that he was not looking forward, and out of which little of any value was likely to emerge. There is a further possibility that Nicholas may have felt a need to ensure the loyalty of the army, and that he imagined himself to be in a stronger position at G.H.Q. than at Tsarkoe Selo. For, though communications between Mogilev and the capital were poor, at G.H.Q. the Emperor was surrounded by an army in being, and away from the complex and fluid factionalism of St Petersburg. At 2 p.m. on 7 March, Nicholas II boarded the Imperial train.

He must have been glad to be back at Mogilev, where G.H.Q. and his quarters were established in the two white blocks, linked by a covered passage, of the neo-classical Government House. Beyond the buildings was open country, with a river flowing sluggishly through a wooded valley. In the well-heated rooms the Emperor could enjoy the sympathetic nature of the mess life that he preferred; in the evenings he particularly liked to play dominoes. But no sooner had he arrived than, on the 8th, riots broke out in St Petersburg.

The lock-out at the Putilov works, in unhappy conjunction with the food shortage caused mainly by bureaucratic bungling and inter-departmental rivalry, started a wave of general rioting. On the 10th the first demonstrators were killed. On the 11th the Pavlovsky Guards staged a passive mutiny. They refused to obey orders and cheered the rioters, but they did not join them. Their commanding officer, Colonel Ecksten, acted promptly and confined his men to barracks. That night he talked over a company of the mutineers and had the ringleaders put under arrest, but as he left the barracks he was killed. This sparked off the mutiny that was to transform the situation into incipient revolution.

In St Petersburg there were about 160,000 troops. They are often misleadingly referred to as the 'St Petersburg garrison'. But a garrison implies an organised body of men deployed so as to maintain the internal and external security of a town or city, and such was hardly the case in the Russian capital. The troops were reserves – mainly new and probably unwilling recruits, or wounded, fit only for light duties, or low-grade men unsuited for front-line service. Some of the so-called 'regiments' were reserve battalions or holding units, others were arbitrary divisions of anything between 10,000 and 16,000 men who had never had any corporate existence or seen actual fighting. The proportion of officers to men was grotesquely, even insanely low – about four to every thousand troops. Many of the officers were themselves only half-trained; all of them had been subject to the blandishments of Guchkov and the other anti-government circles; and Khabalov, the commandant of the city, was new to the post. He had no viable contingency plans for combating a serious uprising – let alone a mutiny – nor had his staff.[1] The Cossacks, on whom the authorities traditionally relied for dispersing demonstrators, had not brought their whips, with which they normally performed this office, since they were bound for the front.

That this state of affairs could obtain is almost incredible. The mutiny, if it had been controlled, need not have been more serious than those in the French army during the same year. Most of the initial actions of the mutineers were passive, and only the total lack of will from above made the transition to active insurrection possible. Khabalov himself fled to his home in the suburbs at an early stage in the proceedings. His staff, unable to find glue with which to post up proclamations of the measures to be taken against the rioters, allowed them to flutter around the streets. Relations between troops and police were bad at all levels. In the early stages of the demonstrations the troops acted mainly as cordons and had strict orders not to fire. The police, on the other hand, were already using firearms. The effect was to enlist the sympathies of the troops on the side of the rioters and to make them unwilling to open fire when they were eventually ordered to do so.

Though various of the St Petersburg authorities were in contact with Nicholas, and though he took, on the whole, a more serious view of the demonstrations than they did, it was not until 12 March that the critical nature of the situation became apparent

---

[1] The story of Protopopov's machine-guns, set up on roof-tops against such an emergency, has never been substantiated. It is pertinent to ask why, if they did exist, they were not used.

at G.H.Q. That day saw the effective collapse of the Tsarist régime in the capital. A few troops still remained loyal. One group was kept hanging around, totally ineffectual, in the courtyard of the Winter Palace; another, a cyclist battalion under Colonel Balkashin, held out in its barracks against a vastly superior force of mutineers who used artillery. Balkashin was unable to obtain any orders, and finally surrendered on the morning of the 15th. In order to allow his men to get out in safety he told the mob that he alone was responsible for the actions of his men, and was shot down as he spoke. On the 12th troops had begun to move to the Tauride Palace and put themselves under the orders of the Duma. Some units were actually marched there by their officers, who were now anticipating the success of the revolution. One of the more sinister aspects of the February/March revolt is the way in which senior officers, mostly commanders of regiments, were shot. Most often these cases were not traceable to the men under their command, and some of the officers were obviously sniped. The responsibility for the murders has never been cleared up, though the technique indicates the Bolsheviks. The effect, however, was immediate, and by the time the last loyal troops took shelter in the Admiralty building on the night of the 12th, their numbers had become derisory. One of the final sorties was led by Kutepov, the future second-in-command to General Wrangel, who lost most of his officers in his efforts to contact Headquarters. Finally, abandoned by those he was trying to aid, he had to give up the attempt.

Political moves were as fumbling as the military response. Nicholas II had made provision for the cabinet, in the event of trouble in St Petersburg, to prorogue the Duma. The Duma was aware of this, and the unscrupulous employment of threats was a contributory cause of its discontent. The decree was communicated to Rodzyanko on the 12th. Amazingly, the members accepted it and did not simply declare it invalid. It was left to a special committee to represent the body that was increasingly becoming the focal point of moderate revolutionaries. Hesitantly headed by Rodzyanko, they began to take decisions. It was to them that the Grand Duke Michael communicated his willingness to act as Regent in the event of the Emperor's abdication. At the time they supported this proposal, but from Mogilev the response was negative. On the night of the 12th the Emperor decided that he should return to Tsarkoe Selo.

The Emperor's decision was largely dictated by the weakness of communications between St Petersburg and Mogilev. Had the extent of the insurrection been known at G.H.Q., Nicholas might well have thought himself better off amongst loyal troops at Mogilev. As it was, he ordered General Ivanov to take the crack St George Battalion (comprised of soldiers all of whom had been decorated for valour with the Cross of St George) ahead to Tsarkoe Selo, where he would be joined by other picked troops. The departure of the Imperial train, which had steam up in the early hours of 13 March, was delayed by several final audiences. Alekseev, although suffering from one of his periodic bouts of feverishness, got up at 1 a.m. to plead with Nicholas to accede to the requests that had been sent by Prince Golitsyn, the fundamentally loyal President of the Council of Ministers, for action on the constitutional front. The Emperor's answer was non-committal and evasive. When Alekseev represented to Nicholas the danger of travelling from the security of G.H.Q. to the turmoil of St Petersburg, the Emperor replied that his anxiety for the Empress and his children demanded that he leave at once. An hour after the Chief-of-Staff's visit, the Emperor saw General Ivanov, who was making preparations for his independent expedition to Tsarkoe Selo. At 4 a.m. and 5 a.m. the two trains containing the Emperor and his suite drew out of Mogilev station.

In St Petersburg power was rapidly becoming concentrated in the hands of the Duma Committee which was already being called the Provisional Government. The Committee had named Alexander Bublikov as its Commissioner for Transport. Bublikov, a right-wing moderate, acted with speed and decision, taking over the Ministry and the principal stations. He was aided by the expertise of Major-General Lomonosov, an engineer who offered his services to the Duma – a typical instance of a process that was happening on a wide scale amongst more junior officers. Bublikov announced the revolution as a *fait accompli*, and used the railway telegraph network to transmit instructions and orders to the provinces. Control of the telegraphs also enabled the Duma Committee to receive reports of troop movements; they were quickly aware, therefore, of Ivanov's advance on Tsarkoe Selo.

This was soon to have an effect on the progress of the Imperial train. Trouble amongst troops guarding stations on the line and the uncooperative attitude of the railway workers induced the Emperor to order that his trains should double back on the course that they were taking, and proceed to Tsarkoe Selo by an alternative route that passed through Pskov. At Pskov had been established the headquarters of the northern front, under General Ruzsky; there Nicholas might reassess the situation from a position of strength. By now he was expecting a meeting with Rodzyanko, to whom he sent a message that he would receive him at Pskov.

Alekseev, still at Mogilev, had of necessity to give half his attention to the situation in the front line. He was, however, in receipt of what purported to be the latest news from the capital; G.H.Q. was acting as a clearing house for information, passing it on to the various Commanders-in-Chief. The picture presented by G.H.Q. was of a calm St Petersburg controlled by a Provisional Government headed by Rodzyanko. The Provisional Government was thought to be committed to the concept of a constitutional monarchy. It must have seemed to Alekseev that the threatened coup had taken place, miraculously, without involving him in any action. All that was necessary now was the Tsar's formal submission to a state of affairs that had already come about – he could either consent to elections, or he could abdicate.

On this basis Alekseev hoped to check Ivanov's expedition to St Petersburg. For if the capital was calm and loyal to the Provisional Government, then Ivanov's advance could only signal the beginning of a civil war, the immediate consequence of which would be the collapse of the front and a full-scale German invasion of the heart of Russia. Alekseev left the decision on whether to continue or not to Ivanov himself – he could not countermand the Emperor's order – but he made his own feelings clear enough. Ivanov, faced with the mutiny of the Palace Guards at Tsarkoe Selo, and the defection of some of his own supporting troops, followed Alekseev's advice – later to be confirmed by a direct order from the Emperor.

Alekseev, and through him the other generals, had been tricked. For Rodzyanko realised that his only chance of holding on to power was to present the limited authority that he did have as greater than it actually was; Alekseev and the Commanders-in-Chief, their confidence already sapped by the various conspiracies that the Duma had set on foot, were unable to see any chances of success in an effort to put down the St Petersburg mutiny – *assuming that an effective Provisional Government had been formed.* And since they refrained from repressive action, their complicity was widely taken for granted. Consequently, yet more units declared for the Provisional Government, including exclusive regiments – such as the First Cavalry Division of Guards – that many people had assumed would remain loyal to the last. But it was in this type of unit, with a definite social *cachet,* that the influence of the Duma liberals and of the dissident Grand Ducal circles was most marked.

Rodzyanko, his position in St Petersburg insecure, threatened in particular by those who supported Prince Lvov as future Prime Minister, decided not to make the journey to Pskov. There was an additional risk; his bluff might be called. Instead of going to face the Emperor in person, he contented himself with long telephone calls to General Ruzsky, on whom the burden of negotiating with the Emperor was now placed.

Ruzsky was in an exceedingly invidious position. One of the reasons why the Emperor had gone to Pskov was to take advantage of the protection afforded by the headquarters of the northern front. Ruzsky was, after all, a Crown servant owing direct allegiance to the person of his sovereign. By using him, in effect, as the representative of the Duma at Pskov, Rodzyanko immediately destroyed that relationship. Whether he had decided to side with the conspirators or not, as soon as he agreed to act as go-between Ruzsky weighed the balance against Nicholas still further. As it turned out, Ruzsky made strenuous efforts to be impartial; but this could not alter the psychological effect that his rôle had on the Emperor.

Throughout 14 and 15 March the negotiations dragged on. Ruzsky was maintaining a frenetic series of communications with both St Petersburg and Mogilev. Armed with the information and advice thus obtained, he paid visit after visit to the stuffy drawing-room of the Imperial train in an effort to gain concessions from Nicholas. But the small concessions offered by the Emperor would satisfy nobody. He was not prepared to grant any kind of democratic constitution and this, as Ruzsky and Alekseev realised, was the minimal demand. The Duma Committee were proposing that he abdicate in favour of the Tsarevich, Alexis, with the Grand Duke Michael as Regent. In the face of the Emperor's obstinacy, Alekseev increasingly came to see in this the only possible solution. Ruzsky shared his opinion. On the morning of the 15th Alekseev had a telegram drafted and sent to all the Commanders-in-Chief: in it he gave a picture of the overall situation and summarised the views of Rodzyanko and the Duma Committee. The telegram misrepresented the situation in St Petersburg, but this was Rodzyanko's doing; otherwise it was precise and well formulated. It ended by emphasising the danger Russia faced from her external enemy and pointing out that a swift solution of the problem at the highest level was the only course of action that would save the army from disintegration.

As soon as the replies were received at Mogilev, Alekseev forwarded them to Pskov. The three most important answers were those of the Grand Duke Nicholas, and of Generals Brusilov and Evert, all of whom had the high distinction of being aide-de-camp generals to the Emperor. The language of the telegrams was uniformly loyal and protesting; their content was also unanimous: the Emperor should abdicate at once. To this batch of messages Alekseev added a hesitant and somewhat convoluted one of his own. Beneath the deviousness the import was nevertheless clear: Alekseev favoured abdication.

At 2.30 in the afternoon of 15 March Nicholas II, having read through the text of the various telegrams, decided to abdicate in favour of his son Alexis, with the Grand Duke Michael as Regent. Later in the evening he saw a deputation from the Duma. The two delegates, one of whom – by a supreme irony – was Guchkov, had come to negotiate the formal abdication. Nicholas received them wearing the grey tunic of a colonel of Cossacks, and behaved throughout with complete calmness. The only moment of emotion came when the Emperor announced that 'up until three o'clock in the afternoon I had made up my mind to abdicate in favour of my son. But I suddenly realised that I was unable to part with him . . . I hope that you will understand

35

this. I have therefore decided to abdicate in favour of my brother.'[1]

Some of those present, once they had overcome the shock of the Emperor's decision, accepted it at its face value. Others, notably the more percipient of the military, realised the dangers. To nobody were the hazards of the decision more dramatically manifest than to the Duma delegates, Shulgin and Guchkov. When they returned to St Petersburg they were greeted at the Warsaw Station by a crowd consisting largely of railway workers – men who were already proud of the part they had played in the victory of the Provisional Government. Guchkov proceeded to read out to them the act of abdication. But when he came to the sentence about the transfer of power to the Grand Duke Michael the mood of the listeners changed at once. Uproar ensued and the two delegates had to escape from the station by a side entrance. The negotiations with the Emperor had taken place in an atmosphere of almost studied artificiality. There were large sections of the population to whom the act of abdication, as it stood, was simply an incitement to further revolt. This must have become clear to many by the time when, on 17 March, the Grand Duke refused to accept the throne unless offered it by a constituent assembly.

It is scarcely surprising if, even in the short perspective of the weeks following the Revolution, General Alekseev and his staff came to feel that they had been betrayed. Alekseev himself was the first to grasp what had happened. When he heard that the Grand Duke Michael had definitely refused the crown, his reaction was: 'What more can I say except "God Save Russia!"' The staff's most immediate worry was that, after the events of early March, the tenuous thread of the private soldiers' loyalty had been broken. Loyalty does not imply vociferous support of a government; it can be just as valuable when it is passive. Such a loyalty had been the foundation of the Imperial Army; it was destroyed, not by the St Petersburg revolution, but by the Emperor's abdication. Despite all the subsequent endeavours of Guchkov and Kerensky, the Russian war effort was doomed by the abdication act.

---

[1] Denikin, *Ocherki russkoy smuty*, I, p. 50.

This is not an attempt to exculpate the Tsarist régime. There is no acceptable justification for that government's incompetence and barbarity. But the liberals, in supposing that they had a viable alternative to offer, were not merely grossly optimistic, but also arrogant and foolish. The measure of their folly was the Bolshevik Revolution; and historians whose sympathies lie with the Provisional Government have only served, in their evasion of this judgement, to further the pernicious myth of the 'inevitability' of Bolshevik rule.

The first, and incalculably harmful, evidence of the weakness of the Provisional Government was in the hands of the staff at Mogilev on 14 March, almost simultaneously with the news of the Tsar's abdication.

III

The Army and the
Provisional Government

The document that so dramatically revealed the inadequacy of the new government was known as Order Number I. Stylistically it was unlike most of the other propaganda and revolutionary material in circulation. It was flat, unemotional, and to the point. In effect it was to prove the most inflammatory and divisive publication of them all, not excluding the Bolshevik Manifesto and the April Theses.

Ostensibly it was an order from the Executive Committee of the St Petersburg Soviet to the garrison of the city. It stated that all military and naval forces should elect their own Soviets (committees) and that these should send representatives to the St Petersburg Soviet. The Soldiers' Soviets were to abide by the decisions of the St Petersburg Soviet, and such decisions should automatically be taken to over-ride those of the Military Committee of the Duma.

It went on to provide that arms were to be guarded by the Soldiers' Soviet and not by the officers; that soldiers, off-duty, should have the same rights as any other citizen and should not have to salute officers; that the familiar second-person singular 'thou' was no longer to be tolerated from officers but was to be replaced by the polite usage 'you'.

The reasons for the success of the order are not hard to understand. The mutiny in St Petersburg had been the occasion for a number of acts of violence by troops against their officers; some of these acts were politically motivated, but others were acts of personal vengeance. The naval mutinies at Kronstadt and Helsingfors were both marked by the wholesale butchery of officers on a scale which, though it was to become all too familiar in the ensuing years, had the horror of novelty in 1917. These mutinies,

38

furthermore, were as short-sighted as most mutinies usually are. The political upheaval was their occasion, but their objectives were generally local – the removal of particularly disliked officers, the righting of what were often petty grievances. When some kind of order became apparent in the political chaos, or even when the brief licence of a day's rioting was over, it became obvious to many of the mutineers that, unless something drastic happened, they were liable to be held responsible for their crimes. No government could produce a new officer corps overnight; those who were already officers would continue in service, and they were the comrades of the men who had been murdered. Nothing was going to eradicate, for either group, the memory of what had been done.

Order No. I seemed to give the soldiers a measure of security from reprisals. If it was not, in itself, an insurance against such action, it did provide a blueprint for the measures to be taken if reprisals were to be avoided. For this reason it was welcomed and, what is more important, acted upon. For the Soviet Executive Committee it was equally vital, for it showed them how they could greatly strengthen their position in the coming conflict with the Provisional Government. Sokolov, the lawyer and member of the Soviet Executive Committee, seems to have been the instigator of Order No. I. Also involved was General Potapov, a staff officer who was the self-styled 'first revolutionary general'. It also seems likely that V. D. Bonch-Bruevich – a Bolshevik and close associate of Lenin, whose brother was a serving general in the Imperial Army – had a hand in the composition of the document; it would be particularly appropriate, for the order was to prove of immense assistance to the Bolsheviks in their seizure of power.

The order appeared on the night of 14 March. During the following days it was widely disseminated. Copies of it were made available throughout Russia, and its contents were telegraphed to the armies on all the fronts. Potapov must have made this possible, and in the chaos of the revolution little attention was paid to the authenticity of the order. In some areas it was represented as having appeared over the signature of Guchkov, the Minister of War in the new government. Some officers managed to prevent their units learning of its contents, but they were in a minority.

The Provisional Government, as yet in only embryonic form, was caught off guard by the order. Some members of the government accused their colleagues of having issued it. When a peremptory demand came from Alekseev requiring the immediate repudiation of the document, the government had no official line on the order, and delayed for as long as possible before denying responsibility. At Mogilev the General Staff was desperate: Order No. I seemed to preclude any possibility of a rapid stabilisation of the internal situation, yet only when such stability had been achieved could they seriously attempt to redeem the military position.

The instability created by Order No. I must be considered together with the instability that was the main feature of political life after the March Revolution. The autocracy had permitted the formation of political parties, but it had never permitted these parties to exercise any significant measure of power. Thus it was only in the proscribed parties, the parties that the autocracy had not permitted, that any adequate sense of discipline had been inculcated. The permitted parties, lacking experience of the responsibilities imposed by the process of government, but free from the shifts and necessities of organisation that persecution creates, were faction-ridden and intellectually frivolous.

Distinctions between parties were often obscure, frequently having their origins in differences between personalities, not in doctrinal disputes. In the circumstances it was natural that the main division between left and right should be implicit in the conflict between the Provisional Government and the St Petersburg Soviet, rather than in a divergence between two conventional political parties. Both Provisional Government and Soviet were coalitions, the former seeing its authority as based on the composition of the last Tsarist Duma, the latter regarding itself as the inheritor of the revolutionary tradition of 1905. Neither Government nor Soviet was a stable entity.

Bolsheviks, Mensheviks and Social Revolutionaries were the prime movers in the St Petersburg Soviet. But Kerensky, Social Revolutionary vice-chairman of the Soviet, was also to be Minister of Justice in the Provisional Government which was predominantly Constitutional Democrat. All the lines of division were blurred and the one truly distinct line, that which divided the Bolsheviks from the rest, was kept steadily in view by the Bolsheviks alone. Therein lay their strength.

The Bolsheviks, even when they were engaged in the brutal elimination of their Menshevik and Social Revolutionary opponents, were careful to present their actions as emanating from the Soviet. By this means they were able to retain the sympathies of the many whose political consciousness was unable to comprehend precisely how Lenin and his followers had come to power. The Provisional Government, which could not claim the organic revolutionary past of the Soviet, was fettered from the start by conventions imitated from Western democracies. It was impossible for any party to use it as the Bolsheviks used the Soviet because it represented, in itself, no focus of loyalty. Active politicking within the Provisional Government served only to accentuate both the weakness of the Government and of the parties that comprised it. When the White armies finally entered the field it is not to be wondered at that their leaders refused to align themselves in terms of the parties that comprised the Provisional Government.

Before abdicating, Nicholas II had signed two orders designed to promote the stability of the new government and to provide a bridge between the old régime and the new. The first of these appointed Prince Lvov President of the Council of Ministers, the second appointed the Grand Duke Nicholas Commander-in-Chief of all Russian forces. The appointment of Prince Lvov reflected the outcome of the struggle for power within the Duma Committee, and Lvov, as the first Prime Minister of the Provisional Government, can be regarded as having taken up his appointment. The choice of the Grand Duke Nicholas, though made for obvious reasons, was to prove unfortunate. As we have seen, the whole picture of what a future Russia might look like was changed when Grand Duke Michael refused the crown. Whatever emerged promised to bear far more resemblance to a republic than to a constitutional monarchy. The Provisional Government, made uncomfortably aware – by Order No. I amongst other things – of the growing strength of the St Petersburg Soviet, decided that the presence of Nicholas as Commander-in-Chief would be a provocation both to left-wing extremists and to monarchists. No sooner had the Grand Duke arrived at Mogilev to take up his duties than he received a letter from Prince Lvov asking for his resignation on the grounds that 'public opinion is firmly and decisively against any members of the Romanov dynasty holding public office'.[1] The Grand Duke Nicholas had accepted his previous dismissal by the Emperor without protest. At what he considered to be the slur on his loyalty to Russia implied by this new dismissal, he was moved to mild bitterness. Yet when he left Mogilev, which he had entered a few days before to the cheers of both soldiers and officers, he made no complaint, merely reminding those who remained that their loyalty was to the Provisional Government.

The government was at once faced with the problem of finding a new supreme commander. The minister directly responsible for making military appointments was now Guchkov. On a vital issue, such as the appointment of a new C-in-C, he clearly had to consult with his colleagues. Otherwise, he had a free hand. His choice for C-in-C was Alekseev, who would therefore hold officially the position which he had filled unofficially since 1915. To this appointment there was considerable opposition amongst other ministers, but it was eventually decided upon as being the best that could be made in the circumstances. Alekseev accepted the post, despite his continued ill-health. In a sense, he had no choice. There was no other officer who shared his knowledge of the military situation, since he was temperamentally unable to delegate responsibility. There was certainly no one who was as widely known and respected throughout the officer corps, and it was through his officers that he would have to attempt to give some kind of shape and direction to the war effort. Furthermore, through his contacts with Guchkov before the abdication he could be said to have the *entrée* to the new and incalculable government.

But this worked two ways. Alekseev's relations with Guchkov had never been precisely straightforward, and they were unlikely to become so now. Guchkov knew very well that Alekseev was at heart a monarchist, and though his own inclinations were similar, he was more interested in maintaining his position in the

---

[1] Denikin, *Ocherki russkoy smuty*, I, p. 71.

government. For, from being a snub-nosed and bearded conspirator, Guchkov had now become a snub-nosed and bearded Minister of War – and found that it made all the difference. His manner became abrupt, his carriage erect, and he grew notably dogmatic about a subject of which, despite his pretensions, he knew little. It was a condition that was to afflict any member of the Provisional Government who had to do with military affairs, and, since this kind of conflict between military and civilian was a novelty in Russia, it served substantially to increase the army's natural distrust of the government.

The government reciprocated this distrust. Other ministers shared Guchkov's doubts about Alekseev, and these doubts were applicable, by extension, to all senior officers. It should have been the first priority of the government to establish good relations with the army, but its actions, throughout its existence, had precisely the opposite effect. Members of the Provisional Government, Kerensky in particular, were subsequently to accuse the army of failing to support the government. What these men failed to grasp was the effect of their own failure to support the army.

The first public action taken by the Provisional Government in the military sphere was a purge of senior officers. This was a necessary and long overdue measure, but it was not the first priority. The immediate requirement was for action to be taken on the mutiny problem. No army can function when mutiny is allowed to go unpunished, least of all an army at war. Since the new government had, in a sense, come to power as a result of these mutinies, they clearly could not deal with them in the usual way. But they could have supported those officers who recommended that the troops in question be disbanded and re-enlisted in different units. This was a wise and reasonable solution to the problem. The government was reluctant to accept it for two reasons: its members were afraid either that the army would stage a counter-revolution once its disaffected elements had been removed, or that when the units which had mutinied were broken up they would resist and, encouraged by the provisions of Order No. I, come out openly for the Soviets. In consequence, no action was taken over the units concerned, and they remained an unstable and threatening feature of the new régime, equally dangerous to both the government and the army.

The Government's fear of a counter-revolution was to determine many of its actions in the months to come. Yet there seems to have been little justification for this fear. There was not a strong upsurge of pro-Romanov feeling in the army, nor was there, at this stage, any serious discussion of the possibilities of a military dictatorship. In any case, the army was too involved in the enormous shake-up that followed the announcement of Guchkov's dismissals.

It is in their attitudes to this reorganisation that the inherently contradictory attitudes of even reformist officers to external and independent interference with military affairs is most apparent. Baron Peter Nikolaevich Wrangel, a recently promoted general who was acting commander of a cavalry division in Bessarabia, was widely considered to be amongst the progressives, at least in his attitude to military reform. As such he would certainly have classed himself. When it came to the acid test of the Guchkov reforms, however, his loyalties were revealed as far more traditional than radical. Wrangel had frequently complained of the rigid system of promotion and the consequent high average age of senior officers, but when he saw a contrary system being put into practice he was appalled, and went so far as to allege that, far from improving matters, Guchkov's reforms were threatening to demoralise the entire officer corps. In the course of the shake-up Wrangel himself was to go up in rank, so it cannot be said that his criticisms were motivated by envy. Rather, they demonstrate the acute insecurity that many officers felt when the transition from the old régime to a new system became something other than a fantasy.

Guchkov was not without his supporters. Krymov seems to have been almost ubiquitous in these days, reassuring commanders at the front – he told Wrangel that the Revolution was 'the forerunner of a renaissance, not a disaster'[1] – or appearing in the Minister of War's office to advise him on some matter of policy. Krymov preferred largely to work in the background. Other generals, including Potapov, Bonch-Bruevich (brother of the Bolshevik) and the temperamental Brusilov were more open in their support of the Revolution. Their colleagues, in the main,

---

[1] Wrangel, *Memoirs*, p. 14.

considered them to be foolish time-servers, deliberately closing their eyes to the realities of the situation. The adherents of the government pointed out that if the army was not seen to be whole-hearted in its support, the masses would suspect collusion and an attempt to move towards counter-revolution. The traditionalists in the officer corps replied that, if the government did not effectively back up the army, the front would collapse and there would cease to be a country to be governed.

March had not brought the Revolution alone. Spring returned to Russia. At the Easter Festivals its coming was welcomed all over Russia, but the military implications were sinister. There were compensations, of course: in the hundreds of miles of rough trenches, where the troops were living under conditions that must have made the equivalent in terms of the front in France seem celestial, life became a little more possible. But the thaw and the first signs of new growth also signalled the opening of the campaigning season and the coming of the spring offensive. Before the Revolution broke out Alekseev had planned a Russian offensive; General Gurko had, as we have seen, undertaken the detailed dispositions for it, in a way not much to his superior's liking. Now there was no chance of the attack getting under way, and Gurko's staff-work meant that a number of entirely new formations were either in the front line or in immediate reserve – formations that were untried, of dubious loyalty, and numerically weaker than those that they replaced.

An offensive had, as a matter of course, been planned by the Central Powers. Its preparation was a straightforward affair and, though both Germany and Austria were attempting to wage war on two fronts, their task, compared with Russia's, presented no real difficulties. The plan provided for two thrusts into Russian territory, one in the north, the other in the south. The attack in the north was intended as a threat to St Petersburg. The immediate objective was the coastal town of Riga, and it was intended that the advancing German forces should be supplied from the Baltic. This would increase the speed and efficiency of the movement, though it also meant that it restricted it geographically and made its direction predictable. It was clear to the Russian staff where the pressure would come.

In the south the situation was, by comparison, fluid. The plans of the Central Powers were not so far advanced, and the local objectives were restricted to the removal of one or two unsightly salients in the Russian and Roumanian line and the preparation of limited advances towards the Black Sea. The long-term aim that was beginning to present itself to the German and Austrian staffs was infinitely more ambitious, for it involved a full-scale link-up with the Turks and a combined march on the Caucasus. This would at once create a situation which would make the capture of the Baku oilfields, which were of the first importance to the British war effort, a feasible project.

Both these lines of advance promised the Central Powers more than a temporary advantage. If their plans came to fruition the consequences would alter the whole complexion of the war. Within the German High Command there was, however, a basic and significant divergence of opinion. Some staff officers held that Germany had most to gain from a forward military policy, others favoured the benefits that would accrue from the negotiation of an immediate peace. The debate was further complicated by the lack of reliable intelligence reports on the Russian situation and by the extent to which the Russian political scene had now become shifting and unpredictable. If a peace could be concluded it would free at least three million troops for operations on the western front. This was obviously a desirable goal, but it had to be weighed against the possible effects of a clear victory in the east, the consequent economic gains, and the strategic advantages of a position that would enable the forces of the Central Powers to threaten India. For a peace with Russia, though it would immediately ease the strain on the German land forces and even make the occupation of France a serious possibility, would do little to alleviate the situation at sea. On 1 February 1917 a last and desperate attempt to redeem this had been initiated with the acceleration of submarine warfare and the switch to a policy of 'sink on sight'. By early March it was apparent that this policy would bring the U.S.A. into the war, though the United States did not make its declaration until 2 April. Nearer home, the Austrian government had become very unstable, and in April the swing to the left was confirmed by the elections. This, in itself, was a mandate for caution. If the British Empire and the United States were to continue the war, then the consequences of a continued blockade might still be sufficiently severe to weight the balance against the Central Powers.

The situation might still have been resolved had the Provisional Government given any clear indication that it was willing to negotiate on peace terms. In April and May the Germans made tentative approaches, though these were patently double-edged, being as much in the nature of intelligence exercises as serious proposals for a cessation of hostilities. This ambivalence of aim did nothing to dispel Russian suspicions of German motives. Such suspicions were deeply felt, and founded in the nature of the Revolution itself. Germany and Austria were both autocratic régimes, representative of that political position from which Russia had so recently emancipated herself. Though the Soviet made it one of its first priorities to issue a manifesto proclaiming to the world the necessity of making peace, this was to be a peace established by a brotherhood of workers. A peace with Imperial Germany would be tantamount to a negation of those principles on which the Revolution was founded. If the Provisional Government had manifested that realism which has latterly come to be regarded as the sole prerogative of Lenin, and had concluded a peace with Austro-Hungary, they would also have encompassed their own downfall; the Soviet would immediately have regarded the treaty as a sell-out to Imperialism.

Nor was the Provisional Government as aware as the German command of the devastating effect of British control of the seas. From a continental perspective a peace with Russia would mean the dominance of Germany and, that accomplished, the run of events could scarcely be expected to go in Russia's favour. There were other, equally urgent, considerations. The reconstruction of Russia would need capital, and this would have to come from abroad. The liberals had been at pains to establish good relations with pre-revolutionary Allied missions – notably the Milner Mission of 1916 – with precisely this end in view. The new government had been accorded recognition by the Allies with gratifying swiftness, and some of the speeches with which it had been hailed abroad verged on the rapturous. President Wilson distinguished himself with an encomium that rang far truer in Russian than it did in his native tongue.

In the fog of the internal struggle it is not surprising that the

Provisional Government was unclear about its proper objectives in external affairs. Had these affairs encompassed anything less than a world war the government might have had some chance of survival; in the event there was no such chance. Lenin, who had a spectator's view of the war from his Swiss retreat, was in consequence able to see the issues clearly. His solution, unpopular as it seemed even in his own party, was eventually to prevail; but it could never have done so had not the Provisional Government tried and failed in its attempt to continue the war. For them there was no option.

It was the Germans' uncertainty about basic aims, rather than the tactical processes by which they intended to promote such aims, that gave the Russian army a breathing space that was long enough for its affairs to have been put in some kind of order – had there been anyone with the authority to do so. As it was, all that happened during this lull on the front was that the emergent forces in the army became polarised. The Soldiers' Soviets established themselves openly, and became centres of dissident opinion. In self-defence the officers formed Officers' Committees to try to unite the officer corps and evolve some kind of policy for the army. In the first weeks of the Revolution there was a great deal of coming and going between St Petersburg, Mogilev, and the various fronts; gradually the officers began to discover what had really happened. In particular the nature of the mutiny had been kept from the headquarters at the fronts, and it was the mutiny that most worried the regulars. General Wrangel met General Mannerheim at a station en route to see Krymov in St Petersburg. Mannerheim, also a cavalry commander, was from a train that was travelling in the other direction, back to the front, and had been in the capital during the Revolution. He had been forced to hide for three days when the murder of officers had become the predominant aspect of the rising. News such as this, from a reliable and courageous officer, was not calculated to improve the reception that his colleagues gave to the new régime.

At the beginning of April the first Officers' Union was established, mainly on the initiative of two lieutenant-colonels attached to the Staff at Mogilev, Lebedev and Pronin. Colonel Lebedev was later to serve as Chief-of-Staff to Admiral Kolchak, so there was from the start a connection between the union and the forces that were eventually to emerge as the White Movement. Some of the Staff were opposed to the union, on the grounds that it could only serve to antagonise the Soviets still further. Most of the officers who associated themselves with the union agreed that this was bound to happen, but pointed out that things had gone too far for the officer corps to ignore the real condition of the army. Over and above this, the apparently haphazard attacks on officers both during the revolution and after, had meant that some form of mutual protection was necessary.

The various branches of the union had no common policy. In the rear areas, where the members came chiefly from the administrative staff or from the exceedingly restive reserve battalions, the general line was much closer to that of the Provisional Government, or even of the Soviets, than it was amongst the unions nearer to the front. It was precisely the insecurity of officers' lives in the capital that caused the St Petersburg union to adopt a line that played into the hands of the Soviets. Where the unions were most needed, where mutiny was most threatening, they were at their weakest. It is not surprising that it was at Mogilev that effective and direct speaking from the delegates to the union was to be heard. On 20 May over three hundred officers assembled in the theatre at Mogilev for a Congress of Officers, held under the auspices of the union.

The period between the abdication and the opening of the congress had seen no increase in the stability of the government. Indeed, the arrival of Lenin at the Finland Station on 16 April constituted the greatest threat to the government's existence that it had yet encountered, and it had proved powerless to do anything about it. For the moment, Lenin was ahead of events: that this was so cannot be better demonstrated than by Sukhanov's anecdote about the soldiers. Troops had come in crowds to greet the returning exile, and they seemed to be amongst his most enthusiastic supporters. But when Lenin began to harangue them about the necessity for an immediate peace, they started to mutter disagreement and even, so Sukhanov alleges, threatened to 'lift Lenin on their bayonets'.[1] And it was true that, for a time, there

---

[1] Sukhanov, *The Russian Revolution 1917*, p. 276.

was apparently widespread support for the continuation of the war or at any rate for some course of action that would obviate the necessity of signing the immediate peace which Lenin advocated. The country was divided not between a peace party and a war party, but between a war party and a 'defensist party', the latter believing that a compromise solution was possible: the army would defend itself, but would not attack. The absurdity of this scheme was apparent both to the officer corps (or at least most of it) and to Lenin; it was seriously considered only amongst those who were hallucinated by the entire unreality of the Revolution. Yet this class of person was so prevalent as to seem at times to be in the majority.

One of the first acts of the Provisional Government had been to abolish the death penalty. This had made desertion from the army an infinitely attractive possibility. The Germans were likely to shoot you if you went to the front, so why not simply refuse to go, and desert? The Revolution had so disorganised the administrative machinery that there was a good chance a soldier's absence would be overlooked; there were political organisations prepared to provide soldiers with documents and cover. In April the government made it all even easier by the simple expedient of abolishing the police. If you were unlucky enough to be caught, then the worst that could happen to you was a period of imprisonment, and that might well be ended before long by a general amnesty.

The flood of desertions now threatened to render Russia's army incapable of performing the Defensists' favourite manœuvre, 'protecting itself', let alone of actually attacking the enemy.

Furthermore, the premature announcement of land reforms meant that every peasant wanted to be back in his native village, ready to grab when the promised legislation came into force. In some parts of the country the process was already beginning, in anticipation of the proposed moves by the government. In the towns, where the Soldiers' Soviets were being backed by the local Workers' Soviets, military discipline had become a thing of the past. Sunflower seeds, chewed by the soldiers and then spat out, lay everywhere, testimony to the aimless but ominous crowds that lounged around the streets and squares.

That a semblance of discipline was maintained in front-line

areas is largely attributable to Alekseev. This short man, with his grey handlebar moustache and his close-cropped hair, had begun to reveal qualities that his intimates – in so far as so reserved a man as the General could be said to have had any – had hitherto only dimly suspected. Perhaps it was his experience teaching at the Staff College that helped him now, that had given him his ability to argue a point without ever losing his temper, to pursue an argument doggedly despite the disinclination of his audience to listen, and to remain absolutely adamant in his attitude to certain central topics. Faced with the 'new men' of the Revolution, many of his more junior colleagues were inclined either to dissimulate an enthusiasm entirely foreign to their natures, or to lose their tempers and refuse to accept that the Revolution had happened. This was never so with Alekseev. There was little that he could actually do in the situation which he confronted; but he managed to set an example of calmness and reasonableness which meant that some kind of stability was retained at the front. It was behind the shield he upheld that all the bickering and the futile debating went on.

The Mogilev Congress was convened on the understanding that the High Command should not be involved. Neither Alekseev nor his Chief-of-Staff, Denikin, wished to be connected with a meeting that was evidently going to be interpreted as a political provocation, even though it was not intended directly as such. Yet, as the date fixed for the meeting drew nearer, it became apparent that the senior officers could hardly avoid putting their point of view. Endless discussions with representatives of the government had achieved nothing. Only a firm statement, supported by the officer corps as a body, could make any impression on the country. Such a statement was made by Alekseev on the first day of the meeting.

Various things made this possible. A meeting between the Commanders-in-Chief and the leaders of the government, held three days before the conference opened, had resulted in deadlock. Alekseev must have realised that he would shortly be relieved of his post. Guchkov had been openly expressing his disgust with the policies of his colleagues in the cabinet. Finally, on 12 May he had resigned, officially because of ill-health but in fact because even his compromise position had become impossible. Guchkov had become aware that there was nothing that he could do to halt the leftwards trend of the government. Almost all the measures that he – a conservative – had put through, had been socialist in their implications. Now he was faced with the necessity of approving a document that promised to be as harmful as Order No. I. This was the so-called Declaration of the Rights of the Soldier, a manifesto which had been drawn up by the same General Polivanov who had been one of the figures associated with the authorship of Order No. I. The Declaration provided for the free expression of political opinion in the army, and the abolition of orderlies, salutes, and arbitrary punishments; it could only accelerate the process of disintegration.

Guchkov was resolutely opposed to this extraordinary piece of legislation – for the declaration was to have the authority of law. But his deputy, Kerensky, was fervently in favour of it, commenting: 'Let the freest army and navy in the world prove that there is strength and not weakness in liberty.'[1] Kerensky's enthusiasm served him well in the short term, for it was he who was appointed to succeed Guchkov. Whether it profited him in the long term is more dubious.

Rumours of the Declaration had reached Mogilev as soon as Polivanov's committee began work on it and had been greeted with incredulity. But Guchkov's resignation served as a danger signal, and though the Declaration was not officially issued until 22 May, two days after the opening of the Mogilev Congress, its substance was known before then. This merely confirmed the opinion of Kerensky prevalent amongst the officer corps. Kerensky had been the only member of the Provisional Government to command any support within the Soviet: to the government he was useful as a link between the two organisations, though he was at the same time regarded as politically suspect. This opinion prevailed, to a much greater degree, amongst the officers. Alekseev called him a 'political juggler',[2] and it was a milder description than others that were bandied around the mess at Mogilev.

---

[1] Denikin, *Ocherki russkoy smuty*, I, part 2, p. 46.
[2] Posthumously discovered note-book; quoted in Knox, *With the Russian Army 1914-17*, II, p. 679.

It was obvious, even before the publication of the Declaration, that the time for plain speaking had come. Hence the decision of the Commander-in-Chief to appear at the Officers' Congress. When Alekseev rose to speak, to the applause of the officers and the deliberately disdainful silence of the representatives from the Soldiers' Soviets who lolled in the boxes of the little theatre, he made no pretence at caution. His message was simple: unless the country united behind the army and gave it their full support, Russia was bound to be conquered by the Germans. The army, or what was left of it, could not hold out much longer. The officers were the only class of the Russian people who had not, so far, asked anything for themselves. They wanted neither more pay, nor shorter hours, nor less danger. All that they required from the government was a mandate for the exercise of authority; only by the exercise of such authority could they hope to win the war. Officers had different political opinions, just as civilians did. Within the army there was as much diversity of opinion as there was outside it about what form the future Russia should take. But this was beside the point. What was needed for the present was the repeal of the legislation that had made the proper conduct of the war impossible. The death penalty had to come back, the Soldiers' Soviets had to be controlled, and political differences had to be forgotten. As the voting was to demonstrate, there was hardly a delegate there who did not agree with these propositions. The Commander-in-Chief's speech was only echoed and amplified in the meetings that followed. Over the conference hung the threat of Alekseev's words: 'Russia is dying. She stands on the edge of an abyss. A few more shocks, and she will crash with all her weight into it.'[1]

From their seats the representatives of the Soviets looked down without comment. They had nothing to say in all this, and few attitudes beyond a generic dislike of officers and a hypersensitivity to imagined counter-revolution. Officer after officer got up and affirmed his loyalty to the Revolution, but this made no impression on the observers or on the reports that were sent back to the government and the St Petersburg Soviet. To the

---

[1] Alekseev also used the phrase at a conference of Commanders-in-Chief. Denikin, *Ocherki russkoy smuty*, I, part 2, p. 108.

observers there was only one possible interpretation of the officers' aims.

Another man who was watching the progress of the conference with interest was Kerensky, the new Minister of War. On 24 May he passed through Mogilev on a self-appointed mission to raise the morale of troops on the south-western front, and he took the opportunity to sound out senior officers about their attitudes to Alekseev. The Commander-in-Chief he deliberately avoided. On 2 June Kerensky was in Mogilev again, having returned from his tour of the front. To those members of the staff with whom he talked he gave glowing reports of the conduct of General Brusilov, who was commanding that sector. It can have come as no surprise to Alekseev that, on the 4th, he received a telegram from the government dismissing him from his post. When he read this curt order Alekseev who, despite repeated recurrences of his fever, had endured so much for so long, broke into tears. General Brusilov was named as his successor.

Before he left Mogilev, Alekseev paid his final respects to the men who, through the Revolution and the subsequent unrest, had served him with such loyalty. To his Chief-of-Staff, Denikin, with whom he had had stormy passages in the past but who had now become one of his most devoted colleagues, he said: 'All this will collapse before long. You will have to start your work all over again. Would you then be prepared to work with me?'[1] Denikin agreed, though he had no means of telling then in what circumstances they would once more collaborate.

Alekseev heard the news of his dismissal in the early hours of 4 June. Later that day the Officers' Congress met for its final session. Alekseev was to have addressed the assembled delegates, but this he could not bring himself to do. Denikin spoke in his place, and he caused an immense sensation. He affirmed, in stirring words, the achievement of the Revolution, and then went on to accuse the government of letting down the officers who were guarding the new state. The officers, Denikin said, would continue to do their duty, if necessary until they were killed. But if they did not receive the support that they so desperately needed, then it was possible that 'the Russian state would perish with them.

---

[1] Denikin, *Ocherki russkoy smuty*, I, part 2, p. 148.

His listeners must have found ample evidence in recent events to support his views. On 17 May Trotsky, the hero of the Soviet in the rising of 1905, had returned to Russia. Almost simultaneously with the Mogilev Congress a parallel meeting of officers in St Petersburg had voted in, by a narrow majority, proposals that accorded with the wishes of the Soviet. The delegates at this meeting were administrators and reserve officers rather than front-line soldiers, but their decisions, because they were made in the capital, carried far more weight with the general public than did those of the men who were direct from active service.

Brusilov, the new Commander-in-Chief, was of greater repute in civilian than in military circles. At Mogilev it was felt that his part in the successful offensive of 1916 had been grossly exaggerated by official propaganda, in an effort to counteract growing gloom about the progress of the war. Now he was profiting by what had been Tsarist propaganda to become Commander-in-Chief of the Provisional Government's army. The unreality created by one régime was being accepted at its face value by another. Brusilov had capitalised on this by his behaviour in the early days of the revolution. He had adopted an exaggeratedly egalitarian pose, and dismissed out of hand any officers whom he considered to have been too attached to the old régime, or, it was said at Mogilev, who had threatened his position through their professional competence. Amongst the men sacked by Brusilov was General Kaledin, an able, if conservative, officer, of whom we shall hear again. Another was General Yudenich, and it is one of the curiosities of the inter-revolutionary period that Brusilov's reason for dismissing this future arch-reactionary was that he was too inclined to favour the Soldiers' Soviets.

Outside the officer corps the new combination of Kerensky as Minister of War and Brusilov as Commander-in-Chief was hailed as though it was the answer to all Russia's military problems. Nothing could have been further from the truth. Kerensky had made his reputation as a revolutionary politician; it was widely assumed (though not by the Bolsheviks) that he had accepted office in the Provisional Government only as a tactical move, and that his real sympathies lay with the Soviets. This, together with the acquiescence of Brusilov, caused the Soldiers' Soviets to grow doubly confident. The officer corps, now further enraged by the appointment of political commissaries, or Commissars, to each army and regiment, lost what vestiges of confidence in the intentions of the government they had previously possessed. Interference by the Soldiers' Soviets in purely military matters, in tactics and technical organisation, was threatening to wreck what offensive power the army still retained. The political commissaries were treating attempts by commanders to restore discipline in their units as tantamount to subversion. The effects of the Declaration of Soldiers' Rights were now being widely felt, and indiscipline was spreading even to the front.

It was against this background that Kerensky decided to mount an offensive. The attack was scheduled to begin at the end of June. This operation, the Kerensky Offensive, was the culmination of the fantasy existence from which the members of the Provisional Government were never really to free themselves. In Kerensky they had found the master fantasist, an orator who could create, through his speeches, a miasma that would engulf a whole land.

Kerensky had a sense of history, even if he was devoid of any sense of historical objectivity. In a confused way he had become aware of the parallels between the Russian Revolution and the French Revolution of 1789. The army of Revolutionary Russia would be the spiritual descendant of the first of the citizen armies, and would emulate its achievements. Out of the revolutionary fog came a clear message: 'Victory'. But what was not specified was how this was to be attained. Kerensky, dressed in the tunic of a private soldier, his arm ostentatiously in a sling – bursitis, rather than a wound, was his particular affliction – would mount whatever eminence was near to hand and harangue the crowds or the troops. The amazing thing was that his impassioned oratory had an effect. It engendered a maximum of immediate enthusiasm and a minimum of serious endeavour. Women enthused over him, the troops roared their approval of him, but it all meant nothing. Much of what he said was counter-productive. He asked for a victory over the Germans, and his audience took his words as a plea for the total victory of the Revolution at home. He spoke of liberty, meaning freedom from the German oppressor, and the soldiers translated this as meaning freedom from discipline. It was all impassioned, exhilarating, and pointless. There were times when Kerensky felt this, when he would collapse of nervous exhaustion, demand the bottle of valerian on which he was dependent to keep him going, or ask his aides, when representatives of the Soldiers' Soviets came crowding round him with petitions and grievances, 'Why can't you send them all to hell?' At the same time there is little doubt that Kerensky loved to feel an audience held by his oratory, loved the sensation of power. Sometimes he seemed entirely to be playing for effect, posing himself before the imagined cameras of an Abel Gance. He was always ready to forsake an essential committee for a mass meeting, to neglect serious planning for the sake of a few minutes of fraught empathy with an amorphous crowd.

It was because he was dependent on empathy, on telling the crowd what it wanted to hear rather than what he wanted it to hear, because his relationship with the people was essentially feminine, that he was never able to take any of the positive and needful steps that might have related his aims to reality. Brusilov was of little help to him here. The General's penchant for popularity, revealed in 1916, had now become a matter of grim necessity. He, too, had to shake hands with the soldiers and ignore his officers, to spend hours listening to the requests of the Soldiers' Soviets – which became a significant force at Mogilev as soon as he took up his command – at the expense of fulfilling his concrete duties as C-in-C.

Consequently, planning for the Kerensky Offensive was perfunctory, an extension of the great politico-military fantasy, rather than a seriously considered move. Brusilov envisaged advances, on broad fronts, both in the north and the south. The northern advance was directed against the German threat to Riga and St Petersburg; the southern advance was intended to break the Austrian line in Carinthia. On 29 June the northern attack, thirty-one divisions and over a thousand guns deployed on a front of forty miles, went in. At first, mainly because of the heavy artillery support, the advance was successful. But as soon as the infantry had outdistanced the artillery barrage, their morale began to fail. The artillery had no way of covering their movement across ground, and were forced to dig in. By 3 July the front had become static once more.

The intention of the planners had been that the southern advance should begin as soon as the northern thrust had thrown the enemy off balance. The plan was basically unsound, because there was no concentration of effort, neither front was given definite predominance over the other, and the advances were too far apart for a pincer movement to be possible. What the Russians were attempting was futile; they were going to make two more or less equal pushes in different directions and hope that something came of it. But there was no provision for the reinforcement of either effort should it prove successful, and the staggering of the two attacks was nothing more than a gesture at subtlety. As it was, when the attack from the south came, the northern front had already been contained by the Germans.

The overall commander on the southern front was General Gutor, an unremarkable officer, out of his depth in the revolutionary situation. Three armies were involved in the advance: the 8th under Kornilov, the 7th and the 11th. On 6 July they began their movement. At first they met with considerable success; the Austrian troops facing them, though numerically strong, were not nearly so formidable as the German units had proved in the north. Kornilov, Kerensky's choice as commander of the 8th Army, handled his men with considerable skill, and the 8th Army made a spectacular breakthrough, capturing ten thousand prisoners and a hundred guns. All went well until the Austrian troops were reinforced with a division of German shock-troops. By skilful use of the railways the Austro-German command managed to concentrate these at the very weakest point of the Russian advance. As soon as the Germans attacked the 11th Army began to fall back; before long it was in headlong retreat. The other two armies, their flanks exposed by the precipitate flight of the 11th Army, were forced to retreat also. By 15 July the Moscow and St Petersburg press was telling its readers that the offensive they had hailed with such enthusiasm had now been transformed into a major catastrophe. Rumours of the defeat played a large part in precipitating the Bolshevik rising of 16 July.

The rising came as a surprise even to those who might have been expected to have anticipated it. Lenin himself was taken unawares: at the time he was resting at V. D. Bonch-Bruevich's villa in the Finnish woods. The rising was provoked by an ill-conceived attempt to take troops away from the St Petersburg area, and to use them to try to check what had now become a formidable Austro-German counter-offensive. At the same time the press, and Kerensky himself, was declaring that the retreat had been brought about by the 'treason' of various units who had refused to fight and by a further, less precise, treachery committed by 'certain subversive elements', an epithet that was widely taken to refer to the officers. Suddenly everybody sensed counter-revolution. The St Petersburg troops suspected a plot by the officers and the government, and refused to leave the capital. Soon they were actively demonstrating their support for the Soviet. Kerensky, who had given them the excuse that they needed for doing this, turned on the mutineers and accused *them* of counter-revolution. The situation on the front got progressively worse.

The July rising, more by accident than design, was quickly suppressed. The arrival of a large detachment from Kronstadt sparked off the outbreak, but the insurgents failed to win over the St Petersburg garrison. The Bolshevik leaders began to realise that the rumours connecting the party with German espionage had seriously damaged their cause, and no determined attempt was made to effect a coup d'état.

By 20 July St Petersburg had returned to the state which now passed for normality; the Provisional Government was still in control. But the rising had severely shaken the Government, and on that day Kerensky took over from Prince Lvov, retaining, however, the Ministry of War. He was now beginning to see himself as the Napoleon of the Revolution. His first cabinet was a stop-gap only: he included a number of left-wingers whose views were far more extremist than his own, and these he discarded at the first opportunity. His tendency now was to the right, towards the moderate socialist parties. In one vital respect he moved much further away from his previous position: on 24 July he appointed Kornilov as Commander-in-Chief of the southern front, in place of General Gutor. Kornilov seemed to be the only man who could possibly stem the flood-tide of the retreat: by now the Germans were on the Dnieper, desertions had caused a number of regiments to disintegrate completely, and the fleeing troops were pillaging the towns of the rear as they went. Kornilov accepted the post but demanded the re-introduction of the death penalty and of summary courts-martial in all sectors connected with the war effort. To these measures Kerensky was forced to agree. Kornilov took advantage of this new amenability to make a number of similar requests, all of which received the Government's approval. Gradually the front stabilised and order returned to the armies; but the losses in territory had been immense, and only the Germans' total bafflement at what was going on prevented their advancing into the Crimea.

On 1 August, after a long conference with Brusilov at Mogilev, Kerensky dismissed him as Supreme Commander-in-Chief, and appointed Kornilov in his stead. He then returned to St Petersburg and strengthened his own political position by the simple expedient of threatening to resign. It at once became apparent that Kerensky was the only man who was remotely acceptable to the more moderate parties, and the only possible government was a coalition under his leadership. It satisfied hardly anyone, but it was the best that could be done. By his appointment of Kornilov and his support of Kornilov's measures, he had seemed to show that he was recovering his sense of reality.

When the immediate threat to his security was gone, Kerensky became once more obsessed with the threat of counter-revolution, and the moment of lucidity in which he had appointed Kornilov and restored the death penalty began to fade into the dream. Kerensky was nothing if not susceptible, whether to the insinuations of the right or of the left. Partly because the Revolution had been just that, a turning away from the established order, he remained prone to believe the men of the left rather than those of the right. Even when he actively disbelieved what they said, his conscience or his past loyalties impelled him to return again and again to their allegations. It was as though, when he supported propositions that could be construed as traditionalist, he felt he was betraying himself. With this went a consciousness of his own individual importance, the importance of his historic mission, that made him doubly vulnerable. It is not surprising that after the first days of August, the old phantasmagorias returned. No one was to feature in his nightmares more frequently than General Kornilov.

IV

The Kornilov Movement

The new Commander-in-Chief, Lavr Georgevich Kornilov, was far from fitting the conventional image of a Tsarist officer. In appearance he was short, wiry, and exceptionally dark; his features had a pronounced Mongolian cast. The oriental effect of his narrow eyes and low-set ears was accentuated by a black moustache and the square trimming of his small goatee. He moved precisely and quickly, as though to compensate for his lack of stature by the smartness of his bearing and the air with which he carried his uniform.

He was born in 1870 at a Siberian garrison town, where his father – an officer in a Cossack regiment – was stationed. Shortly after Kornilov was born his father left the army and took up a very humble post in the Tsarist administration, becoming a local government clerk in his native village of Karkalinskaya.

This move by Kornilov's father was not so pointless as it might seem. He had risen from the ranks, and because of this he could obtain only limited promotion: his corresponding position in a non-Cossack regiment would have been far nearer to that of a sergeant-major. His pay was miserable, and insufficient for the support of his family; as a clerk he could earn more. Once back at Karkalinskaya there was nothing to distinguish him, beyond his ability to write, from the rest of the peasants; his wife was a Cossack by birth, and her background was similar to that of any other woman in the *stanitsa*.[1] The children received a certain amount of teaching at the parish school, though this was of the most basic kind. After Kornilov had been attending this school for just over two years the family moved to the Siberian town of Zaissan. In 1883, by dint of hard work, much of it done on his own initiative, Kornilov gained admission into the Siberian Cadet

---

[1] A *stanitsa* was a Cossack village, usually centred on certain communal buildings.

School. From this he passed with distinction into the Mikhailovsky Artillery School, where he was granted his commission.

His first posting was to Turkestan. During the ample spare time that fell to every Russian officer he continued with his studies, while giving language lessons to his brother officers and the local bourgeoisie. This he did in order to earn money to help his family. He was considered to be an able, hard-working officer, and was nominated by his regimental commander for a vacancy at the Staff College. There, despite his background, Kornilov developed both academically and socially; he began to make the acquaintance of other rising young officers, and acquitted himself well in the examinations. He passed out with the rank of captain in 1898.

When Kornilov became famous, this story of his youth was told with all the sentimental trappings of the rags to riches morality. The Bolsheviks sought to discredit the tale by calling Kornilov's father a 'Tsarist official'—which was true but misleading as to his actual status—and by denying that Kornilov was of peasant origin. The important point is that Kornilov was a general who rose by hard work from a background that was in no sense propitious. He had no family inheritance—no land, no money—beyond his own native abilities, and he had far less of a vested interest in the maintenance of the old régime than a man like Brusilov, who now appeared to be politically to Kornilov's left.

The newly promoted captain was posted back to the Turkestan district, this time to the Staff. As soon as he arrived he was ordered up to the front. The Pathan revolt of 1897 had given the Russians a renewed interest in the situation in Afghanistan and on the borders of India beyond, and in Kornilov's hearing General Ionov, his commanding officer, complained of the lack of precise information about certain Afghani fortifications. The next day Kornilov requested three days' leave and departed for an unknown destination. He returned with detailed photographs and sketches of the locality under discussion, made at the end of a long journey into hostile territory. After this exploit he managed to obtain permission to undertake several expeditions, in the course of which he combined exploration with intelligence work. He published a readable and detailed account of his journeys in eastern Turkestan, and he became familiar with the languages and customs of many of the tribes that made up the total of Russia's subjects in her south-eastern territories. He fought in the war with Japan, and distinguished himself at Mukden. He followed this with a term as Military Attaché in China, and at the

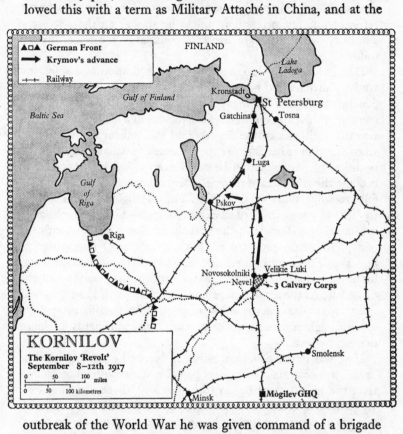

KORNILOV

The Kornilov 'Revolt'
September 8–12th 1917

0   50   100   miles
0   50   100 kilometres

outbreak of the World War he was given command of a brigade on the Carpathian front. It was here that, whilst covering the retreat of his division, he was wounded and captured by the Austrians. Subsequently he escaped from the camp in Moldavia where he was imprisoned, and returned to the Russian lines.

Kornilov's escape made him a national celebrity, and it was this, together with his known revolutionary sympathies, that led to his appointment as Commander of the St Petersburg Military District soon after the Revolution. In the course of his attempts to bring order to the mutinous garrison he first came into conflict with the Provisional Government, and it was as a result of his inability to obtain satisfaction that he asked for, and received, the command of an army at the front. His subsequent progress, remarkable for his performance in the south and his subsequent refusal to accept promotion unless he was given the necessary authority with which to exercise command, we have already followed.

Despite his early leanings towards exploration and scientific study, Kornilov had become a leader very much in the 'fighting general' tradition. To many Russians 'fighting general' was an emotive phrase: it conjured up the picture of a leader of men who was the antithesis of the desk-bound staff officer or bureaucrat, who would never hesitate to expose himself to danger, a hero in the tradition of Skobelev. To be considered a fighting general had become the ambition of many Russian officers, and most of these fell woefully short of their aim. For the fighting general was traditionally something of an exhibitionist, and it was much easier to imitate the show than the real thing. But Kornilov, with his bodyguard of the pink-coated Tekintzy regiment (comprised of ferocious Turkestani tribesmen), his staccato manner of speaking, his abruptness, and his splendid military record, was the authentic article. At the same time, some observers felt he had achieved this status at the expense of his other qualities, sacrificing some of his clearsightedness in order to assert his personality to more dramatic effect.

If he was to make an impression on Kerensky some element of drama was essential. No sooner had Kornilov assumed command than the government began to hedge over those conditions on which he had accepted his post (the death penalty and the jurisdiction of courts-martial to be applicable not only at the front, but also in munitions factories, on railways, and throughout the rear areas). Now Kerensky was claiming that he could not put through these measures for fear of an immediate rising by the Soviets. Yet he dared not admit this fear to the impatient General. In order to stave off Kornilov's enquiries he alleged that the War Ministry was having difficulty in drafting the appropriate documents and proclamations, but that as soon as it had done this he would set about restoring order.

Unfortunately for Kerensky, Kornilov was in close touch with the Prime Minister's deputy at the War Ministry, Boris Savinkov. Savinkov, who had formerly been in the revolutionary underground, was by now a moderate with leanings towards the right. He was rapidly attracted by Kornilov's personality and discussed politics freely with him. Thus it soon became apparent to the General that Kerensky was prevaricating.

It is doubtful, however, that Kornilov saw it in just such terms. He had not grasped the extent to which evasion had become an integral part of Kerensky's character, nor was he to know that, after his brief period of lucidity in early August, the Prime Minister was now once more moving off into fantasy. That Kerensky's intentions were good is not in question; he was sincerely in favour of the restoration of law and order. But he was quite unable to take the necessary steps when these seemed to lead him towards action that might jeopardise his own position. Kornilov's interpretation of Kerensky's motives was more sinister, but in the end came to much the same thing, for if Kerensky did not take action, then the situation was bound to get out of hand anyway.

The military situation was becoming increasingly desperate. The Germans were beginning to recover from their corporate incredulity and, conscious of oncoming autumn and the impening winter that could so soon put a stop to active campaigning, had begun to advance. Their main thrust came in the north, a drive along the Baltic coast. The Russians had concentrated their lines of defence around the greatest natural obstacle to the Germans' progress, the bight of the Gulf of Riga. Already Riga itself was threatened, and once the city fell there was almost nothing that could stop the Germans marching straight on to St Petersburg.

Kornilov still contended that there was little he could do to check the Germans until internal affairs had been brought firmly under control. To his staff he advocated drastic measures against the leaders of the Soviet. Simultaneously, whether he wished it or not, another process was taking place. He was willy-nilly becoming the focal point of right-wing and moderate liberal hopes for the salvation of the country.

This growth of opinion was being unwittingly accelerated by

Kerensky, who was now talking quite openly about the necessity of a *directoire* period if the survival of the Revolution was to be assured. This implied a dictatorship; but the dictatorship that many people were looking towards was not the one of which Kerensky was thinking.

On 19 August Kornilov began to concentrate the 3rd Cavalry Corps at a point almost mid-way between Mogilev, Riga and St Petersburg. Since this decision was to trigger the Kornilov 'revolt', it needs examining in a little more detail.

The precise point of concentration was in the triangle Nevel–Novosokolniki–Velikie-Luki. These three provincial towns were conveniently linked by a triangle of railways, which made for the rapid movement of troops. According to Kornilov, it was chosen as the holding area for the corps because it meant that they could be moved either to the north or to the south-west with equal facility; what was obvious, even to the most casual observer, was that it could equally be used as a base for an advance on St Petersburg. It was also obvious that the real need for troops was in the north, as Riga was already threatened by the Germans; for the moment there was no serious threat from the southern front.

The most important of the constituent units of the 3rd Cavalry Corps was the Native Division, better known by the cheerful title of the Savage Division. This had been created by the Grand Duke Michael, almost on a 'private army' basis. It recruited amongst the Muslim Caucasian tribes (who were exempted, under the law of 1874, from compulsory military service). The officers had been chosen by the Grand Duke himself, mainly from amongst the Guards regiments. Now it was commanded by Prince Bagration, suspect as an aristocrat. As a unit, the Savage Division had a reputation that lived up to the promise of its name. It fought with singular ferocity, and away from the front line tended to visit its frustrated ardour on the unfortunate civilians in neighbouring towns and villages.

The implications of all this were soon brought home to the inhabitants of the capital, if they were not already aware of them. Again and again it was reiterated in the Soviet that the provocation presented by location and the composition of the 3rd Cavalry Corps was too great to be tolerated. The corps – containing a division of its nature reactionary, and probably Tsarist in sympathy – was obviously destined to be used for the suppression of liberty. The outcry was virulent and shrill; it was exactly the kind of amalgam of plea and threat to which Kerensky was most susceptible.

Of course, there were those who felt quite differently. At a conference of various Duma members – all of whom were, in the context of 1917, loosely right-wing – Purishkevich summarised what was being said by a great many people:

> Until Russia gets a dictator invested with the widest powers, until the Supreme Council consists of the finest of the Russian Generals, who have been driven from the front, and who have staked their lives for their country, there will be no order in Russia.[1]

Purishkevich himself was notoriously reactionary. He had been connected with the Black Hundreds and the League of the United Nobility; he had also tried to establish vigilante units in times of civil disorder, and was largely responsible for the foundation of the League of the Archangel Michael, an authentically fascist organisation that foreshadowed the Roumanian party. In the past there had been a general tendency to disregard what Purishkevich had to say; he was compulsively exhibitionist. Now he was being taken seriously. Rodzyanko, the former Duma leader, sent Kornilov a message that 'all thinking Russians' were looking to him with 'faith and hope'. If this had been true, the future of Russia would have been very different. As it was, there were many who might have supported Kornilov but were put off by the re-emergence of men such as Purishkevich.

Kornilov himself disdained political affiliations. Sympathisers were received in a friendly manner at Mogilev, but political talk was limited to matters touching the army. Kornilov continually asserted his loyalty to the Provisional Government, and his main motive in allowing visitors to come to Mogilev seems to have been a genuine desire to acquaint the politicians with conditions in the army and the necessity for the restoration of discipline. This, however, Kerensky was unable to credit. Already rumours were reaching Mogilev, via Savinkov in the War Ministry, that the Prime Minister was contemplating dismissing his C-in-C.

---

[1] Gorky, Molotov, Voroshilov *et al.* (eds.), *Istoriya grazhdanskoy voiny v C.C.C.R.*, I, p. 322.

Kornilov reacted to these rumours with great alacrity. He drove to the capital, together with a squadron of the Tekintzy Regiment armed with machine-guns, and swept up with his convoy to the front entrance of the Winter Palace. While he was inside his guard stood to at the doors, having first removed the two machine-guns that were on the General's car and set them up in the palace hall. Given the condition of St Petersburg, this was probably a wise precaution, but it did not endear Kornilov to the increasingly nervous Prime Minister.

Events were brought to a head by a state conference which Kerensky summoned in Moscow on 25 August. The immediate political objective of this gathering of 2,500 delegates from all the main political parties, who met in the Opera House, was to consolidate support for the government and perhaps to pave the way for a period of Kerensky's personal rule. The credibility of Kerensky's manœuvre was vitiated from the start by the simultaneous outbreak of a series of strikes. These made it dramatically obvious that a vital part of the population was not prepared to regard the composition of the conference as representative, or to lend Kerensky their support.

On the day after the opening Kornilov arrived in Moscow. This event was made the occasion for the first overtly right-wing demonstration that the city had seen since March. Kornilov got off his train to the accompaniment of the full military ceremonial. The Tekintzy Regiment formed a guard of honour, bands played, and once he came outside the station the General was lifted shoulder high and chaired by his men. The bourgeoisie turned up in force with garlands and bouquets; Kornilov's visit rapidly seemed to assume the character of the opening of a political campaign. This impression was reinforced by an action that, whatever the motives which lay behind it, appeared provocative and aggressive in its symbolism. As soon as he had acknowledged the crowds that greeted him at the station, Kornilov went to offer up a prayer at the Shrine of the Virgin of Iversk. This had been part of the Imperial Coronation ritual; it was the act of religious obeisance necessary before the coronation proper could begin. It was also the first act of a reigning Tsar on visiting Moscow. For too many people this action meant too much; it gave a new and unpleasant complexion to the debate between right and left.

Also, it still further reduced the chances of the Kerenskian compromise lasting for any length of time. But whether the visit caused anger or joy, it was fundamentally misleading, for Kornilov had no intention of backing a Romanov restoration. Several people had approached him with this aim in mind, and they had all been rebuffed.

Kornilov stayed in his command train during his visit to Moscow. Even in peace-time he had a marked dislike of cities, and he conceived so violent a distaste for the condition of Moscow and St Petersburg under the Provisional Government that it was with difficulty that he could be persuaded to visit them. Kornilov's refusal to attempt to understand what was going on in the cities, his tendency to think of all politicians as schemers and of urban riots as disturbances that could be quelled by a cavalry charge or a nicely sited machine-gun, was to have serious consequences. The years Kornilov spent in the exploration of Turkestan and Persia may have sharpened his energy and refined his command of men, but they had not given him any feeling for politics beyond an impulse towards rejection.

For the moment, though, he had something that he wished to say and felt should be heard. His purpose in coming to Moscow was to awaken the delegates at the state conference to the realities of the military situation and the necessity for urgent action. It cannot have come as any surprise to him, then, that he received messages, seemingly inspired by Kerensky, telling him that he would be well advised not to speak the next day. He asked if this was an order, and after a great deal of coming and going at the coach parked on a siding in Moscow Station, he eventually established direct contact with the Prime Minister. This in itself was unusual; by now Kerensky and Kornilov were each claiming that the other was deliberately avoiding him. In this they were aided by the conspiratorial confabulations of their staffs, who studiously imitated the deviousness and brusqueness of their respective masters and mentors. Eventually the Prime Minister expressed directly the wish that Kornilov should confine his talk to military affairs.

This was just what Kornilov had no intention of doing. On the morning of the 27th he was asked to address the conference. His appearance on the stage of the Opera House was the occasion for something near a riot. By now Kornilov had gained numerous adherents; the Kornilovists had become a faction to reckon with. The liberals had done their best to forget the extreme right's enthusiasm for Kornilov. They even managed to ignore the ostentation with which Purishkevich had chosen to go and visit the General soon after the latter's arrival in Moscow. Curiously, the circumstances of Kornilov's birth, now much publicised, seemed to hold a greater attraction for the liberals than for the representatives of the Soldiers' Soviets. Or perhaps this was not so surprising; Bolshevik commentators observed that the liberals had always wanted tame imitations of the proletariat – in Kornilov they had the ultimate refinement of this product.

At Kornilov's appearance the liberals and right-wingers jumped to their feet, clapping and cheering. Only the soldiers and the extreme left remained seated. The delegates who were standing began to shout at the others who remained seated, and soon a group of conservatives had begun a rhythmic chant of 'Stand up, Stand up'. Eventually Kerensky restored order.

Kornilov appeared unmoved by his reception. He began his speech without any attempt at rhetoric or drama. First he pointed out that the morning's display was indicative of a deep and serious malaise. He went on to state, in dry and factual phrases, that he could no longer rely on the continued patriotism of the army. Kornilov was perfectly capable, if he wished, of being dramatic. But in this speech he eschewed oratory and concentrated on the bare presentation of facts. He gave figures for the swelling numbers of deserters – by this time at least two million – and he read out a series of telegrams that had been received at Mogilev, informing G.H.Q. of the murder of senior officers. These were so shocking as to be received with disbelief. He next outlined the German threat to Riga and St Petersburg, and finished by repeating the conditions that he considered necessary for the continuance of the army as a fighting force, laying particular emphasis on the need to restore the prestige of the officer corps and to organise the rear.

In the vastness of the Opera House he was a determined and commanding figure, but also a pathetic one. He had tried for the effect of the still, small voice, and though he had succeeded in awakening some of the delegates to reality, he had not communicated with the vast majority. He had carefully avoided saying anything that sounded factionist. He left it to the next speaker, General Kaledin, to make the really controversial proposition that the Soldiers' Soviets should be abolished. Kaledin was another general of Cossack origin; he had been brought into prominence by one of the less publicised but more substantial decisions made by the Provisional Government, the granting of partial autonomy to the Cossacks. Theoretically, such autonomy had existed under the Tsars, but the promulgation of one law after another had whittled it away. The new government had made a genuine effort to reverse this trend, and had reconstituted the Cossack Krug – an approximation to a parliament that wavered on the tribal side of democracy and gave expression to the will of the Cossacks within a given area. The most important of these *Krugy* – there were several, representing the various areas populated by Cossacks – was that of the Don Cossacks, and it had elected Kaledin as its Ataman, or leader.

It was clear that the combination of the loyal elements in the army and the Cossack population would be formidable, and Kornilov was eager to promote this alliance. By doing so he would also ensure the loyalty of the Cossacks who served in the army, and he hoped that the other Cossack territories would follow the lead given by their compatriots of the Don. But in asking Kaledin to propose abolition of the Soldiers' Soviets Kerensky blundered badly, because he immediately postulated a polarity that did not exist. Many of the Cossacks in the army were already involved with the committees, and the river-lands of the Don were, both physically and spiritually, far from Moscow and St Petersburg. Though some of the Cossack units were coming out for General Kornilov, others had been in a state of mutiny since the Revolution. The statements of those Cossack organisations that adhered to Kornilov were, moreover, cast in particularly inflammatory language. Kerensky began to add the fear of Cossack revolt to the sum of his obsessions, and Kornilov was bolstered by an impression of massive support that was not in accordance with the real situation.

Kerensky's final, histrionic appearance on the stage of the Moscow Opera House was a virtuoso performance. The theme was simply himself: he was the only possible alternative, he claimed, to a dictatorship by either the right or the left. Thus he fed his own fantasies – he had neither the authority nor the stability to fulfil the role that he proposed for himself – and thus he fed the fantasies of the right, by making a Bolshevik coup seem nearer to actuality than it was. We cannot tell just how wrong he was about this. It may be that he was misleading only in so far as he presented it as an immediate probability rather than as something ten or twelve weeks off. Speculation is beside the point; the positive effect of his warnings was to confirm the suspicions of reports received by G.H.Q. from their Intelligence Department which indicated that there would be a Bolshevik rising in St Petersburg in mid-September. Even more significantly, at the end of August the Bolsheviks obtained an effective majority in the St Petersburg Soviet.

Another piece of information was to influence Kornilov's actions. Colonel Lebedev, one of the founders of the Officers' Union, had been approached by representatives of an organisation in St Petersburg, composed mainly of moderate liberals, who were making secret plans to combat such a rising – which they, too, expected to occur in the near future. They were anxious for Kornilov to provide them with officers who could lead their resistance movement.

Kornilov consented, and he was spurred on by this approach to make detailed contingency plans for the suppression of the rising. He must inevitably have been influenced by memories of the previous March. In the close atmosphere of intrigue, the intricacies of plot and counter-plot, the fall of Riga on 3 September passed, if not unnoticed, at least largely unheeded. One cleverly manipulated consequence of the disaster was a denunciation of Kornilov by the Soviet as the man who had let it happen; the fact that he had predicted the disaster was remembered, whilst the reasons that he put forward for the inevitability of the event were forgotten. His own prophecies were turned to his disadvantage. Kornilov had no time to take notice of these attacks; he was now deeply involved in what can only be described as the farce of the emissaries.

Since the two main *dramatis personae* were so loth to enter into direct contact with each other, messages between them were transmitted by envoys, all of whom were eminently unsuited for the job. Savinkov was quite probably nearer politically to Kornilov than Kerensky, and he was much impressed by the personality of the General; nevertheless, he owed his position largely to the Prime Minister, and he was anxious to keep a foot in both camps. The fact that he was a morphine addict cannot have beneficially affected a temperament dominated by a passion for the clandestine. Another emissary was Vladimir Lvov (not to be mistaken for Prince Lvov, the Premier), who had held the post of Procurator of the Holy Synod in the original March cabinet. Lvov was not merely indirect, in the Savinkov manner: he was flagrantly irresponsible. To complete the trio – though there are plenty of others who qualify for mention – we can add M. M. Filonenko, Commissar from the Provisional Government to the Commander-in-Chief. This was an obviously vital position, and it took Kerensky and Savinkov between them to fill it with a candidate who had developed to a fine art the accomplishment of being all things to all men.

Of these three only Savinkov seems to have been actuated by motives beyond the narrowly personal. It was his genuine wish to achieve a union between Kerensky and Kornilov who, he argued, if they could be persuaded to combine could bring order to the country without sacrificing the gains of the Revolution. As it was, Savinkov blundered, gained the full confidence of neither man, and left them still further along the path of misunderstanding.

Lvov was deliberately malicious, a figure of a type more often found in literature and mythology than in life – he delighted in mischief for its own sake. One of his minor amusements was to edit the texts of messages he had been asked to deliver. 'Kornilov proposes' would mysteriously become 'Kornilov demands', an alteration which can hardly be said to have contributed to mutual understanding. Filonenko shared many of Lvov's proclivities, and was scarcely more reliable.

It is difficult to believe that chance alone was responsible for the simultaneous concurrence of these men at this time. Though Kerensky eventually broke with all three men he nevertheless at some point trusted each of them. His judgement of character was hopeless; it seems that he deliberately selected subordinates whom he hoped he could dominate. He also showed signs of developing that inevitable corollary of hallucination – an intense dislike and

73

even fear of being driven to face reality. The survival of Kerensky until 1970 as a courteous old gentleman living in New York tended to disguise his condition during the latter days of the Provisional Government. He was confused, incoherent, and highly emotional; his moods were unpredictable, wild optimism followed hard upon periods of acute depression.

After the Kornilov affair an enquiry was held at which Kerensky gave evidence: a partial transcript of this was subsequently published. The enquiry was absurd in the first case: the chairman of the commission asked innumerable leading questions and allowed himself to be directed by Kerensky; many of the most important witnesses were never called. But the revealing evidence is Kerensky's. The words are those of a witness who is tired, muddled, and very arrogant. On the one hand he fails to finish sentences, makes sweeping allegations and does not support them, and continually resorts to rumour as a justification for his actions. On the other he insists on making political speeches irrelevant to the enquiry, and he is continually on the verge of taking the meeting over and chairing it himself. Even in his later historical works, Kerensky's style, such as it is, disintegrates when he describes what happened during the Kornilov affair. This seems to be a reflection of his state of mind during those crucial weeks.

Kornilov was also deluded, but to nothing like the same extent. His delusion was the result of faulty information; had this been accurate, his moves would have been quite logical. He was wrong about two main points: he expected a Bolshevik rising in St Petersburg before 14 September, and he thought the army to be more loyal to him than it actually was. From these two misconceptions the rest followed.

Kornilov's misconceptions were carefully fostered by the emissaries. On 6 September Savinkov visited Mogilev, accompanied by various military officials, and spent a great deal of time discussing what would be done if a rising broke out in St Petersburg. Kornilov now came into the open over the matter of the 3rd Cavalry Corps, and it was agreed that the corps' march on the city should be accompanied by a simultaneous declaration of martial law in the suburbs. Meanwhile, it was to be presumed, the secret organisation which had been established within the city proper would be attempting to prevent the Bolsheviks gaining control of the key points such as the telegraph office, the stations, and the various ministries.

This secret organisation, the centre of excited speculation by left-wing circles in St Petersburg, was becoming a matter of great concern to Kerensky. Its scope and nature had been grotesquely distorted by rumour. Kornilov understood that the group had about two thousand members, and that it lacked adequate leadership; beyond that his knowledge of it was limited to the fact that he had been asked to provide a hundred officers to lead the attempt to check the rising. In the capital it was being represented as an 'army of two thousand officers' trained specially for the purpose, but this was a long way from the truth. Kornilov had managed to arrange for a number of reliable officers to be available in St Petersburg pending posting, and he had made it possible for these officers to get in touch with the organisation. But it is doubtful whether, even at this late stage, there were as many as forty such agents in the city. And the agents were now finding that the 'organisation' was a great deal more amorphous than its representatives had led Colonel Lebedev to believe.

Apart from the dubiety over the extent and nature of the 'organisation', Kornilov's talks with Savinkov appeared to be going well. The only disagreement emerged at the very end, and it came as a surprise because Kornilov thought that the matter had already been settled. It concerned the command of the 3rd Cavalry Corps for their proposed operation. Kornilov suggested that the task should be entrusted to General Krymov, an officer who had been in the fore in the early days of the revolution. He was, as we have seen, one of the original advocates of a coup, and he had been used by Guchkov to subvert the St Petersburg officers. But, just as Savinkov was leaving the Commander-in-Chief, he suddenly announced that Krymov should not be appointed after all. This abrupt volte-face left Kornilov mystified. The appointment was certainly a curious one, in that Krymov had been largely responsible, through negligence, for a German breakthrough in Roumania during January of 1917. Kornilov knew of this, and may have given the 3rd Cavalry Corps to Krymov to allow him to rehabilitate himself. But this did not seem to be the reason for Savinkov's objections.

That evening, while Kornilov was still with Savinkov, Vladimir Lvov arrived at Mogilev, claiming to bear yet more messages from Kerensky; unlike Savinkov's agenda, which was largely restricted to specific details of the plans for suppressing the Bolshevik rising, Lvov's was concerned with far-reaching political proposals. For Kornilov, all this was totally bewildering. It was hard to see what could have impelled Kerensky to send two different messengers in so short a space of time; it became even more puzzling when their respective messages were compared.

Lvov claimed that Kerensky had sent him to find out what Kornilov considered to be the best way of forming a strong government. Lvov went on to outline three possibilities mentioned by the Prime Minister. The first was that Kerensky should become dictator, with a new government; the second was the establishment of a junta of three or four members, one of whom should be Kornilov, which would wield dictatorial powers; the third was that Kornilov should become dictator, retain his post as Commander-in-Chief, and form a new government. If Kornilov should favour the last proposal, Lvov asked, would he consider it desirable to have Kerensky and Savinkov in his government?

Kornilov was far too literal-minded to see that Kerensky was primarily a creature of nerves and imagination, and that the Prime Minister would never voluntarily lay down his office. He had sent Lvov to find out whether Kornilov was considering a bid for power not because he would welcome such an action, but because he feared it. It was a dangerous move, for it was in the nature of Lvov's mission that what was intended as an intelligence operation might easily be interpreted as an incitement to revolt. The courier could become an *agent provocateur*.

Even that would not have been so serious had it not happened that Kornilov, who had come to cultivate directness, was insensitive to a lack of directness in others. And once he had decided to trust someone he continued to do so. At some point he had decided to trust, not Kerensky, but Lvov. At their meeting Lvov, sitting opposite the Commander-in-Chief, read Kerensky's proposals out of a notebook. So far as Kornilov could see, Lvov then entered his replies into the same book. The General asked to see neither the Prime Minister's message nor the transcript of his own answers. He had decided that Lvov was 'irreproachably honest and a gentleman'.[1] It was a fatal mistake.

In St Petersburg the Soviet was publicising the Kornilovist menace, claiming that the fall of Riga had been deliberately engineered by the officer corps as a prelude to a combined operation by Kornilov and the Germans against St Petersburg. Once again the vague charge of treason was being used with deadly and specific effect. The 'Revolution had been betrayed': it could not have been the gallant soldiery who surrendered Riga, so it must have been the officers. The press was denunciatory. The *People's Cause* asked whether the 'mistakes of the commanders, the deficiencies in artillery, and the incompetence of the leaders' were not being blamed on the 'courageous, heroic' soldiers. That these soldiers had, in many cases, refused to fight was of no consequence. *Izvestiya*, as befitted a Bolshevik-dominated publication, went further, and explained to its readers how G.H.Q. was exaggerating the scale of the disaster in order to force the Provisional Government to carry out a series of measures, 'directly and indirectly aimed at the Revolutionary Democracy. . . .'

Lenin, from hiding, issued succinct instructions to his followers. Kornilov was to be resisted with all the force they could command, all soldiers should be incited to mutiny, and they should be encouraged to kill officers who were suspected of supporting Kornilov. The old pattern of mutiny and murder was beginning again. But Lenin looked further than this, for he saw in the developing imbroglio a unique chance to 'show everybody the weakness of Kerensky'.

On 8 September Kornilov signalled to Savinkov that the 3rd Cavalry Corps were now ready to make their move towards St Petersburg, and that they would arrive there, as agreed, on the 10th. On the 11th the capital would have to be placed under martial law. Not long after this signal had been encoded and dispatched, Kornilov was called to the telegraph, and told that Kerensky was on the line. This was a highly unusual event; though the telegraph had always been available, Kerensky had hitherto chosen to communicate through the emissaries. This

---

[1] Lukomsky, *Vospominaniya*, I, p. 239.

was possibly because telegraph messages were punched out onto a tape, which could be filed and subsequently produced.

When Kornilov got to the apparatus he had to wait for some time before St Petersburg was ready to transmit. When the message began to arrive he was surprised to notice that it seemed to be coming from Lvov. What he was not to know was that Kerensky had asked Lvov to come to the Minister of War's house, where the direct line was situated, but had begun sending the message before Lvov arrived. The Prime Minister was subsequently to claim that this was an accident; there were many who disbelieved him. The message, Kornilov discovered as it gradually came through, was substantially a repetition of the points he had discussed with Lvov on the previous day. Kerensky/ Lvov asked the General to confirm these proposals and confirm that he had intended them to be communicated to Kerensky. When Kornilov had done so Kerensky went on to imply that he was in favour of them – he was now speaking in the character of Kerensky – but wanted to know if it was still necessary for him to come to Mogilev. (Kornilov had suggested this as the best way of demonstrating that Kerensky supported him, and also as the best way of ensuring the safety of the Prime Minister. He expected Kerensky and Savinkov to be at Mogilev on the 10th – the day when the Cavalry were supposed to reach St Petersburg.)

Kornilov was puzzled by this message, primarily because it seemed so unnecessary. His answers to the various questions were, as usual, curt; it is also possible that they were a little impatient. He had been kept waiting for half an hour before the exchange of messages began, and he had other, more important, things to do. Kerensky, on the other hand, regarded the messages as crucial: they were to be the concrete evidence on which he would act. As soon as the instrument was closed down he set about defending the capital and the régime from what he described as the 'positive threat of counter-revolution'. Kornilov, meanwhile, assured of the rightness of his actions, began to draw up a list of the new cabinet.

That evening Kerensky gave his talent for melodramatics full rein. He persuaded Lvov to come to his study in the Winter Palace, and there to repeat Kornilov's proposals yet once more. Lvov must have thought that Kerensky was going mad. But even this reflection cannot have afforded him as much surprise as the emergence from behind a curtain of Balavinsky, a lawyer with long-standing association with the moderate revolutionaries and now connected with the reorganisation of local government and the police. He was the independent witness that Kerensky required to have Lvov arrested on a charge of treason. Lvov, who had not slept for four nights, was taken away and locked up in a room in the palace.

Now that Kerensky had committed himself to action, he broke into a frenzy of energetic preparation. The cabinet, in any case a ramshackle compromise, was persuaded to resign in favour of what amounted to a dictatorship, and at 7 a.m. on the 9th General Kornilov received an unnumbered telegram requesting his immediate resignation from his post as C-in-C. The command was to be temporarily transferred to his Chief-of-Staff, General Lukomsky. The telegram had been addressed to both officers. Lukomsky was the first to read it, and it was he who took it in to Kornilov. When the C-in-C had also studied it, he asked Lukomsky what he intended to do. Lukomsky replied that he could not possibly take over command; but his answer to Kerensky was more than a simple refusal to take up the duties asked of him.

In the interests of the salvation of Russia you [Kerensky] must work with General Kornilov, and not dismiss him. The dismissal of General Kornilov will plunge Russia into an agony even worse than that it has experienced hitherto. Myself, I cannot accept responsibility for the army, even for a short time. . . .[1]

This response established a pattern of events that repeated itself again and again, for these sentiments were to be echoed by commanding officers the length of the front. In some units the news of what had happened precipitated immediate mutinies; in others the soldiers remained loyal to their commanders and thus to Kornilov; in more, they waited.

Kornilov's immediate response was to order Krymov to march on St Petersburg. That night he issued General Orders to all headquarters, in which he acquainted them with the situation, and on the 10th he issued a proclamation, which was as near as

---

[1] Lukomsky, *Vospominaniya*, I, p. 243.

he ever got to active propaganda. Both documents – which are in some respects very similar, even to the repetition of identical sentences – are remarkable. But the General Orders, in particular, are notable for the sheer desperation of their language:

> The solemn certainty of the doom of this our country compels me in these terrible times to call upon all her loyal sons to save their dying native land. All within whom a Russian heart still beats, all who believe in God, go into the Churches and pray to Our Lord for the greatest possible miracle, the salvation of our dear country.[1]

In Kornilov's very pessimism there is evidence of sincerity. It is curious how many of his recorded statements, whether public or private, made during these days are expressed in negative forms. He treated the whole business as a refusal to obey, rather than as a crusade against the Provisional Government; he constantly repeated that he respected the aims of the Revolution above all else, and he presented his disobedience as a direct consequence of a sense of his real duty to Russia. There is no evidence that he took political advice about his moves; his orders and proclamations have a bitterness and tortured hesitancy that reflects the struggle within Kornilov himself, and they are documents that no political adviser would ever have allowed him to issue. Yet there were many army officers who responded to his appeal precisely because it was so halting and personal. In his own account of his struggle to interpret his allegiances and his duty he spoke for them all.

Kerensky, in St Petersburg, did not know the difficulty that Kornilov was having in mounting the long-threatened cavalry expedition. Desertions, minor mutinies, and maladministration meant that the force was by no means as formidable as it had looked on paper. Most serious of all, the relationship between the military communications net and the railway system meant that the transport workers were able to black out his whole telegraphic section. General Denikin, commanding the southwestern front, received telegrams from both Kerensky and Kornilov, and replied affirming his loyalty to Kornilov. But, shortly after he had done so, he lost all contact with Mogilev. Kornilov was moving in the dark.

---

[1] Denikin, *Ocherki russkoy smuty*, I, part 2, p. 216.

Meanwhile, Kerensky began to prepare for the defence of the capital. All past differences apparently forgotten, the Soviets leapt to his support. The forbidden Red Guards were soon to be seen on the streets, detachments of sailors from Kronstadt moved into the town, and arms were distributed at Smolny. The urgency of the occasion prevented any close check on the issue of guns and ammunition, but the observant were not slow to notice that great quantities were passing into the hands of Bolsheviks and left Revolutionary-activists. The Soviet established its own Revolutionary Military Committee, and this effectively took over control of the defence arrangements. Kornilov's fifth column never materialised, if it had ever really existed, but the rumour of it was sufficient to start a massacre of officers that was widely ignored in the general chaos. Workers began to demonstrate for arms with which to 'defend the Revolution', and Kerensky was in no position to gainsay them.

On the 10th Krymov's expedition came to a halt within a day's march of St Petersburg. Krymov set up his headquarters at Luga, about seventy miles from the capital, and found that he was unable to move forwards by rail: the railway workers had removed so much track that repair was out of the question. He was therefore forced to make camp. His next discovery was that his communications with Mogilev had been cut, so that he was unable to request assistance from Kornilov or even to inform him of the situation. Worse, whilst his troops were bivouacked in the fields and woods between Gatchina and Luga, they were infiltrated by propagandists from the Soviet, Bolsheviks figuring prominently among them. It was a cleverly handled operation; there was a Mussulman delegation to subvert the Savage Division, and the agitators in the other parties were chosen because they had some connection with the units that they were sent to talk over. Any delay by Krymov was fatal, since it increased the opportunities for fraternisation; but he had no option except to delay. He could not move his artillery or his infantry units, and St Petersburg was a full day's march for the cavalry. It was doubtful whether they could take the city by themselves; in any case, it was just the wrong distance away: if they rode straight there they would arrive exhausted, but if they stopped, the enemy, now fully appraised of their whereabouts, would have the initiative. Krymov was trapped.

Until the 10th the fact that Kerensky had a rebellion on his hands had not been apparent to the general public. There were wild rumours in St Petersburg, and the Soviet had a fair idea of what was on foot, but the government made no formal statement. Indeed, on the 9th Savinkov had explicitly denied to the press that there was anything untoward between the Prime Minister and his Commander-in-Chief. Savinkov made a last minute attempt to persuade Kornilov to accept his dismissal before communications with Mogilev broke down; Kornilov refused, once again returning to the subject of Russia's imminent military collapse. When it became clear that Kornilov would not resign, Kerensky began to draft an official proclamation, the text of which was soon widely known. But by the time the preparations for the defence of St Petersburg had really got under way, Krymov's expedition had come to a halt. This is why descriptions of the business as a 'revolt' have always been misleading: they imply the reality of a state of affairs that never existed outside Kerensky's mind. The movement on the capital had begun before Kornilov was dismissed, and the failure of signalling arrangements meant that Krymov was in no position to collude with Kornilov.

Had Krymov really had a clear idea of his objective, he might still have been able to continue the advance. It would have been a dangerous course of action, but it is possible that even the troops who remained loyal would have been sufficient to break through into the capital. But Krymov was lost without orders. He sent couriers back to Mogilev, and remained where he was. Lack of momentum, and the consequent absence of even the illusion of purpose, had its inevitable effect. The Savage Division, away from the leader who was the visible embodiment of their loyalty, rapidly became unwontedly nervous and irritable. One moment Krymov announced his intention of advancing regardless of the hindrances, another he told his staff that the only thing he could do was to retreat to Mogilev.

It must have come as a relief when a messenger from St Petersburg finally arrived at Luga with what amounted to an invitation to surrender. Kerensky had sent the note indirectly, through Colonel Samarin, a staff officer who had served under Krymov in the past and was now the chief professional adviser to the Minister of War. The Colonel also brought a message from Alekseev, whom Samarin had gone to see after he had received his orders from Kerensky. It was done without Kerensky's knowledge, but it was clearly a wise move for Alekseev commanded great respect throughout the officer corps, and if anyone could act as a moderating influence on either party, it was he. Furthermore, Alekseev was still regarded by many as being the senior officer in the army. Rightly or wrongly, he was the man whom they were most likely to obey. Alekseev heard the substance of Kerensky's note and then gave Samarin another letter which he instructed him to hand to Krymov first. In it he recommended that the General should accept Kerensky's suggestion and come to see the Prime Minister. The streets of St Petersburg were calm, he pointed out; there seemed to be no sign of a rising, and it was unlikely that the Bolsheviks would attempt one now since to do so, as their leaders evidently realised, was to play into the hands of the right.

The tone of Alekseev's letter decided Krymov. The C-in-C whom Kerensky had sacked now stepped in to aid him – there is no saying what Krymov's reaction might have been had he received only the message from the Prime Minister. For General Alekseev the intervention cannot have been easy. He had no high opinion of Kerensky's honesty or of his ability, and his sympathies must have been with Kornilov. At the same time, he was also conscious that Kornilov's action was, in effect if not in intention, illegal. An army officer was the servant of the state: this was something that Alekseev was to repeat again and again, almost as though he wished to hide from himself the situation in which Kornilov was placed. When Alekseev's actions in the present crisis are considered, and it is taken into account that his decisions were made independently of the Prime Minister's, then it becomes clear that the idea of a widespread military conspiracy, master-minded by the senior officers of the General Staff, had its primary existence in Kerensky's hectic brain.

On the evening of 12 September Krymov left his headquarters and, accompanied by an escort provided by Colonel Samarin, drove into St Petersburg. First he called upon Alekseev; it was not until 10 a.m. the next day that he went to see Kerensky. The Prime Minister, who had taken the precaution of having several of his entourage present as witnesses, opened the interview by asking Krymov to explain the movements of the 3rd Cavalry Corps. Krymov replied that the sole object of the march had been to put the corps in a position to suppress the anticipated Bolshevik rising. Kerensky countered that Krymov must surely know that the rising was a deliberate invention of the staff's, that from the start the staff had intended to provoke such a rising in order to create a situation in which their forces would be called on to maintain law and order. The Prime Minister had no doubt that Krymov was privy to the whole conspiracy, and he made it evident that he disbelieved the General's defence. The interview ended in deadlock. Krymov was allowed to leave, after he had been asked to testify before the commission that had already been set up to investigate the 'revolt'.

Krymov walked out of Kerensky's office and went straight to the house of Captain Zhuravsky, a close friend. There he requested pen and paper and asked to be left alone. After a while he came out and, calling to his adjutant who had come with him, asked the officer to make sure that the letter he now gave him was delivered to Kornilov. Then Krymov went back into the room to write another letter, this time to his wife. As soon as it was finished he took out his revolver and shot himself in the chest. Kerensky, naturally, interpreted Krymov's suicide as an admission of guilt. But it is worth reflecting that Krymov must have been conscious of failing Kornilov when the latter had deliberately reposed more trust in him than he truly deserved.

At Mogilev, the failure of Krymov's expedition was known on the 12th. Kornilov tried to persuade General Kaledin to advance on Moscow with his Cossacks, but Kaledin reacted unfavourably, saying that the reliability of even the best Cossack regiments was now dubious. Though officers throughout those areas with which Mogilev retained contact were announcing their support of the Commander-in-Chief, they all doubted the loyalty of their commands. Already, on the south-western front, Generals Denikin and Markov had been arrested by the Commissars, backed up by the Soldiers' Soviets. The arrival of Krymov's adjutant with the General's letter added to Kornilov's despondency. What was in the letter he did not reveal, but it must have told him that there was little hope now.

Even so, Kerensky still behaved as though the country was threatened by a major counter-revolution – and in so doing he materially contributed to the build-up of an atmosphere in which a Bolshevik coup would become a feasible proposition. At the same time, he acted towards the Soviet in a way that could easily be interpreted as being conciliatory and hesitant. Partly this was because of the extraordinary information that he was receiving and believing. Mogilev, so he was told, had been fortified: there were artillery positions around Government House, and machine guns had been set up to cover the valley. Kerensky advocated force one moment, and negotiation the next. He declared himself Supreme Commander of the Russian army, appointed Alekseev acting Chief-of-Staff, and sent him to persuade Kornilov to surrender or to resign.

It was not a mission that Alekseev accepted lightly. Kerensky later claimed that Alekseev had asked to be sent, but this is certainly untrue: in fact Kerensky had to ask Alekseev to perform the task several times, and it seems as though Alekseev deliberately put it off for as long as he could. When he eventually agreed, he went about it very cautiously, and as soon as he reached a place where he could get in touch with G.H.Q. by telegraph, he opened preliminary negotiations. He talked to General Lukomsky first of all, and represented to him the dangers of an attack on Mogilev by Kerensky's shock troops, reinforced by men from the Soldiers' Soviets and the Red Guards. Lukomsky passed the message on to Kornilov, who called to a conference the senior members of the staff. It was Lukomsky who, elaborating on the content of Alekseev's message, persuaded them that armed resistance was useless; he also appealed to their sense of innocence, pointing out that any committee of inquiry would surely find that Kerensky was to be held responsible for the whole imbroglio. After due consideration, it was decided to submit to Alekseev.

On the 14th Alekseev arrived at Mogilev and saw Kornilov. To Lukomsky he remarked that he had once more been offered the post of C-in-C and that he had accepted on condition that the army reforms proposed by Kornilov should be put through as soon as possible. Lukomsky replied scornfully, saying that if Alekseev believed that, he would believe anything. Lukomsky was, of course, right – but it is curious that he should have himself been equally naïve in assuming that a tribunal convened by Kerensky would ever find the Prime Minister to blame. When the order came to Alekseev that evening that he must arrest all prominent members of the General Staff, nobody should have been surprised.

Alekseev carried out Kerensky's command with all the tact of which he was capable. The order privately confirmed him in everything that he had thought of the Prime Minister, and in his belief that it would be impossible to maintain the Provisional Government in its present form. But, for the moment, he could only do his duty. Despite his care and circumspection, there was much latent bitterness, particularly amongst those who did not share his ability to take the long view. Kornilov told him, bitterly: 'You are taking the course which marks the division between the gentleman and the man without honour.'[1] In a sense, Alekseev must have agreed.

On 17 September the Provisional Government released Trotsky from the Kresty prison, where he had been held since early August.

---

[1] Golovin, *The Russian Army in the World War*, p. 280.

V

Headquarters to the Don

Alekseev's second tenure of office at Mogilev lasted just a fortnight. Yet again Kerensky refused to take action to restore discipline, and Alekseev had no option but to resign. Meanwhile, Kornilov and his fellow prisoners were at the centre of a charade characteristic of the situations that developed during Kerensky's term of rule. As soon as the news of Kornilov's arrest got abroad, representatives of the Tekintzy regiment approached the commission of inquiry to demand that they should be permitted to guard the man who, until that time, had been their commander. Their motives were not precisely those which the commission would have preferred, since the regiment remained fanatically devoted to Kornilov and was determined to protect him from the Soldiers' Soviets. So the official guard units stayed carefully outside the Hotel Metropol, in which the prisoners were held, whilst the Tekintzy patrolled the rooms and corridors within.

The commission itself turned out to be far more understanding than the prisoners had expected – or than Kerensky had hoped. Consequently, there were frequent mutterings, in the Prime Minister's entourage, about field courts martial and revolutionary tribunals, which were both bodies that might reasonably be expected to mete out the kind of swift and final justice that Trotsky was demanding from St Petersburg. It was such action that the Tekintzy were determined to prevent. Nor were they alone in their loyalties; each day the Kornilov regiment, which the C-in-C had formed – on a volunteer basis – while he was still commander of the 8th Army, marched past the hotel. Kornilov would stand at a window of the Metropol and the men would salute and cheer him. For Kerensky, still in Mogilev, furiously issuing orders to non-existent units, this was deeply galling. So, too, was the reflection that, had discipline been restored, he would not have had to devote fruitless hours to the search for a single battleworthy brigade.

It was not long before Kerensky had to admit defeat. He could not mount a convincing offensive, and any time that he spent at the front eroded what shreds of political power there remained to him in the capital. The Soviet grew stronger every day, and within the Soviet the Bolsheviks were rapidly gaining ground. It became imperative for Kerensky to return to St Petersburg, but before he did so he arranged for the removal of the prisoners from Mogilev and the transfer of the Kornilov regiment to the south-western front. To the post of C-in-C Kerensky now appointed General N. N. Dukhonin, a man whose chief recommendation for the job was that, for some inscrutable reason, he was prepared to take it on.

Bykhov, the new place of detention for the Kornilovist officers, was a former Catholic monastery not far from Mogilev. Here Kornilov, Lukomsky and other senior officers were joined by Denikin and those members of Denikin's staff who had been imprisoned with him when the news of Kornilov's move reached the south-western front. The conditions of imprisonment were not severe, mainly because a section of the Tekintzy regiment had taken over part of the guard duties, as at Mogilev, and the regiment's second-in-command had been made governor of the prison. Visitors were allowed, and no real attempt was made to screen them.

It was inevitable that the worsening situation should be discussed in great detail, and this was made easier by the fact that the prisoners were in communication with St Petersburg, Moscow and Mogilev. The circumstances of Kornilov's 'revolt' had the curious consequence that many people were not aware of what was supposed to be happening until it was all over, and a great deal of the support that he enjoyed received expression only after the collapse of the Krymov expedition. In a sense Kornilov was in a far stronger position – at least so far as the middle classes were concerned – after his revolt than before it. But his failure also made it clear to him that, however much the bourgeoisie might rally to him, he did not, for the moment, command the confidence of the classes who were the present determinants of the Russian scene. For this reason, amongst others, the generals in the Bykhov monastery did not spend their time in evolving a policy for counter-revolution, though it is possible that they might have been wiser if they had. Their first concern was for their own safety, but the problem that this presented obviously linked up with the question of political stability. Gradually certain common beliefs emerged, and these corresponded closely to the doctrine that Kornilov had so often expounded at Mogilev: discipline in the army must be restored, the war must be continued, and law and order must be maintained. None of the generals wished for a return to Tsardom, and they were all in favour of a Constituent Assembly. Such was their programme, if it can be called by so ambitious a name.

Events on the Don gave to their plans a more solid foundation. Kaledin's speech at the Moscow State Conference had led Kerensky to believe that the Ataman must be involved in the Kornilov conspiracy. The Prime Minister therefore ordered that Kaledin should be arrested together with the other generals. This provided an excellent opportunity for the Krug, which had grown increasingly out of sympathy with Kerensky's conciliatory policies towards the Soviet, to assert its independence. Between 18 and 27 September the Krug investigated and discussed the charges against Kaledin, eventually deciding that there was no case for the Ataman to answer. They then refused to hand him over to Kerensky, saying, in effect, that if anyone wanted to arrest the Ataman, they must come and get him. The Cossacks were a minority in south Russia, but they were the most powerful and unified single group within the area. Their decision over Kaledin, and a series of subsequent pronouncements in which they asserted their right to self-determination in internal affairs, their distrust of 'revolutionary justice', and their detestation of the agrarian policies of the Bolsheviks, gave Kornilov new hope. When it became apparent that there was nothing Dukhonin could do to salve the remaining reliable units from the increasing chaos of what had once been the Imperial Army, it was seriously mooted that officers loyal to the Kornilovist idea should be urged to make their way to the Don Territories.

Alekseev, after his second dismissal, at last seemed to realise that compromise with the Provisional Government was no longer viable. He had given the government his support, partly because it was the body to whom the Emperor had transferred the rule of the country and partly because it seemed the only possible alternative to the Bolsheviks. Now he was slowly and reluctantly coming to the conclusion that, if the Bolsheviks were to be resisted, it was necessary to create a third force. This he set about doing, using as his starting point the various Officers' Organisations and their semi-secret offshoots. Here again the Kornilov 'revolt' had gained an additional dimension of reality after the event: the nascent organisations that had so alarmed the St Petersburg Soviet were now becoming a force to be reckoned with. But the organisations are not to be seen, at this stage, as bands of activists; there was still a deep unwillingness in the officer corps to believe that all was lost. No officer was willingly going to embroil himself in a civil war whilst there was still an external enemy. And it was in the cities, where the Officers' Organisations were now based, that the extent of Soviet power was most apparent. There was nothing to be hoped for from an urban rising save unnecessary bloodshed, but the organisations could be used to raise money and as a centre through which officers could keep in contact with each other.

Thus it was Alekseev, the officer who was generally regarded as being cautious and at his best when dealing with paperwork, who took the first positive steps towards the foundation of the White Army; whilst Kornilov, the supposedly fiery and impetuous 'fighting general', did not decisively commit himself to a specific course of action. Indeed, Kornilov and the other prisoners at Bykhov were still hoping for a fair trial that would exonerate them of the charge of rebellion; had they wished to escape from their monastery-prison it would have been easy enough.

But Kerensky could not have granted them a fair trial, even had he wished to. On his return to St Petersburg he found the Soviet more powerful than ever before, and the Red Guards still in possession of the arms they had been issued when the 3rd Cavalry Corps had advanced on the city. In October a new organ of the Soviet came into being – the Military Revolutionary Committee. It was the contention of the Soviet that the Provisional Government was preparing to abandon St Petersburg to the advancing Germans; the purpose of the committee, it claimed, was to defend the city when this occurred. The government indignantly denied that it had any intention of abandoning the capital – though this denial was almost certainly untrue – and the committee thereupon turned its attention to the possibility of engineering a military coup. Factionalism within the Soviet left the Bolsheviks and the Left Socialist Revolutionaries (SRs) in sole control of the committee, and Trotsky as the predominant personality within it.

The coup was originally scheduled for the night of 5 November, but it had to be delayed, mainly because the plan hinged on the capture of the Winter Palace, and the soldiers detailed for this were deterred by the unexpected arrival of a Cossack cavalry squadron. The coup was rescheduled for the next day, though by now Kerensky was conscious that revolt was imminent. He was not alone in his awareness.

On the evening of 6 November – the day that Lenin, disguised by a wig and bandages, emerged from hiding and the Bolshevik Revolution began – representatives of the Union of Cossack Hosts, mainly consisting of Kaledin's supporters from the Don, begged Kerensky to take action against the Bolshevik headquarters at the Smolny Institute. Kerensky, at last revealing that he realised the critical nature of the situation, summoned General P. N. Krasnov from the northern front to take over military control of the capital. Kerensky also ordered the 1st, 4th and 14th Don Cossack regiments – Krasnov himself was from the Don – to march on St Petersburg and defend the government. The only forces that the Prime Minister could summon up within the capital were two companies of officer cadets and a Women's Battalion. These were vastly outnumbered by the fifteen hundred sailors whom the Bolsheviks had called in from Kronstadt. This had been done partly to counter the dubious loyalties of some of the St Petersburg garrison who, it was feared, might still support the Provisional Government although Trotsky appeared to have talked them round. But the Bolsheviks need not have worried; the garrison was not really interested in supporting either side by now – if the troops were on the side of any party, then it was that which promised them the easiest time. They were tired of politics.

So, too, were the Cossacks, and it was at this moment that a misconception, soon to become endemic, manifested itself for the first time. It had been presumed that the Cossacks would be loyal; in fact this was not the case. Cossacks in their homeland were by no means the same proposition as Cossacks in the strange surroundings of what seemed a foreign city; nor was the patriarchal structure of Cossackdom as secure as the spokesmen for the Union of Cossack Hosts liked to imagine. What the Union said did not necessarily go for the younger Cossacks; in any case the situation was far too complicated for the average Cossack soldier to understand. Had it been a matter of their homes and their farms things might have been different; as it was, the Cossacks preferred to prevaricate. They sent Kerensky a message that they were 'preparing to saddle up' and then took no further action. The squadron guarding the Winter Palace disappeared at an opportune moment, and when the Women's Battalion arrived to take up the posts that the Cossacks had abandoned, the onlookers jeered.

The army played no more part in the Bolshevik take-over, except in so far as its indifference made the whole thing possible. Amongst those who stood by without taking action were many regular officers. The Kornilov affair had destroyed what little faith they had in Kerensky, and the Bolsheviks at least had the merit of appearing to know what they were after. The defence of the Winter Palace by the Yunkers (officer cadets) and women was so ineffective that the building was infiltrated with ease, and by the evening of 7 November all St Petersburg was in Bolshevik hands. Kerensky fled the city and joined up with Krasnov, who had by now mustered a small force of apparently loyal Cossacks. On 11 November the Yunkers staged a rising within the cold and wind-swept city, whilst Kerensky and Krasnov advanced towards Tsarkoe Selo at the head of their Cossacks. The rising in the city was controlled by the Committee for Salvation, consisting mainly of officers, which had obtained several armoured cars that had formerly belonged to a British unit serving on the Russian front. But the timing was muddled and the forces were badly organised: the attempted revolt was put down swiftly and ruthlessly.

The advance on St Petersburg came to a halt the next day. Like Krymov's similar move, which it so grotesquely parodies, it failed because the troops were lacking in discipline and motivation, and were talked over by agitators. The subversion of the Cossacks serving in the army had long been a Bolshevik priority, and though Lenin had not held out much hope in this respect, the effort was more successful than he had anticipated. As early as 4 November the Soviet had managed to prevent a religious procession – intended to bolster the morale of the Cossack troops – from taking place, and the manifesto they issued to the Cossacks on this occasion, pointing out that Cossack generals were nevertheless generals, and that Kaledin was an enemy both of workmen and of soldiers, had a considerable effect. Pro-Bolshevik Cossacks went out to Tsarkoe Selo to try to talk over Krasnov's men; meanwhile the Red Guards hastened to defend the city. A number of officers expressed their loyalty to the Soviet and were appointed – under supervision – to the key commands. Krasnov's force had disintegrated, the General himself had been captured (though he was paroled by Trotsky five days later), and Kerensky, disguised as a seaman, had fled for good. Now the Bolsheviks had only the Germans to fear.

Alekseev had, narrowly, anticipated the revolution. He saw that there was nothing more he could do in the capital, and when the rising broke out he did not throw in his lot with Kerensky but chose to travel south towards the Don. Kaledin had urged him to join him at the beginning of the month, and it was to Kaledin that Alekseev now went. But whether the Ataman realised that he was offering sanctuary to the one man who had serious long-term plans for a counter-revolution is in doubt. Be that as it may, on 15 November Alekseev and his A.D.C. arrived in Novocherkassk, the capital of the Don Territories.

The Bolshevik Revolution made nonsense of the detention of the Kornilovist officers at Bykhov. The chairman of the commission of inquiry, who was officially responsible for the prisoners, therefore agreed to release all but the five full generals held there (to have released the latter would have been tempting the Bolsheviks too far).

The Bolsheviks were determined to make a separate peace with Germany if, as they expected, there was no satisfaction to be had from the Allies. They could not, in any case, fight on, and only peace would give them the breathing space that was essential if they were to consolidate their seizure of power. After the revolt the army had vanished with an almost supernatural swiftness, and even the authority of the Soldiers' Soviets collapsed. The St Petersburg garrison embarked on an orgy of drunkenness which lasted for almost a month. Antonov-Ovseenko (one of the triumvirate who had directed the organisation of the coup and now, along with Podvoisky, Commissar for the Army) reported he 'was caused much more trouble by the garrison, which began to disintegrate altogether, than by the supporters of the Constituent Assembly. . . . The few soldiers who had kept their discipline, and the Red Guards, were worn out by guard duty. Appeals to them were useless.'[1] Lenin had said that the soldiers 'voted with their feet', but what is often forgotten is that they forced a policy on the Bolsheviks at the same time as they made their rise to power possible; there were no choices for Lenin. Gradually the Allies realised that he really did mean to take Russia out of the war. The officers – many of whom had only given their support to the Provisional Government because they believed that the war came first – also began to realise that the Bolsheviks were not bluffing.

So long as the Bolsheviks continued with the war, such officers were prepared to be loyal. But when the news became known that the Bolsheviks were absolute for an immediate peace, they considered themselves released from their loyalties. On 20 November the Council of People's Commissars – now the equivalent of the cabinet – ordered the Commander-in-Chief to seek an armistice. Dukhonin made no reply. On the 22nd they demanded that he make his intentions known, and he answered that he would not obey such an order, as it did not come from 'a Government supported by the Army and the country'. He was at once dismissed from his post and Krylenko, a former government school teacher who had been involved as a student in the revolt of 1905 and had obtained an ensign's commission in the Imperial Army during the earlier part of the war, was appointed in his stead. The Allied governments at once protested in the strongest possible terms, but it was too late. Though Dukhonin disobeyed the Commissars, and stayed on at Mogilev, he did

---

[1] Antonov-Ovseenko, *Zapisky o grazhdanskoy voyne*, II, p. 19.

nothing decisive, and made no move to prevent the Soviets taking action against him. When the Bykhov generals appealed to him to flee with them to the Don, or at least to release them if he would not leave himself, he ignored their requests. Already Krylenko had issued an order distinctly ominous in tone:

> The former Supreme Commander, General Dukhonin, for having encouraged disobedience to orders and for criminal action liable to provoke a new civil war, is declared an enemy of the People. All those who support Dukhonin are to be arrested, regardless of their status, their political position, or their past. . . .[1]

This notwithstanding, Dukhonin remained at Mogilev, and even obeyed the tactical orders given to him by the new C-in-C.

On 1 December the Bykhov generals heard from Dukhonin that Krylenko had set out from St Petersburg with the intention of taking over G.H.Q. Dukhonin proposed that they board a train, which he would provide, and travel to the Don Territories. He suggested that they take the Tekintzy regiment with them. Kornilov and Denikin at once saw that this would be an exceedingly dangerous course of action, since it would be easy for the Bolsheviks to stop the train en route and do what they wished with the prisoners. As things turned out, the train never materialised; instead a further message came from Dukhonin to say that he was now in contact with Krylenko, and that he considered that there was no danger. The generals realised at once that this was a complete misapprehension, and after sending the messenger back to Dukhonin with a warning that his only hope of safety lay in flight, they made preparations to leave Bykhov. The governor was perfectly willing to fall in with their plans, but to protect their guards, the generals forged orders from Mogilev stating that they should be freed.

Kornilov decided that it would be safest if the generals split up and made their way to the Don separately. He himself proposed to make the journey of almost a thousand miles at the head of the Tekintzy regiment. On 2 December the generals set out on their winter journey, Romanovsky disguised as an engineer ensign, Markov as a private soldier, Denikin and Lukomsky as civilians –

---

[1] Krylenko, Order No. 2, *Izvestiya*, no. 226, 28 November 1917.

both using foreign aliases. By the evening of the 2nd they had each left the monastery, and at 11 p.m. that night Kornilov reviewed the guard company of the Tekintzy regiment and, in full uniform, led it away from Bykhov to the south-east.

The next day Krylenko, together with a band of Kronstadt sailors, arrived at Mogilev Station. Dukhonin had already been put under arrest by the local Soldiers' Soviet; when Krylenko's train came in the former C-in-C was brought to the station, the intention apparently being to send him back to St Petersburg to be tried. The appearance of the General was greeted by the crowd of soldiers with roars of fury. Krylenko appealed to the mob to let Dukhonin have a fair trial – but to what extent he was sincere is in doubt. When it was proposed that Dukhonin should be returned to the capital on Krylenko's train, the sailors jeered and drummed against the sides of the carriage with their rifle butts. Dukhonin appeared on the step, as though to address the crowd, and was shot before he could speak. His body was pitchforked with bayonets across the platform onto the rails. There it was left; it was a long time before anyone had the courage to remove it. Later, when the mob had dispersed to find other senior officers suitable for lynching, a train drew into the station, bound for St Petersburg. On it, wearing his uniform and badges of rank, was Lieutenant-General Baron Mannerheim. When he enquired why there was a large pool of blood on the platform he was told what had happened. He was not to forget the incident. The period of acquiescence had come to an end.

On 3 December, the day of Dukhonin's death, the armistice delegations of the Russian and German governments met. The outcome was the negotiation of a truce, and an agreement on the place and time for the commencement of actual peace talks. For those Russians who supported the Allies this was the end of the road. Such people were more numerous and sincere than we might imagine. Admittedly, they could not see, as Lenin saw, that the only hope of restoring Russian stability, and certainly the only policy which would ensure the support of the masses, lay in the conclusion of a peace. On the other hand, they were aware that German ambitions were a serious threat to the integrity of their country, that a peace based on the tacit premise that Russia was defeated would be unlikely to last, and that there was at least a strong possibility of an Allied victory. Some Russian officers posted abroad felt so strongly about this that, on hearing of the Bolshevik proposals, they took service with the Allied forces without standing on rank. Thus Colonel Paul Rodzyanko, who was in England after a mission to Italy, became first a private in the Royal Fusiliers and then a trooper in a cavalry regiment. Admiral Alexander Vasilevich Kolchak, former C-in-C of the Black Sea fleet, now passing through Tokyo on his way back from a mission to the United States, called at the British Embassy to offer his services to George V's government in any capacity, even as a private soldier.

The hopes of those who believed that the war must be continued came to centre more and more on Kaledin. In Moscow, now under Bolshevik control, a group of officers and military cadets planned an uprising. It was rapidly put down. The Bolsheviks claimed that the plot was headed by Purishkevitch, produced letters that he was alleged to have written to Kaledin, and, after a rather unconvincing trial, sentenced him to a very short term of imprisonment. This was an effective piece of propaganda: they succeeded in demonstrating their leniency (less in evidence in future trials of this kind), and also in linking the Don leader with the blackest kind of reactionary politics. That Kaledin had been instrumental in bringing to the notice of the Tsar the liberal Cossack Declaration of 1907 was now forgotten, and at this stage of the Bolshevik Revolution there were many who believed the slander.

In a remarkably short space of time – considering the distances involved and the turmoil of the country – the conflict polarised. On 7 December Trotsky ordered Krylenko to prepare to 'wipe off the face of the earth the counter-revolution of the Cossack Generals and the Cadet Bourgeoisie'. How Krylenko was to perform this edifying task was, like so much in the early stages of the revolution, unclear. The immediate plan was to send a force under Antonov-Ovseenko – who had been a captain in the Imperial Army before he turned his talents to the business of revolution – to the Don, and another force under Muravev to the Ukraine, where the Rada had proved as independently inclined as its close relation, the Don Krug. But all this looked far easier on a map than it was in fact to prove. Kornilov, who with his company of the Tekintzy had set out to make substantially the same journey, had soon run into trouble. Admittedly he had been harrassed by pro-Bolshevik soldiery, and his men were at one point attacked from an armoured train. It was, however, the physical difficulty of the march that finally caused the Tekintzy to propose that they surrender. Kornilov, after he had shown them the folly of this suggestion, was nevertheless constrained to order them to make their own way to Kiev, whilst he and his orderly continued to Novocherkassk alone and in disguise.

General Alekseev had been working for the foundation of the Volunteer Army since his arrival in Novocherkassk. The name Volunteer was a deliberate link with the original Provisional Government, since it was after the March Revolution that it had first been proposed that special Volunteer units should be used to provide shock troops for emergency use. The Kornilov regiment, which had caused Kerensky so much annoyance at Mogilev, was such a formation. Now Alekseev decided to use the term for his new anti-Bolshevik force. On 9 December, two days after Trotsky's order to Krylenko, the first units of the new army were paraded at Novocherkassk. Within the next few days all the Bykhov generals arrived at the town in safety.

The Volunteers did not receive that rapturous welcome from the Don Cossacks for which the optimists amongst them had hoped. They were greeted with suspicion and distrust. It is easy to see why: the Cossacks wished to be left in peace to settle their own affairs and to attend to the neglect of their lands that had been a consequence of mobilisation and the war. The Volunteers not only seemed a threat to Cossack autonomy, but also promised to be a direct provocation to the Bolsheviks, who were not without their adherents in the Don area – though these came mainly from amongst the *inogorodni*, those peasants of non-Cossack birth who now had begun to outnumber the Cossacks in what the latter considered to be their own country. On 10 December Rostov, the industrial town near Novocherkassk, was taken by a revolutionary coup, and Kaledin's troops refused to put down the rising. It was left for Alekseev and the Volunteers to storm Rostov on the 15th, and this short but fierce bout of street fighting can be said to have been the Whites' baptism of fire. It also served to gain them the recognition of the Krug, though the Volunteers and the Cossacks were seriously at variance over the terms on which this recognition was granted.

Kaledin was in serious difficulties. He derived his authority from the elders of the *stanitsas*, but the war had undermined the whole structure of Cossack society. The post of Ataman was an ancient one; it had been revived after a period when it had become irrelevant, and it now seemed, to some of the younger Cossacks at least, an anachronism. He found, therefore, that the number of fighting men who rallied to him was very small. The old Cossack loyalties were not dead, but for the moment Cossack interests lay elsewhere. Like many other Russians, the Cossacks did not become aware of the nature of the struggle in which they were involved until it was too late.

The arrival of Kornilov in the south, though it encouraged many of the Volunteers, did not improve their over-all position. His relations with Alekseev had never been easy, and now they were positively strained. Kornilov, the man of action, and Alekseev, the strategist and staff officer, were at variance from the start. The situation was complicated by the fact that in the chaos of post-revolutionary Russia, Alekseev's virtues had achieved a new relevance. Here was a man who was prepared to take the long view, to compromise, and to concentrate on a process of building in preference to a policy of immediate action. Kornilov, by contrast, looked for rapid results, and believed that a Bolshevik coup could be most effectively countered by a White coup. He did not see the necessity for a firm political base, and he preferred the sensation of command in the field to the more tedious emotions of the committee room.

Kornilov proposed that he should move eastwards and operate independently of Alekseev. But by this time anti-Bolshevik political leaders were beginning to arrive from the north and to take an active part in the Volunteer deliberations. Amongst them were Milyukov, Rodzyanko and Struve. They were determined that Kornilov should align himself with Alekseev and Kaledin, and they refused to pledge their political support to the Volunteer movement unless the three generals issued a manifesto and were clearly seen to be working together. They also pointed out that the Allied representatives in Russia were beginning to take a serious interest in the Volunteers, and went on to say that the

Allies would be prepared to assist with supplies and finance, on the condition that Kornilov came into line with the other leaders. Under protest Kornilov agreed. On the 31st December 1918 the political, military and Cossack leaders met to produce an agreement on Volunteer organisation and policies.

The consequence of this meeting was a document written by General Denikin, specifying that Alekseev should have control over finance, civil government and relations with the Allies, that Kornilov should act as C-in-C of the army, and that Kaledin should retain responsibility for the administration of the Don Territories and for the Don Cossack forces. Major policy decisions were to be settled by mutual agreement between the three of them. On 9 January Kornilov and Alekseev issued a joint statement in which they summed up their common policy:

> The first aim of the Volunteer Army is to resist an armed invasion of South and South-East Russia. . . . It will defend to the last drop of its blood the autonomy of the territories which give it sanctuary and which are the last bastion of Russian independence, the last hope for the restoration of a Free, Great Russia. But together with this, the Volunteer Army also has other aims. . . . [It] will stand guard over civil liberties until the day comes when the master of the Russian land, the Russian people, can express its will through the election of a Constituent Assembly.[1]

This manifesto revealed a firm commitment to the idea of a Constituent Assembly, the continuation of the war against the Germans – with whom the Bolsheviks were classed – and the independence of the Don Territories. It seemed a reasonable and liberal programme – as in many ways it was. But it was also exceedingly nebulous: the Constituent Assembly had not met, and what it would decide was hypothetical, so by their commitment to it the Volunteers disqualified themselves from having any effective political programme. Resistance to the Bolsheviks might be possible, but it was totally unrealistic to suggest that the Volunteers were capable of putting up any resistance to the German army. And it was perfectly obvious from the document itself that the resolution of Cossack autonomy with the idea of a Great Russia

---

[1] Denikin, *Ocherki russkoy smuty*, I, part 2, p. 198.

was vague and unconvincing. The Bolshevik cry of 'Down with the War, Down with the Landlords and the Kornilovist Generals' was far less susceptible of misinterpretation. The generals, desperate for information, bewildered, worrying about their wives and children, could look to the future with little confidence.

1918

The Time
of Troubles

The survivors – shall die; the dead – awake;
One day their sons shall ask, of days long gone:
'So where were you?' The words like thunder shake
And thunderously the answer comes: – the Don!

Marina Ivanovna Tsvetaeva (17 March 1918)

You have been fooled. You are cannon-fodder. You
are shedding the blood of the workers for the benefit
of the rich.

Trotsky to the Czech Legion
and the Whites at Kazan

VI

The Campaign through the Ice

Gradually the Volunteers became an army. Officers straggled in from all over Russia, not knowing what they would find on the Don but feeling that it represented their only possible refuge. One or two remnants of military units also made their way to Novocherkassk, including three companies of the Kornilov regiment which had been caught up in street fighting in Kiev. But though it was heartening for Alekseev and Kornilov to discover that some news of their whereabouts and intentions had spread through Russia, they were deeply disappointed by the small numbers of their emergent army. All in all, they could count on the services of about five thousand men, but many of these had to be sent off at once to perform garrison and security duties in the Don area, and the number that they could assemble for their expeditionary force was much smaller. The White leaders had hoped for a better response. What they failed to see was that many officers were as weary of fighting as the soldiers, that family ties naturally prevented others from leaving their homes for the long and hazardous journey south, and that, of the remainder, most were already either under Bolshevik supervision or – if they were at the front – under virtual arrest by their troops.

The financial situation of the army was desperate. At first the Volunteers received no pay. Eventually Alekseev managed to raise enough money to pay his men a small monthly salary, but this barely sufficed for food and other essentials. There was too great a disparity between the amounts paid to officers and to those in the ranks – many of the latter, of course, had been commissioned in the Imperial Army. The tendency of former officers to regard themselves as having an automatic right to posts of an equivalent standing with those they had held in the Imperial Army exacerbated a state of affairs that was to plague the Whites throughout the existence of the movement. Even in the early days of the

Volunteer Army the staff structure was absurdly disproportionate to the size of the force. Kornilov, Alekseev and Denikin each had their personal staffs, the considerable size of which weakened the fighting strength of the army, encouraged jealousy and intrigue, and had a wholly undesirable effect on morale. The Volunteers were far too short of cash and manpower to carry passengers; but this they did, even in the most desperate days of their existence. It is hard to understand why Alekseev, who was in such difficulty over funds, should have promoted the cause of the trouble.

Volunteer funds officially came from three sources: the bourgeoisie, who consistently promised more than they gave; the Don Government, who proved no less unreliable; and the Allies, whose agents were now in contact with the Whites, and whose reactions were encouraging, though they also failed to produce, for the moment, any hard cash. The Whites were running their operations on what was more or less a wind-fall. The Rostov branch of the State Bank had seen fit to register a protest against the Bolsheviks by 'lending' considerable sums of money to Kaledin and to the Whites. Since the Whites' share of the money did not pass through the hands of the Don Government, they received the full amount promised and were at least able to pay their recruits and to do what they could in the way of purchasing munitions and supplies.

Weapons were a serious problem. Some rifles were obtained from local armouries and by disarming Cossack units of dubious reliability. Others were bought from deserters or from troops loyal to the Don Krug. By now it was clear to the Whites that Kaledin's army was going to be of little use, Kaledin himself admitted that he had lost control of the situation. One of the first acts of the Bolsheviks, on coming to power, had been to set up a Cossack Department under two former Cossack soldiers, Lagutin and Nagaev; the intention was that this should replace the old Union of the Cossack Hosts. The Cossack Department functioned well, and it soon sent agitators to the south in considerable numbers. In the influx of demobilised and deserting soldiers they were impossible to detect. Their main message was that the Soviets did not intend, as the Whites claimed, to 'steal the land from the Cossack'. Certainly they would take away the great estates from the generals and the Atamans, landowners who

were Cossacks only inasmuch as they had temporary homes in
the area; but the ordinary Cossack would receive more land, not
less; an equitable sharing would be to his advantage. This was
an attractive and persuasive argument; the Cossacks had always
understood farming better than politics, and many were happy

to settle for the side who promised them a bigger orchard or more
horses. Moreover, the exclusiveness of the Cossack mentality
prevented them seeing the omission in this argument – that the
Cossacks were outnumbered by the poor and despised *inogorodni*,
and that these, too, would have to have a share in the land under
the Soviet dispensation. For the moment the Soviets were in the
ascendant, and Kaledin's powers came to rest on no secure foundation. Cossackdom had been misjudged once more.

The Volunteers took their arms where they could. They stole

two field guns from a Caucasian unit, they bought two more from Kaledin's men, and they borrowed a couple from the Don artillery depot 'in order to fire a salute at the funeral of a Volunteer officer', and then claimed to have lost them. But such methods could never provide the Whites with the artillery strength they needed, and they remained as short of guns as they were of transport, ammunition, clothing, medical equipment, and all other essential supplies. To these deficiencies we must also add manpower. As January passed the relationship with the Cossacks grew more and more strained, and it became increasingly difficult for recruits to get to Novocherkassk and Rostov. Alekseev began negotiations with the Ukraine, which was now distinctly anti-Bolshevik, with a Polish army corps operating against the Germans on the northern front, and with the Czechoslovak Legion, comprised of Czechs and Slovaks who, anxious for independence from the Austrians, had taken service under the Russian flag. None of these forces were prepared to play. The Ukrainians and the Poles were intensely suspicious of the Whites' adherence to the ideal of a Greater Russia: the Ukrainians began negotiations with the Germans, and the Poles expressed their loyalty to the Regency Council, which had been set up under German auspices in Warsaw. The Czechs remained anti-German but saw no reason, at this juncture, to throw in their lot with the Whites.

Kornilov's army was seriously under strength. In mid-January, when Antonov-Ovseenko's force of Red Guards moved onto the Don, the Whites could field three infantry regiments, three battalions of officers and one of Yunkers, three cavalry 'divisions' – one of these being composed of Caucasian tribesmen, including Tekintzy who had got away from Kiev – a small artillery team, and some scouting units. Antonov-Ovseenko had a much larger force than Kornilov, but his men were not the equal of the Whites when it came to military skill. The Whites were, in the main, trained soldiers; the Reds counted a few Kronstadt sailors amongst their number and also several units of Lettish riflemen, but on the whole they had to rely on workers and party members.

Antonov-Ovseenko's mission was urgent. The Don Basin contained some of Russia's most important coal mines, and fuel was in short supply in the north. Even more urgent was the need for food; Moscow and St Petersburg were both hard hit by famine, and the situation was steadily to worsen. So Antonov-Ovseenko's task was two-fold: to drive the Whites out of the Don area, and to ensure that regular train-loads of provisions got through to Moscow.

The White advantage, however, was purely local. Antonov-Ovseenko was not the only Red commander to have assembled a viable force: other formations had mustered at Mogilev and at St Petersburg. They were composed of volunteers; they were small in number; as yet they lacked cohesion and discipline. Their objectives were primarily defensive. Many of the soldiers were adventurers or released criminals. But the Bolshevik leaders were beginning to sense the necessity for an army. Former Tsarist officers willing to enlist were given a cautious welcome. Their numbers increased when, in January 1918, it was announced that officers would in future be appointed from above and not by election. It was a step away from the ideal; it was also a recognition of reality.

The first White unit to contact the enemy was an officers' battalion under Colonel Kutepov – the man who had tried in vain to organise resistance during the March Revolution. The battalion beat off repeated enemy attacks, but it was so seriously outnumbered that in the end Kutepov had to retreat. He fell back on Rostov, only to find that Kaledin's government was on the verge of collapse. It had been the Ataman's original intention that the Volunteers should defend the western borders of the Don area, whilst his own army took responsibility for the other fronts. But Kaledin's army disintegrated, as the Imperial Army from which most of its component units came had disintegrated earlier. The agitators of the Cossack Department had done their work well – mutiny was rife. The atrocities that were to characterise the Civil War were in evidence from the opening phase. The Cossacks were a paternalistic society, and when the Hosts divided against each other, then war was both parricidal and fratricidal.

Faced with the collapse of his allies, Kornilov decided that he must move south into the Kuban. He did so because it was clear to him that the Volunteers had no future in the Don area, not because he felt that it was any more likely that they would be enthusiastically received in the Kuban Territory. Alekseev went so far as to say that, strategically, the Kuban was useless, but both generals were agreed that to move into the steppes was the only course of action left open to them. They could not defend either Rostov or Novocherkassk; therefore they must take their chance and attempt to establish a base in the southern Cossack lands, on the eastern shores of the Black Sea. Kornilov sent Kaledin a telegram telling him of this decision, and later General Lukomsky came in person to explain to the Ataman why the Whites felt that they could no longer give him active support on the Don.

Kaledin tried in vain to raise a volunteer force of his own. On 11 February he read Kornilov's message to the members of his government; he also told them that, from all the Cossacks of the Don, including the military units, he had had only one hundred and forty-seven volunteers. He thereupon resigned, advised the government to do the same, and left the room. Later that day he shot himself through the head.

This gesture aroused Don loyalties far more than anything else that Kaledin had done, and the new Ataman, General Nazarov, was elected amidst a sudden upsurge of Cossack enthusiasm. But it was too late. The Bolsheviks had succeeded in bringing out on the Red side a large number of troops stationed in the northern Crimea and the eastern Kuban; these were an immediate threat to the new régime. The Don Territories were effectively surrounded: only in the Kuban was there as yet no organised movement against them. In response to a last-minute plea from Nazarov the Whites stayed – to find there was no more strength in the new government than there had been when Kaledin was Ataman. The same problems persisted. When the 6th Don Cossack Regiment arrived at Novocherkassk, its discipline unimpaired, the new Ataman welcomed it as the bulwark of Cossack hopes. The men were sworn in to the service of the Krug, attended a *Te Deum*, and were sent to the front. Within a day the unit had ceased to exist. The men dispersed and rushed to their farms as fast as they possibly could. Elements of the 4th Don Regiment did the same. The Whites returned to their original decision, and left the Don to its fate. On 22 February they abandoned Rostov for the south. They left the city in the evening, Kornilov marching at the head of his staff through the silent streets. As they evacuated the town the local Reds emerged from hiding. Two days later Rostov was in the hands of Antonov-Ovseenko's men. On 25 February Lieutenant-Colonel Golubov, a Red Cossack leader, broke into the Parliament House at Novocherkassk with twenty-seven men, declared the Krug dissolved and shot Nazarov and several other members of the government in a nearby wood. Fifteen hundred Cossacks under General Popov followed the White example and took to the steppes. For the moment, they were all that remained of the Host of the Don.

In St Petersburg and Moscow the Reds had not been idle. On 18 January the Constituent Assembly, the institution in which the Whites reposed so much of their faith, had been permitted to meet. The next day the Assembly was dissolved by the Executive Committee of the Congress of Soviets, on the grounds that it was 'only a screen to hide the counter-revolutionary struggle to overthrow Soviet power'.

In early February Muravev moved on the Ukraine and occupied Kiev; the Reds did not gain any lasting control over the area. This was because the Ukrainian Rada had none of the scruples about the necessity of continuing the war against the Germans that so beset the Volunteers. Having accepted fifty million roubles from the French they then entered into separate negotiations with the Germans, requesting their protection from the Bolshevik threat.

At Brest-Litovsk the peace talks had come to a deadlock. For a time the Bolshevik leaders wondered seriously whether they should continue the war. Eventually they realised that this was impracticable, Krylenko stating that the Russian people 'were not interested in a war on the external front – the main thing was to make sure that the old army was entirely destroyed, and to replace it with a new Socialist army dedicated to the extermination of the Bourgeoisie'. Nevertheless, it was not possible to ignore the German threat, and Trotsky's 'no war, no peace' formula, which attempted to do this, proved a failure. When the Russians refused to fight – but did not sign a peace – the Germans commenced a rapid invasion of south Russia, which lasted from mid-February until March. It was not until 3 March that the treaty was finally signed.

In the course of this invasion the Germans took over the Ukraine, and under the protection provided by German troops a Ukrainian National Government was set up by Hetman Skoropadsky, a former officer in the Chevalier Guards, whose family had held the Hetmanate in the distant past. In 1917 Skoropadsky had expressed his loyalty to the Provisional Government, affirming that he was 'quite free of any desire for self-determination'. He was soon to be flying the yellow-blue flag of the Nationalists and disdaining overtures from the Volunteers, whose subsequent bitterness against him knew no limits. They did not see it as coincidental that Skoropadsky's brother-in-law was the commander of the German troops in the Ukraine or that Skoropadsky himself was one of the biggest Ukrainian landowners. The Volunteers, struggling across the hostile steppes, could do nothing about the German invasion, but it was henceforth – inevitably – an added complication in their plans. Compromise with the Germans was possible: Skoropadsky managed it, as did Svinhufvud's Finnish Government, but neither Alekseev nor the other Volunteer Army leaders were prepared to change their allegiance.

When the German advance took place it meant little to the Volunteers, who were cut off from the rest of Russia by both distance and the encircling pro-Bolshevik troops. Their first objective was survival, and this meant that every contact with the enemy was a matter of life or death. There was nowhere for them to retreat; they had simply to hope that they might capture Ekaterinodar, the Kuban capital, and that the Cossacks, after a dose of Bolshevism, might rally to them. But it was a faint hope only.

The army moved out into the steppes across the thawing ice of the Don. The Cossacks were distinctly unfriendly, refusing the army shelter in the *stanitsas* and demanding exorbitant prices for horses and equipment. Kornilov insisted that these prices be paid, just as he refused – at first – to use conscription to fill out his cadres, in the hope that by considerate treatment the Volunteers would pave the way for future Cossack support. Kornilov realised that, for the moment, he could expect nothing from the Don, and after a fruitless attempt to persuade Popov to join forces with them, the Volunteers headed for Ekaterinodar.

Before they reached Kuban territory they had to fight. Quite who their opponents were they could never be sure, but their most formidable enemies were certainly former Imperial Army units now under Bolshevik control. The Whites now began to learn the meaning of civil war, for they took their first officer prisoners. After court martial these were given the chance to join the Whites and almost without exception they accepted. Why then had they fought against the Volunteers? Partly because their men forced them, but largely because they had been ordered to, and they were not accustomed to question orders.

In the Kuban the Whites met with a better reception than they had encountered in the Don Territories. But it was apparent that the Bolsheviks were rapidly infiltrating the Kuban, and the Kuban Volunteers, whose political alignment was similar to that of Kaledin, were rapidly losing ground. The need for haste became even greater, if Ekaterinodar was to be secured. At the *stanitsa* of Kornivetskaya, only three days from Ekaterinodar, the Whites ran into heavy resistance from the Bolsheviks and suffered considerable casualties. In less than a month they had lost four hundred men, and though they were recruiting from amongst the Kuban Cossacks, they could never survive such a death toll. When they had finally forced the enemy to abandon Kornivetskaya, they heard that the Kuban Volunteers had fled from Ekaterinodar and retreated into the mountains. During the last days of March the Volunteers pushed on southwards, through the rivers and marshes of the Kuban, the mud and ice of a thaw that had long begun but seemed never to be coming to an end.

The survival of the army was a miracle. Perhaps it was only the extreme adversity of their fortune, the knowledge that if they surrendered their enemy would give them no quarter, that made the Whites go on. The whole movement was now manifested in this tattered force, little stronger than two regiments, headed by two former commanders-in-chief of the Imperial Army, staffed by men accustomed to handling divisions and corps, its platoons commanded by elderly colonels, and its privates former lieutenants or seventeen-year-old military cadets.[1] They were short of

---

[1] Let us ignore that propaganda which had it that the Whites were particularly ruthless to use the Yunkers as they did. The Bolsheviks used men of equivalent youth with equal unscrupulousness.

horses, so many of the senior officers walked, including Kornilov, who trudged along, his head sunk deep in the collar of his goat-skin coat and a haversack over his shoulder. Increasingly this short, spare man, with his face prematurely wizened around the slanting eyes, came to dominate the army. Alekseev still commanded loyalty, but he was ill and often constrained to travel in one of the ramshackle carts that made up the tail of the column. With him was one of his sons, who was able to nurse his father and prevent him being a burden on the others. In a battered suitcase Alekseev kept what was left of the army's funds. The baggage in the carts was very simple – there was scarcely any ammunition, for the Whites had set out with only six hundred shells for the whole of their artillery, and two hundred rounds for each rifleman. When they needed more they had to capture it from the Reds.

The daily marches became progressively more dangerous. In the area near Ekaterinodar, the Kuban was traversed by three railway lines that linked the city with the Black Sea and the Caspian: the lines were Bolshevik controlled. Together with the rivers they made formidable obstacles, for there was little that the Whites could do against an armoured train, and if the Whites were caught actually crossing the line then they would have almost no chance at all. After the news of the flight of the Kuban Volunteers the Whites had wondered whether it was justifiable to continue towards Ekaterinodar. Kornilov was attracted by two alternative plans: one was to cross the Kuban river to the south-east of the city and attempt to re-form and reorganise in the comparative security of the mountains; the other was to break out in the direction of Siberia and establish a base there. But no one could be certain what conditions they would find in either instance, and it was Kornilov's eventual decision that the march on Ekaterinodar should be resumed. The army turned to the west, marching parallel with the Kuban river and then swinging round the city in a northerly direction in an attempt to take it from the rear. Their advance was strongly opposed by the Reds, who managed several times to trap the Volunteers at deep fords or in narrow valleys. Each of these actions should have been decisive, but every time superior ability and sheer desperation saw the Whites through.

Kornilov apart, the most outstanding of the Volunteers' field commanders was General S. L. Markov: it was his officers' regiment that, more than any other unit, contributed to the survival of the Whites at this time. Markov had been a lecturer at the General Staff Academy, and his background was primarily academic. In 1914 on his arrival at the front to take up the post of Chief-of-Staff to Denikin, he had earned the contempt of his fellow officers by refusing to go into the firing line, claiming that he had had an operation and was unable to ride a horse. It was promptly assumed that he was a coward. However, a few days later, the same officers were startled by a heavy increase in the enemy bombardment of the track leading to the trenches. The reason for this became clear when a large barouche came into view – inside which, quite composed, sat Markov. He explained that he had got bored, and had come to see what was happening. From then on he was always in the thick of any fighting in which he could find an excuse for involving himself, until he eventually managed to exchange his staff posting for a regimental command. He was true 'fighting general' material; cap on the back of his head and riding switch in hand, he was always to be found in the front line.

It was Markov who superintended the fording operations, who kept the column moving along the roads deep with mud and scummed with ice, who led the last desperate charge with which the officers' regiment cleared a *stanitsa* where the Bolsheviks had established a position, so that the wounded could be brought under cover for the night and the soldiers sleep in shelter. The column moved on through snowstorms and sleet, often travelling long after nightfall before they made camp. At Novo-Dmitrovskaya – the *stanitsa* stormed in the dark by Markov and his officers – contact was established with delegates from the Kuban Volunteers. Both armies were in dire straits, and in imminent danger of destruction, but still they managed to disagree over the terms on which they should unite. The Kuban delegates were anxious to make it clear that they were independent of the Greater Russian bloc, whilst Kornilov was adamant that he would not command 'autonomous' armies. Fortunately the credibility of the delegates was undermined by a message from the commander of the Kuban Volunteers, offering to desert to the Whites with his entire force if the political leaders could not reach agreement. A settlement was arrived at, and over the next week the Kuban troops came in to join the Whites in Novo-Dmitrovskaya. The reinforcements, together with a considerable quantity of ammunition captured from the Reds a few days before, made an assault on Ekaterinodar possible.

Kornilov's plan for the capture of the city was simple in concept, complicated in practice, and entirely dependent for its success on the fact that he had highly trained troops whom he could trust implicitly, and who he knew could be left, when necessary, to act on their own initiative. The first aim was to scatter the enemy forces operating between the Whites and Ekaterinodar, and to capture as much ammunition as possible. Then, when the dangers of observation had been reduced to a minimum, it was planned to make a forced march to a *stanitsa* seventeen miles west of the city, where there was a ferry across the river. From there the attack on Ekaterinodar would be launched. Cavalry were sent at once to seize the crossing, whilst the mopping-up operations were arranged to look as though they were the prelude to an attack on the city from the south. This was indeed the direction from which the Reds expected Kornilov to come, and they took elaborate precautions to defend the town. They did not imagine, however, that Kornilov would risk a crossing of the fast-flowing Kuban, fed by mountain torrents and now in full spate with the thaw, when only a single ferry remained. Yet this was what he did, even though he knew that by so doing he was committing his men to a route along which it would be almost impossible to retreat. The crossing took three days, despite the fact that a second ferry had been found downstream and that fishing boats were commandeered to help move stores across. Kornilov was past caring about Cossack susceptibilities: Ekaterinodar was too important a prize for him to risk, and he began to conscript local Cossacks in an effort to improve his cavalry strength. Morale was buoyant and when, on 9 April, the enemy attempted an attack on the crossing place, they were repulsed with severe losses. The Reds retreated towards the town, eventually establishing defensive positions in some farm buildings on a ridge that commanded the city. On 10 April the Whites, after heavy fighting, succeeded in clearing the ridge and taking the farm. In the whitewashed farmhouse itself Kornilov set up his H.Q. From the building he could look down on Ekaterinodar, with its straight streets typical of Imperial garrison architecture, and the golden domes of an oriental town. The spring had come at last, the weather was fine, and the Whites knew an optimism they had not experienced before. The artillery dug in near the H.Q., and in the evening, news came through that the outskirts of the town had already been occupied by White troops.

This presaged well; in the past, once a suburb of a town had been taken, the Reds had always refused to give battle in the town itself and had retreated without further resistance. But, on the morning of the 11th, officers in the farmhouse H.Q. were woken by the crash of Bolshevik artillery. Ekaterinodar was not to conform to the usual pattern. Avtonomov, the Red commander, was determined that the Whites should be defeated, and his orders left him in no doubt that this was also the desire of his superiors. When, that day, Kornilov mounted a heavy frontal assault on the town, his men made little progress. He was hampered by having to leave a large proportion of his army back at the ferry to guard the baggage and the crossing. Now the defeat of his first attempts to take the town meant that the Reds had time to build breastworks and fortifications, and the longer that Kornilov failed to take the town, the more formidable these became.

Avtonomov was able to employ the civilians in the town as labourers on the fortifications, and he was aided in this by the fact that Kornilov had attempted a complete investment of the town and had left no escape route for the usual outflow of refugees. This, together with some judicious propaganda, induced the inhabitants to believe that, should the Volunteers get through, they were all doomed. Avtonomov made the best use of his advantage. He was comparatively strong in artillery; he was fortunate both that there was an ordnance depôt in the town, and that the forces at his disposal included sailors trained in gunnery, together with a number of Imperial Army artillerymen.

That these men were present in Ekaterinodar was largely due to the formation on 1 March of the Supreme Military Soviet. This decision was at first eclipsed by the signing of the Treaty of

Brest-Litovsk, and the subsequent removal of the Soviet Government to Moscow on 12 March. On 13 March, with the appointment of Trotsky as both President of the Military Soviet and
Commissar of War, a new phase in the development of the Red
forces began. The Military Soviet could not at once alter the
whole conduct of the Civil War, but they could at least ensure
that the units at their disposal were deployed as effectively as
possible. Ekaterinodar was a far more serious obstacle than the
Volunteers had optimistically imagined.

The Whites attacked again and again. Markov and the officers'
regiment seized an artillery barracks on the outskirts of the town;
the Kornilov regiment was decimated in its attempts first to
capture – and then to hold – an ancient burial mound overlooking
the Bolshevik trenches. Late on the 11th a group of White
partisans under General Kasanovich managed to break through
the ring of defences and enter the town. Kasanovich assumed
that he had support on his flanks, but did not think to check;
consequently he had reached the Haymarket, near the centre of
the town, before he realised that he was on his own. He decided
that he could not possibly hold out in daylight and, after capturing some baggage wagons and horses, he endeavoured to retreat.

Both sides wore what uniforms they could find: there was no
mark to distinguish them except for the occasional five-pointed
star of the Reds and the epaulettes of the Whites. Kasanovich's
men removed their badges of rank and managed to bluff their
way through the Bolshevik firing line: it was only when the
baggage wagons appeared that the Reds woke up to what was
happening. Kasanovich was not necessarily wise in his course of
action. Had he and his 250 men stayed and fought he could have
caused chaos within the town, and it is possible that the Whites,
who held the positions of vantage round Ekaterinodar, would
have seen what was happening and managed to relieve them.
In any case, the effect on Red morale would have been devastating.
But Kasanovich – and in this he was typical of all the less able
White officers – was still thinking in terms of another kind of
war. As the Bolsheviks had more than 20,000 men at their disposal, and the Whites had only 2,600 who were in any condition
to fight, the Whites could hardly expect to win by conventional
methods.

Fighting went on through 12 April to no avail. In the afternoon the Whites held a council of war in the cramped farmhouse rooms. Kornilov outlined the situation and stated it as his view that the only possible course of action was a general attack on the town at dawn the next day. When asked for their opinion the other generals, except for Alekseev, replied that this was impossible. But they were not prepared to stand up to Kornilov, nor did they wholeheartedly try to persuade him to change his mind. Eventually Alekseev suggested that the attack be postponed until the 14th – a compromise which was gratefully seized on by all present, including Kornilov. But the other generals still could not see how, short of ammunition and severely depleted in numbers as they were, the Volunteers could conceivably mount another attack on the town.

The 13th was to be a by-day, devoted to regrouping before the final attempt to carry the city. The enemy's artillery was still as active as ever, and the prominent farmhouse was dangerously exposed. In the early morning of the 13th Kornilov's staff tried to persuade him to move to a safer place, but he refused, on the grounds that they would be attacking within twenty-four hours. Since the council of war Kornilov had seemed moody and depressed: this was attributable to both the failure of the attempts on the city, and the death of Nezhintsev, commander of the Kornilov regiment, to whom he was particularly attached. For the first time since the Volunteers left Rostov their C-in-C was showing signs of strain; his face was grey with tiredness, and he had become exceptionally taciturn. On the 13th he had got up, as usual, at dawn; after briefing his staff he went back into his room at the farmhouse to think about the dispositions for the attack on the following day. Just after 7 a.m. members of the Headquarters staff heard the whine of a shell. Accustomed to enemy near-misses, they instinctively assumed that it would land beyond the farmyard. But when the explosion came it was at once apparent that they were wrong. Soon everyone was running towards the C-in-C's room.

Kornilov lay on the floor beside the stove, his body covered in dust and flakes of plaster. The shell had entered the room through the outside wall next to the window, and had exploded when it hit the floor. When his staff reached him Kornilov was still alive, though his thigh was smashed and a wound on his temple suggested that a splinter had lodged in his skull. His breathing rapidly became fainter, and it was obvious to those present that he was about to die. Denikin, Romanovsky and the officers of the staff looked on until, after a few minutes, it was over. The two generals endeavoured to keep the news from the rest of the army, but the attempt was hopeless; soon every Volunteer knew, and the attack petered out before it had properly begun. There seemed no chance now that the Whites could accomplish what they had set out to do.

Denikin, as second in command, took over the post of C-in-C; an army order confirming the appointment was issued by Alekseev the same day. Alekseev received the news of Kornilov's death with his usual impassivity; in a way it must have come as a relief, since the rift between the two men had not been mended even by the shared sufferings of the campaign through the mud and ice of the Kuban. At the same time, Alekseev could not but admit that Kornilov's example had fired the Whites with a genuine loyalty, and that his handling of the army had made it the most formidable single military force in Russia. When Alekseev passed by Kornilov's cortège – the General lay on a wagon under his goatskin coat – he halted the improvised hearse, guarded by those of the Tekintzy who had made their way to the Whites, knelt down on the ground and kissed the dead man's forehead. It was a sincere and moving gesture, and as near to a conventionally Russian expression of emotion as Alekseev ever came. Later, Alekseev, Denikin and the other generals sat on their coats by the roadside and discussed what was to be done. They were all agreed that the only hope lay in retreat, to get away from the areas where the Bolsheviks had organised, into more hospitable country. Previously they had considered the plan and rejected it; now they had no choice.

Long after sunset on the 13th the army made off to the north. Their march was silent and hurried, but it was disciplined: here the officers' training told repeatedly. Several times they avoided Bolshevik parties, and there were one or two sharp skirmishes before they were clear of the Ekaterinodar district. The immediate problem was to get away from the system of railway lines, for these were commanded by Bolshevik armoured trains. Speed was essential, and the most severely wounded had to be left behind under the care of a doctor and some nurses. No one had much hope that these men would survive, but this seemed the only thing to do. In the Kuban neither side took prisoners, the Whites because they could not encumber themselves further; the Reds either because the Whites did not, or because they believed that the only good bourgeois was a dead one. This state of affairs was to be the norm throughout the war. Kornilov was buried secretly and by night, in an unmarked grave. The next day the Reds, searching for valuables they believed the Volunteers to have hidden, found the body and identified it from the general's shoulder-straps on the tunic. They took it back into Ekaterinodar, where it was hung on a tree, then kicked around the street before being burnt in the municipal slaughter-house.

The Volunteers pushed on to the north and then to the north-east. They travelled by forced marches, and, finding that they only had thirty shells left, they abandoned all their guns but four. Each railway line was a major hazard, for the column was some seven miles long, and took a long time to pass any given point. Though the line might be cut, this could not be done too far from the place at which the army crossed if the cutting details were to remain in contact with the main force, and there was no real answer to the problem of what happened should an armoured train come along the line. Not long after they had left Ekaterinodar the Volunteers had their narrowest escape of all. The retreating army had nearly been cut off by strong Bolshevik forces, and for the only time in its history morale collapsed. For several hours Denikin was afraid that there was going to be a full-scale panic, but the situation improved once the column was on the march again. At 4 a.m. they reached a railway line, which had to be crossed before dawn. The station close to the crossing proved to be occupied by the Reds, and Denikin decided that the place must be captured. General Markov, in a characteristic position at the very head of the army, came up to a signal box, captured the signalman, and having found out the man's name and other necessary information, telephoned to the station to quiet the garrison's suspicions. But Volunteer squads sent to storm the station building ran into Red sentries, and shortly an armoured train, which had been waiting in the station, crept down the line.

Only the light of its furnace flickering on the embankment showed the Whites where it was. Such trains were heavily armed, often with substantial artillery pieces, and the Whites had nothing with which to oppose them. By the signal box Alekseev, Denikin, Markov and the staff waited: if they were seen, one shell could wipe out all the leaders of the White movement. Eventually the train glided up level with the signal box.

At this moment Markov broke the paralysis that seemed to have gripped the White staff by rushing towards the engine, waving his riding-crop, and ordering the driver to stop. Automatically, the man did so. Before he had had time to recover Markov leapt up onto the footplate, grabbed a hand-grenade from one of the riflemen standing on the engine and threw it into the firebox. The train was now immobile, but the troops on board kept up a heavy fire with rifles and machine-guns from inside the steel-plated carriages. Eventually the Whites managed to bring one of their guns up to the signal box, and began to shell the train at point-blank range. Since the Reds could not get to their heavy weapons, which were mounted on exposed platforms, they had no means of retaliating, and in a short while the train was carried, the Bolsheviks being put to the bayonet.

An unexpected consequence of this action was that the Whites were able to replenish their stocks of ammunition – their most pressing need. When they continued their march north they were still under considerable pressure from the Reds, but the action against the train seemed to have given them a new confidence. The White objective was once more the Don – to be precise, the southern Don steppes, where three of the new 'republics' and three Bolshevik military districts had their juncture. This, Alekseev and Denikin reckoned, would be as safe as anywhere. There was news from the Don that made the Volunteers, despite their weariness, quicken their pace. A cavalry patrol, raiding deep into Don Territory, came back with a hundred White Cossacks and the news that the *stanitsas* beyond the river had risen in revolt. On the Saturday before Easter the Whites captured the village of Egorlyskaya, in the trans-Don territories; they were almost back where they had started. Later Denikin rode to the church for the midnight mass. On the way he talked to General Romanovsky, now his Chief-of-Staff. Romanovsky reflected that two months before the Volunteers had been passing through the very same places to which they had now returned. Half to himself he asked whether the Whites had been stronger then than they were now. According to Denikin, Romanovsky answered his own question: he decided that they were stronger now. In the campaign through the ice they had lost their leader and at least four hundred troops, but they had also found unprecedented unity of spirit.

The manner of Kornilov's death was typical of his strengths and limitations. Had he moved his headquarters to a less exposed position, he might well have escaped the attentions of the Red artillery and survived to continue the campaign. Yet it is possible that he was to prove more potent in his death than he had ever been whilst he was still alive. His life was marred by his weakness for the 'fighting general' tradition, by his sacrifice of forethought for daring, and by his impetuous actions. None of his characteristic poses was wholly bad, but many of them would have served him better had he been a colonel rather than a general and a commander-in-chief. Once he was dead his faults ceased to matter, and his memory served as an inspiration for the great majority of those who fought and died on the White side in the Civil War.

In the first Kuban campaign the Whites found themselves both as an army and as a movement, thereby doing something to close the gap that separated them from the Bolshevik party – which had been welded into a workable whole by the harsh necessities of a clandestine existence. The Whites who had fought in the Kuban campaign became the élite; the campaign remained, it can be said, the foremost expression of the White ethos. It is significant that this should have been so: the Bolsheviks had an ideology, but all the Whites could show as the basis for their beliefs was the bitter anabasis of the Kuban campaign.

There were some who responded to this as they could never have responded to the repetitive insistencies of the Bolshevik message. But the Whites were proposing a romantic ideal in a world where hunger and bloodshed had made the ideal irrelevant. They were offering sacrifice to a people who already knew too much about it. This was to prove deeply damaging to the White cause; there was too much concentration on the tale – heroic enough – of their own Caucasian martyrdom, and not enough of an effort to understand the experience of others. Yet those others were the people on whom the Whites would have ultimately to rely. Far to the north of the Don, another general of the Imperial Army was also fighting the Bolsheviks. His campaign, unlike the first Kuban campaign, was to end in clear-cut and mensurable success. That this was so was largely because of his ability to listen to others, and because of the attention that he paid to the views of those outside his own immediate circle of colleagues and friends.

VII

General Mannerheim and the Finnish Victory

Gustav Mannerheim has already appeared in this narrative. It was he who gave to General Wrangel, when Wrangel was travelling to St Petersburg from the south-western front, a first-hand account of the Revolution. Mannerheim had been in the capital during the March Days and had narrowly escaped arrest; he was to pass through it again in November. There can be no doubt that his experiencing both Revolutions at first hand decisively influenced his anti-Bolshevik viewpoint. Yet it cannot have been a simple matter, for the revolution left him enmeshed in a net of apparently conflicting loyalties, which admitted of no easy resolution.

The Mannerheims were a Swedish family that had taken up residence in Finland whilst it was still a Swedish province. They soon showed, however, that their loyalty was primarily to the land of their adoption; when, after the war of 1809, Finland was made a Grand Duchy of the Russian Empire, Gustav Mannerheim's great-grandfather was chiefly instrumental in negotiating the settlement with Russia that allowed Finland a Diet of her own. Subsequent Mannerheims held important posts in the government; Gustav Mannerheim's father, by nature a saturnine and retiring man, nevertheless made a point of regular attendance in the Upper House of the Finnish parliament.

This institution, the Diet, was of fluctuating importance. The limited autonomy of the country was the subject of continual attacks from St Petersburg. Whenever the autocracy determined to take a tighter grip on the empire, Finnish rights were automatically threatened. Gradually the liberties granted in 1809 were eroded. The effect of this was to intensify nationalist feeling within the country.

Gustav Mannerheim was born in 1867, in the Manor of

Willnas, a large, square, seventeenth-century house built on an inlet of the Baltic. That year there was a severe famine throughout Finland; it cannot have much affected the Mannerheims, but it caused appalling distress to the peasants, especially the Lapps, who eked out a precarious existence in the fastnesses of the extreme north. The Russians made no attempt to alleviate the famine, and its severity was so great that it had the effect of awakening a new interest in the country. This ushered in a period of reform which was to make the subsequent destruction of liberty in Finland even more devastating. The precarious nature of Finnish autonomy did not prevent many Finns taking service in the Imperial Army. For some pride was salved by the nominal existence of a Finnish Army, comprised of elements of the Imperial Army recruited exclusively from Finland. Gustav Mannerheim was determined from his earliest years, that he should pursue a military career, and it was appropriate that he should be sent to the Cadet Corps of the Finnish Army at Frederikshamn.

He was a natural soldier, and academically gifted as well, though his high spirits and predilection for going his own way caused him to be expelled from Frederikshamn for taking unofficial leave. This left him in a quandary over the direction of his future studies. He experienced a brief but powerful desire to be a sailor, and only through the intervention of a family friend could he be persuaded that it was best that he should continue with a military career or go to a university – he eventually chose to join the Nikolaevsky Cavalry School at St Petersburg. Here it must have become obvious to him that he was in a foreign country; he was teased about his accent when he spoke Russian – Swedish was the language of the Finnish aristocracy – and he was a Lutheran in an establishment that was, as a state institution, Orthodox. This did not prevent Mannerheim being more successful than he proved at Frederikshamn; he was soon regarded by his superiors as a man marked for high command, and his initial service showed him to have a practical as well as a theoretical grasp of his subject. Promotion was rapid. In 1899 he became a staff captain in the Chevalier Guards. Service in this élite unit meant that he was in close touch with the Imperial family; he was chosen to form part of Nicholas II's personal bodyguard for the coronation ceremony, and he was often called upon to attend court functions. His social prowess was the open envy of his fellow officers, and was marred only by the break-up of what had been thought to be a brilliant marriage to the daughter of a wealthy Muscovite family.

1899 may have been a year of personal success for Mannerheim; nevertheless, it cannot have proved entirely satisfying. For it was in 1899 that really drastic steps were taken by the Tsar and his

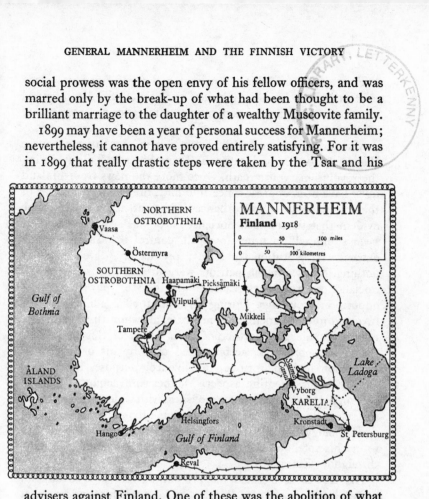

advisers against Finland. One of these was the abolition of what remained of the Finnish Army, without even a nominal concession to national feeling. Finland was subjected to an intensive period of Russification aimed at destroying all traces of national identity. One of the main organisers of resistance to the Russian moves was Mannerheim's elder brother, Carl, who was exiled for his activities.

It is a characteristic of the Russian situation that this anomaly in no way hampered Gustav's career. In 1903, the same year that his brother was exiled, he was appointed to command the crack Model Squadron of the Imperial Cavalry School. Here his superior was Brusilov, who, before his involvement in the affairs of 1917, was most widely known as a theorist of cavalry warfare.

Mannerheim shared this enthusiasm, and transformed his squadron from an anachronistic joke into a unit that fulfilled its intended function as a testing and demonstration force for new concepts of cavalry tactics.

Mannerheim served with distinction in the Russo-Japanese War, and travelled back along the Trans-Siberian Railway during the revolutionary aftermath. Once more the news from Finland must have been of great concern to him: the province was one of the first places where disturbances broke out, and it soon became evident that the Finnish Socialist Party was stronger than had been supposed. In order to regain control the Tsar promised extensive constitutional reforms; predictably, these came to nothing. Many Finnish patriots were to find themselves in the Socialist camp simply because it was the most powerful of the opposition groupings. During 1906 to 1908 Mannerheim was involved in a remarkable journey of exploration through southeastern Russia and northern China. Much of this he accomplished on horseback, accompanied only by his orderly. The expedition had an obvious 'intelligence' purpose, but it also had a serious scientific aspect. Mannerheim acquitted himself well on both counts, and the seriousness with which he approached the scientific side is worthy of note. He took a crash course in anthropology and archaeology before setting out, and on his return his notebooks became valuable source material for scholars throughout Europe.

His travels accelerated his promotion, and also made him something of a social lion. But this, he remained first and foremost a professional soldier – too professional, some thought. His dislike of 'civilians in regimentals', and his often distant nature, did not endear him to everyone. A subordinate remarked that he 'could do everything by the book, and even drank in such a way that he stayed sober'.[1] Mannerheim's aloofness had more than a little to do with a consciousness of his nationality. In 1911 he became a major-general, and in 1912 he was made an honorary A.D.C. to the Tsar. At the same time renewed efforts were under way for the Russification of Finland, and the foremost advocates of this were the conservatives in the Imperial Duma. We know

---

[1] Ignatev, *Pyatdesyat let v stroyu*, I, p. 88.

that once Mannerheim dared to represent to the Tsar the gravity of the Finnish case, risking his career, as well as his position at court. The nationalities problem must have been particularly brought to Mannerheim's attention when he was appointed to the Warsaw military district. The position of the Poles was not altogether dissimilar to that of the Finns, though the Polish landowners were of far more significance as a social group than the Finnish upper classes.

The outbreak of war found Mannerheim still in Poland, and he was soon involved in the offensive operations with which the Russians opened their campaign. In little over a month the Russian armies were in full retreat, and Mannerheim was to distinguish himself in a number of holding and covering operations. In this he resembles Kornilov, and he was in fact serving on the south-western front alongside the future C-in-C during the months between the two revolutions.

After an initial flirtation with the idea of counter-revolution, he had seen his duty chiefly in terms of the continuation of the war and of loyalty to his comrades and men. The abdication and detention of the Tsar made more of a personal impact on Mannerheim than on many other senior officers – perhaps because as an A.D.C. and a shooting companion of the Tsar he had a greater understanding of, and sympathy with, the man beneath the Imperial trappings. For Nicholas, Mannerheim had a qualified admiration, and on hearing of the Grand Duke Michael's abdication he approached Sakharov, a senior general, and suggested that he might lead a counter-revolution. But Sakharov demurred, and Mannerheim did not pursue the idea. Nevertheless, it is an interesting revelation of his immediate reaction.

Though Mannerheim was clear in his detestation of certain aspects of Imperial Russia, he was attracted by the ideal. The frame of an Empire had encompassed his whole career, and he had no easy way of thinking himself out of the Imperial context. He had also experienced directly the German military threat. For these reasons, and for the by no means negligible reason that he came to approve of democratic rule, he fought on. He was not simply the 'model mercenary' that both left- and right-wing critics have chosen to brand him. He was a professional soldier, and aware that his professional obligations appeared to run counter to his private loyalties; this awareness did not compromise what he regarded as his over-riding commitment – to the Tsar to whom he had sworn his oath when he was commissioned, and to the government to which the Tsar ordered, as his last act, that his subjects should transfer their loyalty. It was only when discipline in the army collapsed, and all traces of the institution in which he had served seemed to have disappeared, that he finally made the break which, once accomplished, appeared so natural.

In October Mannerheim used a fall from his horse as an excuse to resign his command. He went to Odessa for treatment, and in that city by the sea he saw, and was disgusted by, the number of former officers who spent their days in idleness. He was in Odessa when the November Revolution broke out, and he made none of those conciliatory gestures to the new régime that became so popular with his former colleagues. It is indicative of the strength of Mannerheim's character that he had kept his command, the 6th Cavalry Corps, loyal throughout the summer of 1917; only the Savage Division had managed to maintain the same corporate integrity. When his former soldiers met him as he walked the streets of the town in unfamiliar civilian dress, they saluted. There were few other officers for whom they would have done the same.

It was now that Mannerheim's apartness stood him in good stead. On 3 December he decided that he must move from Odessa. He did not go, as so many were going, to the Don Territories and the standards of the Volunteer Army. Instead he chose to make the journey northwards. He travelled on the crowded Bolshevik-controlled trains in full uniform, wearing the hated epaulettes and all his insignia of rank. It was safer, he felt, to rely on the old habits of obedience than to risk the hazards of disguise. Accordingly, he commandeered a private coach. His strategy proved correct. Mannerheim succeeded in reaching St Petersburg in safety – taking under his protection some English nurses whom he found to be travelling in the same direction.

In St Petersburg, where the old ruling classes still lived out a hollow imitation of their former lives, Mannerheim tackled at least one Grand Duke on the theme of counter-revolution. But he met with no response; despite the tenuous nature of Bolshevik power, those who might provide an alternative were apathetic and quietist. The Bolsheviks were not resisted when they made their arbitrary arrests, and the General Staff was without any effective direction and divided in its loyalties.

Mannerheim decided that he must leave St Petersburg; events in Finland were now his main interest, and though it did not seem that he would be any more secure there than in Russia, there appeared to be more room for political manœuvre. He would also be amongst friends and compatriots.

On 6 December Finland had declared her independence of Russia. The decision was reached by the Diet – reconstituted after the March Revolution – only after a long and bitter debate. In the final vote, 100 for independence to 88 against, the majority was obtained by a coalition of all the non-Socialists. The Socialists were in favour of a union with the Russian Soviets – a course of action to which they were urged by Stalin in person.

The Prime Minister, Svinhufvud, had an uneasy parliamentary majority. It can have afforded him little peace of mind. The Red Guards, active in the south of Finland during 1905, had been resurrected. They were led by mutinous elements of the Russian army, the discipline of which collapsed in Finland more swiftly than it did elsewhere, mainly because of the tedium of garrison duty and the ease of access to St Petersburg. An elaborate plan for the fortification of Finland against a possible attack through Sweden (whose neutrality was always in doubt) meant that large numbers of Finnish workmen had been working along-side these same demoralised troops, and had become closely associated with them. Thus the Socialists were in a position to use force, whilst Svinhufvud was comparatively powerless.

The main hope of the Finnish right lay in the Jaeger battalion. The outbreak of the World War had been followed by the grotesquely ill-timed and possibly accidental publication of a Russian programme for the final obliteration of all traces of Finnish nationalism. As a direct result many Finns had decided that their only salvation lay in a German victory; organisations were set up in Sweden which would recruit Finns to fight along-side the German armies. In 1915 the first two hundred Finns had arrived at a camp in Holstein, where they were given preliminary military training, and in May 1916 the battalion, now eighteen hundred strong, was sent into action against the Russian western front.

The relationship between the Finns and the Germans was never an easy one; like the corresponding Czech Legion, which fought for the Russians against an equally oppressive system of empire, the Finns were deliberately kept out of the front line when political crisis threatened. Throughout 1917 the Jaegers grew increasingly restive.

In mid-December Mannerheim boarded a train from St Petersburg to Helsingfors. His papers were invalid, and the journey was once more hazardous. Yet he was to repeat it within a week. On his arrival in the Finnish capital he was approached by former colleagues in the old Finnish Army who had set up a Military Committee to co-ordinate national defence. The Military Committee was looking to the Jaegers and Germany for support; this was not an attitude that Mannerheim, who had been fighting the Central Powers for the last three years, was prepared to endorse. He therefore returned to St Petersburg in the hope of enlisting the help of the French Military Mission. He also took the opportunity to renew his contacts with the various organisations of ex-officers in the city, with the object of persuading sympathisers to help the Finnish effort. In this he met with little success. Although any fighting done in Finland was bound to be anti-Soviet, the more traditionalist officers were already firmly committed to the concept of the restoration of a Greater Russia.

This attitude is the more natural when we consider that most of them managed to regard the period of Bolshevik rule as symptomatic of a brief attack of national insanity from which Russia would shortly re-emerge in all her ancient glory. Mannerheim was already decided that this could not be the case. He returned to Helsingfors with no assurances of any value from either the French or the Officers' Organisations.

On 31 December 1917 the Russian government officially recognised the independence of Finland. In practice this meant nothing. The Red Guard was still a threat to democracy within the country, and there were also a large number of Russian Army units stationed within Finland. Civil war seemed imminent, though such a conflict could equally well be construed as centring on the issue of independence. A mere four days after Lenin had assented to the recognition of a separate Finland, Stalin persuaded the Executive Committee of the Soviet to alter the terms of the document, and a proviso was entered to the effect that the negotiations for the practical separation of the two countries must be attended by 'representatives of the Finnish proletariat'. The terms on which the Bolsheviks were prepared to grant the Finns independence can be gauged far more accurately from the tone of Stalin's speech to the Finnish Socialists at their congress in Helsingfors than from any subsequent disclaimers:

In such an atmosphere [of war, economic disruption, and revolution] there is but one power, Socialist power, which alone can sustain itself and conquer. In such an atmosphere there can be only one kind of tactic – that of Danton: 'Audacity, audacity, and again audacity.' And should you need our help we shall give it you, extending to you a fraternal hand. Of this you may be certain.[1]

It is not too extreme to say that independence for Finland meant freedom for the Finnish Social Democratic party to re-unite its country with Russia. The December agreement was, like Brest-Litovsk, a means of obtaining a *peredishka*, a breathing space.

Consequently we have in Finland the paradox of a war that can be regarded as either a civil conflict or a fight for independence; the former description being preferred by the left, and the latter by the right. This does not mean that all Socialists supported the Red Guard; many of them were to fight for Svinhufvud and the Military Committee. But in the initial stages loyalties were confused and allegiances muddled.

During January the issue became clearer. This was largely because several countries, in rapid succession, recognised Finnish independence and the Svinhufvud government. These were, in order, France, Germany, Greece, Norway, Denmark, Austro-Hungary, Switzerland and Holland. Many Finns felt that they could no longer withhold their support for a government that had gained the acceptance of Allied, Central Power and neutral countries. A further clarification followed when operations by the Military Committee commenced.

At the end of December Mannerheim had been asked to attend

---

[1] Stalin, *Sochineniya*, IV, p. 5.

the meetings of the Committee. The Committee had already offered the post of C-in-C of the Finnish army to General Charpentier, another former officer of the Imperial Russian Army. Charpentier was sixty – ten years older than Mannerheim – and somewhat lost in the bewildering complexity of events. Mannerheim accepted Charpentier as C-in-C, but eventually declined to take part in further meetings of the Committee, which he considered to be wasting invaluable time over bureaucratic trivialities. He told the Committee that there was only one possible course of action for them. In Helsingfors, a town dominated by Red Guard and Russian units, none of them was personally safe. They ran the risk of arrest daily, and they were out of contact with their potential recruits. The immediate necessity was for the establishment of a field force. The Military Committee could only operate in a part of the country where they could secure a base area, and therefore they must move at once. He finished his assessment of the situation by saying: 'Let us go there tomorrow, if the last train for today has already left.'

This was basically the same reasoning that lay behind the decision of Alekseev and Kornilov to go to the Don Territories; once again we find conservative leaders forced to employ the tactics of guerrilla – and traditionally revolutionary – warfare. It serves to emphasise the urban bias of the Bolsheviks, and the old association of traditionalists and the land. Mannerheim was fortunate that he was able to express his views to an organisation that already had a rudimentary but effective network of communication. He did not have to hope, as Alekseev did, that somehow news of his decision would filter through the murky confusion of revolutionary Russia. The Military Committee also had a vital advantage as a result of the social structure of Finland. There was no tradition of serfdom for them to live down. Landlords had been good masters, and the proportion of peasant-owned holdings was infinitely higher than in south Russia. Yet, for the moment, there was one overriding problem. Mannerheim, who so evidently had the inspiration and the will to succeed, was not in a position to command.

That he should do so was at once recognised by the Military Committee. It is to their credit that they took immediate action, and asked Charpentier, to whom they had already committed themselves, if he would be prepared to go into Svinhufvud's cabinet as Minister of War, instead of commanding in the field. Charpentier responded that he considered the Military Committee in no way bound by their previous decision – thus making the way clear for Mannerheim. The awkward division of power that so afflicted the Volunteer Army was avoided. In Mannerheim the Military Committee had, as a member said, the 'very man we wanted, a commanding, energetic, and self-confident soldier'.[1] The more politically conscious noted, too, that Mannerheim's prolonged absence from Finland meant that he had no particular political associations. This, though the Russians – who held him to be the 'hangman of the Finnish Revolution' – could never accept it, was largely true. When the war was over he was prominent in attacking the idea that former Red Guards should be tried, and gave frequent evidence of political impartiality. But in so far as he was a confirmed and articulate enemy of Bolshevism, he was inevitably political and, by his own admission, a White. We return to the basic dilemma: a White, who as often as not regarded himself as being a-political was, for the Red, the most politically tainted of all animals.

On 16 January Svinhufvud verbally appointed Mannerheim to the post of C-in-C. (Such was the state of Helsingfors that no written confirmation was possible.) Before Mannerheim left Helsingfors, a fortuitous encounter with Axel Ehrnrooth, a banker and old school friend, resolved one major problem, that of finance. A conference of bankers was called for the evening of the 17th, at which Ehrnrooth said to his colleagues 'If all goes well, you'll get your money back, and if it doesn't, all will be lost in any case.'[2] This argument – which was surely correct – prevailed, and 15,000,000 marks were made available to Mannerheim. Why such a course was never pursued in Russia is a mystery.

On the 18th Mannerheim set off for Vaasa, a city two hundred miles north-west of Helsingfors, in south Ostrobothnia. He and the four officers who formed the nucleus of his staff travelled by Bolshevik-controlled train with false passports. There is a certain absurdity in the idea of these five hated counter-revolutionaries

---

[1] Hannula, *Finland's War of Independence*, p. 39.
[2] Mannerheim, *Memoirs*, p. 139.

going to set up their army by means of the enemy's transport. It nearly turned into a disastrous journey for Mannerheim. A patrol searched the train whilst Mannerheim was asleep in his berth, and when he awoke he unthinkingly spoke in Russian. Suspicion was aroused, and he was questioned; in order to pass a case of vital documents to his aide he pretended modesty and closed the curtains of his berth while he dressed. The patrol were dangerously inquisitive: only the mysterious intervention of a 'young man wearing a uniform cap' kept them from detaining the General. The name of the youth, and whether he realised Mannerheim's identity, remain unknown. At Vaasa Mannerheim set up his G.H.Q. He proved a ruthless and implacable task-master. His first objective was to establish a workable staff structure and an effective commissariat. Shortage of trained and reliable officers threatened to be his main problem. In marked contrast to the Volunteer leaders he tolerated no insubordination, and refused to appoint officers to commands simply because they had held a commission in the past. Part of his requirements was met by a training school that the Military Committee had set up at Vimpali under General von Gerich – another Finn who had served in the Imperial Army. The other main sources were the officers of the old Finnish Army, Imperial Army officers of Finnish origin, men who had served with the Jaegers, and the leaders of the local Defence Corps.

The Defence Corps were essentially vigilante organisations – disguised, in some instances, as fire brigades. They were made up mainly of peasants, largely untrained except in hunting, and they were seriously short of arms and equipment. Their chief source for these was the Russian army, since the soldiers were willing to make what they could by selling their rifles. The more conscientious entrepreneurs, the money safely received, then informed the local party men where they suspected that the Defence Corps might have hidden arms. It was an affray consequent on such information that sparked off fighting in Karelia, Finland's southern border province.

At the same time Podvoysky, Soviet Commissar for War, ordered that Russian troops in Finland should disarm the Defence Corps. This decision was made on 23 January, and it was tantamount to a declaration of war. Three days later Svinhufvud's cabinet published a proclamation setting out the position in which the government found itself, and calling on all Finnish citizens to resist attempts at rebellion and the overthrow of the democratically elected régime. This was immediately followed by an appeal from the General Staff of the Red Guards and the Excom of the Socialist Party. The appeal was a clear call to revolution.

In Karelia the Defence Corps met with initial local successes. Four ministers of the Svinhufvud government arrived at Vaasa, which strengthened the political position of the White Army; Mannerheim, who was still able to talk by telephone to the Prime Minister in Helsingfors, decided that the time had come to assert control of southern Ostrobothnia. But on the 28th, when Mannerheim's forces went into action at Vaasa, the Red Guards carried out a coup in Helsingfors and Svinhufvud went into hiding.

At Vaasa Mannerheim had found it hard to control the enthusiasm of the local Defence Corps, which was led by a former N.C.O. of the Guards Regiment of the Finnish Army, Matti Laurila. Laurila, a farmer, had brought out all the men of his village, and they were eager for action. Mannerheim was able to persuade Laurila that he must wait, and Laurila recognised in Mannerheim the leader that Finland needed. The General's ability to command the loyalty of these peasants and small farmers meant that the White army enjoyed the confidence and support of most of Finland's rural population. It was to prove an inestimable advantage.

To those who knew him, it seemed that there was a distinct change in Mannerheim during early 1918. His standards were still as high as they had ever been, his capacity for work remained phenomenal, and he lost none of his professional capacity for painstaking attention to detail. He was, however, far less withdrawn, far more approachable, and he gave an impression of being at ease with himself. The old air of tension and reserve had largely disappeared. At the same time, he seemed even more direct and decisive than he had been hitherto. When the Senate in Helsingfors had second thoughts about the appropriateness of military action at this juncture, he disregarded them. He knew what had to be done, and he saw no point in delay.

At the same time there was more evidence of humanity in him than there had been before. Mannerheim cannot be said to have cultivated the common touch; his staff were always immaculately dressed, compliments were given and returned punctiliously, command was rigidly exercised. But the General's dry humour was much appreciated by his fellow countrymen, and he undoubtedly felt more at ease as Commander-in-Chief than he had ever done in subordinate positions. In his white *papakha* (fur hat) and fur-collared greatcoat, he was to become a familiar figure in the front lines; his leadership was personal, though his maintenance of a chain of command was meticulous. His tall figure, remarkable among the Finns, his wry remarks and his habit of always having a cigar or a pipe in his mouth soon made him as well-known throughout his new command as he had been to the Chevalier Guards.

Mannerheim's main tactical precept was that the initiative must at all costs be won and preserved. He had seen in Russia how inertia and apathy had enabled the Bolsheviks to conquer even though they were a minority group, and he was aware that Bolshevik organisation, at present weak, was certain to become more effective. Delay would prove fatal to the White cause. On 27 January Russian communications were cut and their outposts seized. At 3 a.m. on Monday, the 28th, a bell in a Vaasa church tower broke the stillness of the northern night to signal the attack on Russian detachments in the city. Before the dim half-dawn the Finns were in control of all key positions. The insurgents transmitted the news to the Helsingfors Excom on the captured military telegraph before they closed down the line. By the end of the month five thousand Russians had been captured, and all of southern Ostrobothnia was in White hands. News of the Red defeat encouraged other units of the Defence Corps to take the field; the extent of the victory was far greater than Mannerheim had anticipated.

It was now that the strategic reasons for Mannerheim's choice of Vaasa as a base became apparent. A coup, similar to that at Vaasa, was carried out at Uleaborg in north Ostrobothnia by 300 Defence Corps men with only 90 rifles and 15,000 cartridges between them. They succeeded in surprising the Russian garrison of 1,000 and the Red Guard of at least 500; though outnumbered, they held on in the town until they were relieved by units from the south of the province. Soon north Ostrobothnia was also under White rule, and Finland was virtually cut in two.

The deep indentations of the coastline, the lakes, swamps, and forests, all make Finland a country particularly vulnerable to lateral movements. Mannerheim seized on this and related it to his deep understanding of the mentality of the Russian soldier. Courageous in the mass, Russian units were at their weakest when forced to act independently. So, though Mannerheim had enemies both to the north and to the south of his position, he could count heavily on the demoralising effect of his move; an effect that would be heightened when the spring thaw would make the passage of frozen waterways impossible.

Once the initiative was gained, Mannerheim made certain that he kept it. Two moves, one to the north, the other to the south, further strengthened his base. In the north the town of Tornio, where the Gulf of Bothnia railway crossed into Sweden, was taken by another *coup de main* on 7 February. This made the delivery of supplies from Sweden possible, and aided the attempts of pro-Finnish groups, such as that set up by Mannerheim's brother Johan, to get men and munitions into the White areas. The move to the south brought about the capture of Haapamäki, the junction town of the Haapamäki-Pieksämäki railway, which served as what can be termed a projected axis for the Finnish railway system. Before the construction of this line, there had been two parallel systems, extending north and south through Finland – one in the east, the other in the west. The Haapamäki line, which was finished only in January 1918 (it is extraordinary that the revolution did not affect such things), linked the two.

There was no front line between Red and White Finland. By the end of February northern Finland was entirely in White hands – over half the country, though containing only a small proportion of its resources of man-power and industry. This did not unduly worry Mannerheim, who felt that his basic premise – that Red power depended on bewilderment and inertia – pointed to a victory won as a consequence of the right use of speed and surprise, rather than as the conclusion of a lengthy war of attrition. This was one reason why he never allowed a formal front line to develop. The other determining factor was the situation of the enemy. The Red Guards were primarily urban based – the factory town of Varkaus was the last place to fall in northern and central Finland – but factory towns were not the predominant feature of the Finnish scene. The Russian army was by no means solidly Bolshevik. Its confused soldiers preferred the security of fortified positions to active campaigning, and its leaders, despite orders from the Soviet, were not always prepared to co-operate with the Red Guards. It was only in the big garrison towns, and near the Russian border, that Red morale was high and its leadership determined. In these places the belated coming of the Revolution had brought with it a Red terror that was far more horrifying in the small, tightly knit Finnish communities than it had seemed in the relative anonymity of the Russian urban scene. Already there was an influx of middle-class volunteers from the cities at Mannerheim's G.H.Q.

At this point we may take stock of the overall situation. Mannerheim had obtained a large and secure base area, with a line of communication to Sweden. He had also secured vital sectors of the Finnish railway network. His front line was fragmentary, but he was not interested in positional warfare; his campaign was dependent on movement. He was short of manpower. There was an excellent cadre of both officers and men, but the problem was to fill out the skeleton structure of the army. He had accepted the services of several Swedish officers, who resigned their commissions in order to be free to fight for the Finns; there was also a battalion of Swedish volunteers. He was hoping for the return of the Jaegers from Germany; some had already come over individually in order to fight for him. He had the all-important Defence Corps, but many of these were ill-trained, and most were badly equipped. He also had a number of men who had served in the old Finnish Army, or in the Imperial Russian Army. He was still short of troops. Eventually, in mid-February, he decided to start conscription, on the basis of those laws which had been in force when Finland was a Grand Duchy, before the period of Russian oppression. On this foundation he hoped to raise twenty-one battalions of 650 men.

The Reds faced rather different problems. Mannerheim suffered from a shortage of officers, but this was nothing to the dearth experienced by the Reds. It was not simply a case of not having enough officers; they lacked *anyone* trained in the requisite staff and administrative work. Things might have been better had there been effective liaison between the Russian army and the Red Guards. This had been urged by Lenin, but co-operation was minimal. The language difficulty, a hindrance even to the educated – as it was to Mannerheim when he had to be coached in Russian before going to the Nikolaevsky – was acute amongst the lower classes. Nor were Finnish Reds inevitably unpatriotic; there were those amongst them who, whatever they might wish to feel, found that the brotherhood of man stuck in their throats when it was taken to include Russians. Though overall command of the Reds in Finland was deputed to the Russian staff, co-operation at lower levels scarcely existed. And though the Russian army in Finland was numerically strong, its troops were amongst foreigners, many units were demoralised, and all were unaccustomed to the extremities of the Finnish winter.

The recruiting base of the Red Guards was amongst the Finnish trade unions. As with the Whites, they soon had to resort to conscription. But, however loyal their recruits, this did not solve the problem of an effective leadership, or of extremist elements amongst the Reds who were more interested in robbery and terrorism than in serious military operations. A far more real Red advantage than the presence of the Russian army lay in the unhindered flow of supplies from St Petersburg. At this stage of the Civil War the Soviet was profligate in its distribution of weapons, though it can be argued that Mannerheim gained more from this than the Reds. For, apart from one or two consignments from Sweden, he was dependent on what he could capture. His position was so serious that he set up an armaments factory, under the Swedish Count Adolf Hamilton – an entirely ruthless officer who devoted himself to one of the most difficult and thankless tasks of the war. In a remarkably short time Hamilton was producing grenade-throwers and mortars. Once again Mannerheim's army showed what could be done with sufficient determination – there was no equivalent of a Hamilton amongst the Russian Whites.

The temporary breakdown of the negotiations at Brest-Litovsk meant that, after 18 February, the Russians began to withdraw their troops from Finland. This was mainly through fear of provoking a German landing; consequently a great many Russian officers, commissars and N.C.O.s were surreptitiously left behind to aid the Finnish Reds. In many ways the withdrawal simplified their situation, but they still failed to evolve an adequate command organisation. The Russian withdrawal left the Reds with some 90,000 men under arms; Mannerheim had no more than 40,000. His disadvantage was not as great as it seemed: amongst the Red troops were conscripted men and peace-time socialists who had no stomach for civil war. Consequently desertion was commonplace. Mannerheim, by contrast, was able to watch his forces grow daily.

Mannerheim, having seized the tactical initiative, was now to see other hopes fulfilled. By the end of February most of the eighteen hundred Jaegers had returned from Germany to Finland. Though he had anticipated their return, it presented practical problems, since the Jaegers, not unnaturally, wished to preserve their distinct identity as a unit, whilst Mannerheim felt that they could be used to best effect if they were split up amongst his new battalions, to provide a stiffening of trained troops. Mannerheim soon won the confidence of the Jaegers, and the initial scepticism that some of them felt about serving under a 'Russian general' quickly disappeared.

The second phase of the war begins with official Russian withdrawal from the conflict. The Reds were now under the nominal command of Eero Haapalainen, though the executive commander was in fact a Russian, Colonel M. S. Svechnikov. Svechnikov had previously commanded the 106th Infantry Division, which was based on Tampere, in the south-west of Finland, and he was one of the most able officers to have come out as a supporter of the Bolsheviks. His plan involved, after a march on Haapamäki, the recapture of the railway, and then a two-pronged advance into Ostrobothnia. The counter-offensive lasted into the beginning of March, but the Reds were unable to make any real impression on the White position. Mannerheim, impatient of defensive warfare at the best of times, was determined to mount a deep attack into southern Finland as soon as possible. The thaw, which would consolidate his own defensive positions would perform the same function for his enemies. The result would be a summer of deadlock, during which the Reds would be able to utilise the resources of southern Finland. There was an additional danger in that the Reds enjoyed the services of the Russian navy; a seaborne assault was a far more serious threat to the Whites than any overland attack, and the Baltic would soon become navigable.

The Whites had to act fast. There was no time for them to worry about their deficiencies in trained troops and in equipment; they had to destroy the Red Army by the middle of spring. Mannerheim determined on two immediate objectives: the removal of the threat to Haapamäki and the capture of Tampere, which had become the focal point of the Red movement.

Svinhufvud and his Senate had the same considerations very much in mind. Their own solution to the problem differed sharply from Mannerheim's, however, for they felt that the main hope of Finnish salvation lay in German intervention, while Mannerheim considered that no lasting stability could come to Finland if her internal problems were solved by military action on the part of a foreign power. Svinhufvud justified the move by pointing to his parliamentary majority; Mannerheim, more realistically, considered that this argument would never satisfy the Finns who supported the Reds, for they would eventually have to take part in Finnish affairs if Finland was to remain a democratic country. Already he was looking to the political settlement with which the war must end, and he saw, in German intervention, a serious obstacle to a satisfactory agreement.

The German forces would take some time to reach Finland. Mannerheim used the delay to accelerate his new offensive. Any victories won before the Germans arrived would mitigate the effect of intervention. On 5 March he sent a telegram to Ludendorff, asking that the German expeditionary force be placed under the command of the Finnish C-in-C as soon as it arrived in the country, and that the German commander issue a manifesto stating that German aims related to Russia only, and that the German force had no intention of interfering in internal Finnish affairs.

In the first days of March the Red counter-offensive came to a halt. There were places where the White defences were strained, particularly in the west, along the coast of the Gulf of Bothnia, but all sectors held, and the Reds were repulsed. The failure of their plans caused a split within the Red command, and eventually Haapalainen was dismissed as C-in-C. On 14 March Mannerheim took the initiative once again. The Reds had over-extended themselves in their offensive, and they were now temporarily without a leader. The first step in the advance was a pincer movement designed to cut off and surround the Red troops who had advanced towards Haapamäki. The plan was to continue this movement and if possible to envelop the vital Red position at Tampere. The Whites advanced successfully against what was initially strong opposition, but the right flank was not able to move quickly enough to get behind the retreating Reds. A major hold-up was caused on the 18th by an armoured train sent up by the Red command and partially manned by Russian sailors of the Baltic fleet – the men who, more than any others, deserve to be called the Praetorian Guard of the revolution. Fortunately this train had to be withdrawn during the night to replenish its stocks of fuel and ammunition. The Whites, taking advantage of this respite, counter-attacked and wrecked the line.

G.H.Q. had been gradually moved south; from Osteermyra to Vilpula, and from Vilpula to Vehmais four miles east of Tampere. Throughout the Tampere operations Mannerheim had also to give his attention to the situation on the Karelian front. Here the Whites, after the success of their original risings, had been hard pressed; though they consolidated a certain amount of territory they were forced onto the defensive, save for small-scale raiding which they used to keep the Reds in a state of confusion and to deceive them over White deficiencies in manpower. Eventually the Karelian Whites were forced to appeal to Mannerheim for reinforcements. These Mannerheim could not give. He might have managed to divert some of his troops to the Karelian front, but it would have reduced his chances of capturing Tampere, and he saw this town as the key to the Red position. To reinforce Karelia would not have been to reinforce failure; the Whites were holding their own. But Mannerheim believed that in the circumstances – and outnumbered as he was by nearly three to one – he could only afford to reinforce success.

Even this he would have found difficult, since his ten thousand men were fully extended by the end of March. On the 24th, White units had managed to get south of Tampere, so the city was now surrounded, but it proved, in Mannerheim's words, a 'harder nut than I expected'. The Red artillery, set up in prepared positions, was well trained and formidable. The Red soldiers in the town fought with exceptional bravery, partly because they feared reprisals for their brutal massacre of eighty disarmed members of the local White Guard.

The storming of Tampere was directed by Mannerheim in person. Throughout this period he was up with the front line, and his staff were much alarmed that he was exposing himself unnecessarily. The small size of his army considered, Mannerheim's decision was correct. His command was numerically the equivalent of a division in the former Imperial Army, and by exercising tactical control he both boosted the morale of his men and helped prevent the kind of muddle that was so often to develop in Russian White organisations.

White losses were heavy, particularly amongst the units attacking from the south; the first attempt to rush the enemy, made on Maundy Thursday, 28 March, came to a halt once the outer defensive ring had been broken. Mannerheim marked time to allow more artillery to be brought up, together with all possible reinforcements. On Easter Day he was visited by Svinhufvud, who had escaped from Helsingfors and had eventually reached White territory via Germany and Sweden. The reappearance of the Prime Minister was an additional encouragement to the half-trained troops of the Defence Corps, and helped convince them of the importance of the final assault on Tampere. Another less public but equally important contact was made at the same time. A party of diplomats, recalled from St Petersburg, reached Tampere on their journey through Finland to the Swedish frontier. They were granted a safe-conduct across the front line, and Mannerheim entertained them to dinner at the White Headquarters. He was able to have a long conversation with Lindley, Counsellor at the British Embassy, and explain to him the position over German intervention. This was to be of great service as a check on adverse British reactions to the news of the expeditionary corps.

In the early hours of 3 April rockets signalled the renewed attack on the town. This came in from three separate directions, and though it was not immediately successful, it proved to be the beginning of the end. A company under command of a certain Captain Melin managed to fight its way to the centre of the town, and to hold out in the museum buildings. The Reds were unable to dislodge them, but White attempts to relieve the force proved fruitless. Melin moved out after nightfall and retreated across the frozen river. The Red commander, a worker named Hugo Salmela, inspired his men to fight on, though White units had now penetrated well into the town. By 5 April, however, Mannerheim was sure enough of the outcome to pay a flying visit to a threatened sector of the Karelian front. On the 6th the Reds in Tampere surrendered. The Whites captured eleven thousand unwounded prisoners, thirty artillery pieces and seventy machine guns. Salmela was killed, together with two thousand of his men. Unlike the Whites in South Russia the Finnish forces did not shoot those they captured. The main centre of Red resistance was now in White hands. It was high time. On 3 April the Germans had made an unopposed landing at Hangö, a peninsula in the extreme south-west of Finland. The expeditionary corps, under General Graf Rüdiger von der Goltz, at once advanced on Helsingfors.

It might have seemed the natural course of action for Mannerheim to link up with von der Goltz. This was certainly what the Red General Staff expected. In fact, Mannerheim's intentions were quite different, and his next move had been started as soon as he realised that Tampere would not hold out against him indefinitely. Already all troops that he could find were massing for an offensive on the Karelian front. The Reds, who had anticipated that Mannerheim would move at once into south-western Finland, were taken by surprise; once again Mannerheim had seized the initiative.

Mannerheim's action was not dictated solely by a desire to exploit the value of shock to the full. His position in south-western Finland was strong, mainly because an extensive White underground had been established, and he reckoned that this was sufficient to keep the Reds in the area tied down. Von der Goltz had at his disposal the Baltic Division, nearly ten thousand strong; to reinforce it was unnecessary. In any case, an attempt to do so might have resulted in an unseemly race for Helsingfors. It was far better to direct the effort to cutting the Karelian isthmus, through which ran the supply lines that were the umbilical cord of the Finnish Revolution. If Mannerheim could stop the flow of supplies, trained men and directives from Russia, then he anticipated that the revolution in Finland would wither away for lack of support. A further, nationalist motive for an advance on the Karelian front was that, by so doing, Mannerheim could ensure that he would acquire for Finland the maximum territorial advantages.

The Reds were aware, before they saw the direction or the significance of Mannerheim's move, that the loss of Tampere had jeopardised their position in southern Finland. They therefore pulled out of the south-west without waiting to see if Mannerheim intended to invade and concentrated on building up a defensive line between Toijala – amongst the lakes south of Tampere – and Helsingfors, on the coast. At the same time they attempted yet another reorganisation of their command structure, making Kullervo Akilles Manner – former Socialist Speaker of the Diet and head of the 'People's Commissariat of Finland' – dictator with supreme political and military power. Colonel Svechnikov became his 'military adviser' and was at work organising the defence of Helsingfors. Meanwhile, urgent requests were made for more direct Russian help. But Mannerheim was already astride the Red communication lines, having manœuvred his troops between the new Red defensive front and the Russian border. Nor did he have much respect for the demarcation line. White units raided deep into Russian territory in order to cut the railway tracks far enough from the frontier to inhibit any Russian attempt at intervention.

By now it was clear that any such attempts would be directed at Karelia. The eventual signing of the Treaty of Brest-Litovsk had meant that the Soviet leaders were anxious not to offend Germany, and for this reason the Baltic fleet sailed out of Helsingfors the day before Tampere fell. On 13 April the capital was taken, though it was General von der Goltz who marched in in triumph. The Germans had met with virtually no resistance, and they were aided by a muster of the White Guards within the city who, though more impressive in number than in training or equipment, came into the open at just the time when their appearance would do the most harm to Red morale.

The Reds' spirit had definitely begun to falter. Mannerheim was finding it remarkably easy to persuade Red soldiers to desert, and he also discovered that a little bribery went a long way – officers and guns were turned over to him for ridiculously small sums of money. Another more surprising feature of Red demoralisation was the plan for an exodus to Siberia, where Finnish colonies might be set up under the Soviet aegis. It was largely a fear of White retribution that made the refugees take the road, but it is to Mannerheim's credit that there was never a White terror in Finland. It was the political leaders, after the war, who determined on a policy directed against former Reds.

To cope with the exigencies of the new situation Mannerheim divided his army in two. The Western Army had what was primarily a watching brief, though it maintained a steady pressure against the Reds, whose counter-attacks were often fiercer than Mannerheim had anticipated. It was under the command of Major-General Wetzer. The Eastern Army, a larger force, for it was strategically the more important of the two, was commanded by Major-General Löfström, a Karelian familiar with the terrain in which the army was to operate. Mannerheim moved G.H.Q. to Mikkeli, a small town on an arm of Lake Saimen, whence he regulated the activities of both armies.

The Germans' advance on Helsingfors had forced the Red front line back along the coast, and it had also loosened the Red grip on the area to the north of the capital. Elements of the German Corps marched north, and finally made contact with a unit of the Western Army, which had pushed southwards against orders. Nevertheless this was entirely gain, and Mannerheim was delighted with the outcome. All his forces were now linked; he had direct telephone communication with each of his headquarters, and the remaining Red troops were now cut in two by White forces. Mopping up, however, was not easy. The Reds conducted a fighting retreat south-east, in an attempt to join up with their units on the Karelian front, and a combined German-Finnish force which attempted to block their route suffered heavy casualties.

Once more, Mannerheim did not allow minor setbacks or an apparently untidy operations map to cloud his judgment. The immediate objective was Wiborg (Viipuri). The town was important as a manufacturing centre, as a port that gave access to the Finnish inland waterway systems, and, most of all, as the junction of the railway from St Petersburg. Three miles outside the town Manner had set up his headquarters, though his only method of communication with the Reds to the west was by messages dropped from aeroplanes.

Against Wiborg Mannerheim threw all those troops that he could make available. On 24 April the Whites within the town attempted a coup, with the intention of helping Mannerheim's advancing troops; but though they seized some batteries to the east of the citadel of Wiborg, they were outnumbered and forced to surrender. Once the internal threat was under control the Reds devoted themselves to the essential task of breaking through the cordon that the Whites had now established round the town. On the succeeding two days desperate attempts were made to force a way out in a westerly direction – towards the units of the Red forces who were now tied down by Mannerheim's Western Army. These units were also surrounded, and the continual pressure from the Western Army and von der Goltz's Baltic Division was beginning to take effect. Though the Red units numbered twenty-five thousand they could achieve no positive action, and their morale rapidly disintegrated.

Meanwhile the situation at Wiborg deteriorated for the Reds. The projected exodus meant that the town was crowded with refugees; Red effectives were outnumbered by the White force, which was now twenty-five thousand strong. Though the Reds had an enormous advantage in artillery, they lacked the trained men required to man the guns. Mannerheim had resigned himself to the prospect of a conventional attack on the town; surprise was no longer possible. But at this stage of the war a quick decision was essential, before the Russian position grew stronger, so it became necessary to mount a large-scale frontal assault that was expensive in White lives. In fact, this policy proved more successful than the Whites realised, for, on the night of the 26th, Manner, Svechnikov and the other Red leaders fled by boat to Kronstadt. Only Dr Gylling, the Finance Commissar, chose to remain in the beleaguered town – Manner's final order was that he should hold off the Whites until the Red leaders had made good their escape. Gylling did better than this, for the Reds maintained a fierce resistance until the 29th, when White troops finally fought their way into the town. The Reds attempted to retreat into Russian territory, and hand-to-hand fighting developed as the Whites tried to cut them off. Inside the citadel the local White Defence Corps men, who had been imprisoned there after the failure of their coup, had broken out of custody and captured the mediaeval castle. On the 29th they were relieved by the advancing Whites, and on the 30th victory was complete. The news caused the remaining Red units still holding out in the west to lay down their arms on 2 May. Only mopping-up operations remained, and the final stages of the war became a race between the Whites and the retreating Reds, who devastated the countryside as they fled.

On 1 May Mannerheim issued an order of the day, on the occasion of his victory parade in Wiborg. In this he said:

> On arriving in Wiborg, the ancient capital of Karelia, on seeing the proud castle of Torkel–for hundreds of years the sure shield of Finland against the attack of foreigners until, two hundred years ago, it was captured by the Russians–I was filled with feelings of joy and gratitude. For now the flag of Finland waves over this stronghold, and once again Wiborg will be our sure shield against the East, but not, as in the past, as part of another empire, but in a great, free, independent Finland.[1]

These sentiments were to underlie all Mannerheim's subsequent political pronouncements, as well as his remarks to the Finnish Senate when he finally made his ceremonial entry into Helsingfors on 16 May 1918. To foreign observers the army at the head of which he rode into the great Senate Square of the city, bounded by massive neo-classical buildings, seemed a motley collection of ill-equipped troops. But these men, with their rough clothing, and their fur caps with branches for badges, had defeated an army that greatly outnumbered them and had achieved the first White victory of international significance.

Whether they could have accomplished this without the assistance of Germany has, not unnaturally, been the subject of much partisan debate. The Senate decided that Finland's hopes of survival could be best secured by an alliance with Ger-

---

[1] Mannerheim, *Memoirs*, p. 176.

many. They therefore demanded the dismissal of Mannerheim's Swedish officers, and proposed that a German staff officer should be attached to the Finnish C-in-C. But Mannerheim had always maintained that the Finns could win alone; he was reasonably certain that the Allies would win the war; he was horrified that men who had resigned their commissions in the Swedish army to fight for Finland should now be treated so shabbily, and he personally resented the interference of the Germans in the army that he had built up from nothing. He therefore decided to resign his command, and on 30 May he left Finland for Sweden.

The new orientation of Finnish foreign policy had already caused an armed clash between Finnish Whites and Allied troops – the extraordinary Petsamo incident, which we shall subsequently see from the point of view of the British in north Russia. It was to prove fortunate for Finland that Mannerheim dissociated himself from Svinhufvud at this point, for when Allied victory was seen to be inevitable, it was Mannerheim to whom the country turned for the negotiation of a settlement with the victors. And this, in November 1918, he accomplished.

Mannerheim was undoubtedly the most successful of the White generals. This is sometimes attributed to the fact that Mannerheim was, quite fortuitously, able to take advantage of Finland's unique position after the November Revolution. But the speed with which he relinquished his command, and his selflessness in giving his help to the politicians when they needed an emissary to negotiate with the Allies, are proof that he had no personal ambitions. In any event Mannerheim exemplifies the basic peculiarity of the White movement – that it was in a sense a-political; and it is certainly arguable that only Finland's parliamentary tradition, which both gave the Whites a mandate for their actions and made possible a clear separation of army and government, enabled Mannerheim to achieve what he did. At the same time, it needs emphasizing that Mannerheim was, in his own estimation, a White. After the abdication of Nicholas he plotted a counter-revolution; later he saw that the issue was more complex, and became a supporter of constitutional government and the rights of nationalities. He was successful because his approach was flexible.

For me personally it was no easy matter, after thirty years' service in the army of a Great Power, with its characteristic atmosphere and fixed forms, to adapt myself to the conditions of 1918, moreover without the support which the Commander-in-Chief received partly from his government, partly from military discipline, uniform training, and unbroken traditions.[1]

His main asset was his detachment. This did not mean that he was devoid of political passion; on the contrary, his hatred of Bolshevism was deep-rooted and violent. But he was able to take the long view and to see the Finnish situation in its full perspective. What he did had a decisive influence upon political decisions, but he always managed to regard himself as the servant of the politicians, even when he was, for all practical purposes, the dictator of White Finland.

His detachment also enabled him to emancipate himself from the Imperial context, and to see that Finland must be independent of Russia. He greatly strengthened the political base of the Finnish White Army when he committed himself to this doctrine, and it is essential to an understanding of his success. Of Imperial Russia he said: 'Forget that, it has crumbled away.' His realism, a product of his detachment, contrasts oddly with the chimerical notions of other White leaders. It was also the basis of his ability as a strategist, and accounts for that ruthless concentration of forces which is the main feature of Mannerheim's conduct of the war. Mannerheim saw that a civil war will always produce a multiplicity of fronts, but that there is also always one front more important than the others. It was in finding and destroying this front that he excelled.

So Mannerheim, by a combination of sound strategy and political realism, defeated the Reds in Finland. The Finnish episode is not a self-contained parenthesis in the history of the Civil War but an essential part of the whole. It gave the Whites throughout the Russian Empire new hope, yet it was also an object lesson, the importance of which the Russian Whites never understood. On the contrary, in a curious way it added to the common stock of their fantasies and of their inherent lack of realism. For at critical moments in the war, they would be sure

---

[1] Mannerheim, *Memoirs*, p. 183.

to remind themselves that in Finland Mannerheim was waiting, poised to swoop on St Petersburg from the Karelian frontier twenty miles away. It was a course of action the possibilities of which Mannerheim canvassed on several occasions. Yet it should have surprised no one that he was unable – and, in the last analysis, unwilling – to act as the other White leaders hoped he would. It was precisely because he differed from them over the nationalities policy and the strategy of civil war that he had succeeded; to throw in his lot with the Russian Whites would have been to deny the principles that made his victory possible. Even so, there were to be occasions when Finnish intervention seemed almost certain, and there was to be a moment when, if Finland had intervened, the Russian Whites might well have won.

VIII

Cossacks, Germans, Czechs and Allies

On the same Easter night that Denikin and Romanovsky, as they rode to mass, discussed the morale and the future of the Volunteer Army, fighting broke out once more in Rostov. From the west – a totally unexpected direction – White Russian troops advanced into the town. It was a few hours before the Reds woke up to the fact that the enemy had only a small unit at their disposal, and the next morning reinforcements sent up from Novocherkassk enabled the Bolsheviks to retake the town.

The White force was led by Colonel Drozdovsky, the former commander of the 14th Infantry Division who had been on the Roumanian front when the Imperial Army finally began to break up. Alekseev had several times appealed to the commander of the Roumanian front for assistance in the formation of Volunteer units, but the officer in question had refused to co-operate. It was left to Drozdovsky, acting on his own initiative, to get permission to form such Volunteer groups. Soon he had mustered a force of just over nine hundred, and set about equipping it by the expedient of ambushing units of the Russian army which were deserting to their homes and seizing their arms and equipment. Sometimes, with these units, there would be officers who chose to join the Whites.

The Roumanian front ran parallel to the Ukraine-Roumania border. When, on 18 February 1918, the Ukrainian Rada signed a separate peace with Germany, the position of the Roumanians became untenable; with German armies to either side of them they were forced to come to terms with the Central Powers. Drozdovsky's force became a major embarrassment. The Roumanians proposed to disarm the Volunteers – a policy which Drozdovsky resolutely resisted. At the beginning of March he came close to ordering his men to fire on Roumanian troops, and this had the effect of making the Roumanian authorities provide trains on which Volunteers might leave the country. Drozdovsky decided that the only course of action left open to him was to march across the south of Russia in an attempt to join up with the main Volunteer Army.

On 21 March Drozdovsky's column left the Roumanian frontier; on 4 May they appeared at Rostov, having travelled nine hundred miles in sixty-one days. Close behind them marched the Germans.

That the Germans should invade south Russia was natural. What neither Bolsheviks nor Volunteers had anticipated was the extent and the speed of the invasion. The Germans wanted grain, foodstuffs and coal; they also hoped for oil from the Caspian. Their object was the economic exploitation of as much territory as they could control, and they rapidly concluded that, with Russia in chaos, they could safely manage a great deal of the country. In any case, a state of national turmoil was not conducive to the rapid satisfaction of their needs: men who were primarily engaged in fighting when they could be gainfully employed on the land, were of no use to them. South Russian peace meant German plenty.

At the same time they did not wish to establish any one unified force in south Russia that might come to threaten the German hegemony over the area. Consequently they aimed at a balance of the opposing forces in the area, rather than at the support of an overlordship of any particular group. In pursuance of this policy they were aided by the shortcomings and confusions of the Treaty of Brest-Litovsk. This had been phrased so as to make allowance for the existence of theoretically autonomous republics within the Union of Soviet Republics, and the Germans at once took advantage of the latitude that this permitted them. An advance into the Don area could be presented as a matter to be settled between the Germans and the rulers of the Don (whoever they might be), rather than between the Germans and the Soviet leaders in Moscow. It also enabled them to use the Ukraine as an instrument through which to make territorial claims; thus the Ukraine might 'annex' part of the Don Territories, claiming them as part of the Ukrainian Republic – though the actual annexation would be effected by German troops, operating on behalf of the German Government. This was what the Whites called the 'Balkanisation' of Russia: the term itself implying an ironic reference to earlier 'Greater Russian' designs on the south-east European states.

Such a policy clearly ran against the admitted aims of the Whites. But, however anti-German they might be, the Whites realised that there could be no resistance to the German army. Equally, German officers were far more likely to see the Bolsheviks and not the Whites as the enemy; they did not find it difficult to ignore that it was the Bolsheviks with whom Germany had signed a peace treaty. When we consider the sympathetic attitude towards the Whites evinced by many German officers, the class aspect of the Russian Civil War is brought home to us. In the end, for all their disclaimers, the Whites became dependent on the Germans. It was a state of affairs that – in south Russia – did not last for long, but whilst it continued it caused embarrassment and discontent. German troops aided Drozdovsky when he was attacked by Skoropadsky's Ukrainians; Austrian officers saluted the column and wished them 'good luck'. When they came to cross the Dnieper at Borsilavl, Drozdovsky's men discovered that the Germans had reached the bridge before them, and were now being held up by Bolsheviks on the other side of the river. After parleying with the German commander, Drozdovsky forced the crossing and cleared the Red opposition, thereby leaving the way open for the Germans to follow after him.

After Drozdovsky had been driven out of Rostov, having held it for only a night, it must have seemed as though his attempt to join up with the Volunteers had ended in failure. His men were confused by the conflicting accounts of the fate of the Volunteer Army that were current in the Don Territories; they were unable to reconcile the news of the death of Kornilov with rumours of the successful return of the Whites to the lower Don. But Drozdovsky rallied his troops, and led them on Novocherkassk, where they were to make as dramatic and unexpected an arrival as they had at Rostov.

Golubov, the Cossack lieutenant-colonel who had distinguished himself by shooting General Nazarov, failed to follow up his initial successes. He declared himself 'Soviet Ataman', shot over a thousand Cossack officers on the strength of this remarkable title, and then discovered, apparently to his surprise, that the men to whom he had offered his allegiance were prepared to have him 'Soviet', but not to tolerate his being distinguishably 'Cossack'. There was not room for Atamans – of whatever colour – in the Soviet scheme of things. His subjects accused him of knuckling under to the *inogorodni*, whilst his masters were suspicious of his separatist, Cossack tendencies. Nor was he proving co-operative over the matter of food supplies, which the Moscow government needed as desperately as did the Germans. It was largely for this reason that the Soviets withdrew their support from Golubov, and began agitation among the *inogorodni*, who were prepared to be more understanding about 'food detach-ments', and to make the best use of the presence of these foraging parties by joining them and employing them as a means of paying off old scores against the Cossacks.

In the Don Territories the Bolshevik handling of the situation was crassly incompetent. Soon Popov and his men, still living out in the steppe, were becoming the focus of a genuine Cossack resistance movement. More daring than Popov, two younger officers, Denisov and Mamontov, concentrated on organising resistance within the *stanitsas*, mainly through a network of former Cossack officers who had been spurred into activity by the Golubov massacre. When Golubov fled into the steppes and, shortly afterwards, was shot by the Reds, the situation became still more complex. The Red Cossacks came into conflict with the equally Red *inogorodni*, whilst the organisations in the country continually clashed with those in the town over the basic question of food – a matter about which, not surprisingly, the townsmen tended to be more radical. When the Red Army, retreating from the Germans, came through the north of the province, the inevit-able looting caused still greater discontent. It was not long before the partisans under Denisov and Mamontov were the men to whom the Cossack population turned with hope.

In April the partisans had captured Novocherkassk and held it for three days; in May they threatened it again. That the attack was launched was mainly due to Denisov, who, after linking up with Popov, had assumed command of the 'Don Southern Army'. Relations between Denisov and Popov were strained, Popov insisting on breaking up the available forces and using them piecemeal, some in the north, others in the south, rather than uniting all of the Don units for an attack on Novocherkassk – which was Denisov's recommendation. On 6 May Denisov captured the town, but a strong Bolshevik counter-attack developed on the 8th and threatened to overpower him. It was at this moment that Drozdovsky's force marched on the rear of the Bolshevik position from across the steppes. Novocherkassk was once more in White hands.

Precisely what complexion of 'White' was not at first apparent. But it was not long before an assembly of the Don Host had been convened at Novocherkassk, its express purpose the 'salvation of the Don'. The title at once revealed its political alignment: 'salvation' had become a traditionalist and right-wing word. Nor should it have been any great shock when the Krug elected as its Ataman none other than General Krasnov, leader of Kerensky's abortive expedition against St Petersburg. Krasnov began his régime as he meant to continue it, by refusing to take office unless the Krug gave him what amounted to dictatorial powers. He also required the abolition of all post-revolutionary legislation. After a certain amount of hesitation the Krug fulfilled these conditions, Krasnov having used their two days' deliberation over this issue to demonstrate that he was the only man who was likely to be able to hold the Cossacks together.

On receiving confirmation of his appointment Krasnov at once set about consolidating the position of the Don Territory. His first move was to establish good relations with the Germans, since he held that, without support from Germany and her puppet state in the Ukraine, the Don Cossacks could not survive. He began by writing a letter to Kaiser Wilhelm II, outlining the position of the Don and his plans for its future; it may have been of some assistance to him here that he had met the Kaiser in the days before 1914. He reinforced this personal appeal with proposals for trade between Germany and the Don. This was attractive for both sides, since the Germans could get their grain without having to administer the province, whilst Krasnov would receive in return much needed supplies of arms. So far as internal affairs were concerned, he commenced a programme of land reform that broke up the biggest Cossack holdings and divided them amongst the *inorogodni*. At the same time he embarked on a campaign to remind the Cossacks of their ancient heritage, intending by this to promote unity and to do something to negate the effect of Bolshevik propaganda. In his campaign he was largely successful, and it is perhaps possible to see why he was to turn to the writing of novels of military life when his political star had waned.

Krasnov's leanings towards Germany did not please Denikin. Nor was it clear to the Volunteers just what the new Ataman's ideas on the future of Russia amounted to. If the country was to be 'great and indivisible' it would be hard to find a niche for the Don as Krasnov conceived of it. What Denikin did not at first realise was that Krasnov was prepared to subscribe to any scheme that seemed to promise well for the Don, without worrying too much about ethical niceties. The Ataman believed in monarchy, but since a large Cossack faction clearly preferred their new independence, he did not force his private beliefs on them. Instead he concentrated on building up the strength of the Don Host, so that he would be able to aid the Whites when they made a serious bid for power. Presumably he felt that Russia could be made into some form of federated state, loosely linked with a central government, but he never cared to elucidate the point. He promised Denikin what military support he could give him with his newly founded Army of the Don, whilst at the same time continuing further negotiations with the Germans.

From the Germans he was receiving arms, on the understanding that these must not come into the hands of the Volunteers; yet about half of these arms were in fact being passed on to White units. This caused great heart-searchings, since the Whites were determined that they should remain independent of the Central Powers, yet were increasingly conscious that the presence of the Germans could be made to work – if it was not already working – in their favour. Krasnov summed up the position perfectly: 'The Volunteer Army is pure and undefiled. And I, Ataman of the Don, accept with my dirty hands German shells and ammunition, wash them in the waters of the quiet Don, and hand them over clean to the Volunteer Army.'[1] From the Germans Krasnov received at

---

[1] Speech to the Don Krug, 31 August 1918; quoted in Lukomsky, *Vospominaniya* II, p. 92.

least eleven thousand rifles, forty-six field-guns, and eighty-eight machine-guns.

If the Germans ever explicitly committed themselves, it was to the Whites, though even this particular episode had a back-handed aspect. Irritated by Denikin's consistently anti-German attitude, they set up two 'White' armies of their own. One, the Astrakhan Army, was commanded by the self-elected 'Ataman of the Astrakhan Cossacks' – who had managed to get an audience with Wilhelm II and to persuade him to support his plans. The other, the Southern Army, was placed under the control of the Duke of Leuchtenberg, a cousin of the Tsar who had embraced extreme reactionary politics after his house had been burnt down during a peasant rising in 1905. Both forces were very small, but their existence greatly annoyed the Whites. At the same time, the Germans covered all possibilities by remaining in contact with the Bolshevik leaders in Moscow, and keeping the channels for negotiations open. And it should not be forgotten that the German occupation of South Russia brought advantages to the Reds as well as to the Whites. It enabled the Soviet leaders to consolidate their hold on the territory of which they were masters, and it also enabled them to concentrate their troops east of the German-occupied territories, and to form a short and easily defensible front that would contain any attempt by the Volunteers at an advance to the north.

The German invasion of south Russia indirectly triggered off another sequence of events which was to prove of immense importance to the Whites. The Czechoslovak Legion, as we have seen, occupied a position vis-à-vis Germany and Austro-Hungary analogous to that which the Finnish Jaegers occupied in relation to Russia. Though the legion had been under the tactical command of the Russian Staff from the time of its foundation in 1916, its final allegiance was to the Czech National Council, which was based in Paris. The legion recruited extensively amongst the nearly two and a half million prisoners-of-war held by the Russians; the Czech nationalist leader Thomas Masaryk was sent to Russia by the council as its representative with responsibility for overseeing the legion's affairs. During the period of the Provisional Government the legion fought well, and maintained a cohesion that was sadly lacking in the Russian units. It did not follow, however, that the legion was loyal to any particular political ideal, beyond the broad aims of Czechoslovak nationalism. In fact it included amongst its soldiers men with a wide diversity of political affiliations, ranging from communists to monarchists. When the November Revolution broke out 37,000 Czechs were serving on the south-western front, and their attitude to the Bolsheviks at once became of crucial importance.

Masaryk himself was in no doubt that the legion should remain neutral, and directed the commanding officers that the force could not be used in 'Russian internal conflicts, but only against Russia's external enemies'. Meanwhile, the National Council came to the conclusion that the legion could do best employed in France, where other Czech units were already fighting. The Allies welcomed this suggestion, and began to canvass ideas for the best way of bringing the Czechs out of the Ukraine. Lenin was quite amenable to the transfer of the legion, and relationships with Red troops in the Ukraine area – now commanded by Muravev, the defender of the Bolshevik Revolution in St Petersburg – were generally friendly, if somewhat restrained. In February and March Masaryk negotiated with the Soviet leaders for a safe-conduct for the legion; and having, as he thought, accomplished this, he left for the United States to continue his fight for the recognition of Czechoslovakia there.

On 26 March Stalin sent a telegram to the Czech National Council in Paris, in which he stated that the Soviet of People's Commissars

... regards the proposal of the Czechoslovak army corps as fair and completely acceptable, on the essential condition that the unit sets out at once for Vladivostok and that all counter-revolutionary commanders are removed. The Czechoslovaks will not travel as fighting units, but as a group of free citizens, carrying only such arms as are necessary to ensure their protection from the counter-revolutionaries.[1]

On the next day the Czech delegates and the Military Soviet reached agreement over the definition of the number of arms required for self-protection, but the Soviet added the codicil

---

[1] Krachtovil, *Česta revoluče*, p. 42.

that these arms should be surrendered at Penza, a town on the route east beyond which it was not anticipated that the Czechs would be in any danger. The Soviet was naturally concerned at the prospect of this sizeable army – for by now the Czechs were over 50,000 strong – passing armed through the Siberian hinterland. Vladivostok seemed, both to the Allied planners and to the Soviet, the only possible port of departure for the legion; but it meant, of course, that to get to the western front the Czechs would have to travel most of the way around the world. The situation in France in 1918 was such that details like this were no object. At the same time, both Churchill and the French staff were wondering if there might not be another possible use for the legion in the Russian situation.[1]

Stalin's condition that the 'counter-revolutionary commanders' should be removed, points to one of the main sources of Bolshevik unease. Though the Czechoslovaks had so far resisted the blandishments of the White leaders, there was at least one unit composed of Czechoslovak monarchists serving with the Volunteer Army. It is not surprising that the Czechs were soon to find that, though Stalin had seen no objection to their passage east, the local Red units and town Soviets often felt rather differently. The progress of the trains in which the Czechs were travelling was hindered incessantly, and those units which had handed in their arms to the Red Army before leaving the Ukraine were beginning to regret that they had done so. Furthermore, there were indications that Moscow was reconsidering its decision, and it was certainly proposed by Trotsky that the legion should cross Siberia not merely disarmed, but also broken up into small groups.

The Czechs were not slow to react to this change in the climate of opinion. At Penza troops in many of the echelons hid their arms. Since the necessary details had not been forwarded by Moscow to the local Soviet, this was not discovered for some time, and when the Reds realised what had happened they still remained uncertain as to just what the Czechs had retained – which put the psychological advantage with the legion. Two Czech officers,

---

[1] Many historians dismiss this possibility. But see Beneš, *Souvenirs de Guerre et de Révolution, 1914-1918*, II, pp. 175-95.

Captain Rudolph Gajda and a colleague by the name of Kadlec, began to agitate for an attack on the Bolsheviks. Gajda, who originally joined up as a hospital orderly, had emerged as a seemingly able soldier, though he combined a melodramatic outlook with a predilection for political intrigue, and this was to complicate his career. In contrast Kadlec was a professional, interested primarily in a return to the western front, but sharing with Gajda a deep suspicion of Red motives. The two worked well together. Gajda formulated the political objects of the Czech coup; Kadlec prepared the military aspects. Soon they had a workable plan, which they communicated both to their own fellow-officers and also – though this was done with great circumspection – to local anti-Bolshevik parties. The original assumption underlying the plan was that its object should be the security of the legion. Gajda did not at first envisage initiating military action, though one of the aims of his correspondence with the local anti-Bolsheviks was, if possible, to provoke it. In the end he did not have to bother.

On the morning of 14 May two trains stood side by side in the station at Chelyabinsk, a small and dirty town just to the east of the Urals. One train formed part of the Czech Legion's transport; the other was filled with Hungarian prisoners of war, who were being repatriated under the terms of Brest-Litovsk. Both groups of men were impatient, both were cooped up in inadequate accommodation, and the Czechs were the enemies of the Hungarians. As the train carrying the Hungarians moved out of the station one of the prisoners aboard expressed what he felt by flinging a large lump of cast iron from a broken stove at a group of Czech soldiers. The missile hit and injured a Czech, whose comrades at once climbed onto the engine of the moving train and forced the driver to stop. They then lynched the offending Hungarian.

All would have remained calm, had not the local Soviet taken it upon themselves to enforce law and order in their small corner of the Siberian plain. They arrested the soldiers involved in the lynching, and this was interpreted as deliberate obstreperousness by the rest of the echelon, who did not, in any case, put much faith in 'revolutionary justice'. On 17 May the Czechs imprisoned the Red troops at the station, marched into Chelyabinsk, and demanded their men back. Almost by accident, Gajda's plan had gone into action.

Everything was made much easier for the conspirators by the fact that the Czechs had decided to hold a conference to discuss their journey east and the policies they should adopt during it. This conference they intended to convene at Chelyabinsk. The incident with the local Reds intensified Czech suspicions, and made the legion resolve to retain its weapons at all costs. The conference also gave Gajda a chance of propagandising for his own schemes, which became increasingly ambitious as the weakness of the Reds was revealed. When the congress broke up the échelons resumed their slow progress east, and on 25 May Gajda finally came into the open and seized the town of Novonikolaevsk, which lies two-thirds of the way between the cities of Omsk and Tomsk. Emboldened by his success, and that of Kadlec further down the line, he went on to issue orders to all legion units between Omsk and Irkutsk – on Lake Baikal – to act similarly. Within the last week of May large sectors of the Trans-Siberian Railway and several of the largest towns on it came under Czech control. They were able to seize considerable quantities of arms and ammunition, and, firmly established all along the vital line of communication with the far east as far as Lake Baikal, they at once became the predominant factor in Siberian politics.

These were no simpler than politics anywhere else in Russia. Gajda's nefarious contacts with anti-Bolshevik Russians had involved him with a number of parties whose aims were often wildly divergent, and once the Bolsheviks had been overthrown other political groups, the existence of which he had not taken into consideration, emerged. The governments were at first purely local affairs such as the West Siberian Commissariat at Omsk, though this was soon to give way to a government that claimed to represent the whole of Siberia. On 8 June the Czechs occupied Samara where a Government of the Constituent Assembly came into being; but it, in turn was soon to be followed by a body with a different title, this time the Samara Directory. The Samara government was also in contact and approximate alliance with the Orenburg Cossack Host who, encouraged by the news from the Don, had risen against the Bolsheviks earlier in the year. Their leader, Ataman Dutov, had nothing of Krasnov's personality or diplomatic finesse, though he endeavoured to compensate with brutality and low guile. All of the governments established in Czech-occupied territory were at best makeshift affairs. They based their respective claims to legality on the membership of the dissolved Constituent Assembly, and they started as fairly left-wing institutions – mainly Socialist Revolutionary in tendency – and then, under the force of circumstances, swung to the right. Gajda realised that he could not control the movement that he had started. He was not even in a position to direct the operations of the legion itself. But he had succeeded in creating a situation in the context of which he might realise some of his own ambitions.

Three separate events in Siberia deserve our attention, since they were – in very different ways – to exercise an important influence on the course of the White movement. The first of these was the murder, during the night of 16/17 July, of the Tsar, the Tsarina, the Tsarevitch, the four Grand Duchesses and four loyal attendants of the Imperial Household. The murder took place in the former house of a wealthy merchant in the Siberian town of Ekaterinburg. The ostensible reason for this was the Czech threat to the town, though how real such a threat was is hard to estimate. It is quite clear, however, that had the Bolsheviks wished to move the Imperial family to an area where they would have been comparatively secure, they could easily have done so. But the Bolsheviks might well have felt that it was courting trouble to bring the Tsar to Moscow or some other large city. Trotsky had been much attracted to the idea of a public trial, preferably featuring himself as prosecutor. The project did not appeal to Lenin, who saw that there was little political capital to be gained from such an obviously contrived operation. On the other hand Lenin was afraid of the possible consequences of a thorough-going restorationist movement. He rated the chances for the success of such a movement much higher than did any of the White leaders. Apparently Lenin decided that the Bolsheviks should not 'leave the Whites a live banner to rally round, especially under the present difficult circumstances'.[1]

---

[1] Lenin as quoted by Sverdlov to Trotsky. Trotsky, *Diary in Exile 1935*, p. 80. But for an apparently contradictory account see Trotsky, *Stalin*, p. 414.

There were, in fact, Whites who had serious plans for the rescue of the Tsar – notably Colonel Kappel, who was later to serve with distinction as one of Kolchak's senior commanders. Early in June there had actually been an ill-judged attempt to carry Ekaterinburg by a coup – the leader of the revolt, a Captain Rostovtsev, was captured and shot. The Kremlin obviously knew of the June attempt, and it is more than likely that they had wind of Kappel's plans. Thus their suspicions of White aims might have seemed borne out by the information available to them. There was certainly another plot on foot during this period that they may have connected with the presence of the Imperial family, for there is no doubt that the Bolsheviks knew of the projected risings in Yaroslavl and the Volga towns, which were being organised by Savinkov, Kerensky's last Minister of War. Savinkov had precious little sympathy for the Romanovs, and he certainly had no intention of freeing them. But the concatenation of events was enough to induce the Politbureau circumspectly to inform the Ural Soviet that they would have no objection to the liquidation of the Emperor and his family. Once the decision was taken, it seemed the obvious solution. That the policy was one of extermination is shown by the systematic way in which all other members of the dynasty who were accessible to the Soviets were subsequently murdered.

The interesting thing about Lenin's brutal retribution is that it reflected his own view of what it would be logical for the Whites to do, and not what the Whites were actually doing. The groups who had an interest in the rescue of the Imperial family were in a very small minority. The chief political factions amongst the Whites were all adamant that there should be no restoration, and the Constitutional Monarchists, in their search for a figurehead, did not proceed on strict dynastic lines. Those few legitimists who moved in White circles were reactionaries who would have caused even Purishkevich a moment's sober reflection. Though some of them were very vocal – notably a group which established itself in Kiev – they never exercised a serious influence on White thinking, and were generally regarded as divisive and dangerous by the White leaders. So the drunken Letts and Russians who shot and bayoneted the Imperial household in the cellar of the *Dom Ipateva* were exorcising Lenin's fantasies about the Whites, rather than removing a real threat to Soviet rule. Nevertheless, the execution can be seen as marking a new stage in the struggle, a phase in the course of which the Soviet leaders gradually came to realise that their position was not as secure as it had hitherto seemed.

The second significant event in the Siberian theatre was the Czech victory on Lake Baikal. The lake lies in the eastern extremity of Siberia. It is long, broad, and exceedingly deep, and it had proved the major obstacle to the completion of the Trans-Siberian Railway. Eventually the engineers had succeeded in blasting a way through the rocky spurs that come down to the shore all round the southern end of the lake, and a line was run round through thirty-nine tunnels from Baikal to Kultuk. If any part of the Trans-Siberian line was defensible, it was this.

Around Baikal, and in the settlements of the Trans-Baikal region, the Bolsheviks were relatively strong; they were able to organise a far more effective resistance than did the dithering Red forces elsewhere. Even so, they were short of trained troops, and when Gajda and his men eventually came into contact with them, the Reds were forced to beat a precipitate retreat. They did not entirely lose their heads, for they succeeded in demolishing a tunnel behind them. Admittedly they botched the operation by performing it the wrong way round; instead of blowing the nearest tunnel to Baikal, from which they were retreating, they destroyed the one furthest away – thus providing themselves with no cover behind which to blow up the remaining tunnels, and also cutting off the retreat of the party whom they sent up the line to destroy the rest. This party was captured by the Czechs. The whole incident is indicative of the state of Red military science in 1918, not to mention a sad lack of common sense. Nevertheless the move did have the effect of denying to the Czechs their line of communication with Vladivostok. It also split the Czech forces, for some had already got through to the port. Behind their demolished tunnel, the Reds set about organising resistance in Trans-Baikal. If the Czechs were to break through, they had to do so as soon as possible.

Fortunately for the legion their other operations in Siberia had proved successful, and there was no threat from the rear. Gajda himself superintended operations at the lakeside, which were made very difficult because the Reds had command of the water and were able to bombard the shore. The work of clearing the tunnel took almost a month, and it was not until the end of July that the route became practicable again. Yet to open up the tunnel was not enough; beyond, the Red forces were altogether more formidable than they had been before. To cope with this situation Gajda evolved a plan that was by no means simple. As with comparable operations of the Volunteer Army, it was dependent on the fact that the Czechs were a well-trained body of men, preserving a corporate identity, whilst the Reds, for all their fervour, were lacking in troops of the same calibre, and – at this stage of the war – were still trying to arrive at decisions 'democratically', by holding interminable mass meetings. Thus, though the forces available to Gajda were small, he felt justified in splitting them up, and sending two regiments of the five at his disposal on a lengthy march through the mountains by night. The battalions eventually reached a point where the railway ran through a long and deep valley; there they set up an ambush.

On the morning of 4 August Gajda's main force advanced, hesitated, then began to retreat. The Reds promptly followed them up with a considerable force of cavalry and infantry, supported by artillery, three armoured trains, and several echelons of troop carriers. Once the Reds were into the valley – and their progress was so cautious that they did not reach it until after dark that night – the Czechs cut the line behind the trains, and attacked them from both sides. At the same time Gajda's main force moved over to the attack. The Reds, who had the advantage of the protection afforded by the armoured trains, as well as a considerable superiority in artillery, fought back with tenacity. The battle continued through the night, and most of the next day as well; the Czechs were hampered by heavy and continuous rain, which had the effect of making their temporary bivouacks in the sodden pine-forests untenable, and movement difficult, though it proved equally debilitating to the Red cavalry. By the 6th the Reds were beginning to weaken, and during the course of the day the Czechs found themselves in possession of sixteen urgently needed engines, a great quantity of rolling stock, and the route to Vladivostok.

The Czech line of communication was now completely secured.

It led to Vladivostok – where great quantities of Allied war materials, originally destined for use by the Russians against the Germans, lay mouldering on the quays and in the town – and it put the Czechs into contact with the outside world. Their westernmost units were now at Samara, beyond the Urals, and their easternmost units could look out over the Pacific Ocean. Already Čeček, commanding in the Samara area, saw his units as the spearhead of an attempt to 'form a new eastern front against the Germans'. And in Vladivostok itself the Czechs' commanding officer, General Dietrichs (a Russian of Czech origins), was beginning to think of the possibilities of action westwards.

Meanwhile the Allied planners, whose notions about the potential of the Czech Corps had been of the vaguest, suddenly became aware that an area of Russia, three thousand miles long and of considerable breadth, had fallen into pro-Allied hands, in Winston Churchill's phrase, 'as if by magic'. But, despite Churchill's interest and enthusiasm, and that of several other influential politicians in the various Allied governments, there was no clear-cut response to the Siberian situation. It was felt to present an opportunity too good to throw away, but not sufficiently secure as to justify an all-out effort to exploit the situation. When the Supreme War Council, at the beginning of July, considered the matter, their appreciation concluded with a reference to the 'urgent necessity' of intervention, both to 'save the Czecho-Slovaks, and to take advantage of an opportunity of gaining control of Siberia for the Allies which may never return'.[1] Gajda's action at Lake Baikal made this far more possible. But the essential confusion implicit in the phrases 'save the Czecho-Slovaks' and 'gaining control of Siberia for the Allies' was never to be resolved.

The third significant event in the Siberian area was the capture of Kazan, the former Tartar capital north of Samara. The battle for the city was being fought by combined Czech and White forces at the same time as Gajda was clearing the way to Vladivostok. From the military point of view, its capture was a necessary

---

[1] 'Allied Intervention in Siberia and Russia', Supreme War Council Appreciation, 2 July, 1918. Quoted in Swettenham, *Allied Intervention In Russia, 1918-1919*, p. 112.

sequel to the capture of Samara, since Red forces in the former city could easily threaten the latter. Both cities are on the Volga, which provides an easy route between them. When the insurgents finally captured Kazan they also took with it an unexpected bonus, for in the city was the gold reserve of the Imperial Government, which had been evacuated to Samara to avoid the risk of its being captured in St Petersburg by the Germans. The Whites found themselves in possession of six hundred and fifty million roubles in gold, one hundred million roubles in paper 'Romanovs' (which still held their value, even in Red areas), a quantity of state treasure, and the government's platinum stocks. Discounting the paper money, this was worth the equivalent of at least one hundred million pounds, and it meant, for the first time, that a White government had a chance of being able to operate on a secure financial base.

The Samara government were not, however, to have the benefit of this windfall for long. A Red counter-attack developed in the Samara area, and the gold was moved to Chelyabinsk. Whilst the government were debating the safest place to hide the bullion, some enterprising adherents of the West Siberian Commissariat – who regarded Omsk as a city of infinitely more importance than Samara – bluffed their way onto the trains in which the gold had been loaded. They then steamed off to the security of their own capital, thus resolving the Samara government's problem, though in a way not entirely to the liking of its members. And at Omsk the gold was eventually to be taken over by Admiral Alexander Kolchak, no longer an unemployed naval officer, but 'Supreme Ruler of All the Russias'.

In the summer of 1918 Allied intervention in Siberia became a reality. By the end of the year sixteen nations were to have some kind of stake in Siberian affairs, and Britain and France were also to be deeply involved with Denikin in the south. For historians the Allied intervention has proved a considerable source of interest, and the wealth of readily available material has given rise to a great number of books on the subject. Nevertheless, we must not allow this to distort our perspective on the Civil War itself. Only in the north, in Archangel and Murmansk, was intervention the predominant factor in the Civil War.

It was obvious to the Allies that America would have to be the senior partner in any Siberian expedition. Britain and France were prepared to help, but they were in no position to lead. Though British troops from the Middlesex Regiment were the first forces of an intervening power to land in Siberia, the number of units that the War Office could free for such a purpose was very small, and the men were officially classified as unfit for war service. France was able to field a somewhat more effective force, but after this initial commitment the government confined itself to the dispatch of high-ranking officers whose chief function seems to have been to promise more than they could ever perform. Japan's intervention force was powerful enough, but since Japanese objectives were limited to expansion in the Russian Far East, it is not surprising to find that Japanese units did not venture much farther west than Lake Baikal. Only the Czechs were of military significance and, though they were vital during the earlier stages of the Siberian White movement, their importance diminished rapidly after November 1918.

The issue of American intervention hinges on the behaviour of Woodrow Wilson who, as we have noted, had greeted the March Revolution with a good imitation of rapture. Enormous pressure was put on Wilson to intervene; but at one moment he was being asked to support the Whites, at another to side with the Bolsheviks who, it is said, would resume the war against Germany if the United States sent troops to their aid. At the same time, conflicting reports from Wilson's own representatives in Russia and from the agents of the other Allies, left him in serious doubt as to whether it was the Bolsheviks or the Whites who were the true heirs of the March Revolution. In so far as anything decided him, it was the plight of the Czechs. So it came about that, when the Allies finally discovered that the United States was about to intervene – a decision that Wilson took on his own initiative, without consulting the other Allied governments – they were horrified to find that the American troops had only been assigned to a drastically limited task. This was defined in the *aide mémoire* that was given by the Secretary of War to General William S. Graves, the commander of the force, in the course of a ten-minute briefing in a room at the Kansas City railway station. The briefing had concluded: 'Watch your step; you will be walking on eggs loaded with dynamite. God bless you and good-bye!'[1]

The document itself was drawn up in curiously elusive language, recommending, among other things, that there be dispatched to Siberia 'agents of the Young Men's Christian Association accustomed to organising the best methods of spreading useful information and rendering educational help of a modest sort'.[2] For them to discover how much they were needed all that was necessary was an encounter with Dutov's Cossacks or the Bolshevik partisan bands.

Be that as it may, the purpose of the American intervention was to protect the Czechs and to help Russian attempts at 'self-government or self-defence' – though such assistance was limited to the guarding of 'military stores' and the 'organisation' of local defence. If the document was interpreted strictly it committed the American commander to nothing beyond the active protection of the Czechs – who were more than capable of looking after themselves in the first place, and had far more men already on the ground than the Americans ever dreamed of putting into Siberia. Graves had no intention of going beyond a strict interpretation of the *aide*. If he erred it was on the side of caution, and the document itself was cautious in the extreme. American military intervention could scarcely have been less effective than it was.

Allied intervention did, however, have a very decided impact in two important fields: firstly the provision of supplies, financial credits, and instructors; secondly the psychological, for it radically changed the Whites' outlook, not least of all because the Allies could serve the Whites as convenient scapegoats.

The Allies provided the Whites with an immense quantity of military equipment, with food, with money, and with trained men. The largest amount of aid went to south Russia and Denikin's armies, but the total extent of aid to the Siberian theatre runs it very close. Much of the *matériel* landed never saw its destination. Graft and corruption were an essential feature of all Russian towns, and the Whites had no Cheka to take the

---

[1] Graves, William S., *America's Siberian Adventure, 1918-1920*, New York, 1931, p. 4.
[2] *Papers Relating to the Foreign Relations of the United States, 1918. Russia*, II, p. 290.

ruthless measures necessary to prevent it. The Reds were not only ideologically conscious of the evils of exploitation, but also were facing famine and industrial crisis at a time when there were no possible sources of supply other than in the areas that they controlled. They saw that graft must be stamped out. But the Whites exercised no comparable discipline. In south Russia, and in Siberia also, aid seemed to go anywhere but to the front.

Few Whites were prepared to admit that this was so. Rather, they tended to blame the Allies, demanding direct military intervention (yet distrusting those Allied troops that actually reached White territory), and still greater consignments of supplies. Their demands were impracticable. In almost every instance, the Whites pitched their hopes too high and the often generous aid never came up to their expectations.

They would have done well to remember the example of Mannerheim, who realised that a civil war could never be satisfactorily ended by outside interference.

Allied intervention had, moreover, the effect of consolidating the morale of those in the Soviet camp, who could look for no outside aid. It gave their fighting a new, patriotic meaning. Here were the imperialists, ravening for booty, using civil strife as an excuse for the invasion of Russia. After the Armistice of November 1918 this interpretation became even more plausible. The murder of the Emperor had meant the final end of hankerings for the old régime: it was a new Russia for everyone, and the individual could no longer dodge the issue of whether he was for the Reds or for the Whites. The Emperor had been killed partly to make just this point; the war was in deadly earnest. The arrival of the Allied forces served to harden attitudes even more, and it may well be that intervention served the Reds better than it served those whom it was intended to assist. Nevertheless, in the short term, it was the Whites who stood to benefit; and it was Allied aid that gave much of the impetus to the next phase of the war.

IX

Denikin and the Conquest
of the Kuban

Once again we must return to Easter 1918, that point in time when the re-emergence of the Volunteer Army from the Kuban steppes gave a new lease of life to the White Movement in south Russia. For the two months after its return to the Trans-Don territory the Volunteer Army rested and regrouped. Denikin and Alekseev were preoccupied with problems of politics and finance. They were anxious to regularise relations with Krasnov, to obtain definite promises of Allied aid, and to put the army onto a firm footing financially. In none of these aims were they successful; Denikin obtained certain minor concessions from Krasnov, Alekseev received, via the anti-Bolshevik 'National Centre' in Moscow (that it had not come straight to him annoyed him very much) ten million roubles sent by the Allies – which was enough to keep the army for about six weeks.

Anton Ivanovich Denikin, the new C-in-C of the army, was an altogether different type of officer from Kornilov. He was short, though not as short as his predecessor, inclined to fatness, and full in the face. His hair he wore cut close. He had a small, neatly trimmed imperial, and his complexion was pale and slightly waxen: a clerkly man, more easily visualised as a retired official in a Chekhov play than as a high-ranking army officer.

He was half Polish. His father had been a serf, his mother a housemaid. At the age of thirty his father had been drafted into the army under the regulations and conditions prevailing prior to 1874. At the age of fifty-two he was promoted ensign, and eventually retired, as a major, in his sixties. What life as a commissioned officer must have been like for this former serf it is hard to imagine, particularly as he had served for so long in the ranks. Promotion may have brought him temporary benefits,

174

but it did not help him much financially; like the Kornilov family, the Denikins found it almost impossible to manage on the meagre military pension. They had several children, and their son Anton was born in 1872.

Denikin himself had no other ambition than to join the army. He took service as a 'volunteer' and, after a year spent messing with the private soldiers, succeeded in obtaining a commission. Subsequently he passed through Staff College, where he showed an aptitude for gunnery and organisation. Nevertheless, his military career was not an easy one, since he gained the reputation of being politically unsound and was regarded by his seniors as a dangerous radical. When Denikin felt that he had been unfairly passed over for promotion, he became involved in a clash with the Ministry of War. To a large extent his model service in the Russo-Japanese conflict rehabilitated him, but by the time the World War broke out he had begun another struggle with authority by attempting to use the press to bring pressure on the senior generals in the course of a campaign to improve conditions for the private soldier.

Certain aspects of Denikin's upbringing and early life were to influence his career as a White leader. His half-Polish origins may well have had something to do with his attitude to the nationalities problem. He was not a 'pure' Russian; in his early days his Russian colleagues could, and sometimes did, accuse him of not being 'one of them'. But he was not a Pole, either, and he had little time for Polish nationalism. Out of this insecurity was born his dedication to the ideal of a Russian Empire, an ideal from which he was never to waver.

The other main conditioning effect of Denikin's background was the fact that his only status was as an officer. His father had risen, the hardest way, to a commission; Anton Denikin had chosen to do the same. For him the military environment was total and, because he was of a serious turn of mind, he came to place a great deal of emphasis on his personal honour as an officer and on the obligations that this entailed. He was also a devout Christian. These were not superficial attributes; they were central to his whole character. It is not surprising, then, that he was to prove an inept politician and an intransigent negotiator. At more or less any point in the history of the Volunteer Army Denikin

could have enlisted considerable additional support by the simple
expedient of recognising the independence of the Don, the
Ukraine, and the break-away provinces of the extreme south,
Georgia and Azerbaijan. When he had achieved his object, the
conquest of central Russia, he could then have repudiated his
promise and reduced the new republics one by one. In the words
of one commentator who saw the possibilities of this course of
action: 'Denikin was undoubtedly too much of a soldier and too
little of a politician to be able to adopt it.'[1] Today one must
qualify the usage of 'soldier' – it was Denikin's particular con-
ception of the soldierly virtues that mattered; but the essential
point remains valid.

There were other side-effects of Denikin's rigid concept
of a soldier's honour, revealed, for instance, in his dislike of
the devious White relations with Krasnov. For all his flirtation
with the Germans, Krasnov was offering Denikin a great deal,
and had Denikin been a little less unbending, a workable alliance
might have been established. But Denikin considered that Krasnov's policy was 'either too astute or too unprincipled', and
consequently the makeshift connection between the generals'
armies was to cause continual trouble. This is not to say that
Denikin was incapable of subtlety; in a military context, so long as
the forces at his disposal were small, he could operate in an
unorthodox but highly effective manner. Towards the end of the
first Kuban campaign he outwitted the Bolsheviks by putting all
his infantry into carts and travelling fast right across the strongly
defended enemy lines of communication; in the second Kuban
campaign he was to go against the normal conventions of military
science on numerous occasions. But in political matters he was
quite without finesse or guile; and, even in military affairs, the
larger his forces, the more rigid he became.

It should not be thought that Denikin's example of personal
integrity was followed or even admired by all his officers. Amongst
them there were adventurers and time-servers who enlisted with
the Whites in search of plunder and excitement. There were also
men whose personal experience of Bolshevik atrocities led them
to commit similar outrages. Denikin proved unable to check this

---

[1] Bechhofer, *In Denikin's Russia*, p. 16, footnote.

process, and a White terror developed, as vicious, if not so widespread, as the Red.

Morale in the ranks of the Volunteers was high during May and June, though it did prove necessary, as a result of Krasnov's activities, for Denikin and Alekseev to address all officers holding commissioned rank on the political situation in south Russia.

Denikin had half-feared that the army might melt away; in fact the great majority of the troops who had served in the Kuban stayed on, and there was a continual flow of recruits from the north. Practically the entire contingent of St Petersburg and Moscow military cadets got through to the south, as did many officers. In mid-June the total strength of Denikin's force stood at 9,000 men, and it was evident that the time for further action had come. On 23 June the army set out into the steppes again;

with it was an artillery team of twenty-one guns and a squadron of three armoured cars, the only reliable one of which was known as 'Trusty'. The army's objective, once more, was Ekaterinodar.

The Whites might have been expected to march north, for the capture of Moscow was their ultimate hope. But Denikin did not think that, at this stage of the war, Moscow could be taken by the Whites. He believed that, by liberating the Kuban, he could secure a base area sufficient to support the Whites whilst they prepared their big push to the north. Moreover, he would have possession of several Black Sea ports and would be able to take delivery of Allied aid if, and when, the passage of the Dardanelles became possible. A third, local reason influenced his decision. Half of his army were Kuban Cossacks, and their motive in joining the Volunteers had been to free the Kuban from the Bolsheviks. Denikin considered that he had a moral obligation to them, but there is no doubt he also realised that, if he headed north, they might well desert *en masse*. From now on the local ambitions and attachments of levies was to be a perpetual hindrance to the accomplishment of the Whites' broader strategic aims.

At this time there were about 100,000 Red troops in the Kuban, the largest single unit being an army under Peter Sorokin, now concentrated to the south of Rostov. A further large concentration was in the area of Torgovaya, and it was on Torgovaya that Denikin first moved. His aim was to capture the station and seize the railway line; by so doing he would cut off the Kuban from central Russia. Having made provision to defend his right flank from any attack by the Sorokin army group, Denikin split his forces into four and commenced operations against Torgovaya. On the 25th the columns had all reached the railway line and were moving along it, from both directions, towards the station. This, though strongly held, was taken by nightfall. The demoralised Reds fled to the north. The Whites at once mounted machine-guns onto plate-layers' trolleys and started up the line after the enemy. Others of the Volunteers improvised an armoured train out of sand-bags piled onto flat-trucks.

The next station up the line was at Shablievskaya, and there the retreating Bolsheviks ran into the northernmost of Denikin's columns, commanded by General Markov. Markov had been held up at Shablievskaya by an unexpectedly strong Bolshevik garrison and an armoured train. No sooner had he reduced their defences than he was faced with the Reds from Torgovaya. These, however, were demoralised, and soon began to surrender or to abandon their arms and try to escape. It was in the very last stages of the action that Markov was hit by a random enemy shell, and killed. With Markov's death Denikin lost one of his closest friends, but the Whites gained another martyr.

The Kuban was now isolated. To the north Red troops had been contained at Tsaritsyn (on the Volga) by Krasnov's Army of the Don; to the west of Denikin's position Sorokin's force still represented a considerable threat, and Ekaterinodar itself remained a major obstacle. But those Reds who were to the west and to the south of the Volunteers were now cut off. Denikin pushed on, by the most direct route, towards Ekaterinodar, meanwhile keeping a close watch on the activities of Sorokin. Eventually the disorganised Reds who attempted to oppose his swift advance (once again he had put his infantry into carts) made a stand at the *stanitsa* of Belaya Glina. Denikin employed his usual enveloping tactics and, though he was outnumbered, had no hesitation in dividing his forces into three columns of 3,000 troops. A small nucleus of men from the Red 'Iron Division' led the defence, and succeeded in rallying a large number of Kuban villagers to the Bolshevik flag. But, despite the fact that the enemy were over ten thousand strong, Denikin had no difficulty in taking the *stanitsa*.

The action was to prove significant for two reasons. Firstly, of the five thousand prisoners taken by the Whites, a considerable number was drafted into the White Army. Nothing says more about the conditions under which the war was fought than this: it was a war between two minority factions, and the rest of the population really had no idea what it was being fought about. They understood the meaning of land and crops, and little more. If they were told to defend their village – no matter by whom – the probability was that they would do so. If they were conscripted – again, no matter by whom – the probability was that they would obey. It was only in the urban centres that the issues were ever widely understood, but even in the cities famine would induce men to join armies for no other reason than that they would at least be fed.

The other respect in which the fighting at Belaya Glina is important is that when the Whites moved into the *stanitsa* they found that some of their number, who had been captured in the early stages of the action, had been brutally tortured and then killed. Now, for the first time, the Whites began to take reprisals, and a large number of Iron Division prisoners were arbitrarily shot; they were dealt with in small groups, each batch having first been compelled to watch the execution of their comrades.

Whilst the Whites were marching on Belaya Glina, Sorokin attempted to cut their line of communication, but was repulsed by a combined force of Volunteers and men from the Army of the Don. This action served to neutralise the threat from the west, and enabled Denikin to continue towards Tikhoretskaya, half-way between his starting point and Ekaterinodar. Against Tikhoretskaya Denikin used a plan similar to that which he had employed at Torgovaya and Belaya Glina: a division of his forces into separate columns and then a synchronised enveloping movement. Once again he was outnumbered, but he had long come to realise that this was irrelevant. So long as he had trained men at his disposal he always had the advantage over the makeshift Red units. He also, for the first time, sent a flying column to round up Red partisans. The move was very successful. Speed and surprise proved to be an effective psychological weapon, and the raid greatly contributed to the disarray of Red forces.

By now the Bolsheviks were thoroughly confused and discouraged. At Tikhoretskaya, Kalnin, the Red C-in-C in the Kuban, attempted to gather his troops in an effort to destroy the Volunteers before they could threaten Ekaterinodar. But the division of the White forces deceived him as to the Volunteer numbers, and though some of the units at his disposal fought well, Kalnin himself was resigned to defeat. The Red vanguard was forced to abandon its positions and fled so fast that the Whites could not keep up with it. Late in the afternoon of 15 July White units were advancing across fields of tall summer wheat towards the station at Tikhoretskaya, where Kalnin had set up his H.Q. The station itself was taken by a column approaching from the rear. The Reds, who put up a formidable resistance to what they imagined to be the main Volunteer force, discovered that the buildings they were defending had been quietly infiltrated by the

Whites. Some hand-to-hand fighting developed in the shunting yards and amongst the houses of the station employees, but the greater part of Kalnin's forces broke and fled. Kalnin himself decided that the time had come for him to follow their example; when the Whites broke into his command train, which was drawn up in the station, they found the C-in-C's cap, but not Kalnin himself. The Red Chief-of-Staff, a former Imperial Army colonel named Zverev, had committed suicide and was lying on the floor of the carriage in a pool of blood. Zverev's wife, whom he had shot before killing himself, was still alive.

No amount of individual bravery by Red troops could compensate for the loss of nerve at the top. They dispersed into the steppes, or surrendered to the Whites and were either shot or drafted into the ranks of the Volunteers. Denikin, who had set out with 9,000 men, now had 20,000 under his command. Some of the new recruits were Kuban Cossacks, and others were Cossacks of the Don who had grown tired of Krasnov's pro-German policies; but the great majority were prisoners who had changed sides.

Just as important to Denikin were his captures of *matériel*. At Tikhoretskaya the Whites seized three armoured trains, rolling-stock, armoured cars, 50 field-guns, rifles, ammunition and an aeroplane. The Volunteers were becoming an army in something more than name.

It was now that a serious difference of opinion arose between Denikin and Alekseev, and this was to have a bearing on the whole future conduct of the war. Alekseev, who still had responsibility for the management of the army's political affairs, and played a major part in the making of strategic decisions, did not agree with Denikin that the next step was a march on Ekaterinodar.

He was concerned by two things: firstly the desperate shortage of money, and secondly the overall strategic situation. There was no more money to be had on the Kuban, but he might well be able to raise funds from the bourgeoisie of the wealthy Volga towns, if the Whites could liberate that area. Alekseev also argued that a move in the direction of the Volga, rather than onto Ekaterinodar, made better sense from the strategic point of view. If the Volunteers turned north-east, then they would be in a position both to replenish their exchequer and to connect up with the Czechoslovaks. Early in the year Alekseev had tried in vain to recruit them to the White cause. Now what he had hoped for had, quite unexpectedly, come about. It was Alekseev's view that:

> The principal theatre of war is now the east; it is there that the fate of Russia will be decided. We must not delay in leaving the Kuban and appear in the theatre where we are most needed.[1]

Denikin was not convinced. His viewpoint, as commander in the field who was not involved with the day-to-day fluctuations of the Volunteers' position in the Kuban, was bound to be different. Denikin based his rejoinder to Alekseev on the substantial argument that the Whites must have a base, and that the grain and oil-producing region of the Kuban was far too valuable an asset to throw away. He seemed to regard Alekseev's attitude as that of a paper strategist. Because Denikin was with the army, and the army was in contact with the enemy, and Ekaterinodar was a rich prize near to hand, Denikin's view prevailed. But Alekseev, though he was not, like Denikin, marching at the head of an army, was by no means out of touch. There is no saying what might have happened had the Volunteer Army met up with Čeček's troops in the Penza area. Alekseev, however, could do no more than register a protest at Denikin's decision.

Denikin's obsession with the Kuban is revealed by his action on hearing that Sorokin, with his north-west Kuban army group, had disengaged from the Don Cossacks and Germans whom he was fighting in the north, and was falling back to defend Ekaterinodar. Sorokin's front had been the river Yeya, which is crossed at Kuschkeva by the main Rostov-Ekaterinodar railway. As soon as he knew that Sorokin was in retreat, Denikin ordered a White unit to blow the bridge, in order to prevent a German advance into the Kuban. By doing this he was, as he realised, cutting his best line of communication with Rostov and the Don; and if he was to win the Kuban, then this railway would play a vital part in the launching of any expedition bound for the north.

Sorokin's move south greatly assisted Krasnov, who was now

---

[1] Letter from Alekseev to Denikin. Quoted in Lukomsky, *Vospominaniya* II, pp. 78-9.

able to deploy all his forces to the north and to the east. Krasnov's main objective remained Tsaritsyn, on the Volga, though he was in no hurry to join up with the Czechs, since he could hardly expect a favourable reaction to such a move from the Germans. The Bolsheviks were holding Tsaritsyn in force. It was the key to the granaries of the north Caucasus, and if it fell their food situation would become still more drastic. But, without Denikin's aid, it was doubtful whether Krasnov could mount an assault on the city – and, as we have seen, Denikin was occupied elsewhere.

The real battle being fought out at Tsaritsyn at this moment was one which was not to have any appreciable effect on the Russian situation for some years, though it was a crux in the development of the U.S.S.R. It was fought not between Red and White, but between Trotsky, Commissar for War, and Stalin, officially Commissar for Nationalities but now also Director General of Food Supplies for South Russia. Perhaps, in view of what this post really entailed, the wording should have been changed to 'Food Supplies *from* South Russia'. Stalin, who had a high opinion of his own abilities as a military overlord, found affairs on the southern front in what he considered to be an unwarrantable state of chaos. Therefore he abrogated to himself military powers, and appointed one Voroshilov, a former iron-worker, as commander of all troops in the Tsaritsyn area. This was in spite of the fact that Trotsky had already appointed an ex-Imperial Army colonel as commander of the southern front. Stalin, typically, avoided a direct confrontation with Trotsky but tried to enlist Lenin's support. Trotsky was for a long time unclear as to what was actually happening, attributing to Voroshilov actions for which Stalin was responsible. Stalin, meanwhile, was encouraging Voroshilov to act as though his command was independent of the southern-front Headquarters. As a result no one had an overall picture of what was going on in the south; both Trotsky and his commander, Sytin, were in the dark about developments in the Tsaritsyn area, and units were receiving contradictory orders from Voroshilov and Sytin. The confusion did not end until October, when Trotsky finally made a 'categorical demand' for Stalin's recall. Temporarily, Stalin was defeated; but it was the first in a series of conflicts that was to turn Trotsky into an exile, Tsaritsyn into Stalingrad, and Stalin into a dictator.

In the Kuban Denikin continued his single-minded advance on Ekaterinodar. On 21 July the Whites achieved an entirely unexpected victory when Colonel Shkuro, an anti-Bolshevik guerrilla leader acting on his own initiative, captured Stavropol in the eastern Kuban. This he was able to achieve in an economical and trouble-free manner by sending word to the Red commander that, if the garrison was not evacuated by the next morning, he would bombard the town with heavy artillery. The Bolsheviks moved out and Shkuro, who had no artillery whatsoever, moved in. What had really done the trick was the sheer terror evoked by his name, for Shkuro's methods were simple and brutal.

Shkuro had gathered a band of Kuban Cossacks, all of whom were fanatically loyal to their leader. The chief inducement offered them was loot, for Shkuro was not particular where he looted, or how, provided that the results justified the effort. If he had to kill people, he preferred that they should be Bolsheviks. He did not pay his officers, because he saw no need for them ever to be in want of money. Even those serving in the Volunteer Army found it prudent to keep out of the way of Shkuro and the men whom he called his 'Wolves'. Denikin promoted him to general. He was subsequently to dismiss him at least twice, but was each time forced to reinstate him, for fear that his men should go over to the Bolsheviks.

Even the capture of Stavropol was not without its drawbacks. Before long the Reds realised that they had been tricked, and began a counter-attack. Since the Wolves were by this time conducting a thorough examination of the contents of the local wine cellars – which the inhabitants of Stavropol had made available rather than sacrificing their possessions and their womenfolk – there seemed every chance that the Reds would succeed, and Denikin was forced to send reinforcements to Shkuro. It was an unfortunate moment for him to weaken his army, for whilst the Volunteers moved on towards Ekaterinodar, they were quite unexpectedly attacked from the rear by a large Bolshevik force. This was Sorokin's doing.

Sorokin was one of an extraordinary class of Bolshevik commanders who emerged in the Civil War. He had originally been an ensign in a Cossack regiment and had served under Yudenich on the Turkish front. His father was a peasant who had done well and bought land. Sorokin had had a limited education, which put him a step above the other men of his *stanitsa*. The Bolshevik Revolution, however, had effected a transformation. He was not interested in the subtleties of politics, but he understood what class warfare was about, he had a little military training, and he could command the absolute loyalty of his men. But he could be every bit as cruel and despotic as his White counterparts. He was wont to shoot down commanders of whom he disapproved whilst they were on parade with their men – which made life unpleasantly exciting for his officers. Now he had succeeded in manœuvring his army between Denikin's columns in such a way that the central pair were entirely isolated and the Army Headquarters itself threatened by powerful Red forces.

The ensuing battle, fought out in the extreme heat of July amongst the great cornfields of the Kuban steppe, was much more closely contested than any of Denikin's actions in the campaign to date. Sorokin succeeded in checking the Whites, and in bringing them to battle on terms that were favourable to the Reds. He had superiority in numbers, the advantage of surprise, and some of his troops were in prepared positions which lay across the Whites' line of march. Against the centre divisions of the Volunteers he launched the full force of his attack. The Whites suffered heavy casualties and slowly retreated westwards.

By nightfall the two isolated columns had still not succeeded in making contact with Denikin and the rest of the army. Drozdovsky, commanding one of them, proposed a further retreat by night in the hope that they would be able to link up with the army commander. General Kasanovich, of the other column, held to the view that Denikin should find them, rather than they him. Since Kasanovich was the senior, his view prevailed. The next morning the Reds again attacked in force, charging with the bayonet. The Whites fell back in disorder, cut off and outnumbered. It was at this moment that Denikin's possession of the only aeroplane in the Kuban saved the day. The White pilot brought a message from Denikin that reinforcements were on their way. At noon men of the Drozdovsky and Kasanovich columns saw tell-tale clouds of smoke in the sky to the south of their position, and knew from the direction of the high-explosive bursts that help was near at hand. Within three hours the Reds had been put to flight and the White Army was united once more.

For the Reds, however, this seemed only a local set-back. Sorokin was still convinced that he could destroy the Volunteers; he succeeded in regrouping his forces and in launching an attack in the north. He was everywhere on the battlefield, urging his men on, leading cavalry against the White positions – a demonic figure in oddments of Imperial Army uniform and a Circassian coat. During the course of the battle he heard from Moscow that he had been appointed C-in-C North Caucasus, in succession to Kalnin, and this had something to do with his dogged continuation of the battle. But no amount of enthusiasm could compensate for the skill of trained troops: though the Bolsheviks kept up harrassing attacks for a week and the Volunteers' advance was brought to a halt, on 7 August the Reds broke and fled towards Ekaterinodar.

It was a headlong retreat and, since Sorokin had broken his army against the Volunteers, there was no hope of putting up a serious defence of the capital.

On 14 August Timashevskaya, where the Red Taman Army had been holding Sorokin's left flank, fell to one of Denikin's columns. The way to Ekaterinodar was clear. In the afternoon of 15 August White troops encountered Red Guard units on the outskirts of the town; after a series of short but bloody actions the suburbs were carried, cavalry dashed along the main boulevards to seize the town centre, and the Whites entered at sunset, meeting with virtually no resistance. On the 16th Denikin, Lukomsky (his newly appointed assistant commander) and the White staff made their formal entry into the town. With the Volunteers were the representatives of the Kuban Cossack Government. But, having won the military battle, Denikin was immediately faced with a political conflict from which, given his temperament and outlook, it was impossible that he could emerge victorious.

As soon as Denikin had captured Ekaterinodar the Kuban government revealed that they were far more interested in their own independence and a peaceful existence, than in embarking on Denikin's ambitious and seemingly impossible scheme for the capture of Moscow. There were even covert proposals, by various members of the new government, that negotiations should be opened up with the Soviets. They were at least as concerned as Krasnov that their new state should be autonomous, and there were signs that they would soon emerge as being altogether more extreme in their insistence on this.

Denikin's plan was that, for the moment, both the Don and the Kuban should retain their existence as separate territorial entities, but should be subordinated to a council headed by Alekseev. Right-wing groups proposed that a dictatorship should be established under the Grand Duke Nicholas, who was living at Dalber in the Crimea – which was, of course, now occupied by the Germans.

To this plan Denikin was firmly opposed, since such dictatorship would inevitably be seen as the prelude to a restoration of the monarchy. Alekseev, who had been against the march on Ekaterinodar, now insisted that any political council should include the emergent White forces in the east, and went ahead with his plans to move to Siberia. His opinion remained that the Volunteer Army should be used to link the two territories, since it was obvious that, for the moment, no close alliance was possible with the Cossack forces. Denikin, however, insisted that the rest of the Kuban should be cleared of Bolsheviks before the Volunteers moved on elsewhere. He was still thinking in terms of base areas, whilst Alekseev seems to have regarded the Volunteers as a flying column. Such a column could concentrate on striking at the Bolsheviks where they were weakest militarily and, until the Reds were defeated, leave the political questions to whatever forms of authority emerged locally.

No doubt Alekseev saw the strength of Denikin's argument that the army must have a secure base. Considered in the abstract, this point of view was obviously correct. At the same time he realised that all Denikin was really doing was liberating territory for other people, who had no hesitation, once they had come into what they considered to be their own, in refusing him the co-operation that he so urgently required. If this was so, then it seemed reasonable, to adopt the alternative policy – for all that it was theoretically unsound. Alekseev felt that once the various anti-Bolshevik groupings were in contact with each other, they might then feel sufficiently confident to embark on the greater matter of the march to Moscow. But first that contact had to be made.

After the capture of Ekaterinodar the pursuit of the Red units that remained in being went on. The most formidable of the Bolshevik forces was the Taman army group, which attempted a retreat to Novorossisk on the Black Sea coast. This important port had been one of the bases of the Black Sea fleet. The Germans felt, understandably, that the possession by Denikin of a formidable instrument of war might make the White threats about reopening a front against Germany rather less rhetorical than they sometimes seemed. They therefore demanded that the Bolsheviks surrender the fleet, and the Reds, rather than do this, had scuttled it. Now a German garrison occupied the town, but they tactfully withdrew when the retreating Reds and pursuing Whites approached. On 26 August the Volunteers seized Novorossisk, and the Reds continued their flight southwards down the coast. They were now in a drastic situation. The only factor that worked in their favour, as it had for the Whites earlier in the year, was their lack of a safe refuge. To the west there was the sea; to the south and east lay inhospitable steppes; to the north were the Germans and the Don Cossacks. Their only substantial hope was that they might make a break-through to the line of the Volga, where the Reds were still in the ascendant. In September the harried Bolsheviks heard news from the Volga that must have encouraged them still more; the Red Army, led by Trotsky, was seriously threatening Kazan. On the 10th the town fell to the Bolsheviks. All the Red forces in the Kuban thereupon began to concentrate in the east, the plan being that, if they massed in sufficient force, they might be able to break through to the Volga towns.

By now the Volunteers were tired of the incessant campaigning. The Bolsheviks had put different armies into the field against them time after time, but the nucleus of the White forces had remained the same. Though Denikin could call 50,000 men to arms, his cadres consisted of the men who had marched into the Kuban in January. They were battle-weary, their uniforms were falling to bits, and munitions were in desperately short supply.

The pace of the retreat was as exhausting for the Whites as for the Reds, and the Reds, who moved in front of the Whites, were able to commandeer transport and provisions. In the eastern Kuban the Reds mounted a series of sharp counter-attacks, in which their superiority in numbers told against the worn-out Whites. Towns changed hands several times; the Whites were acutely hindered by their lack of signals equipment, and all Denikin's enveloping movements failed.

The capture of the Black Sea ports had enabled a certain number of Imperial Army officers who had been caught in the Crimea by the German invasion to cross over and join the Volunteers. So there was, throughout the autumn, a slow reinforcement of the commissioned officers. Since Denikin was now conscripting, many of the officers who had hitherto served in the ranks were promoted, but others of them continued to serve as private soldiers. Against the idle or the cowardly who found for themselves pleasant and entirely superfluous jobs in the rear areas, we have to set those men who had known command all their lives and chose to serve in the ranks. As late as 1920 there were former colonels serving as privates, and though it is generally true that there were far too many officers in footling staff jobs, it is also true that many did serve in the line of battle, taking orders when all their lives they had been accustomed to giving them.

Of the new recruits the most remarkable was Lieutenant-General Baron Peter Nikolaevich Wrangel, who had distinguished himself as a cavalry leader during the war against Germany. Kornilov had attempted to locate Wrangel when he was originally organising the Volunteers, but had failed to make contact with him. Wrangel had been in the Crimea and in Kiev, where Skoropadsky endeavoured to persuade him to join the Ukrainian forces. Wrangel had refused the offer. Now he had managed to get to Ekaterinodar, and Denikin at once appointed him to the command of a division. When Wrangel eventually reached his command, he discovered that it consisted of two and a half thousand men, together with three field batteries. But it was a start, and though he had an unpleasant experience in his early days, when his Cossacks broke before a Red cavalry charge and he had to escape by jumping onto a moving ambulance-car, he soon succeeded in making a unified force out of the very mixed batch of units that he was given.

Not all the changes in personnel were as auspicious as the arrival of Wrangel. On 8 October General Alekseev died. The apparent cause was pneumonia, though his doctor had long suspected that he was suffering from cancer. But it was obvious, to all who knew him, that his end was a direct consequence of his two years as Chief-of-Staff and C-in-C, followed by his service in the appalling conditions of the first Kuban Campaign. Even that experience was not to end his troubles; it was Alekseev, rather than Denikin, who conducted the difficult negotiations with Krasnov and the Don Cossacks. That he did so was just as well; he undoubtedly got much further with the Ataman than Denikin would ever have done. Much of the support from the Army of the Don – support which enabled Denikin to win the second Kuban Campaign – was negotiated by Alekseev. It was Alekseev who, more than anyone else, had been responsible for the foundation of the Volunteer Army. Whilst others had postured, or devoted themselves to wishful thinking, he had got on with the hard work involved in actually creating, arming, and financing the Army. He deserves to be remembered not only for his local achievement in giving concrete expression to the aims of the Whites through the foundation of their army, but also for his contribution to the Allied cause in the World War – for it was he who, in his quiet and unobtrusive way, held the Russian front together until May 1917.

Now Denikin appointed himself Commander-in-Chief both of the army and of the civil administration. It was an unsatisfactory move, but it had the effect of quieting those who looked for a dictatorship. With Denikin firmly in both posts there was less reason to clamour for the return of the Grand Duke Nicholas. Though the death of Alekseev was a personal loss to many Whites, and though Denikin was to have cause to regret that he had not, through the agency of someone as distinguished as Alekseev, effected a working connection with the Siberian Whites, the tactical command structure of the Volunteers was left unchanged.

This was in sharp distinction to the situation that obtained in the Red camp, where Sorokin had become dissatisfied with his lack of success, and felt that the time had come to take drastic action. The Reds had concentrated in the Stavropol area, though the Whites still held the city, and now received orders that they should try to break through to the north. Eventually, it was hoped, they would link up with the Bolshevik front at Tsaritsyn. Sorokin began to execute commissars and commanders whom he disliked, notably those of Jewish birth. He also started conspiracies against Shelest and Kozhuk, respectively commanders of the Iron Division and the Taman army group.

His eventual aim was revealed when, on 26 October, just after his armies had begun their move to break out to the north, he arrested the five most prominent members of the Soviet of the North Caucasian Republic. The main offence of these individuals – to whom he was technically subordinate – had been that, tired of high-handed executions and his unwillingness to undertake systematic planning, they had attempted to form a committee to settle basic strategic and administrative questions. Sorokin consequently decided to shoot them also. But when this had been done, it was obvious that he had overplayed his hand. The army Soviet declared him an outlaw, and he was finally captured and killed by men of a Taman army regiment, whose popular commander he had unwisely shot.

The Red move to the north began with their capture of Stavropol. Since its seizure by Shkuro's Wolves the town had only been lightly held. The Whites garrisoning it were driven out shortly before a relieving column reached the town, and the Reds managed both to beat off this attack from the steppes and to consolidate their hold on the town. By early November Denikin had the town surrounded, but, despite efforts at negotiation, the Bolsheviks refused to surrender. Their efforts were directed to the organisation of a northwards break-out, and they assembled a large number of locomotives and a mass of rolling stock, together with baggage waggons, lorries, and other transport. Meanwhile Denikin closed the ring around the city, and panic spread within it.

General Wrangel had rapidly made of his division one of the most formidable fighting units in the Volunteer Army. He was, however, desperately short of men with which to fill out the cadre structure. In the fighting before Stavropol he captured a large number of Bolshevik prisoners – nearly three thousand in all. It seemed to him that the time had come to embark on a recruiting drive. He therefore lined up the officers and N.C.O.s amongst the Bolshevik prisoners. There were three hundred and seventy altogether. When they were paraded he ordered them to be shot. That done, he offered the rank and file the chance of joining the White army so that they might 'have a chance to atone for their crime and prove their loyalty to their country'.[1] If there was an alternative to this choice he did not make it explicit.

It was Wrangel's men who were the first to enter Stavropol, though not before Drozdovsky had been mortally wounded in an attempt to take one of the suburbs. On 14 November Wrangel, sabre drawn, charged in at the head of his cavalry. On 15 November the town fell. The Reds managed to break out eastwards, and Denikin at once ordered the cavalry to follow up their retreat. In the town itself the Whites found weapons, munitions, and much of the vast transport train collected by the Reds.

The Bolshevik retreat was at first covered by rear-guard actions; but on the 20th the Volunteers finally broke the Taman army group in a strongly contested action, and the Red withdrawal disintegrated into a panic-stricken flight. The Bolsheviks were mercilessly pursued by White cavalry and – though individual units were to rally and put up a fierce resistance in various towns and villages of the eastern Caucasus – the North Caucasian Army had, for all effective purposes, been destroyed. Denikin could now truly claim to be master of the Kuban.

The change in the Whites' position – from insurgents to incumbents – coincided with another change of as great importance. This was the Armistice of 11 November – the direct consequence of which was the appearance off Novorossisk of Allied warships. It seemed to Denikin as though his dearest hopes were now to be fulfilled. His control of the Black Sea ports put him in a position to receive all the war materials that the Allies could send him, and he knew that on the Salonika front alone the British must have vast stocks of surplus armaments and munitions. He fully expected that such aid would immediately

---

[1] Wrangel, *Memoirs*, p. 59.

be forthcoming. As early as 14 November the British War Cabinet had agreed in principle to give Denikin what backing they could. But they had not committed themselves to a total support of his war effort, nor were they ever to make such a commitment.

Even in the short term, the Armistice presented difficulties for the Whites. German units were soon pulling out of South Russia and the Ukraine: this created a void that both Reds and Whites raced to fill. They were not the only interested parties: nationalist groups in the Ukraine and elsewhere endeavoured to form governments; the Allies had their own private aims. The elimination of the Germans simplified the Russian chaos only superficially; the Armistice brought new uncertainties.

In the first place, channels of communication between the Whites and the Allies were confused and inefficient. The Russian embassies in the various Allied countries still housed the diplomats who had been appointed by the Provisional Government, and these had been joined by anti-Bolshevik Russians of every political allegiance. The Paris Embassy acted as the natural headquarters for the largest of such groups, which came to constitute the Russian Political Conference, generally known to the Allies as the White Council.

As a designation this was misleading. The Council was itself divided into bitterly opposed factions, and its members were in no way representative of the anti-Bolshevik forces as they had emerged in 1918. In the Council there were spokesmen who claimed to represent the views of the Social Revolutionaries, of moderate conservative groups, and of Savinkov. But there was no-one who could speak with any authority on behalf of Denikin, or Krasnov, or the Siberian Whites. Indeed, it is doubtful whether the Council was better informed on current developments in Russia than the Allied governments to whom they gamely offered advice. What the Council most nearly represented was the Provisional Government in exile – a connection that was reinforced by the arrival of Kerensky in Paris. The problems attendant on this situation were manifold, and not the least of them was the tendency of the Council to speak as though it exercised some control over the activities of the White leaders. It very soon became obvious that, if anything was to be achieved, the Allies must establish formal contacts of their own.

In late November 1918 a conference of Allies and Russians was held at Jassy in Roumania with this end in view. It was an improvement on the meetings with the Paris Council, if only for geographical reasons. In other respects it was hardly better. Denikin was too hard pressed to organise an effective mission, and the various representatives were appointed because they happened to be on the spot, not because of any qualifications that they might have for arguing their respective cases. Those present included some distinguished politicians: there was A. V. Krivo-shein, formerly Minister of Agriculture in Stolypin's cabinet, a staunch but unconventional conservative; there was Milyukov, who could speak both as the leader of the Constitutional Demo-crats, and as the former Foreign Minister of the Provisional Government. But there was no provision for effective communica-tion with the leaders who mattered, the men commanding the armies now ranged against the common foe.

In the Ukraine Hetman Skoropadsky's puppet government fell shortly after the Germans withdrew. It was replaced by a Directorate of Ukrainian nationalists under Simeon Petlyura. The aim of the Directorate was to fill the gap left by the retreating forces of the Central Powers before the Allies or the Whites arrived. Petlyura adopted a pro-Bolshevik line which pleased no-one save for the fellow members of his makeshift junta. It was at first unclear whether this move was dictated by conviction or temporary policy, but the move, which lost Ukrainian nationalism the sympathy of the Allies, immediately contributed to the atmo-sphere of unrest in south Russia, and it became obvious that action had to be taken fast. Perhaps only such pressure could have caused the Russians at the Jassy conference to come to any decisions at all; the two that they did reach were both to create a great deal of future misunderstanding.

At the conference the Russians adopted a prima-donna role that was to become all too familiar in the ensuing years. With the vaguest credentials, inadequately briefed, and often representing no identifiable political grouping, anti-Bolshevik Russian diplo-mats were to spend the next three years behaving as though they were the spokesmen of a great empire, formidable in its power and resource. At Jassy the Russians decided that the Allied aim should be to see Russia restored to her pre-1914 borders (with the grudging exception of Poland), and that Denikin should be regarded as the leader of the anti-Bolshevik movement. Having made these momentous resolutions, and having attributed to the anti-Bolshevik movement more unity than it was ever to achieve, the Russians then sat back, assuming firstly that the Allies would approve and secondly that vast quantities of aid would shortly flood into the Black Sea ports.

The two main consequences of the Jassy conference were that the French decided to intervene and 'restore law and order' in south Russia, and that the anti-Bolshevik groupings in south Russia decided that they had better try to present to the outside world that unity which their representatives at the conference had claimed for them. The French intervention got under way with a landing in Odessa on 18 December; but the French government were far more interested in the emergent nations of eastern Europe, and the possibilities of an anti-German Polish alliance, than in the activities of the Whites. They embarked on their interventionist career with the combination of Gallic esprit and massive incompetence that was to characterise all their future excursions into White Russian affairs.

So far as Denikin's new role – ironically imposed from outside, though he himself was only too willing to fill it – was concerned, the immediate consequences were more the outcome of military events than of any diplomatic decisions. The Don Army was increasingly hard pressed, and Krasnov was attempting to hold off large Bolshevik forces on two fronts. There were hard-fought battles in the north, and it was not until he was faced with dis-affection that Krasnov's ability to contain the Reds weakened. A local Cossack, Mironov, led a revolt against Krasnov on the Upper Don, and Krasnov's army began to suffer from a spate of desertions. In these circumstances, and urged on by many of the most noted anti-Bolsheviks in the Don Territories, Krasnov turned to Denikin for help.

X

Northern Diversion

Nothing reveals more fully the futility of intervention, and the total lack of understanding of the Russian situation by the intervening powers, than the course of events in Murmansk and Archangel. These two towns on the White Sea had come into considerable prominence during the World War, since they were the chief entry-ports for the large quantities of munitions and supplies that Great Britain was despatching to Imperial Russia to aid her war effort. The emergence of Murmansk as a port can be attributed to the vagaries of the Gulf Stream, which freakishly keeps the Kola inlet, on which Murmansk is situated, free from ice all the year round. Between 1914 and 1917, therefore, a port was constructed so that the flow of supplies to Russia could be maintained even for the six months of the year that Archangel (which, paradoxically, is further to the south) was iced in. From Murmansk a railway had been built that connected up with the Trans-Siberian trunk line, and thus provided for the transport to St Petersburg of cargoes docked in the north. The railway was constructed largely as a result of British initiative and persistence. But it was not the British, but the Reds, who stood to profit by the stockpile of *matériel* that had built up in both ports in February 1918. The stores, particularly the armaments, were precisely what was needed to keep the White Finns at bay, and to equip the Red units which were moving towards the Don to fight the forces of Cossack secession and White reaction.

In Murmansk, situated hard against the Finnish border, the local picture was shaped by external factors. The inhabitants of the town, more interested in combating the rigours of the Arctic winter than in matters of ideology or nationality, were concerned lest the fighting in Finland should disturb the relative peace that they enjoyed.

The Allies were equally concerned by the Murmansk situation, but for a rather different reason. The lives of the Murmansk Soviet were of less interest to them than the fate of the Allied stores, but over-riding both of these considerations was the fear that Graf von der Goltz, who was now known to have landed in Finland, might endeavour to capture the port and use it as a base for German submarines. If Murmansk were to be put to such a use, the U-boats would be able to evade the mine barriers that now restricted their exits from Hamburg and the Grand Belt, and to roam in the Atlantic, harrying Allied shipping at will. The Allies and the Murmansk Soviet had, therefore, a commonalty of interest, and their co-operation was ensured by what appeared to be a sign of approval from a very unlikely quarter.

On 2 March 1918 the Murmansk Soviet received a telegram from Trotsky instructing them to accept 'all and any assistance' from the Allies. Since this telegram was subsequently used both by the Allies as a justification for intervention, and by Stalin as evidence of Trotsky's treason, it is well to note both the date and the circumstances of its despatch. On 2 March it was still not clear to Trotsky whether agreement would be reached in the peace negotiations with the Germans. It was at least possible that the outcome would be a continuation of the war, and that would have meant that the Bolsheviks must call on the Allies for help. Further, the telegram to the Murmansk Soviet was sent in response to a somewhat panicky message in which it was alleged that the town was threatened by a large force of Finns and Germans. Obviously a German occupation of Murmansk was unacceptable from any point of view, treaty or no treaty. But the main importance of the telegram, later countermanded and disowned, was that it acted as a salve to the consciences of the Murmanskers, and encouraged them to embark on a course of action from which there was to be no turning back.

Allied forces had moved into Murmansk proper at the beginning of April. They were able to do this so promptly for the simple reason that there was, based on the port, a squadron of ships of the Royal Navy under Rear-Admiral Thomas Kemp. The Marines from these ships constituted the first British intervening force. By the end of May there were over five hundred Marines ashore.

The physical presence of British troops was to have far more effect on the Murmansk Soviet than any harangues from Moscow. As early as 12 May British Marines and Russian troops had been in action against Finnish Whites near Petsamo, to the north-west of Murmansk.[1] These Finnish Whites were not, as was supposed, the advance guard of a German force moving on Murmansk, but a party who wished to establish Finnish claims to the Petsamo area – claims based on an agreement made by the Russians with the Finns in 1864, but which had never come into effect. Nothing came of this incident, which was the subject of a highly absurd 'protest' note from the Finnish to the British government, but it did awaken the Allied command to the dangers of an advance by von der Goltz.

All the operations in the Murmansk area were complicated by the British belief that von der Goltz's Baltic Division numbered 55,000 men. As it was, the Germans never had more than 15,000 effectives in Finland, and even had they been able to enlist the support of the Finnish Whites – in their post-Mannerheim phase – it is doubtful that they could have raised a force 50,000 strong. But the British misapprehension conditioned the Allied response, and soon the Allies were heavily committed in the Murmansk peninsula, and had also recruited extensively among both local Russians and Finnish Reds. This force, though intended for use against the Germans, was eventually deployed against the troops of the increasingly hostile Red Guards – that is, those from beyond the Murmansk area. Yurev, the leader of the Murmansk Soviet, came into open conflict with Lenin, and by August the Allies and the Murmanskers had established a front – more by accident, it can be said, than by design.

In May the War Office had sent Major-General F. C. Poole to Murmansk to command all Allied troops in north Russia: this was in anticipation of the event, since – apart from the Marines – the first detachment of the new expeditionary force did not arrive until 23 June. The men of this contingent – known as 'Syren force' – were, like those of the British battalions sent to Vladivostok, low-grade troops unfit for service in 'an active theatre of war'. No fit men could be spared from the western

---

[1] See above, p. 151.

front. Shortly after the Syren landing, personnel for a second expedition arrived in Murmansk.

This second expedition, 'Elope force', about 1,500 strong, set sail across the White Sea on 30 July, bound for Archangel. It

ARCHANGEL
AND MURMANSK

0   50   100 miles
0   50   100 kilometres

Murmansk

Kola Inlet

The
White Sea

Archangel

Onega

River Dvina

Tulgas

Shenkursk
Ust Padenga

White/Allied Fronts
Winter 1918-1919
Railway

St Petersburg

Vologda

appeared off the city on 1 August, to find it in White Russian hands; a rising had been timed to coincide with the approach of the Allied force. It had been a little unwise of the local Bolsheviks to leave the British Consul a free man, in telegraphic contact with the outside world.

The rising was largely the work of former officers of the Imperial forces, notably Commander Chaplin, a naval officer.

199

It succeeded in clearing the town of Bolsheviks, who had never been well received in Archangel at the best of times, and enabled the Allies to take over without bloodshed. But a force as small as the Allied contingent could do little in the way of holding territory. Patrols of the British, French, and Polish troops who constituted the Elope force were sent down the railways and roads leading out of the town to reconnoitre and to establish what defensive positions they could. Poole then set about organising internal affairs.

A certain piquancy was added to the situation in Archangel by the fact that the Allied ambassadors in Russia, who had caused both their own governments and the Russian government far more trouble than they were worth, and had eventually managed to get themselves evacuated to the north, were now in the city. General Poole was, in consequence, the unwilling recipient of much well-meant and contradictory advice about the political scene. Eventually a government of a Right Social-Revolutionary inclination emerged, led – if the word is not too forceful – by M. Nikolay Chaykovsky. Chaykovsky was a worthy of great age who had been a consistent and loyal moderate revolutionary all his life. A university teacher by profession, he was much practised in the art of keeping reality at a distance. He was described by one senior British officer as 'utterly unmilitary; he did not seem to realise that force would be necessary to defeat the Bolsheviks. . . . Now that the chance had come to him, he had no vigorous plan to put into effect.'[1]

The officers who had organised the coup in the town had no time for this septuagenarian socialist relic, and they were particularly irritated by his two military advisers, Durov and Samarin. The latter had had the dubious distinction of having been promoted from captain to general by Kerensky. The officers who had actually paved the way for the instatement of the new government now found themselves ignored and despised as dangerous reactionaries. As they were unemployed, they grew bored, and at length determined to do something to relieve the tedium. On the night of 5 September 1918 they demonstrated that if they could manage a coup once, then they could repeat the

---

[1] Ironside, *Archangel*, p. 38.

performance. They kidnapped Chaykovsky, Durov, Samarin and other ministers, and held them captive on Solovetsky's Island, conveniently central in the White Sea.

On 6 September General Poole took the salute at a parade of part of the American contingent, which had arrived in Archangel two days before. With Poole on Government House steps was David R. Francis, United States Ambassador to Russia, and a man of liberal sympathies. Towards the end of the parade these two dignitaries engaged in some of that light conversation with which it is apparently customary for senior officers to while away such functions, and Poole took the opportunity to remark that there had been a revolution in the night. To which Francis replied: 'The hell you say. Who pulled it off?'

'Chaplin,' Poole answered. At this Francis motioned for Chaplin, who was on the parade-ground, to come over to the steps.

'Chaplin, who pulled off this revolution last night?'

'I did,' said the errant captain. 'I drove the Bolsheviks out of here. I established this government. . . . I see no need for any government here anyway.'[1]

It was Francis who persuaded his colleagues to press for the reinstatement of Chaykovsky, and eventually the old professor was brought back from his barren islet, and told to resume the reins of government. There was little doubt that Poole had been aware of what the plotters were up to, and after a short lapse of time he was replaced by Brigadier-General Edmund Ironside – a large man, well over six feet tall, and known to the troops as 'Tiny'. Ironside was given the acting rank of major-general, and set about organising his command with flair and energy.

One of his first acts was to dismiss Durov, whose military endeavours had resulted in the recruitment of one single company which, when it was ordered to parade for an inspection by Ironside, mutinied. Durov's replacement, though more efficient, was no great improvement. The effective commander in the north Russian theatre remained General Ironside.

Ironside was insistent that, if Archangel was to be of any significance whatsoever, a Russian force must be raised. The difficulty was to persuade anybody actively to set about forming such a

---

[1] Francis, *Russia from the American Embassy*, p. 204.

force. On the Murmansk front there was a Karelian regiment, formed of Red Finns and used with effect against Whites who encroached on Russian territory; but the political circumstances dictated that these were for local use only. And though the American force was sizeable and an Italian unit arrived at the end of the year, there were not enough Allied troops on the ground to defend the perimeter that had been established – against which the Bolsheviks were now moving in earnest.

The lack of any indigenous Russian army made the most ambitious of the north Russian strategic schemes an act of faith. This was an attempt, initiated by Poole, but carried on by Ironside, to link up with anti-Bolshevik forces in Siberia. The line of march was defined by the course of the Dvina River, which is navigable as far as Kotlas, nearly four hundred miles south-east of Archangel. From Kotlas there is a rail link with the Trans-Siberian Railway. Poole's intention was to march as far up the Dvina as he could before the onset of winter, and then to establish defensive positions and to hold them until the movement could be resumed. His troops advanced from Archangel, supported by a shallow-draught monitor which provided them with artillery cover. Eventually the column managed to penetrate two hundred miles up-river, finally halting at the village of Tulgas. To protect their lines of communication they also took and garrisoned the town of Shenkursk, a resort on the banks of the Vaga, a major tributary of the Dvina. When the snow came, and the northern forests were transformed from swamplands into the conventional backdrops for a Russian winter scene, the Allies had established fronts at Tulgas, at Rodvino (south of Shenkursk), and also on the Vologda railway, which ran south from Archangel, roughly parallel to the Dvina. The three front lines, each of which only effectively covered its respective column, could be projected by the optimistic to make a single front, arc-shaped, two hundred miles from Archangel.

Winter tested the low-grade Allied troops to the uttermost. The Armistice removed the only convincing reason for their presence in Russia. Each day there were only two pale hours of light. The cold was extreme, the forests were vast and unknown, communication between the various fronts was almost impossible. There were continual cases of frostbite, and several of insanity.

The Reds mounted surprise attacks on the blockhouses in which the troops lived, and though the Bolsheviks undoubtedly suffered the most casualties in these attacks, the nervous strain on the Allied forces – most of them raw recruits – was enormous. Eventually many units became dispirited and mutinous.

The behaviour of the Russians did nothing to reconcile the Allied troops to their situation. In Archangel and Shenkursk there was a return, amongst the bourgeoisie, to the social life of the Imperial epoch; this was made possible only because Allied troops were manning the defences. Those Russian units whom the government did succeed in raising seemed to cause nothing but trouble. It was obviously the weakness and irresolution of the government that lay behind this state of affairs, and it was only when Chaykovsky left, in January 1919, to occupy himself with the greater affairs of the White Russian Council that matters improved. Chaykovsky was replaced by P. J. Zubov, and shortly afterwards the Governor-General, Marushevsky, was succeeded by General Eugene Miller.

Miller came from a Baltic Russian family who had owned land in Lithuania. Before the war he had served mainly as a military attaché, and in 1914 he had joined the Staff of General Gurko. He succeeded in being a thoroughly able Chief-of-Staff, but he could hardly be regarded as a front-line soldier; for him, as for so many Imperial Army officers, there seemed to be no half-way home between the 'fighting general' syndrome and the popular General Staff illusion that wars were won behind desks. After the March Revolution he had been made an army commander, but he became progressively disillusioned with the Provisional Government, and towards the end of 1917 he went abroad. Until he took over in Archangel he had been living in Rome.

Under Miller the other members of the Archangel government became less important than they had seemed hitherto. Miller had little confidence in the existing régime, and soon made sure that he, as Governor-General, had the final word in political as well as military affairs. Though he was not reactionary in his views, and even succeeding in winning the respect of the more left-wing political groups, Miller did not believe that the Social Revolutionaries were presenting a sufficiently convincing anti-Bolshevik front, and his policies followed a much tougher line. There had been some suggestion that Kerensky might come to north Russia – Chaykovsky's political views had been closely allied to those of the erstwhile Prime Minister – but Miller simply remarked that if Kerensky was found on north Russian territory, he would be shot. Kerensky refrained from paying his promised visit. (The same threat, incidentally, was made by Denikin. It did not require unusual percipience to see that Kerensky was unlikely to be an asset to a Russian régime.)

Miller, a tall, thin figure with a remarkably luxuriant moustache, proved to be the first effective Russian leader to emerge in the north. He succeeded in raising a small army, which began to take over sectors of the front line from the British, and he re-employed Chaplin and the other conspirators. But, politically, Miller could only propound that series of negative theses on which the White Russian military leaders always seemed to fall back when they were questioned about civil affairs. He wanted a Russia 'Great and Indivisible', and he believed that the political future of Russia should be settled by a Constituent Assembly. As for his own private beliefs, he told Ironside that: 'the Tsar had been his master, and he would remain faithful to his memory, but it was for the people of Russia to decide whether there would be a Tsar once more'.[1]

Ironside himself was anxious to transfer to the Russians as much responsibility as possible for the security of the city. In pursuing this course he was undoubtedly wise, for on 4 March 1919 the British War Cabinet decided to pull Allied troops out of North Russia as soon as local conditions permitted. The troops in Archangel were in bad condition and their morale was low; the cost of the expedition was high, and it was causing the government at home embarrassment, since British Communists were agitating against intervention, and many members of the Labour party had come to support their view. Sir Henry Wilson, Chief of the Imperial General Staff, was concerned to free troops for Ireland and India, where they were urgently required; Lloyd George was, in any case, dubious about the whole enterprise. It was Winston Churchill, since 1917 Minister of Munitions but from January 1919 Secretary of State for the War Office, who

---

[1] Ironside, *Archangel*, p. 108.

was left as the chief advocate of thorough-going intervention in Russia.

Up until the Armistice British (and American) intervention in Russia had one over-riding objective: the re-formation of an eastern front against Germany. Other motives certainly influenced the despatch of intervening troops; in Britain there was much distrust of the Bolsheviks – in particular of their appeals for world revolution, of their suspected collaboration with the Germans (about which British Intelligence had become very excited), and of Lenin and Trotsky as personalities. Moreover, the contacts which had been established between the Milner Mission and Russian Liberal elements had pre-disposed a number of influential people in favour of the Provisional Government.

But after the Armistice the picture changed entirely; it became far harder for a politician to justify Allied interference in Russia's internal affairs. Furthermore, it seemed to many politicians that a weak Russia was to be preferred to a strong and militaristic power, and they therefore hesitated to support those elements in Russia who had, as almost their single point of agreement, the slogan 'Russia, Great and Indivisible'. And such politicians were certainly not prepared to give unlimited assistance to a movement that refused to recognise, and asserted that it always would refuse to recognise, the independence of the small national states that were emerging out of the Russian chaos.

In general, the British military did not share the politicians' dubiety; much of the initial enthusiasm for intervention had come from military quarters. Nevertheless, even given the degree of latitude that the British command structure permitted to senior officers in the years 1918-20, the amount of persuasion, or even mild blackmail, that could be exercised by a Director of Intelligence, or the Head of a Military Mission, was limited. This was particularly the case since Wilson was known to regard other actual or incipient crises as more important. Churchill, clearly, was able to persuade the military planning staff to support schemes which he favoured – or had initiated – but there was a limit to what one man could do. For Churchill certainly did not spare himself in his efforts to aid the White Russians; his involvement was so apparent that in September 1919 Lloyd George was to write to him in 'one last effort to induce you to throw off this obsession with Russia which, if you will forgive me for saying so, is upsetting your balance'.[1] Yet there was precious little logic in Churchill's grand strategy for intervention.

In his office Churchill had a large wall-map of Russia, upon which he was wont to illustrate his strategic designs. In essence these were simple; they were based on the assumption that the best way to combat Bolshevism was to assail it from as many different points as possible. All anti-Bolshevik movements should be supported, until the Bolsheviks were eventually surrounded by an 'immense circle' of enemies.

This sounded splendid when it was expounded in Churchillian prose, and with the map to hand. But the plan was fundamentally unsound. It was unashamedly dependent on a dispersal of effort, and it failed to take into account that a ring around Russia, particularly if it was not overwhelmingly strong at any one point, might serve to raise, rather than lower, the morale of those within its compass. And given that the Soviets had interior lines of communication and control of the all-important railway system, there is no reason to suppose that the 'immense circle' was going to unduly discommode them.

It is at this point that we return to Archangel. For here was a front set up on Allied initiative, largely manned by Allied troops, and yet achieving very little in terms of the Civil War as a whole. The distances involved were immense, the population of the northern tundras was sparse; the whole operation was taking place in a vacuum. Slowly the government managed to build up a basis of popular tolerance, if not of notably active support, and though Bolshevik partisan bands were a nuisance, attempts at agitation accomplished comparatively little. The Whites began to meet with success in their efforts to recruit an army, but the troops were not of a high calibre, and the forces raised seemed to have been afflicted with that accidie which was to be so noticeable a feature of the whole Archangel episode. Ironside was forceful and energetic, but there was a limit to the extent that he could impose his will on other people. The British officers made

---

[1] Letter of 30 August 1919. Owen, *Tempestuous Journey*, p. 520. Quoted in Ullman, *Britain and the Russian Civil War*.

scornful comments about the Russian forces, these remarks were inevitably passed on, and the Russian officers countered by saying that the British were interlopers and not pulling their weight. All of which was very confusing and infuriating for both sides.

In the early summer of 1919 – for it seems justifiable, in view of the isolation of the northern front, to anticipate the overall chronology of this account – Ironside knew that the expedition would certainly be evacuated. This presented him with a great number of problems, both military and political. He had to withdraw his men from defensive positions, deep inland, at a time when he anticipated strong offensives by the Red forces. He also had to ensure that the Whites, if they decided to stay, were in as advantageous a position as possible; those who wished to leave he promised to aid. It was the least he could do when it was considered that the British had created the régime from which they were now withdrawing their support.

Some Russians chose to be evacuated. But Miller decided to stay on, and to endeavour to hold the territory that the Whites controlled. Had he wished, there is little doubt that he could have prevailed upon the British to transport his troops to join those of Kolchak or Yudenich; he remained, despite the comparative weakness of his army, though this was obviously going to make it very hard for him to launch an offensive. If he could not attack, why did he remain? The answer seems to be that he regarded White territory as something to be defended at all costs – in other words that he, too, was more alive to lines on maps than to the priorities essential for military success.

In order to facilitate the withdrawal of British troops, it was planned that a relief force should be sent to north Russia. Ironside decided that his best plan would be to try to inflict one crushing defeat on the Bolsheviks before he retreated, and thus gain time in which to extricate his men from the front line. Churchill permitted himself to hope that the relief force might succeed in linking up with the Siberian Whites, with whom a small party from Archangel had already made contact. But though Ironside's attack was successful, it did not get half the distance needed to effect this link. (It is pertinent to ask what difference it would have made to the war if the link had been made, and Churchill had persuaded his cabinet colleagues to allow the North Russian expedition to remain in Archangel and risk another winter with their transports frozen in by the Arctic icefloes.) As it was, General Sir Henry Rawlinson was sent to superintend the evacuation, which went ahead as planned.

In the forests the Bolsheviks bided their time. Miller's government suffered a prolonged twilight existence which lasted until early 1920. The Allies had tied down twenty thousand Red troops for about a year.[1] They had given a great deal of false comfort to the Whites, and had encouraged them in unwarranted expectations. For themselves they had created a considerable fund of ill-will amongst the Reds. So much force, military and economic, applied at another point, might have had an effect. As it was, the Allies had achieved nothing.

---

[1] Lenin was at one time very worried lest the Allies mount a major thrust through Archangel (see *Sochineniya*, XXV, p. 360). But this, of course, never materialised.

XI

Supreme Ruler of All the Russias

Throughout 1918 there had been an increasing tendency amongst the Whites to look to the east as the direction from which help might come to them. It was to Siberia that Alekseev had decided to go, before his death put an end to all his strategic schemes; it was with the Siberian anti-Bolsheviks that General Poole, and subsequently General Ironside, proposed to effect a link-up from the north.

The Czechs had made the establishment of an anti-Bolshevik régime in Siberia possible. It was at once apparent that it was up to the Russians to make the most of this opportunity, since the Czechs themselves had no real idea of their future intentions. It was typical of the conditions obtaining in 1918 that the Russian response should have been the formation of no less than nineteen separate governments within the area liberated from the Reds. Two of these, based on Samara and Omsk, we have already encountered; there are two more which deserve our attention.

The most far-flung of the Cossack Hosts was that which eventually established itself – with government support – in the Trans-Baikal. Here, on the empire's eastern border, a Cossack community had been set up in the middle of the preceding century, with the object of colonising and of developing the economic resources of the newly opened frontier. Because of the relatively recent date of this process the Trans-Baikal Cossacks tended, in the main, to be wilder and more independent than their confederates nearer to central Russia. They were also a great deal less civilised, which is why, during the Russo-Japanese War, there was a dearth of officer material amongst the Trans-Baikal regiments. It is to Peter Wrangel, transferred into a Trans-Baikal unit in an effort to remedy this dearth, that we owe our best description of Semenov, Ataman of the Trans-Baikal Cossacks and one of the most vicious and unpleasant of the White leaders in the Civil War. He was also, it must be added, one of those who did most harm to his own cause. According to Wrangel, Semenov appeared

... dark and thickset, and of the rather alert Mongolian type. His intelligence was of a specifically Cossack calibre, and he was an exemplary soldier, especially courageous when under the eye of his superior. He knew how to make himself popular with Cossacks and officers alike, but he had his weaknesses – a love of intrigue and indifference to the means by which he achieved his ends.[1]

Semenov was half Mongol, and in 1917 he was in Trans-Baikal recruiting amongst the Mongol tribes when the Bolsheviks seized power. Semenov promptly removed himself across the Chinese frontier, and began to raise an anti-Bolshevik army. In this course of action he was aided by a singular piece of political geography. The final section of the Trans-Siberian Railway had actually been built across Chinese territory and, though a loop was subsequently constructed which ran round the Manchurian border, within Russian territory, the Chinese Eastern Railway – as the line running through Manchuria was known – remained the most direct line to Vladivostok. The line itself and the towns along it were protected by various agreements, all of which were, in the fashion of the time, greatly to the advantage of the Russians. And here, when the November Revolution broke out, flocked those who found the new régime in some way inimical. There were a great many of them. But, more important from Semenov's point of view, he could use the area as a base for raids into the Trans-Baikal. Having thrown out the local Bolsheviks he set up his headquarters at Manchuli, a small town on the railway just within Manchuria, and commenced operations against the Reds. In so doing he was certainly motivated by sincere anti-Bolshevik feelings. But Semenov, this 'Heathcliff of the steppes' as he has been aptly called,[2] also had hankerings for that ancient Cossack occupation, banditry; and he conducted his war in such a way that the one concern was inclusive of the other.

In his exploits Semenov was greatly aided by his companion, Baron Ungern-Sternberg, who had served with him in the Car-

[1] Wrangel, *Memoirs*, p. 6.
[2] By Fleming, *The Fate of Admiral Kolchak*, p. 52.

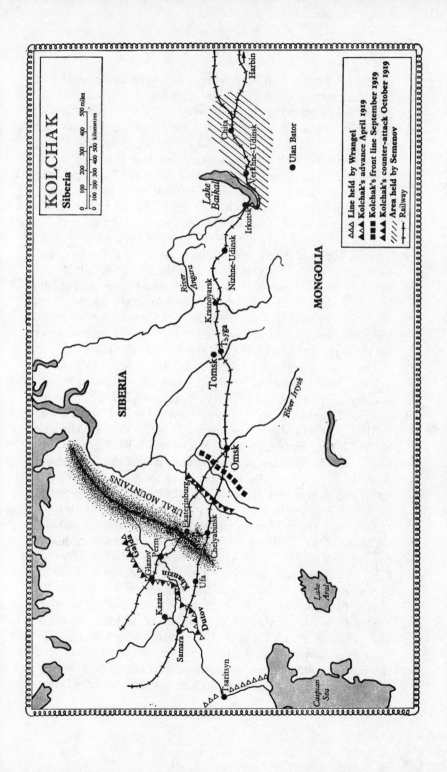

KOLCHAK
Siberia

0 100 200 300 400 500 miles
0 100 200 300 400 500 kilometres

△△△ Line held by Wrangel
▲▲ Kolchak's advance April 1919
■■■ Kolchak's front line September 1919
▲▲▲ Kolchak's counter-attack October 1919
//// Area held by Semenov
┼┼┼ Railway

SIBERIA

MONGOLIA

Harbin
Chita
Verkhne-Udinsk
Ulan Bator
Lake Baikal
Irkutsk
Nizhne-Udinsk
River Angara
Krasnoyarsk
Tayga
Tomsk
River Irtysh
Omsk
URAL MOUNTAINS
Ekaterinburg
Perm
Gajda
Glazov
Chelyabinsk
Khanzin
Kazan
Ufa
Samara
Dutov
Tsaritsyn
Lake Aral
Caspian Sea

pathians. The two men were both under thirty, and both shared the same taste for bloodshed and plunder. Ungern-Sternberg, generally known as the Baron, looked totally ineffective but was, it seemed, more or less physically indestructible. He was also exceedingly cruel, and a sabre-blow on the head, received during a trivial quarrel with a fellow officer, may have mentally unbalanced him. The Baron, with his pale face, red hair, and long cavalry moustache, was soon one of the most feared men in eastern Siberia. In their early days the distinctive characteristics of this pair were not widely known, and Semenov was the pleased but ungrateful recipient of a considerable sum of money from British sources. He used this to expand his activities as a war-lord, and soon controlled a considerable area of the Trans-Baikal. By the time the British discovered the true nature of their protégé, the harm was already done. In any case, he had, in the interim, been discovered by the Japanese; they saw in this Asiatic *condottiere* an instrument who might well be used to further their own schemes for the control of Manchuria and the Russian Far East.

The other government east of Lake Baikal was an altogether different kind of concern. At first it had neither a base in Russia, nor any hold on Russian territory; its centre was Harbin, on the Chinese Eastern Railway. There General D. L. Horvath, who had long been retired from the army and was now General Manager of the Chinese Eastern Railway, had set up his Far Eastern Committee for the Defence of the Fatherland and the Constituent Assembly. This was about as nebulous as it sounds. What it amounted to was that Horvath, an avuncular figure who much preferred negotiation to action, was concerned to protect the railway from the Bolsheviks and to do what he could to stabilise the situation in the Trans-Baikal. He was not helped in this by the presence in Harbin of so many refugees, the fact of whose flight indicated that they were not much interested in active opposition to the Reds. It was a psychological factor that was always to work against White hopes of success: the refugees tended to be those who could either afford to leave Russia or had no stomach for a fight; yet these were the men who had the most direct influence on the behaviour of the Allied powers and the border states. There were those who stayed and fought; M. V. Rodzyanko, for instance, the former President of the Duma, joined the Volunteer Army service corps and served under Denikin through both Kuban campaigns. Purishkevich, after he had been released from prison, got to south Russia and remained there. Naturally, he managed to make a nuisance of himself, but he did have the courage and faith to stay. Not so the émigrés – at least the wealthier of them – and Horvath's government, which was established in a foreign town filled with refugees, was tainted by the émigré mentality. Nevertheless, Horvath himself was not lacking in either common sense or political awareness and, seeing that the Red hold on the Trans-Baikal was weak, he began to explore the possibility of military operations.

Horvath did not intend to conduct these himself; the years in railway management had not increased his appetite for soldiering. In any case, he was wise enough to see that a military dictatorship was unlikely to answer in the present circumstances. He needed a military adviser, who would act as Commander-in-Chief of his troops – always assuming that he could raise any; specifically, he needed somebody who was *persona grata* with the Allies. By a curious combination of coincidence, he found such a man in a very short time, though he was not a soldier, but a sailor.

British interest in Admiral Alexander Kolchak had been aroused when a small naval officer with a permanently worried expression on his face had arrived at the Tokyo Embassy, asking for employment in any capacity in which he might further the Allied cause. There had firstly been a move, for some no doubt excellent but now forgotten reason, to send him to Mesopotamia. He had got as far as Singapore when he was called back at Horvath's request – first to Peking, then to Harbin. But, once he had arrived at the Manchurian town, he found that he could achieve little. This was because of the omnipresence of Japanese money and agents. Manchuria was regarded by the Japanese as exclusively their business, and the Russians were to be tolerated only for as long as they seemed likely to be of use to Japan. With neither the head of the Japanese military mission, nor with Semenov – the mission's unruly, but nevertheless totally dependent puppet – did Kolchak have any success, personal or diplomatic. When Kolchak finally decided to go and beard the Japanese General Staff in Tokyo, he failed just as badly. It was only when the Czech revolt brought the British directly into the Siberian theatre that Kolchak became anything more than an unfortunate and irritated go-between.

The man who created the new interest in Kolchak was Major-General Sir Alfred Knox, the former Military Attaché in St Petersburg, now once more actively involved in Russian affairs. Knox, who had been appointed British Military Representative at Allied Headquarters in Siberia, had become one of the most influential men in all Russia. His experiences in St Petersburg during the Revolution had made him uncompromisingly anti-Bolshevik. He was confirmed in this attitude by his Siberian experiences, to the extent that, at one stage he cabled to London: 'Civilisation demands that we should intervene to prevent the horrors now committed every day in Russia.'[1]

Knox approved of Kolchak, considering him the only hope for the anti-Bolshevik Russians. In August both men were in Vladivostok and were able to discuss the Siberian situation. Kolchak was dissatisfied both with the behaviour of the Japanese and with Horvath's 'railway buffet' government; Knox was anxiously searching for even one reliable Russian with whom the British could co-operate – for it should not be assumed that, because Knox was anti-Bolshevik, he was greatly taken by the Whites.

Kolchak was the best, and perhaps the least conventional, type of Russian naval officer. If nothing has until now been said about the Imperial Navy, this is because during the World War it was rendered largely impotent by German control of the western Baltic and Turkish control of the Dardanelles, and during the revolution it was paralysed by mutiny. The larger ships were, almost without exception, taken over by left-wing elements; these mutinies were characterised by the massacre of officers in gross and bloody circumstances. It was as though the close quarters under which a ship's company had to live reduced all the baser passions of the revolution to their elemental state. The smaller ships often remained loyal, but the total effect of the mutinies, together with the continual strikes in the ship-building

---

[1] Knox, telegram of 4 November 1918. Quoted in Ullman, *Britain and the Russian Civil War*, p. 30.

and repair yards, was to render the fleet useless. In fact, the greatest impact made by the naval mutinies was on land warfare, for the bands of sailors from Kronstadt and Odessa, who put themselves under the orders of the Soviets, became of considerable importance during the early days of the Civil War.

The naval mutinies were largely a product of the brutal disciplinary measures adopted in the service. It is to Kolchak's credit that the ships in the Black Sea Fleet, which he commanded in March 1917, though naturally shaken by the events, did not mutiny during the revolution. Kolchak, the son of an army officer, and brought up to regard the services as his only possible career, was concerned for the welfare of his crews as well as for the efficiency with which they performed their tasks. He was himself distinguished both as a man of action and as a scientist. He had made several daring journeys of Arctic exploration, and he had returned from them with valuable geographical and climatological data. He was also an expert on naval mines, and he had played an important part in the reorganisation of the Russian Navy after the Tsushima disaster. When he heard of the abdication his standpoint was quite clear: 'I was after all serving not one form of government or another but my country, which to me was above all else.'[1]

But no amount of co-operation with the Sailors' Soviets, or of interminable meetings with members of the Provisional Government, could prevent the situation in the fleet from deteriorating. Bolshevik agitators were not the least of his worries, and he had to try to keep the fleet operational whilst dealing with its internal problems. In June 1917 the fleet finally mutinied, claiming that the officers were planning a counter-revolution, and demanding that they be disarmed. Kolchak still had sufficient control of the company of his flagship to assemble them on deck. He then addressed them from the bridge, telling them that German agents had been responsible for the mutiny, and that he took the demand that the officers be disarmed as a personal affront. Having said this, he drew his sword and hurled it from the bridge into the sea, thus ending his command of the Black Sea Fleet.

---

[1] Varneck and Fisher, *The Testimony of Kolchak and other Siberian Materials*, p. 48.

The gesture may seem to have been superfluously dramatic. The cart-wheeling arc of a silver-hilted uniform sword flashing into Odessa harbour – it sounds like dramatic renunciation by an histrionic leader. But Kolchak was not in this tradition. His action was the expression of an ungovernable temper that was seldom in evidence but that, when he did become angered – often at apparently trivial things – goaded him to bitter words and violent actions. At other times he was quiet and reserved. Physically, he was most remarkable for his deep-set eyes, and there were many of his subordinates who were disconcerted by the unwavering intensity of his gaze.

We may say Alexander Kolchak was a conscientious officer of the Russian Navy. He was brave, loyal, intelligent and, above all, he was serious in his approach to his work. His behaviour, both professional and personal, was conditioned by a strong sense of decorum. (During the Civil War period he had a mistress, the wife of a brother officer. But the relationship, though he did not attempt to dissimulate it, seemed – so far as the outside world was concerned – studiously correct.) Kolchak was in no sense a counter-revolutionary leader. When Alekseev became disillusioned with the Provisional Government he set about organising an army; in the same circumstances Kolchak offered his services to an Allied power. Duty was his primary motivation, and it would have been pertinent for Knox to ask whether, in a counter-revolutionary situation, this was an adequate or sufficient driving-force.

But there was no one else; by now Knox was backing Kolchak for all he was worth, and to a large extent making the running for him. At last the various Siberian governments had begun to realise that their only hope lay in unity, and the urgent need for such unity was becoming increasingly apparent. The Czechs, who were still having to fight fierce battles in the Urals and elsewhere, were daily growing more impatient of Russian prevarication and delay. And since, in the beginning of September, the Reds launched a big offensive towards the Volga and the Urals beyond, the Czechs' disenchantment was of more than passing importance to the anti-Bolshevik governments. On 7 September the Red Fifth Army moved against Kazan; on 8 September the Whites began a 'State Conference' at Ufa, three hundred miles eastwards.

At Ufa were gathered as many members of the Constituent Assembly as could be found, together with representatives of all the main political parties. The result of their deliberations was the proclamation of an All-Russian Government, with a directory of five ministers at its head. Kazan fell on 10 September; the State Conference did not end until 6 October.

The sequence of dates is more revealing than any amount of rhetoric. Looking back, Trotsky was to write that after the fall of Kazan to the Whites there was nothing to stop them moving on to Nizhny Novgorod: 'Nizhny was next. Had the Whites taken possession of Nizhny Novgorod, they would have had a clear road to Moscow. That is why the fight for Kazan acquired decisive significance. . . . We tore Kazan out of the hands of the White Guards and the Czechoslovaks. That day was the turning point in the course of the Revolution.'[1] Yet whilst the Reds were desperately massing all the available troops against the city, even going so far as to bring a flotilla of destroyers through the newly completed canal system connecting the Baltic and the Volga, the Whites were engaged in time-wasting, and often futile, debate. Relations between the Samara government – which was strongly socialist, and the Omsk government – which was considered by Samara to be reactionary, grew so bad that Omsk took the line that they did not mind what happened to Kazan (in the Samara territories). In such an atmosphere it is hard to understand why the Czechs bothered to remain at all.

However, the Ufa Conference did eventually produce the Directory; though if the State Conference could by any stretch of the imagination be described as a mountain, then what it had given birth to was a mouse. The Directory was proposed as a temporary measure pending the convocation of a Constituent Assembly. Its policies much resembled those of the Provisional Government, and though its members claimed that the formation of a strong army was their first priority, their military organisation was chaotic and their approach to military problems temporising. General Boldyrev, who was appointed Siberian C-in-C, was ineffectual. His first action was to overmobilise, and this promoted in both himself and the other members of the Directory

---

[1] Trotsky, *Stalin*, p. 310.

a totally misplaced belief that they were in possession of a formidable fighting force. This was far from being the case. To call two hundred thousand men to arms when no proper provision could be made for their training and equipment was an act of crass stupidity. Knox, who was engaged in organising aid in both fields, was anxious that the army should be reduced to a feasible size. But from the Directory he could obtain little satisfaction.

Knox was not the only man to realise that the whole Siberian situation was seriously unstable. Many of the Russians knew this, though their frantic caballing did not improve matters. Of the Czechs Gajda, ever on the look-out for a means of furthering his own career, but at the same time sincerely anti-Bolshevik, was particularly anxious. When, encouraged by Knox, Admiral Kolchak came west from Vladivostok to Omsk – travelling, as it happened, with Gajda – he was immediately recognised as a figure who, because he was outside party factions and had held high military command, might prove of singular value to the Directory. By the end of October he had been invited to become Minister of War. He did not at first wish to accept this post; he had to be persuaded to take it. Here was no thirst for power, no hunger for the proffered rank. He could see, all too clearly, the parlous state of Siberia. But, in the end he allowed himself to be persuaded. When he accepted he did so unwillingly, but he accepted nevertheless. In a sense, he lost control of the situation at the start.

As Minister of War Kolchak's powers were limited. He was beset with complications on all sides. There was the central problem of just how much the Allies could be persuaded to do to aid the Directory; there was the difficulty posed by the Trans-Siberian Railway, which was as often as not single-track, jerry-built, and clogged with traffic of a kind for which it was never designed; there was the Bolshevik advance from Kazan to be resisted. Kolchak was often neither tactful nor pragmatic in his approach to the diplomatic problems. The Czechs, grown increasingly restive, were beginning to move towards Vladivostok and out of the front line. Kolchak must have been aware of the reasons for this, and it would seem to have been the logical thing for him to do all he could to encourage them to fight the Reds. It was, of course, natural that he should resent the Czechs' refractory attitude at so critical a juncture, but it would have been in his best interests not to reveal this. Instead, he made it quite apparent that he disapproved of the Czechs' behaviour; it is scarcely surprising that this angered them still more.

In the second week of November 1918 Kolchak, in his capacity as Minister of War, went up to visit the front. He was escorted by men of the Middlesex Regiment which was supposedly the spearhead of the British intervening force. The force had never got any further than the planning stage at Whitehall, but the Russians still believed that the rest might come. Consequently, the sight of the new Minister accompanied by a British bodyguard and the regimental band must have warmed the heart of many an onlooker. But disillusionment was as rapid as the first trustful enthusiasm for the Allies had been; the British troops, it was soon apparent, were for show only. When they finally reached the front line Colonel John Ward, an ex-regular now back in the army for the duration, and otherwise remarkable as having been M.P. in the Labour interest for Stoke-on-Trent, decided that the cold rendered conditions 'quite impossible for British military operations'.[1] So the band played, but 'British military operations' were not conducted; nor were they ever to be. Kolchak had to learn the difficult lesson that, though he might get aid from the Allies and though he might receive a great deal of personal encouragement from General Knox, in many respects the Russians were on their own.

He had ample occasion to consider this in the middle of the month. For the Armistice was just as significant an event in Siberia as it was anywhere else in White-controlled Russian territory, and in one major respect it was far more important in Siberia than elsewhere. The over-riding reason for Allied intervention in Siberia had been the 'rescue' of the Czechs. It had soon become apparent that this was an entirely unnecessary operation. A secondary aim had then been canvassed: the formation of an eastern front against Germany. Now this, too, was rendered irrelevant. At the end of October Czech national independence had been declared; there was every reason for the Czechs to return to their homeland. The European peace made

---

[1] Ward, *With the 'Die-hards' in Siberia*, p. 118.

it ridiculous for unfit British soldiers still to be involved in a distant and irrelevant theatre of war. Had the Russians chosen to look, there were danger signals enough.

Some did choose to look; but the way that they interpreted the signals and the action that they decided upon was by no means to everybody's taste. Now that the snows had come again to Siberia, the military situation was temporarily static. There was no guarantee that it would remain so for long. The cold and the biting winds kept the troops crouched around fires or huddled together for warmth in the trenches; the drifts made movement difficult. But a determined commander could always break the deadlock; there were a hundred places where either side could outflank the other unopposed; and there was always the possibility that an armoured train might advance deep into White territory before it could be halted. The same situation obtained in the Red camp, but for the moment the Reds were attacking and the Whites were on the defensive.

In Omsk itself, the barren capital of the Siberian plain dominated by vast buildings of neo-classical and neo-Byzantine design, numbers of discontented officers were appalled by the failure to capitalise on the military opportunities now offered to the Whites, and disgruntled by the socialistic leanings of the Directory. Amongst these officers was a group of Cossacks headed by a certain Ataman Krasilnikov. Krasilnikov entertained feelings about the Directory that must have closely resembled those which Commander Chaplin had nurtured for the Chaykovsky régime at Archangel. The plan that Krasilnikov decided to adopt was also similar – though he met with a great deal more success than the North Russian conspirators. And many observers were to count it more than a coincidence that both coups – for such was the course of action upon which Krasilnikov decided – were conducted with the apparent connivance of British officers.

On the night of 17 November the two Social Revolutionary members of the Directory were at an unofficial meeting of a party caucus. This was, however, held in an official building guarded by Government troops. Such trivial details did not deter Krasilnikov, who had the satisfactory experience of breaking in on their nervous deliberations, and marching the offending politicians off to the lines of his own Cossack regiment.

At six o'clock the next morning there was an emergency meeting of the remaining members of the Directory and of other members of the government. It was at once apparent to these gentlemen that they enjoyed no substantial measure of popular support, and that, by now, all of the Cossack regiments stationed in Omsk had come out against them. That there had not been any violence beyond the kidnapping was probably accounted for by the presence of machine-gun units from the Middlesex Regiment, who had taken up positions commanding fields of fire down all the main streets. Colonel Ward subsequently asserted that his only motive for taking action was the maintenance of public order; whilst this was certainly one sound enough reason, there was no doubt that it also effectively ruled out the possibility of an attack on the Cossacks by any armed force that remained loyal to the Directory. The *status quo* after a coup is, clearly, a rather different thing from the *status quo* prior to it.

Krasilnikov did not present, to the bewildered and largely uninterested people of Omsk, an alternative government. He was content to express his dissatisfaction and to leave the remnant of the Directory to work out a solution. After a lengthy discussion it was proposed that, in the circumstances, the only possible form of government was a military dictatorship. Apparently this decision was so long delayed not because it was reluctantly arrived at after a discussion of all the other possibilities, but because those present at the meeting had simply not thought of the idea before. This is difficult to believe, but seems to have been the case. It would have been hard to find a more well-meaning or less realistic gathering of politicians anywhere else or at any other time. For, reactionary Cossack though Krasilnikov may have been, there is no doubt at all that he was right in his view that a military dictatorship was the only hope for the Siberian Whites if they were to survive, let alone play an active part in the assault on Bolshevism. Any military dictator would, at that juncture, have been an improvement on the existing government. To those present at the hastily convened meeting at Omsk, it seemed that there was only one possible man for the job: Admiral Kolchak.

The sequence of events was not quite spontaneous. Kolchak seriously proposed that Boldyrev be made dictator, and was then asked to leave the room while his own suitability was discussed.

He must have known as he waited, alone, in one of the ministerial offices in Government House at Omsk, that he would be asked to accept the office. He must have also known that there was no one else to whom they could reasonably offer it. When he was called back in and told that the Ministers had decided to subordinate themselves to a Supreme Ruler, and that it was their wish that he should be that ruler, he had already decided that he would have to accept. Thus, and thus unwillingly, did Alexander Vasilievich Kolchak become the Supreme Ruler of All the Russias.

Some of the right-wing members of the Government had certainly known that a coup was planned; equally, they almost certainly had Kolchak in mind as dictator. Kolchak himself had been approached by various officers, whom we must assume to have been involved in the coup, but he had rejected their proposals. Knox knew that a coup was planned, but he did not consider that the time was right; on the other hand, some of his intelligence officers were not above playing a lone game – superior officers can be surprisingly flexible when presented with a *fait accompli*. The British Foreign Office was dismayed by the news of the coup; but reactions in the War Office were, on the whole, more favourable.

What Krasilnikov had done was really very simple: by removing the Social Revolutionaries from the government he neutralised those elements in Siberia that were more concerned with short-term political freedoms than with an ultimate victory for the anti-Bolshevik cause. Between May and October the Siberian governments had been the most liberal régimes in all Russia; but their policies worked against the organisation of an efficient and disciplined army, and without such an army the governments could not survive.

In the ensuing days the situation in Siberia stabilised. There was little doubt that Kolchak's assumption of power had removed a number of the sources of the tension which had hitherto characterised Siberian affairs. But, in some respects, the Admiral's elevation had a far from beneficial effect. The Czechs, who had been quick to react to Kolchak's evident antipathy, reiterated their demands to be sent home, and in some of the Legion's units Soldiers' Soviets were set up – an obvious and provocative sign of dissent. On 21 November the Czech National Council met at

Ekaterinburg and stated its disapproval in unequivocal terms. The Czechs opened negotiations with the remaining Social Revolutionaries and, for a time, it looked as though there might be an attempt at a counter-coup. Other Czechs, in a definite minority, declared themselves in favour of Kolchak; not unexpectedly, Gajda was one of these – though he was, at the same time, careful not to lose contact with the Social Revolutionaries. But it was now more than ever apparent that the Czechs would have to be withdrawn from the front line.

Further trouble developed between the Allies. The French, working on the assumption that a general was as good as a battalion, had dispatched General Maurice Janin to Siberia, in the hope that they, rather than the British, would eventually emerge as the major European political influence. But Kolchak, known to be a friend of Knox, was most unlikely to prove to be their man. Though Janin was appointed to the command of Allied troops in western Siberia, French influence showed every sign of declining, and the French settled down to being unobtrusively but persistently obstructive. In their inhibitions they differed from the Japanese, who now encouraged Semenov to regard himself as an independent princeling, not to be imposed on by the stranded sailor of Omsk.

In December the new régime was able to take the credit for an unexpected military success, the capture of Perm, to the northwest of the Urals. The town was taken by the most northerly of three army groups established by Kolchak: the Northern Army, under Rudolph Gajda, who was now a general in Kolchak's service; the Western Army under General Khanzin; and the Southern Army under Dutov, the Orenburg Cossack leader. Gajda caught the Reds by surprise, and having seized the initiative, retained it. He captured the vital Perm-Vyatka railway intact, as well as taking 30,000 prisoners, 260 locomotives, 4,000 railway trucks, fifty guns, ten armoured cars, and much other booty besides. Perm was also of strategic importance, for it was a step towards a link-up with the Archangel forces, as well as a possible starting place for an advance on St Petersburg. The capture of Perm was a major success for the Whites, and the railway engines, in particular, were of enormous value to them. The Reds' hold on the Urals and the western marches of Siberia was

severely shaken. Kolchak looked forward to the spring with good
heart.

There were, not unnaturally, adverse as well as encouraging
indications – some of these could be read both ways. On 21
December there had been yet another attempt at a coup in Omsk.
Both Bolsheviks and Left Social Revolutionaries were held
responsible. Be that as it may, it was suppressed quickly and
ruthlessly, and in the process a large number of demonstrably
innocent people were shot. Amongst Kolchak's entourage there
was a great deal of self-congratulation. White counter-espionage
had sabotaged the conspiracy before the attempt was made, and
the whole incident was regarded as a triumph for the Intelligence
and Secret Police officers.

The Omsk rising demonstrates both the strengths and weaknesses of the Kolchak régime. White counter-espionage was
remarkably good in Siberia, and Kolchak's men had already
started to break the Bolsheviks' Siberian network; but they were
completely unscrupulous in their use of power and were far more
extreme than the Supreme Ruler. Kolchak knew this, and from
time to time made disapproving comments, but in practice he
condoned their behaviour.

Kolchak's policies were moderate, but they bore little relation
to what actually went on in Siberia. The Whites, when they
advanced into Perm, were horrified by the evidence of Red
atrocities – prisoners bayoneted and their faces ground with
the heel of a boot, instruments of torture, reports of the execution of members of families who were known to have menfolk
serving with the Whites. But the Whites were to perpetrate their
own atrocities, and though these may not have been so barbaric
from a superficial point of view, they were just as terrible in the
end, and the more so in that they often lacked any specific motive.

Militarily, Kolchak appeared to be strong. At this stage he
had no recruiting problem, and his troops were trained and
equipped by the Allies. But there were flaws, apparently minor,
in the overall picture. They were to emerge, in time, as being far
more serious than Kolchak ever suspected. One of the fundamental points relates to the motivation of his troops.

The Bolsheviks were never notably strong in Siberia, mainly
because of the individualistic attitudes of the inhabitants, who

still retained traces of the frontier mentality. They were not caste-proud, in the sense of the Cossacks, and they traditionally held the authority of European Russia in scant respect. There was a great deal of small-scale farming and private enterprise, and the landlords were by no means so important a social factor as they were elsewhere in Russia. But, whilst there was little fertile ground for the Red seed to fall on, there was no markedly richer tillage for the Whites. The Siberians were not as explicitly independent as the Don Cossacks, nor were they so worried about the colour of their flags, but their attitudes were just as parochial. Though only a small minority affirmed that Siberia was for the Siberians and that the conflict between Red and White did not much concern them, a great many Siberians nevertheless behaved as though they believed this. Amongst such people we can number many of Kolchak's supporters; they had been in favour of his appointment because it seemed that he might be a figure under whom the various political factions could unite. Yet the sole reason for Kolchak's presence in Siberia was that he wished to see the White armies march into Moscow. There was a basic divergence of aim, all the more harmful because it never became explicit.

Another of Kolchak's major problems was an almost total lack of reliable subordinates. We have already seen that there was a tendency for elaborately uniformed but quite useless officers to congregate in the base areas of White territory. Nowhere was this more evident than in Siberia. And when Kolchak wished to recruit officers, he had to do so largely amongst those who had held war-time commissions. Some of his officers he had, in any case, inherited from the earlier Omsk governments, and of these there were many with dubious credentials. In the south the Volunteer influence meant that officers tended to be called by their official, i.e., pre-November 1917, ranks – Alekseev was devastatingly rude to those who 'assumed' ranks, as did many of the officers amongst the Don and Kuban Cossacks. During the course of 1918 the Whites had to make appointments of their own, but these were carefully recorded, and promotions were gazetted in orders. In the early days of the White movement in Siberia this had not been so; as a result, many of the ostentatiously clad officers who adorned the cafés, headquarters, and bordellos of Omsk were both untrained and unfit for command.

Bribes were routine; military stores were regarded as the raw materials of private enterprise; muster-rolls were falsified to provide for a number of profitable 'dead souls'. There were those who worked hard and honestly, but much of their time was wasted by futile bureaucratic procedures and by the necessity to attend to work that other men neglected. Some of Kolchak's staff officers were as conscientious as those of Mannerheim, but because they lacked the direction of a man who knew precisely what he wanted, they achieved comparatively little. But many of the 4,000 administrative officers in Omsk can have done nothing at all. Much time was consumed by the problems of liaising with the Allies; this, too, was time wasted.

An honourable exception must be made for Knox. Knox summed up his own feelings, and the problems created by Britain's partners in the Siberian venture, when he wrote in a report to the War Office:

I confess that all my sympathy is with Kolchak, who has more grit, pluck and honest patriotism than any Russian in Siberia, and whose difficult task is being made almost impossible by the selfishness of the Japanese, the vanity of the French, and the indifference of the other Allies. You have to take what you can get in Russia, and if you find an honest man with the courage of a lion he should be supported, although he may not appear to have the wisdom of the serpent.[1]

To say that Kolchak's task was made 'almost impossible' was no exaggeration. Semenov's activities on the Trans-Baikal sector of the all-important railway – activities that went on with the connivance and material aid of the Japanese – threatened to disrupt traffic entirely. Semenov regarded this stretch of the line as his private playground. He raided villages irrespective of their political affiliations; he murdered and looted. He kept several armoured trains, all of which had portentous names such as *The Ataman* or *The Terrible*. They were in steam and ready to leave his headquarters at a moment's notice. In order to maintain these trains he commandeered materials and locomotives from the hard-pressed railway workshops at Vladivostok; since he

---

[1] Knox to W.O., 10 January 1919. Quoted in Ullman, *Britain and the Russian Civil War*, p. 43 and, in a different version, from Canadian records: Swettenham, *Allied Intervention in Russia*, p. 165.

controlled the line between the port and Siberia proper, nobody was prepared to take issue with him over this. He cornered supplies of boiler steel and used them for the armour on his trains – thereby making it impossible for repairs to be effected on any of Kolchak's engines that had damaged boilers. At times he refused to let trains go further than Baikal, for no apparent reason. He was determined that the Supreme Ruler, in the gloomy grandeur of Omsk, should be dependent on him in his humbler headquarters at Chita. His hold could not be denied, for his men were fierce and loyal fighters, most of Trans-Baikal was under his control, and there was always the unvoiced but nonetheless real threat that he might blow up the Lake Baikal tunnels.

The other major hindrance to Kolchak's plans was the obdurate presence in Vladivostok of General Graves. Graves refused to commit himself to anything that was not clearly defined in Wilson's *aide mémoire*; since nothing was clearly defined in this obfuscating document, Graves did nothing. He adopted a manner and tone of stern moral rectitude. His caution was such that he had never travelled further than four hundred miles from Vladivostok. He had not been to Baikal, let alone Omsk, and he had no idea of conditions in Siberia. His reports to his government were often based on unreliable information and in any case were found contrary to information received via the State Department. But Graves's self-righteous interpretation of Siberian affairs aroused some deep responses in influential quarters, and though the Americans eventually decided to support Kolchak, the damage had been done. The isolationists, who knew that foreign parts and peoples were immoral and corrupt, believed the General's relation of events, and such aid as was eventually forthcoming was tardy and insufficient. Until this belated decision was reached, Graves was determined to ensure that Kolchak received nothing that was not clearly and specifically destined for him. The huge stocks of armaments and materials of all kinds which lay rusting in Vladivostok could not, in his opinion, be justifiably used to aid the Omsk régime. So there, until Knox managed to get a certain amount of the material released, the vital stores remained.

At the end of 1918, the seriousness of these matters was not fully apparent to Kolchak. His Western Army might be able to join up with Dutov's Cossack forces in the south. This accomplished, there was the further possibility of linking with the Archangel government, by an advance in the direction of Kotlas, and with the Volunteers and the Army of the Don in the direction of Tsaritsyn. Nor was he forgetful that Moscow was vulnerable to a thrust from the Urals. Already he was in contact with Denikin; couriers were running letters across the Caspian, and telegraphic communications had been established – via London and Paris. Denikin had refused to recognise the previous Siberian governments, but he at once accepted the Kolchak régime, and established good relations with the Admiral. At present, there was no question of the one being preponderant, though the Omsk ministers had, in effect, claimed supremacy for their dictator. The future of Russia was, after all, to be settled by the Constituent Assembly when it met in Moscow. It was Moscow that was the White objective; and, despite all the local difficulties, there was a new spirit of optimism in the White Headquarters as 1918 came to its wintery end. A great many White officers did not see how they could fail to succeed.

1919

Christmas in
Moscow

I doubt if history will show any country in the world during the last fifty years where murder could be committed as safely and with less danger of punishment than in Siberia during the régime of Admiral Kolchak.

General William S. Graves, U.S. Army

XII

View from the Centre

The New Year of January 1919 found the Soviets surrounded by a ring of enemies. Twenty miles from St Petersburg the Finnish border was heavily patrolled by units of the victorious Finnish White Army; Allied troops were astride the Murmansk railway; combined Russian and Allied forces held the Archangel front; Gajda's army had entered Perm and Kolchak controlled Siberia; Denikin was the master of the Kuban and free to reinforce Krasnov; the French had landed at Odessa; French influences were at work in Poland, and the leaders of the newly emergent state were known to be opposed to the Bolsheviks; the Baltic Provinces of Latvia, Estonia and Lithuania – previously over-run by the Germans – were fighting for their independence and prepared to accept any help which would enable them to resist the Soviets.

On a map – as, for instance, on Churchill's map in Whitehall – the situation looked desperate for the Reds. So, indeed, it was, but not to the extent that the more optimistic adherents of the White cause claimed. For the Russian Civil War was a war of the weak. The norms of twentieth-century warfare had ceased to apply. It was also, for the Whites, a war from the borders. This meant that the Reds were able, throughout the whole period of the war, to fight on internal lines of communication. They had one government – centralised in Moscow – and a unified command; flexible responses to White moves were possible as pressure increased or decreased on the different fronts. If one army was forced onto the defensive, this was not catastrophic: commensurate gains might well be made on another front. For the Reds, therefore, the defensive was psychologically permissible. But for the Whites a forward policy on all fronts was the only one that seemed viable, even when the military dictates of the overall situation indicated otherwise. The Whites could not move troops from one front to another, nor could they readily exchange views and intelligence; both their actions and reactions were inhibited by geography. In winter the climate favoured the defensive; advances were possible, but they tended to be immensely costly; the Whites' urge to attack brought them rapid gains but decimated their officer-strength, and effective leaders could not quickly be replaced. The Reds, who could afford to wait, did not suffer to nearly the same extent.

In Moscow itself there was a very different atmosphere from that which prevailed in the White capitals. For one thing, it was an atmosphere largely purged of illusions; the Reds had their backs to the wall and knew it: there was no feckless faith in the delusory cornucopia of Allied or German aid. For another, it was an atmosphere which was conditioned by the ideas for which the new rulers of central Russia were fighting. They saw a future; they saw it with what we now realise to have been a totally misleading clarity, but that was beside the point. The existence of the ideal was enough, for it ensured that there could be no reliance on vague generalisations about a return to 'what was best in the old Russia'. The people to whom the Whites addressed this appeal had only known the worst.

In January 1919 Moscow was cold and dark. The inhabitants were all hungry, and often diseased. But the situation was infinitely more stable than it had been a year before. There is an account of a visit to Russia in the beginning of 1919 written by Arthur Ransome,[1] whose later preoccupation with children in sailing dinghies has obscured his earlier achievements. Ransome had been a newspaper correspondent in Russia through the war years and is remarkable as one of the few Englishmen to realise that 'It is folly to deny the actual fact that the Bolsheviks do hold a majority of the politically active population.'[2] Robert Bruce Lockhart described him as 'a Don Quixote with a walrus moustache, a sentimentalist who could always be relied on to champion the under-dog, and a visionary, whose imagination had been fired by the revolutionaries'.[3] This may be so, but it is pertinent to add that without such qualities as Ransome possessed it was impos-

---

[1] Ransome, *Six Weeks in Russia in 1919*, 1919.
[2] Ransome, *Daily News*, 10 November 1917.
[3] Lockhart, *Memoirs of a British Agent*, p. 266.

sible to assess the revolutionaries' strength. Furthermore, his sympathy gained him access to the highest counsels of the Bolshevik leaders. (He later married Trotsky's secretary.)

The extraordinary thing about Ransome's account of his time in Moscow in 1919 is the sense of normality he conveys. At just the time when the Whites were about to launch the offensives that would lead to their biggest drives on the capital, Ransome was writing, 'My general impression that the Soviet revolution has passed through its period of internal struggle and is concentrating upon constructive work so far as that is allowed by war on all its frontiers, and that the population is settling down under the new régime, was confirmed . . . '[1] What Ransome sensed was not simply the Bolsheviks' increased grip on the territory they controlled, though this was undoubtedly a relevant factor. The work of the Cheka under Dzerzhinsky, and the initiation of a systematic Red terror by Sverdlov and Petrovsky after Fanny Kaplan's so-nearly successful attack on Lenin's life on 30 August 1918, had removed the more substantial threats to the Soviet régime – even if in certain quarters it intensified opposition. On the whole, however, it is safe to say that the Bolsheviks did 'close ranks' as Sverdlov ordered: like the murder of the Tsar, it was an indication that the time for prevarication was past and irrecoverable.

But of more importance than this, and far more closely related to the sense of 'normality' conveyed by Ransome, was Lenin's ability to see beyond the narrowly military. The White leaders were trained soldiers, and though this helped them in some respects, it hampered them in others. For their perspectives remained those of C-in-Cs rather than heads of state. Lenin was not a military ignoramus; he knew enough to know that he was not an expert. In 1915 he had read Clausewitz with considerable care, and his study of the great Prussian seems to have reinforced the lessons that he might already have learnt from Engels. Lenin's own theories of war, of its causes, its nature, differed radically from those of Clausewitz. But his attitude to the practice of war to a large extent derived from Clausewitzian precepts. Above all, he never forgot that 'politics is the reason, and the war is only

---

[1] Ransome, *Six Weeks in Russia in 1919*, p. 108.

the tool, not the other way round. Consequently, it remains only to subordinate the military point of view to the political.'[1] This is precisely what Lenin did, both in theory and in practice.

It was Lenin's great strength that he always had the ability to take the grand view: there are times when he seems to have regarded the Whites as no more than provincial trouble-makers. He would not be bothered by detail and technicalities, because they were not his business; he restricted both his comments and his interventions to the main points. Above all, he had an unswerving conviction that the Bolsheviks would win. When he did issue an order relating to the war it generally concerned the civil rather than the military aspects. He consistently supported Trotsky's demands for an organised and professional army. On one occasion, in the course of an interview with Lenin, Antonov-Ovseenko was unwise enough to speak slightingly of the loyalty of his superior officers. At this Lenin jumped from his chair saying: 'This is a military affair. Your part is to obey orders or be arrested.' As soon as he saw an opportunity, Antonov-Ovseenko left the room.[2] In the south he demanded 'summary execution for every hidden rifle' – this was directed at the Cossacks who, when their *stanitsas* were overrun by the Reds, hid their weapons in the thatch and waited for an opportunity either to come out in sympathy with the Whites, or to set up as partisans. Lenin realised that, so long as the Cossacks continued to possess their own weapons, their independent outlook would always be a threat to Soviet rule. He saw that the pacification of territory was every bit as important as its conquest – a lesson that the Whites never fully learnt.

But Lenin was only able to play his part as a man to whom the Civil War was of secondary interest because of the presence of Trotsky. For it was Trotsky who made of the heterogeneous bands of Red Guards, Kronstadt sailors, Lettish riflemen, former Austro-German prisoners-of-war with communist sympathies and party members an effective fighting force.

The process was long drawn out and beset by vicissitudes, but it did mean that by the beginning of 1919 the Red Army was a fighting force. In 1918 it had been an *ad hoc* affair dominated by

---

[1] Quoted by Sokolovsky, *Military Strategy*, p. 17.
[2] Antonov-Ovseenko, *Zapiski o grazdanskoi voine* III, p. 30.

several distinct elements. These were: the Red Guard, which had evolved from the revolutionary Red Guard and had been reorganised to contain the German threat to St Petersburg after the breakdown of the negotiations at Brest-Litovsk; the units of the Imperial Army which had gone over to the Bolsheviks – notably the forces in the Kiev area, commanded by Muravev, part of which were later transferred to the east; and the various regional 'armies' such as Sorokin's in the Kuban. Some of these units were strong on paper, but this meant little. As the Kuban campaign reveals, the Reds suffered inordinate casualties in their battles against White units which often numbered a bare fraction of the Red troops. In the last analysis the Red forces were ill-trained and ill-led. Sometimes – as in the south-east, where they fought against the forces of Krasnov's Don Army at Tsaritsyn, and the Czechs and the troops of the Samara government at Kazan – they learnt from their experiences, and even achieved victories. Elsewhere, as in the Kuban, they were defeated.

Trotsky had to fight as many battles within the Communist Party as did his troops against the Whites, before the preconditions for a successful army were established. He saw that the Whites were strong as a result of their discipline and training. Neither side had a monopoly of fanaticism, of courage, or of tenacity; but the Whites were possessed of military skills in abundance, and these their training and discipline enabled them to use. But there were several amongst his colleagues who refused to see this, who would not acknowledge that the cause by itself was no guarantor of victory. And, beyond the Bolsheviks, the Left S.R.s were firmly against a regular army, preferring defeat to the employment of such a 'low bourgeois weapon'. According to Ransome the Left S.R.s would have welcomed occupation 'in order that they, with bees in their bonnets and bombs in their hands, might go about revolting against it'.[1]

The specific point of disagreement within the Bolshevik party concerned, however, the employment of former Tsarist officers. There were those amongst the Bolsheviks who felt, with the Left S.R.s, that a partisan army would best serve the Revolution. They were in a minority; the traditions of party discipline, inculcated

---

[1] Ransome, *Six Weeks in Russia in 1919*, p. 198.

during the clandestine days, went deep enough for it to be apparent to most Bolsheviks of importance that the army must approximate to the condition of a regular formation. What these men were unable to stomach was the idea that former officers should – or could – play a significant part in the war. Yet, even as early as November 1917, it had been to Lieutenant-Colonel Muravev that the defence of St Petersburg was entrusted. Perhaps we can understand the feeling of the anti-Trotsky faction better if we remember the eventual fate of this officer. Himself a Social Revolutionary rather than a Bolshevik, Muravev changed sides in the summer of 1918, and went over to the Czechs and Samara S.R.s. In the event, his treason did not profit him, since those of his men who sided with him were surrounded by loyal Bolshevik forces, and Muravev shot himself rather than face whatever gruesome fate the Cheka would have concocted for him. The direct consequences of his action were not, then, notably serious. But the moral effect – for Muravev was, despite various personal extravagances, a revolutionary hero of considerable stature – profoundly shook many Bolsheviks. If Muravev could behave in such a manner, they reasoned, what could be expected of officers 'persuaded' by avowedly draconian measures to offer their services to the cause?

Despite the weight of this opposition, Trotsky remained adamant. He regarded the appointment of 'spets' – as the 'military specialists' were known – as being essential if the Reds were to succeed. By expanding and reorganising the commissar system he hoped to keep a close check on any potential traitors, and also to provide each unit with a fount of ideological encouragement. The commissars would be the avatars of the new army, teaching both by precept and example, and ensuring the loyalty of the 'spets' at the same time. Thus the army, though it would still retain the form and fighting capacity of a regular force, would also be an instrument for the propagation of the revolution. Or so, at least, the theory went. Whether the system did in fact imbue the Red Army with a 'truly revolutionary consciousness' is more than dubious, but the commissars certainly made the employment of 'spets' feasible. Subsequently Trotsky was to claim that it was he who, virtually single-handed, pushed through the scheme for the employment of 'spets'. This was not strictly true: there is a strong suggestion that Lenin may have originated the plan,[1] and he was certainly instrumental in supporting it as it evolved in practice, despite Trotsky's later confusion of the issue.[2]

At first the number of Imperial Army officers prepared to join the Reds was small; the most notable of them was General Bonch-Bruevich, who was persuaded into this course of action by his brother, Lenin's close friend. Other officers joined Bonch-Bruevich, but they seemed chiefly interested in organising resistance to the German threat, rather than in the possible development of a Civil War. Brest-Litovsk changed that, as it changed so much else; gradually it became apparent that service with the Reds meant service in a civil war. This did not, however, check the flow of ex-officers returning to the new army: in 1918, about 75 per cent of the total of officers in the Red Army had previously been commissioned in the Imperial Army. Though because of the very rapid expansion of the Red Army this figure decreased to 34 per cent by the end of 1919, the actual number of returned officers steadily increased; by early 1919 there were over 30,000 in service.

They joined the Reds for a variety of reasons. A few were convinced that the Bolshevik analysis of the Russian situation was fundamentally correct; these gave of their skills willingly and tirelessly. Others were men who had done badly in the Imperial Army and felt that, because of this, they must succeed with the Reds. They were perhaps the least successful group, and though their influence is perceptible in 1918, they were soon weeded out. But the vast majority of the 'spets' were men who were totally bewildered by the course of events in Russia, who had lacked the will-power or the initiative to travel south or east, and were now unemployed and starving. The Bolsheviks' policy of 'registration', of making lists of the inhabitants of houses in a given area, and their families, made it easy for the authorities to bring pressure on such men. Once they were in the new army their reactions depended largely on the commissars. If the commissars were tactful, as well as able in other respects, then such officers could be invaluable. In Trotsky's words: 'Such unions of

---

[1] See, for instance, John Erickson in Pipes, *Revolutionary Russia*, p. 231, and the references there cited.
[2] Trotsky, *Stalin*, p. 278.

commanders and commissars often lasted for a long time and were distinguished by great stability. [But] where the commissar was ignorant and boorish and baited the military specialist . . . friendship was out of the question and the hesitating officer was finally inclined toward the enemy of the new régime.'[1]

There was an additional class of officer-recruit to the Red Army that caused a great deal of trouble. If an officer's sympathies were with the Whites, then to join the Reds provided the easiest way of making contact. To travel as a civilian would almost certainly have been fatal. Trains in forward areas were continually searched by the Cheka and, in any case, the traveller would eventually have to make his way through the front lines. There were various other possibilities: it was sometimes possible to get to the Whites via Finland or the Ukraine, but this was still an exceedingly hazardous business. But for a Red officer, though the operation was not easy, it was rather more practical. There were commissars and suspicious soldiers to be outwitted, but the trick could be, and often was, achieved. In some cases it was even a simple case of an entire regiment changing sides, for it was by no means improbable that the sympathies of conscripted men lay with the officers and not the commissars. It was such eventualities as this that convinced Trotsky's opponents of the danger of the course he was taking; but they forgot that, for each instance of desertion, there were hundreds of others that argued considerable loyalty on the part of the 'spets'. Ironically enough, such loyalty was far more likely to be a consequence of Imperial Army training than of any deeply-felt adherence to the Bolshevik cause.

Trotsky naturally lost no time in setting up training schools run on 'Bolshevik' lines; yet in these, to an even greater extent than elsewhere, he had to employ 'spets' as instructors. He also appealed for Imperial Army N.C.O.s to come forward and join the Red Army as officers. By such means he was able to establish a new officer corps free from the taint of Tsarist service, though by no means emancipated from either the techniques or the professional outlook that prevailed in the Imperial Army. But these effects were only to become apparent over a long time; the

---

[1] Trotsky, *Stalin*, p. 280.

immediate consequence, which was to have so vital a bearing on 1919, was that the quality of leadership decisively improved, no matter for what reasons.

As significant, both in long- and short-term effects, was the introduction of conscription for the Red Army. Though a crude form of this was practised by regional commanders from the early months of 1918 – e.g., by Avtonomov in the Kuban – it was not an officially recognised method of recruitment. When it became obvious that volunteers were no answer to the Bolsheviks' problems, Trotsky began to conscript amongst factory workers who might be presumed reliable supporters of the Reds. His first ventures were deliberately cautious; it was only when enough such workers had been drafted to develop a cadre system that he began the mass conscription of peasants.

Not until November 1918 was a serious plan evolved for the organisation and deployment of the Red Army considered as a single whole; even this was more of a paper project than anything else. Basically it allowed for fourteen (subsequently sixteen) armies, to be made up from a grand total of forty-seven infantry divisions and four cavalry divisions. Throughout mid-1918 the Red Army had had a total strength of just under 500,000 men; by November it had reached that figure and was to continue to expand. But the component 'armies' themselves were very small, seldom numbering more than 50,000. The relatively small number of effectives, contrasted with the vast distances, has always to be borne in mind.

Even given the returned Imperial Army officers and the formidable commissars, it is sometimes difficult to see how these units maintained discipline and fighting ability. Certainly, when the recruit joined he was made to swear that he would 'observe revolutionary discipline strictly and unceasingly', and that, if he should break his oath, 'let general condemnation be my fate, and the stern hand of revolutionary law punish me'.[1] Nevertheless, as soon as the mobilisation of peasants began, mass desertions became common, as did cases of units refusing to go into battle.

The Bolsheviks solved this problem in two ways: firstly by the application of a ferocious discipline, and secondly by the example

---

[1] Trotsky, *Kak vooruzhalas revolyutsiya*, I, p. 125.

of the various cadres within the army. The ferocious discipline was instilled from the top, by Trotsky, and though it did not obtain at all times or within all units of the Red Army, its effects penetrated the whole structure. This discipline was dependent on courts martial and summary executions – precisely those features of the Imperial Army that the Soviets had, in the days of the Provisional Government, been so determined to do away with. These methods were employed far more generally than they ever had been in the Imperial Army, and Trotsky himself established the precedents for their use. When in August 1918 the Red Army had withdrawn from Kazan, it was Trotsky who had stopped the rout and given the troops the will to advance once more. This he had achieved mainly by issuing orders of the day which, at the same time as praising troops who fought well, contained the most dire threats against those who were 'idle and criminal servants of the Soviet Republic'. That he had every intention of fulfilling these threats he demonstrated by shooting any commanders or commissars who had, in his opinion, failed in their duty. On at least one occasion he carried this principle further, and shot one in every ten men of a regiment that broke and ran from the front line.

Trotsky was totally, and sometimes indiscriminately, ruthless. He could also be totally inspiring, and if we are to understand why the Bolshevik troops recaptured Kazan, why, at critical points Red morale so often and, to the Whites, so inexplicably, stiffened, we must try to grasp the demonic energy and the personal magnetism of the man whose name has now been all but erased from Soviet records of the Civil War. To describe the Red side of the war without acknowledging the part played by Trotsky is like trying to give an account of *Hamlet* without the Prince. The analogy is the more appropriate, since Trotsky was shamelessly – and hence effectively – theatrical. The small figure with the distinctive mane of hair and goatee beard, usually dressed in a leather coat, breeches and boots, with a fur hat or a battered peaked cap, was to become familiar to thousands of Red Army soldiers. The man who had held the crowds on the Cirque Moderne in St Petersburg was now demonstrating that his oratory was no less effective in the context of the militarism that he had then so fervently condemned.

Trotsky and the command train that he travelled in were on the way to becoming a legend. By the end of the Civil War they were a legend. The train was, in itself, a symbol. Not only was it equipped with all the necessities for military command – wireless, map-room, a headquarters platoon of riflemen and machine-gunners dressed in leather uniforms; it had as well, a printing press, a secretarial staff, a waggon holding several motor cars for travel independent of the railway line, reserves of ammunition, medicine, weapons, boots, clothing and other commodities in short supply at the fronts. What the train carried was only a small proportion of the quantity required, but the effect on morale was vital. And there would also be a hundred or so reserves on the train, picked men who could reinforce a threatened sector or bolster a flagging regiment.

The train was the complete politico-military unit, defensible in itself – it was armed and partially armoured – but primarily designed to provide immediate and effective support at any critical point. The emphasis here is on 'any'. The train united the troops holding the Red front on the Dvina river with those fighting Krasnov on the Don; it was a link between the emergent armies in the Urals and the Red troops on the borders of the Ukraine. The Whites knew no such unifying agency, nor had they a Trotsky, whose style of command ran counter to both the training and the instincts of the White leaders.

But no one man, neither Trotsky nor his picked generals, Vatzetis and Tukhachevsky nor, least of all, Stalin and his fellow dissidents from Tsaritsyn, could effect the transformation of the Red Army into an effective fighting force. If any one factor can be isolated as having been decisive, then this was the cadre system, and the men who brought about the change were the loyal communists – by no means all of them Bolsheviks, though the greater part probably were – who constituted these cadres. The first such cadres had been formed from volunteers but, by the beginning of 1919, mass mobilisations of Bolshevik Party members were being ordered. This meant that local parties were asked to provide a certain number of workers, assessed on a quota system, without delay. Where these levies should be concentrated was decided by the central organisation, and the result was that it was possible to assemble a number of absolutely trustworthy cadres at any given point. Sometimes the Party members would be ordered to join an existing regiment; nevertheless, the effect was that of a cadre, for by their example of loyal service they provided the backbone that a demoralised unit needed.

An extension of this system was the foundation of *Komsomol*, the Communist Association of Youth, in early November 1918. The membership was small – only 22,000 at the time of its first national conference. But within a year it had expanded enormously, so that by the end of 1919 there were 100,000 members. Komsomol members were used in much the same way as ordinary Party members, but they were regarded as commandos. They were employed as commissars, as agitators, and as shock troops, and their impact on the Red Armies was out of all proportion to their numbers. Together, the cadres of Party members and young men from Komsomol made the transformation of the Red Army possible. The 'spets' provided the skill, the cadres and commissars the morale, and the conscripts the greater part of the overall force. Often the combination failed; in the Russian Civil War everything failed at one time or another. But more frequently it succeeded, and it represented an achievement that the Whites could not match. In the south they experimented with cadres of officers and with cadres from the veterans of the Kuban; in Siberia, officer cadres were also used, though on a much smaller scale. But officers remained officers whatever their titular rank, and neither scheme can have been said to have worked. It was possible to use officers as shock troops, but not as cadres, and this remained an inherent weakness of the White armies.

Command, manpower and morale were all major problems which had to be solved. So, too, was that of supply and transport, without which no army could have a useful existence. The Reds lacked, as we have seen, any source of supply beyond their own resources. There had been one or two fortunate but fortuitous windfalls. When the German armies retired from Russia, their discipline largely broke down, and it became possible to buy weapons and ammunition from them. Rifles were a mark each, field-guns 150 marks, and a field wireless station was 500 marks. Apparently the rates seemed equitable to both sides. But this was only a limited and temporary source of supply. In early 1919 the total production of rifle ammunition was the equivalent of two cartridges a day per Red Army effective. There was, however, a great quantity of field-gun ammunition surviving in Imperial Army arsenals, and there were still considerable stocks of naval munitions which were adapted, often hazardously, for army use. Uniforms and boots were barely obtainable. An army, as Napoleon had it, marches on its stomach; but Red commanders were far more impressed by the fact that an army marches on its boots, and of these they had no reserves and no prospect of fresh supplies. Uniforms were all make-do; recruits brought what clothes they had and wore a red five-pointed star; if they were lucky they obtained some articles of kit later. But boots were the outstanding problem, and only the evolution of 'war communism' ensured a supply. The same process took place in all departments; the whole of central Russian industry had to be geared to the war effort.

Transport had to be run on similar lines. Without Russia's internal railway net the Bolsheviks could never have survived, and though the railways were not good, they were not so bad as people sometimes imagined. Nor did the Reds have Kolchak's problem: there was no Semenov to hinder their operations. They did, however, have trouble with the railwaymen, who were inclined to be S.R.s rather than Bolsheviks, and in consequence it was found necessary to run all railways in forward areas as exclusively military affairs.

There were horrors enough in central Russia. Typhus was rife and such hospitals as there were remained overcrowded and filthy. There was famine in many areas. In the autumn of 1918 thousands of square miles of grain had been left to moulder and blacken in the weather; fruit had hung on the trees until it rotted there; livestock had been left untended and had strayed or become diseased. In some provinces there was a surplus of foodstuffs, but there was no means of moving this to the areas where it was needed. In the towns every household was bitterly cold; there was a general lack of fuel, and hunger intensified the effects of its absence. For many there were the midnight or early morning visits of the Cheka to be feared. At all the railway stations of the big towns the platforms were crowded with those who wished to get out into the country, where there might be some chance of

243

survival. When the fortunate ones finally found a train, they would travel in packed and fetid trucks, and there were even those who managed to hang onto the engine or sit amongst the coal or wood in the tender.

Nevertheless, as Ransome observed of Moscow:

A year ago the streets were deserted after ten. . . . They used to be empty except for the military pickets round their log-fires. Now they were full of foot-passengers going home from the theatres, utterly forgetful of the fact that only twelve months before they had thought the streets of Moscow unsafe after dark. There could be no question about it. The revolution is settling down, and people now think of other matters than the old question, will it last one week or two?[1]

But this did not imply that the Civil War was to be prosecuted with any less fervour or bloodshed than hitherto; the opposite was the case. On 23 January 1919 there was an effort to bring about peace. It had begun with a suggestion by the British government that a truce should be arranged – a suggestion that was firmly discountenanced by the French, but that became acceptable when it had been mediated through the person of President Wilson, who was able once more to indulge in his favourite amusement of drafting proposals for peace. Of the Allies, only the Japanese had objections to the proposals as they finally emerged. The Japanese excepted, the Allies were all in favour of an ending to the Civil War, their embroilment in which was causing unrest at home and had become, since the Armistice, of no real point. The proposals envisaged a conference, on the island of Prinkipo which lies in the Sea of Marmora, off Constantinople, involving all of the belligerents, including representatives of the Great Powers.

The project was doomed to failure. The Allies, who sent messages through their representatives to the Whites, and broadcast the terms of the truce to the Reds, were more than usually purblind in their assumption that it would have any effect. What mandate they had for interference in Russia's internal affairs was unclear: their action was only likely to provoke resentment. Nor were hole-in-corner dealings on a remote Turkish island calcu-

---

[1] Ransome, *Six Weeks in Russia in 1919*, p. 94.

lated to inspire either side with confidence. If they wished to try and settle the fate of Russia, then they could surely have allowed that Russia was the proper place. Again we see, at its most insidious, the influence of the map: the choice of Prinkipo mirrored the thinking that made control of the Don or of Siberia seem as important as control of central Russia. The surprising thing is that the Soviets appeared to give the proposal serious consideration. However, this is partly explained by the probability that, if they gave the impression of being willing to negotiate, the Allies might check their supplies of aid to the Whites, thus increasing Soviet chances of a military victory.

The Executive Committee discussed the matter in detail, and agreed on certain possible concessions to the Allies, but they were unable to accept the truce proposed. As it turned out, this was beside the point; the Whites rejected the Prinkipo proposals out of hand. Since they were fully aware that, as matters stood, they were insurgents and not incumbents, they saw that they had nothing to gain from it. Siberia as an independent state would have been no more use to Kolchak than an independent Don and Kuban to Denikin. Yet it was the most that they could hope for from Prinkipo. The Whites' aim, their basic and controlling aim, was the conquest of central Russia – which was just what Prinkipo and an Allied recognition of the *status quo* would prevent. Moreover, they regarded the Bolsheviks in a way that the Allied leaders could only dimly apprehend. The Whites' reaction is, once more, best summed up by General Knox who telegraphed that 'suddenly the whole of Russia is informed by wireless that her Allies regard the brave men who are here fighting for part of civilisation as on a par with the blood-stained, Jew-led Bolsheviks'.[1]

So the war went on, and during 1919 it became even wider in its scope and more terrible in its effects than it had been hitherto. For the Whites the goal was Moscow, but the nearer they advanced to the Soviet capital, the harder their task became. The war had brought a change within the Bolsheviks themselves; though they still spoke of 'international goals' and 'world

[1] Knox, telegram of 29 January 1919. Quoted in Ullman, *Britain and the Russian Civil War*, p. 115.

revolution', the conflict had made their real aims national. Because this was so, they had gained many supporters even amongst those who disagreed with the specific tenets of their beliefs. The process may have been prevaricatory, but it left the balance with the Bolsheviks. In the centre, as Ransome remarked, the revolution was an established fact. Before we leave Moscow in the New Year of 1919 we should take note of something else that he had to say:

New rulers are advancing on Moscow from Siberia, but I do not think that they claim that they are bringing with them new principles. Though the masses may want new principles, and might for a moment submit to a reintroduction of very old principles in desperate hope of less hunger and less cold, no one but a lunatic would imagine that they would for very long willingly submit to them.[1]

---

[1] Ransome, *Six Weeks in Russia in 1919*, p. 196.

XIII

Spring

For General Denikin 1919 opened well. On 3 January he began a powerful offensive, designed to clear northern Caucasia of the remaining Red troops. Fighting had been going on in the area since the fall of Stavropol. As had happened so often before, the Whites were outnumbered; the Reds could field 70,000 troops to their 40,000 and amongst the forces available to the Reds was the newly reorganised Eleventh Army. Denikin's plan was very simple: he detailed a small group to contain any threat from the north, and loosed his main attack on the concentration of Bolshevik troops in the Terek territory, which lies between Stavropol and the Caspian Sea. In tactical command of the operation he placed General Wrangel, who led his men with dash and determination; within a week the Bolshevik line had been broken, and the Red forces had been split into three. Wrangel then proceeded to reduce each of these formations, and by 20 January the Reds were in full retreat. Shkuro's cavalry harried them continually, and though Wrangel's men were exhausted he had to continue the pursuit until the Red armies were entirely destroyed. The fighting in the Terek was fierce, and after the capture of Kislovodsk – formerly a celebrated medicinal resort – quarter was seldom given. Before the Reds evacuated the town they had initiated a horrific terror. Hundreds of inhabitants had been shot, many of them elderly men, and most of them likely to have relatives amongst the White forces.

The Reds retreated in total disorder. When prisoners were captured they were generally found to be so demoralised that a couple of Cossacks were sufficient to guard two thousand of them. Typhus had taken an enormous toll of the Reds and of the civilians who, fearing White vengeance, fled with them. The sick, if they could not find places in the trains, crawled along beside the track, which was soon lined with corpses. Late in January

White cavalry forced a large party of Reds back against the Terek river; the Reds attempted to cross by a wooden bridge which gave way; almost the entire force was drowned. Typhus spread amongst the White ranks, until eventually even Wrangel fell a victim. But by then the whole of northern Caucasia and the Terek was free. Those few remnants of the Red Armies who had escaped were left to make their way across the barren and inhospitable Astrakhan steppe; the Whites found themselves the possessors not only of the conquered territory, but also of 30,000 prisoners, several locomotives, and large quantities of artillery.

As the Terek operation progressed, an increasing number of White units became available for use in other theatres. It was time for Denikin to consider his wider intentions. An additional urgency was given to the situation by a dramatic change in the political position.

Krasnov's Army of the Don had continued to make progress until December 1918. Then, as we have seen, there was internal dissension within the Don Territory, and the morale of the Don Cossacks began to decline. Moreover, Krasnov's army had been on the furthest boundaries of the territory that the average Cossack was likely to construe as belonging to the Don, and his troops saw no reason for going any further. Krasnov himself realised that the long-term security of the Don demanded further advances, but it was another matter to persuade his Cossacks of this.

Now that the White Armies of the south were in control of significant areas of territory the establishment or re-establishment of effective government became of paramount importance. With this in mind Denikin set up the Special Conference or South Russian Government, a body which included prominent politicians who had fled to the south. For four main reasons this government was doomed to failure.

Firstly, its area of jurisdiction was always in doubt. As long as the Don and Kuban Cossacks – together with the Caucasian nationalists – claimed autonomy, and as long as that autonomy remained the subject of dispute, no White government could operate effectively.

Secondly, the government itself was anomalous. It could not be an elective body; its members were, for all practical purposes, co-opted by Denikin. But, rather than appoint men whom he knew to be loyal to him, he made the fatal mistake of trying to create a pseudo-representative organisation, choosing politicians of both conservative and liberal views whose loyalty was predominantly to those parties of which they had previously been luminaries. Denikin's motives were liberal: the consequence of his good intentions was a body divided against itself.

Since this was so, he had achieved little by failing to be still more liberal and to allow spokesmen for the non-Bolshevik socialist parties to take places on the conference. As Denikin saw it, the socialists were far too ready to compromise with the Bolsheviks – and it was certainly true that the socialists were intensely suspicious of the views they believed the White leaders to hold. But by denying them representation he increased their grievances. If the admission of socialists to the Conference had threatened to split an otherwise unified government his attitude would have been entirely reasonable. In the circumstances it was not; the politicians to whom he had accorded recognition were already at loggerheads.

Thirdly, in order to counteract dissension Denikin found it necessary to appoint General Dragomirov (who was subsequently replaced by General Lukomsky) as President of the Conference with the power to veto. Dragomirov was a soldier, not a politician: his presence automatically made the Special Conference seem no more than a cover for a military dictatorship. That such a dictatorship should exist was not part of Denikin's intention; yet, given his handling of the Special Conference, a military dictatorship was inevitably the result.

The fourth reason for the failure of the South Russian Government was a compound of all the others. Denikin's object was a swift re-conquest of the whole of Russia. But by creating the Special Conference he seemed to imply that south Russia could be, at least temporarily, a territorial entity of its own. Budgets were drawn up, the probable yields of the harvests calculated, taxation and land policies adumbrated. This was admirable, except that it implied a strategy Denikin was loath, in practice, to adopt. The budgets revealed enormous deficits, local authorities had ceased to exist, courts of law no longer functioned. To remedy this state of affairs would require much

time and much devoted work. These things were not forthcoming: they were subordinated to short-term military goals.
The Special Conference was, in fact, a symptom of the fundamental dichotomy that we can sense in all Denikin's policies. An
overt military dictatorship, the formation of an avowedly military government, might well have served him better. And since
it was apparent from the method he employed to establish the
Special Conference that his own position was not subject to
review, then an avowedly military government would at least
have had the appearance of honesty.

There were further weaknesses in his régime. The Armistice
had disrupted the German connection, and even so adroit a
diplomatist as Krasnov was hard put to it to convince the Allies
that his real adherence had been to the Entente. Red propaganda
had spread widely; there were over 15,000 desertions from his
army – which was no more than 50,000 strong in all – during the
winter of 1918-19. Much of the propaganda put out by the Reds
was specifically slanted at the Cossacks' spirit of independence;
it promised them that they would be able to retain their distinctive uniforms if they joined the Reds, and that they would be
allowed to practise their religion. By such promises they attempted to nullify the emotional appeal of Krasnov's romanticised
Cossackia – the scarlet, blue and yellow flag of the Don, and all
the supporting mythology – and to remedy the effect on the
Cossack outlook of such unfortunate miscalculations as the
deliberate use of the cathedral at Novocherkassk as a stable for
the Red cavalry. Another reason why the Reds were able to
build up powerful cells amongst the Cossacks was that the Krug
had discriminated, in their policy of land distribution, against
Cossacks who had served with the Reds. This clause was often
interpreted maliciously and unjustly, and it had the entirely
deleterious effect of establishing the doctrine of 'once a Red,
always a Red'. Consequently Cossacks who had been impressed
into the Red Army now found that their only future lay with
those whom they had so unwillingly served.

It was partly as a result of these factors, though specifically
because of pressure brought to bear on him by General Poole –
Chief of the British Military Mission to the Volunteers, and newly
arrived in Rostov – that Krasnov decided to subordinate the

Army of the Don to General Denikin. A formal announcement to this effect was made by Denikin on 8 January; he could now claim to be Commander-in-Chief of all Russian anti-Bolsheviks in the south. By the end of the month he could also claim to control the greater part of south Russia, though his command was by no means free from difficulties. His left flank was secured by the French troops which had landed at Odessa and to which he had sent reinforcements. But they were meeting with far stiffer opposition than they had anticipated; Petlyura was menacing the area from the Ukraine, and the morale of the French troops was low. Volunteers had also been sent by Denikin to the Crimea, where S. S. Krymov had established an anti-Bolshevik government; from a military point of view, however, the fate of the Crimea was bound up with the progress, or otherwise, of the formation of an anti-Bolshevik front by the French. For Denikin had no troops to spare; he had taken over command of the Army of the Don at a critical time.

Denikin's right flank was menaced by the Bolshevik front at Tsaritsyn. It was the Red presence at Tsaritsyn that was to be one of the main points of controversy in the Council of War that Denikin called at the end of January. He had troops in Odessa, in the Crimea, and on a broad front extending along the River Don, along the Don's eastern tributary, the Manych, and through the steppes of northern Caucasia to the Caspian Sea. A small number of troops were also tied up on the Georgian frontier. The Black Sea was commanded by the Allied navies, and a British flotilla had been established on the Caspian; nevertheless, development of an independent White naval force was an obvious necessity. The main front line, formed by the Don and the Manych, was strongly held in the west but was less well covered to the east. However, the line of lakes along the Manych river made for strong defensive positions, and the spring floods, heavy this year, had given the line an additional, though temporary, strength.

The Council of War was stormy. Denikin began by summarising the situation and by giving the details of reports that he had just received from General May-Maevsky, advancing with his Volunteer troops into the Donets basin. May-Maevsky had previously been guarding the line of communications with

Rostov; now he had moved forward and was meeting with quite unexpected success. Denikin proposed that all available troops be concentrated in the Donets basin to follow up May-Maevsky's advance. The Manych front would be held by screens only, and the whole weight of the White assault would be channelled through the Donets basin.

On the face of it, this was sound strategy. For the Reds had decided to launch their attack on the Don, on Rostov and Novocherkassk, not through the Donets basin but across the steppes north-east of the two towns. This decision is hard to understand. In the Donets basin the lines of communication were good, and there was, amongst the population, a high proportion of industrial workers who might well be expected to come out for the Reds. Perhaps the Reds thought that by marching across the steppes they were more likely to achieve surprise; possibly, since conciliation with the Allies was in the air, they did not wish to get embroiled with the French, the weakness of whose forces was not at first apparent to Moscow. In any case the Soviets were hindered by the activities of Kolchak. Or it could have been a simple case of stupidity; it is always easy to read too much into decisions of this kind. But, be that as it may, Denikin proposed, with obvious logic, that the White forces should be concentrated on the Don and the Donets.

But Peter Wrangel – tall, thin, with a lined face emphasised by the high black cravat that he habitually wore, by now regarded as one of the most brilliant of the Volunteer generals – did not agree. He argued that, despite May-Maevsky's success, and despite the obvious economic value of the Donets coalfields, the Whites should concentrate along the Manych. From there they should strike north-east against the Volga in an attempt to link up with Kolchak, now known to be advancing in that direction. Debate was general, those present at the Council of War being almost equally divided for and against. Complete conquest of the Donets area meant that the Whites would gain coal, which was essential for the railways, that the Reds would be deprived of it and, or so Denikin and Romanovsky claimed, possession of an excellent jumping-off ground for the attack on Moscow. Wrangel agreed with the first points but demurred at the last; a thrust without Kolchak, he asserted, would be a weak thrust, and a thrust doomed to failure. The Donets basin promised immediate and tangible gains, and Red stupidity had made it unexpectedly accessible. But to throw the whole weight of the White effort in that direction was to lose sight of the basic strategic dictates of the war, which made the concentration of force essential. Yet it was Denikin's view that prevailed.

The lure of Moscow exercised an enormous fascination right through the ranks of the Whites (when Denikin began to print currency, it was the great bell of the Kremlin that he printed on his notes). But we must also bear in mind that Denikin was never amenable to criticisms of his suggestions. Perhaps it had something to do with the harshness of his early years in the army, when he had to fight his own battles against his colleagues; certainly it had to do with his solitariness, his lack of close friends, and the bureaucratic traditions of the Russian staff officer. Long before the composition in exile of his immensely lengthy memoirs, Denikin had spent a great deal of his time writing – not just minutes and memoranda, but articles and reminiscences for the military press; and writing is a predominantly solitary occupation. Denikin's contacts outside his staff were limited to his family and a very small circle of friends whom he had known for a long time, and with whom he hated to talk of political or military affairs. He had a considerable faith in his own talents as a strategist, and a corresponding suspicion of other people's suggestions – a suspicion much increased by his tendency to work enormously long hours without a break, and to over-centralise his command. He was, moreover, personally uneasy about Wrangel. Wrangel was a guardsman, former commander of the Tsarevich's Own Regiment, and of aristocratic birth. As it happened, he was also very intelligent. But Denikin preferred to treat him as an able cavalry leader and little more – as, let us say, a less dissipated Shkuro, from a dangerously exalted social background. Denikin, whose soldiering had largely been done in line regiments with no social cachet, distrusted guardsmen and aristocrats. He was still, even as C-in-C of the Volunteers, sensitive to any imagined slight or insult. He tolerated Wrangel because he was an able tactical commander and because Kornilov was known to have thought well of him. But he had no regard for his strategic opinions and he made this apparent by his reception of Wrangel's suggestions. There was to come a time when he would, in part at least, regret this. But, for the moment, Wrangel's assertion that the 'main and only direction' for the White army was Tsaritsyn and the Volga was firmly rejected.

Whilst May-Maevsky was advancing into the Donets basin, some units of the Army of the Don were still falling back from their positions to his north. It was the virtual collapse of the Army of the Don – and the realisation that, if it was to be re-organised, this would have to be done by the Volunteers – that precipitated the resignation of Krasnov on 14 February. A vote of censure was passed by the Krug on the commander of the Army of the Don, and Krasnov, rightly, interpreted this as an indication that it was time for him to leave. Unable to ensure their own security, and far too compromised now to hope for any mercy from the Soviets, the Krug elected as Krasnov's successor a man known to be a supporter of Russia 'great and indivisible', General Afrikan Bogaevsky. Bogaevsky was prepared to co-operate with Denikin and, though there were Cossacks who groused at this, the greater majority accepted it as the only hope for the future of the Don.

In the Kuban, however, relations between the Volunteers and the Kuban government had become increasingly strained – so much so that Denikin proposed moving headquarters from Ekaterinodar to Sevastopol. But the French did not prove amenable to this idea, and for the moment Ekaterinodar remained the White base. But the tension continued, and it was increased by the presence behind the White lines of the 'Greens' or 'Green Guards'. These were bands of deserters, of anarchists, or simply of marauding peasants, who could be classified as neither White nor Red, but were liable to attack both sides whenever such an action gave promise of easy booty or a satisfactory vengeance. The most famous of these bands was the peasant army led by Nestor Makhno; this originated in the Ukraine, but elements of it came as far south and east as the Sea of Azov. Makhno was unusual in having political objectives; most of the other Green armies were quite apolitical. Denikin, for all that, was inclined to believe that the Kuban government tolerated the Green menace to his lines of communication as a way of indirectly bringing pressure on him.

May-Maevsky, whose successes in the Donets basin precipitated the strategic debate, was a rotund and cherubic man, short in stature, of whom Wrangel remarked that, had he not worn a uniform, he would have been taken for 'a comedian from a little provincial theatre'. He waddled as he walked, was capable of the greatest cruelty, and had a penchant for orgies. He had the Russian officer's traditional liking for the *tsygane*, the gipsies, and maintained a gipsy orchestra. Despite the conditions of ostentatious luxury in which he preferred to live, May-Maevsky was the idol of many of his troops – to whom he allowed a licence commensurate with his own – and an able, if lazy, commander who was capable at times of brilliant tactical manœuvre. In the Donets basin he was equipped with all the armoured trains, armoured cars, and planes that Denikin could spare; planes were beginning to play an important part in the war, and British machines had been brought over from the former Salonika front. British instructors had also begun to arrive, and these found it hard to refrain from demonstrating their teachings in the heat of action. But railways were the key to May-Maevsky's success.

The Donets basin contained one of the most elaborate railway networks in all Russia. This May-Maevsky utilised by concentrating his troops not at the front, but at the main railway junctions. The concept of a conventional front line he rejected; he established lightly held defensive positions, the function of which was to act as bases for patrolling and reconnaissance, not as static fortifications. His air force was extensively employed to gather information as to the enemy's whereabouts and, armed with this intelligence, he dispatched his troops by rail from the junctions to any point at which the enemy threatened. He gave ground as easily as he conquered it: if he could extend the enemy's lines of communication before attacking, then he would do so. He was also careful to use cavalry on the flanks of his trains: the effectiveness of an armoured train was limited to the field of view of the commander unless vigorous reconnaissances were carried out; without flanking patrols, armoured trains were spectacular but often futile contraptions. By building up stocks of fuel, water, and ammunition at key points, May-Maevsky was able to obviate the other weakness of the armoured train, which was its limited endurance. A train could rely on no more fuel or ammunition than it carried; consequently armoured trains were always having to return to base at full speed half-way through a battle. By intelligent preparation May-Maevsky reduced the incidence of this, and in the Donets basin he not only tied down, but also made progress against, a Red force of five times his number.

To the extreme north of Denikin's front White cavalry, dominated by Shkuro and his shaggy-capped horsemen with their wolf's head insignia, broke the Red forces that threatened Rostov and Novocherkassk. The battle was close-run, but the Whites eventually forced the Reds to withdraw. It was on the flanks, in the west and east, that the real danger to Denikin's armies was revealed.

The French landing at Odessa had been a splendid and memorable event. French plans for the occupation of south Russia were grandiose though, in their own way, logical; only the premises were mistaken. The C-in-C of the French Orient forces, General Franchet d'Esperey, had little understanding of Russian politics, and still less sympathy for the Whites whom his troops had been sent to support. This attitude, not unnaturally, was shared by General d'Anselme, the field-commander of the south Russian expedition. Relations between the French and the Volunteers rapidly deteriorated; the situation was made worse by the appointment, as Governor of Odessa, of Grishin-Almazov, a young White general who had his full share of the White sensitivity to Allied slights, real or imagined. Further complications were pioduced by events in the Ukraine, where the Directory, which had formerly seemed pro-Bolshevik, had declared war on the Soviets. The French, filled with their new enthusiasm for East European buffer states, and obsessed with the cunning of their own diplomacy, at once began to negotiate for an alliance with the Ukraine – which constituted yet another betrayal of the ideal of Russia 'great and indivisible'.

In the midst of the inevitable row, the Bolsheviks struck at the French lines near Kherson. Shortly before, they had invaded the Ukraine. Kiev had once more changed hands; this had happened so often now that most inhabitants had lost count of the number of times the city had been besieged and captured. But it was the turn of the Directory's troops to retreat whilst, in the south, the French fell back before a comparatively small force of locally raised Bolsheviks. The French command had no choice; they had just heard that the French fleet in Sevastopol had mutinied, and there were disturbances amongst the sailors on the French ships in south Russian ports. The troops were equally unsettled. The disagreements between the French and Denikin had meant that there was no local White force to take over from them; the units of the Volunteers sent by Denikin were small in number and badly equipped, despite ample French stocks of munitions which d'Anselme refused to pass on. D'Anselme soon decided, with the approval of Paris, that he should pull out of Odessa if the situation deteriorated further. No mention of this decision was made to the Whites, who were encouraged, by the various fortifications that the French had begun to build around Odessa, into believing that they were determined to stay. But these fortifications were simply a gesture, set up in the vain hope that the fighting qualities of the French troops might improve.

On 2 April General d'Anselme received definite orders from Paris; on 3 April he informed the Whites that he would be withdrawing his men in seventy-two hours. There was no reason why so short a time should be regarded as desirable; the consequences were panic and disorder. Local Bolsheviks rose within the city, Bolshevik partisans moved in from the country; looting had begun long before the last French soldier was embarked. It had been proposed that the White forces should be sent to the Crimea, but there was no ship-room for them; instead the White troops were forced to make their way to Roumania, where they were disarmed and temporarily interned. Of far more concern to many of the Whites in other parts of Russia was that their families, thinking Odessa a safe refuge under Allied protection, had taken shelter in the city. A few were herded aboard the French transports. The great majority were left to the mercy of the Reds.

French disengagement laid open the whole of Denikin's left flank. In particular it exposed the Crimea, already threatened by Bolsheviks advancing from Kherson. Once more the French equivocated, but Franchet d'Esperey who, after a quick visit to Odessa in late March, had gone on to Sevastopol, proved himself a better officer than d'Anselme, and managed, with the help of the Royal Navy, to get much of the civilian population evacuated. Amongst those who left Russia for the last time were the

Empress Dowager and the Grand Duke Nicholas Nikolaevich. In the early hours of 16 April, the Volunteers left the Crimea under cover of French troops, and on 25 April, by the terms of a truce between the French and the Bolsheviks, the Reds entered Sevastopol. Denikin was now obliged to establish a new front line in the west, and pressure on May-Maevsky was still further increased. It was fortunate that, for the moment, the Reds had no way of exploiting their success.

White cavalry had repulsed the first Red offensive against the Don. But, in early April, a new threat emerged, this time on the Manych front. This was exactly what Wrangel had prophesied would happen. It was not long before the Reds had forced the line of the Manych river; some of their units came within fifteen miles of Rostov, and for a time the town was completely unprotected. The direction of the Red advance threatened once more to separate Caucasia from the Don. Wrangel was offered command of the assailed front, but he refused, on the grounds that Denikin would never give him the quantities of troops that he would need, since the Commander-in-Chief would suspect him of attempting to pursue his own plans for the Manych front, under pretext of the urgency of the situation.

Denikin himself was forced to take command of the operation and, at the time he did so, something near to a panic began to affect the White troops. Immediate steps were taken to check this. At Ekaterinodar, officers' detachments were raised from the staff and administrative personnel; some of these were given rapid training on the tanks that the British had recently begun to deliver to the Volunteers. Wrangel, still suffering from the effects of his bout of typhoid, insisted on returning to his headquarters, and did so just in time to repress an incipient Bolshevik uprising in the industrial quarter of Rostov. Though there were only insignificant numbers of troops available to him in the town, he arrested seventy Bolshevik infiltrators and agents. Despite the uproar amongst the workers, he had six of them shot. The town was soon firmly under White control.

On the Manych river fighting was fierce and inconclusive. Twice White units under the youthful General Chatilov attempted the fording of the river, and twice they were forced back. The mud and the swamps along the river line made the use of artillery impractical, and the Reds had established themselves in strength. Denikin was forced to call on all his available troops, to the extent of putting the other fronts at risk, in order to contain the Bolsheviks. Here the wisdom of Wrangel's earlier behaviour became apparent. By ensuring that Denikin was personally responsible, Wrangel also ensured that the front was adequately reinforced. The front steadily stabilised until, by the end of April, a state of deadlock had been reached. Nevertheless, in the long-term deadlock favoured the Reds, and it was obvious that somehow the Whites must achieve a break-out.

In these circumstances the limitations of Denikin's generalship first became apparent. Until now he had always proved equal to events and his handling of the Volunteers during the end of the first Kuban campaign and the beginning of the second had been both unconventional and effective. But the White 'Army', at that time, was of little more than brigade strength. Now Denikin had to exercise a different kind of command for which, by training, he was supposedly better suited. In practice this was not the case; his strategy was by no means infallible, and his judgement of men weak. Worse than this, he was becoming predictable. The only possible way in which the Whites could break out of the Manych line was by the decisive use of cavalry, in which – as it happened – they were relatively strong. But Denikin made no provision for the unified command of the cavalry: the individual commanders held equal powers, and there was no command structure. It seems an incredible lapse. Denikin still thought in Imperial Army terms, in which the army list decided seniority and, in a given situation, everyone knew where he stood. But now Denikin had to make decisions, and he refused to take them. It was only after Wrangel had several times pointed out the absurdity of the situation that anything was done about it; Romanovsky (still Denikin's Chief-of-Staff) suggested to Wrangel that he was the man whom the various cavalry generals would obey, and Wrangel agreed to take over the cavalry command. Almost at once a new spirit of confidence was evident on the Manych front.

Denikin, as it turned out, had been lucky. His western front, hastily thrown together across the Kerch Isthmus held, mainly as a result of British naval operations in the Azov Sea and off the Sivash Inlet. The Royal Navy did its job well, bringing down concentrated heavy artillery fire on any map reference indicated by the White command. The Reds had no effective means of replying, and it is remarkable that they endured, huddled in their inadequate trenches, for so long.

The other event that enabled Denikin to recover his position was a rising on the upper Don. Involved in this were many of the Cossacks who, less than six months before, had deserted from Krasnov's Army. Now they had had an opportunity to sample the reality of Bolshevik promises and, once more, they declared for the Whites. Despite Red punitive expeditions they were soon 30,000 strong, and Denikin's airmen landed behind the Bolshevik lines to make contact with their leaders. The helmeted and goggled emissaries were welcomed to the *stanitsas*, with bells and flowers. Lenin, from Moscow, was urgently enjoining 'a quick victory in the Donets basin, collection of rifles in all the *stanitsas*, and the creation of a stable army'.[1] But, for the moment, it was too late, and Denikin was able to turn his attention to the continuing problem of the Manych front.

Lenin's concern was not restricted solely to the area of the Don and the Donets basin; from the point of view of Moscow, in the spring of 1919 the greatest threat to the future of the revolution came not from the south, but from the east. After the capture of Perm and the fighting around Ufa there had been a lull on the eastern front. This was occasioned by the extreme cold of early February, which put a stop to all active campaigning, and made the frost the predominant enemy for both sides. Kolchak's troops were, in the main, peasants. At the training centres set up by Knox for Kolchak's recruits, the British officers and N.C.O.s. were horrified by the difficulty that they had in developing in the recruits any sense of co-ordination. Their rifle-fire was slow and their aim consistently bad. But, for all this, they could live and fight under conditions where British and other Allied troops could only exist – as they were doing, at this moment, on the Archangel front – in the shelter of blockhouses. But February 1919, which found them on the Europe-facing forward slopes of the towering Urals, defeated even their capacity for the patient conquest of the cold.

[1] Lenin, *Sochineniya*, XXXV, p. 329.

The pause gave an opportunity for both sides to take stock. In Moscow Lenin and Trotsky were able to peruse a lengthy report, written by Stalin and Dzerzhinsky, on the reasons for the loss of Perm to Gajda. It listed the remarkable number of Red Army men who had defected to the Whites, including the C.O. of the engineers and his staff, the chief railway engineer and his staff, the C.O. of the army transport group and his staff, the commander of the guard battalion, the commander of the artillery brigade, all the accountants of the army commissariat, and many other senior officers and officials. This, of course, gave a great deal of ammunition to those who were anxious, for one reason or another, to attack Trotsky's policy of recruiting ex-officers. But the far-sighted realised that the desertions were not a systematic effort to sabotage the Red defence, but symptoms of something more serious. What had happened was that the morale of the Third Army, defending Perm, had broken. Men had thrown themselves in the snow and asked their comrades to shoot them because they could not go on. To the staff at Perm, it had seemed as though the Whites had won the war.

It emerged in the report that the Reds, for six months, had been trying to hold a front of three hundred miles without adequate reinforcements, and that there had not been enough of them to hold the front in the first place. The answer, as valid from Trotsky's point of view as it was from Stalin's, could only be a complete reorganisation of the Third Army with the object of making it an efficient fighting force once more. The process was put in hand during February, and serious attention was given to the strategic problems of the Urals area. Trotsky became convinced that, in the past, part of the trouble had been the piecemeal commitment of Red forces wherever the Whites threatened, and a tendency to envisage the defence in terms of a static front line. This was totally misleading; the vastness of the Urals front could never be treated in such a way, nor was it any use thinking in terms of the tactics of attrition. Assuming that Kolchak attempted to continue his three-pronged advance, then the best strategy would be to hold back the main Red forces until Kolchak's advancing columns could be taken in the flank and defeated in detail.

Trotsky's assumption was correct. Despite vigorous representations from Knox, Kolchak proposed to continue his three-column offensive as soon as movement in the field became possible once more. The situation was complicated to an extraordinary degree because, though there were a number of advocates of the 'one thrust' policy, different factions argued for this 'one thrust' to be made in quite distinct directions. The most powerful of these factions was headed by Gajda, and it was supported by Knox. They envisaged a link with Miller and Ironside, followed by a swing south-west on Moscow. A second faction argued Wrangel's case in reverse: their aim was a juncture with Denikin's forces. A third were content to express the great, simple, and delusory idea that lay behind so many White actions, 'to Moscow' by the most direct and the quickest route. So the three armies under Kolchak's command embodied, albeit indirectly, the conflicting outlooks of the various schools of self-appointed strategists. Furthermore, the most powerful thrust was to be made into the desolate tundra, in the hope of effecting a break-through to a relatively small force which was already fully extended. Gajda was flamboyant and plausible; he impressed both Kolchak and the British. But his military experience was limited – far more so than he cared to admit – and one of the main reasons for his employment, that he commanded the loyalty of a number of the Czechs, notably their Second Division, was rapidly ceasing to seem relevant.

By now Kolchak was determined that the Czechs must go. He and his staff made no secret of their antipathy to them. They felt that they could manage on their own. So, in a sense, they could. But they did not see that in questions relating to supplies, as in the diplomatic field, they were at the mercy of the intervening powers.

By the end of January the Czechs were formally out of the front line, though a few of their number, mainly ambitious young officers, threw in their lot with the Russians. The Russians were now in sole command of the Urals front, and the Allies had even less to do with the management of the front line than they had had in the past. General Janin, the French representative, indiscreetly let it be known that he had no faith in the Admiral's régime. Even Knox's comments began to reveal evidence of disillusionment. The old problems of discipline and organisation were as acute as ever. The capture of Perm had been marked by a horrifying outbreak of looting and rapine amongst the White troops. This was merely one symptom of the indiscipline that ran through the whole Siberian Army. It began at the top. Lebedev, Kolchak's Chief-of-Staff, and a former organiser of the Officers' Union, spent much of his time engaged in complex intrigues. Gajda was a law unto himself; with his connivance men of the Northern Army removed at gun-point stores destined for Khanzin's Western Army. Lebedev, informed of this, did nothing to stop it. Nor did he demur when Kolchak composed orders of the day that seemed, from a military point of view, confusing or even meaningless. British uniforms and equipment arrived at Vladivostok in large quantities, but were a long time in getting to the front. They were much fewer in number when they finally arrived, since it was obvious that all the staff and support groups had to be clothed first. Indeed, the uniforms were often never issued when they did reach their destination. In the spring of 1919, the great majority of Kolchak's men were dressed in whatever garments they could lay their hands on, and some were wearing no more than rags. Rough Siberian bast shoes, not boots, were all they had for footwear.

The politicians were even less reliable than the officers of the staff. Colonel Ward was of the opinion that there was not one whom he would 'trust to manage a whelk-stall'. Speculators were making vast sums of money, and the way to make even more was to combine speculation with governmental office. The black market flourished, prices in Omsk were astronomical, and profits were equivalently high. The railways were ridden with corruption; when British sappers and American engineers were put in charge of sectors of the line they uncovered the most remarkable frauds. Wagons containing ammunition and guns were left off trains in order that trucks containing luxuries in vogue at Omsk might be substituted; minor pilfering took place on almost every train, and major pilfering – such as the diversion of a whole train and the sale of its contents – was by no means unknown.

It is hard, in all this, to get any perspective on Kolchak. We know what he looked like: a small, pale-faced man with eyes remarkable for their intensity, usually clad in a British uniform with a Russian admiral's epaulettes. We know that he was moody, personally unhappy, ill-tempered, and given to breaking pens and any other articles that he might find on his desk. We know, also, that he was aware of the deviousness of his subordinates, the corruption that surrounded him, and the turpitude of many of his commanders. But he did nothing about it. His commissions of enquiry never got any results, obviously incompetent officers continued to hold important posts, and relations with the Allies grew steadily worse. Kolchak knew that he was bad at handling meetings and rallies, and that the impression he made in public was often poor. Rather than attempt to do anything to overcome this, so far as possible he evaded such functions. It is not surprising that the people began to feel increasingly alienated from their government, and the soldiers from their higher command. When Kolchak did make a public appearance the precautions taken to ensure his safety meant that his visits were brief and that the machinery of security was much in evidence.

In early March the Urals were still deep in snow. The passes were blocked, and supply of Kolchak's front line was difficult. Neither side was prepared for an offensive. But Kolchak was insistent – it was one of the very few things of any significance that he was ever insistent about – that the Whites take the initiative. Unprepared as they were, they began an advance. Khanzin was the first to break the Red defences, and he inflicted so demoralising a defeat that two Red battalions came over to him, weapons and all. By 13 March Ufa had been recaptured, and the Volga was obviously the White objective.

Kolchak had been trying in vain to persuade Gajda that he also must move. But Gajda, with characteristic petulance, refused; it was not until his vanity was aroused by the fall of Ufa that he launched a serious offensive. Yet, of Kolchak's available 120,000 men, by far the greater part were serving in the Northern Army. Khanzin had many less troops at his disposal, and with these he had defeated the Soviet Fifth Army, a much more serious proposition than the remnants of the Third, who faced Gajda. When Gajda eventually did attack, he soon succeeded in breaking through the Soviet line, rapidly cleared the Kama basin, and finally took Glazov. There, however, he had to stop, hamstrung by the inadequacies of his transport arrangements. Even had he had the means to go on this would have been futile, since by now he was badly outflanked.

Khanzin had had the same difficulties, but he did not allow them to cripple his advance. Following up the rout of the Reds, his troops became increasingly spread out, until they began to act as independent units, rather than as part of a unified army. The same problem hindered Dutov's Southern (Orenburg) Army, long before they commenced on offensive operations. Dutov was a man capable of exercising absolute control over a regiment, and absolutely no control over a brigade. Consequently his Cossacks, though many single units fought brilliant actions, were never used effectively. For weeks they threatened their main objective, Orenburg. But, though his patrols came within sight of the town, Dutov did not succeed in his aim. With Orenburg in his hands he would have been well placed both for an attempt to break through to Denikin, or to turn the flank of the Soviet forces that were facing Khanzin. Both opportunities were lost.

Nevertheless, April was a month of victories for Kolchak. Trotsky, who had hurriedly left the Eighth Party Congress at Moscow, in order to bolster the defence of Ufa, endeavoured to check the disarray of the Red forces that followed on the fall of the town. He appealed to Moscow for reinforcements of Party members and took steps to reorganise the local Soviets. He also complained of Left S.R. elements in the Third Army, and sub-sequently purged them. At the command level, he arranged for the dismissal of Frunze as C-in-C of the eastern front, and replaced him with Vatzetis. Gradually these measures began to have an effect.

After the capture of Ufa, where his Cossacks massacred 670 captives, Khanzin's armies moved on west and south. By the end of April they were within striking distance of both Kazan and Samara. Dutov, though he was still held back from Orenburg, managed to envelop Uralsk from the south; his task was made the easier by yet another local rising. Only the continued resis-tance of Orenburg – now almost surrounded – and of Saratov prevented a link-up with Khanzin. Kazan was threatened both by Khanzin in the south and by Gajda in the north. Kolchak's forces had moved forward on a front 700 miles long; in the north they had made an advance of 150 miles, in the south they were

250 miles from their start line. The territorial gain was immense.

Yet there is no evidence that Kolchak's strategic aims were any clearer; he made no serious effort to discipline Dutov's movements in the south or to co-ordinate Khanzin's advance. Communications with Denikin remained poor.

In the north, at the end of March, a British officer, a Russian civilian, and a platoon of British and French troops, reached the Pechora river, 400 miles south-east of Archangel. There they encountered Gajda's reconnaissance patrols. It was, then, possible for the troops to get through from the Archangel front, though it must not be imagined that the expedition was at all easy. But Kolchak never ensured that Gajda followed up this lead, and a connection that might have forced the hand of the British Cabinet, and persuaded them to let their Archangel commitments stand, was thrown away. By the time the relief force sent out by Churchill did make an attempt to break through to Gajda the Reds had reorganised and the opportunity was gone.

Kolchak was content to watch the progress of his troops, reinforcing them where he could and where it seemed justified. In so much as he had an objective, it must be taken to be Moscow, for he sent yet more troops to Gajda, whilst refusing Khanzin the reserves with which he might have captured the Volga towns. The reinforcements sent north were men thrown away; Gajda grew increasingly insubordinate and failed to break through the Soviet defences beyond Glazov, whilst at the same time canvassing such wild schemes as an attack on St Petersburg by a flying column. In the meantime, nothing was done to remedy the inadequacies of the White 'tail'; supplies failed to get through, and there were small but violent mutinies by troops whose officers neglected to ensure that they were either clothed or fed. The situation was aggravated by Trotsky's institution of a partial 'burnt earth' policy, which had the effect both of denying forage and shelter to the Whites, and of revealing to the local peasants that the war was in earnest. As the Reds were driven back, so their supply problems became relatively less acute, and the effects of Trotsky's reforms of the base areas more evident. Vatzetis rapidly grasped that Kolchak's already grotesquely extended front line would be weakest where the different armies joined; accordingly he concentrated his better troops at these places. Then, before Kolchak's forces could menace the line of the Volga, he counter-attacked in the south. At Glazov the reorganisation of his Third Army was still under way, but he was strong enough to make a demonstration in force against Gajda's left flank.

The counter-attack was dramatically successful. Kolchak's great salient into European Russia dissolved in a few days. On 14 May the Bolsheviks attacked from the direction of Samara and turned the flanks both of the Western Army under Khanzin, and of Dutov's force. Khanzin was forced to retreat at once. The peasants, who had materially aided his advance by rising in protest against Bolshevik grain raids, either changed sides once more or began to trek to Siberia, blocking the roads with their carts. Lateral communication along Khanzin's front proved almost impossible, and each regiment, fearing for its flanks and not knowing whether it was being supported, fell back. The length of the front line accelerated the process. Soon Vatzetis was sending forces north and Gajda, conscious – like the other forward commanders – of the vulnerability of his flanks, retreated also. In the south, Ufa was evacuated on 6 June. Kolchak's forces were in full retreat.

It was the contention of Winston Churchill that in the Russian Civil War 'twenty or thirty thousand resolute, comprehending, well-armed Europeans could, without any serious difficulty or loss, have made their way very swiftly along any of the great railroads which converged on Moscow; and have brought to the hard ordeal of battle any force that stood against them'.[1] But the Allies realised how extensive Kolchak's gains had been only when he began to lose them; and even then they did not see that the crowds of weary and demoralised soldiers, trudging down roads blocked by fleeing refugees, were to establish a pattern from which there could be no escape.

While Khanzin was moving back towards the Urals passes, and Trotsky was sending reinforcements against Gajda and Denikin, the first scenes of an extraordinary counter-revolutionary charade were being played out in the north-west. There the Reds had but few troops; despite periodic complaints from the inhabitants of

---

[1] Churchill, *The World Crisis: The Aftermath*, p. 234.

St Petersburg – for whom the city was, of course, Petrograd and nothing else, it was only the Whites who recalled the old name, so pusillanimously altered in 1914 – who felt that their lives and what remnants of property the Bolsheviks had left them were in jeopardy, Trotsky regarded the threat to the city as minimal. For the time being his analysis was quite correct. Nevertheless, in a round-about way, the Whites were emerging as a military force in the north-west.

The Armistice of 1918, which had, as we have seen, drastic and not necessarily happy effects on the course of the Civil War in the south and the east, had two noteworthy effects in the Baltic area.

Firstly, it entirely altered the political orientation of the Germans. The Germans on the western front knew that the Armistice was at least an ending. But on the eastern front the Germans were still advancing, and they could say with conviction that they were undefeated. While units of the German eastern forces mutinied and returned home and others were led home by their officers, there was one area in which the natural reluctance of German troops to leave their conquests happened temporarily to coincide with Allied interest.

This was the area of the Baltic states. Under Article XII of the Armistice, it was laid down that 'the Germans are to withdraw from the territory that was formerly part of the Russian Empire as soon as the Allies should consider the moment suitable having regard to the interior conditions of those territories'. In other words, the Germans were to stay in the Baltic states because the Allies did not want the Bolsheviks to reconquer them and were unable, for the moment, to guarantee this themselves. The German commander, on whom this duty of resistance to the Bolsheviks fell, was none other than their old antagonist of the Finnish Revolution, Graf von der Goltz. Von der Goltz was intelligent, able and patriotic, and naturally he saw in his new mission possibilities beyond those envisaged by the Allies. It appeared to him that it might be possible, by skilful manipulation of the situation, to retain the Baltic states for Germany, even though they might have to be independent in name. It also seemed to him that, if he were to proceed against the Bolsheviks with success, then he might well be able to ensure that their successor government would be an adherent of the German cause.

The wider implication of his scheme needed careful consideration; of this he was fully aware. For the moment he limited himself to local objectives. But the germ of his idea was implanted, and there were not lacking those among the Whites who, dissatisfied with the scale of Allied aid, disillusioned by Prinkipo and other allegedly pro-Bolshevik Allied moves, and largely oblivious of the scale of Germany's defeat in the west, saw in the remaining German forces their rod and their staff.

The second effect of the Armistice with which we have to be concerned was that it brought home to the Finnish Whites who were pro-German that they had chosen the losing side. The more percipient had seen this a month or so before the event, and had been sufficiently sensible to ask Mannerheim, who predicted an Allied victory, to return to the country which had rewarded his services so shabbily. Mannerheim agreed; when the Armistice was signed, he proceeded to Paris to treat with the Allies; and there, despite the activities of the White Russian émigrés who were daily anticipating the fall of Bolshevism and the return of Finland to the Empire, he was successful in his mission to the victors. Whilst he was in Paris the Finnish Diet decided formally to offer him the post of Regent of Finland, which it was understood that he would accept. On 22 December Mannerheim once more entered Helsingfors in triumph, and was able to tell his people that as well as securing Finland's political future, he had persuaded the Allies to offer Finland a loan that would enable her to obtain supplies of wheat. This would be used to stave off incipient famine. White loaves, the first that many Finns had seen for years, were known as 'Mannerheim bread'. The General had come home at last.

The Reds were intensely suspicious of the newly instated Mannerheim, whilst the Whites still optimistically nurtured the idea that Mannerheim might yet be induced to come to their aid. But the obvious concession that they in their turn must make, namely the recognition of Finland, they adamantly refused to consider.

The only White Russian (as opposed to White Finn) troops in the Baltic area at the beginning of 1919 were those of the Northern Corps. This had been set up, in the first instance, by the White underground in St Petersburg, which was a sibling

269

of the organisation that had played so nebulous a part in Kornilov's 'revolt'. Its prime movers were officers, all of whom were committed reactionaries; their political attitudes were largely a consequence of first-hand experience of Bolshevik rule. They had established themselves in October 1918 under the aegis of the Germans who obligingly released to them Russian prisoners of war who might be induced to fight in the White ranks. After the Armistice the commander of the Northern Corps had managed to persuade the Estonian government to take over the little army – an agreement that was distasteful to both parties, but that was forced on them by the rapidity of the Soviet advance. There was considerable friction, since the officers of the Northern Corps made it quite apparent that they regarded the independence of Estonia as a purely provisional arrangement. But the combined forces of the Whites and the Estonians did succeed in containing the Red advance, and the Whites were able to take into their ranks many soldiers who had deserted from the Reds.

The commander of the Northern Corps during this period was General Alexander Rodzyanko – a slow, ironical Guards officer, who was a notable horseman and a relative of the former President of the Duma. A further family connection, with Mannerheim, was hopefully recalled. In March there arrived from Helsingfors a more senior officer, Nikolay Yudenich, bearing Kolchak's commission as Commander-in-Chief of all Russian forces in the Baltic area. Accompanying him was a group of cantankerous and self-important old gentlemen who, it was announced, would constitute the government of such territory as might be liberated by the Corps. Many of the officers viewed this descent from Finland with disgust, but this did not hinder preparations for an offensive in May. Much against his will, Yudenich opened negotiations with Mannerheim, though this had no immediate consequences. Relations with the Estonians were patched up; and it at last seemed as if something might happen. For, though the anti-Bolshevik forces were small in number, the fact that since the Armistice the Allies had had naval supremacy in the Baltic made a great difference to the strategic picture as a whole. Even if the Northern Corps did not seriously disturb the Reds, the presence of Admiral Cowan's squadron caused them the utmost concern.

XIV

Summer

In the south Denikin was faced with a war on three fronts. Compared with the enterprise of Kolchak, as Churchill was to write, 'the military effort of Denikin was far more serious and sustained'.[1] In May 1919 he was making progress on two of his fronts: the Donets basin, where Red troops had been distracted by the turmoil in the Ukraine; and the northern Don, where the rising behind the Red lines shook the morale of the Soviet forces. On the Manych front there was still deadlock, and a break-out in the direction of Tsaritsyn was Denikin's major priority.

Denikin had two significant assets. The first was the presence of Wrangel as the commander (virtually self-appointed) of the cavalry; the second was the arrival, along with great quantities of other war material, of British tanks – together with instructors who were eager to see what their monsters would do under conditions entirely different from those on the western front. Since the Russians were not notable for mechanical aptitude it was British officers and other ranks (mainly N.C.O.s) who took the vehicles into action; the results surpassed all expectations. The arrival of the ironclad in Hamilton Roads was a bagatelle compared to the advent of the tank on the Russian scene. There were problems, of course; the arrangements necessary to get the tanks to the front were generally muddled, and the Russian staff had the greatest difficulty in understanding that the endurance of a tank was limited, that they overheated with great speed and were then temporarily unusable, and that gasoline was a basic requirement. Nevertheless, the effect of these creations, once they reached the front, was gratifying to the representatives of both Whites and British.

Wrangel began his operations on the Manych front by solving

---

[1] Churchill, *The Aftermath*, p. 250.

the problem of fording the muddy river. He proceeded on the sound basis that if he wanted anything done it was best to do it himself – and ask Denikin afterwards. The enemy were concentrated in the village of Velikoknyazheskaya, in entrenched positions covered by artillery. The only hope for a White assault lay in an attempt to envelop the position from the east – the direction from which the Reds were least likely to anticipate attack. So Wrangel tore down the village fences behind the White lines and, after conducting experiments in a nearby lake, decided that these were exactly what he needed.

On 17 May the White General Ulagai, with a column of cavalry, was raiding north of the Manych. Against him the Reds launched six of their finest mounted regiments. At mid-day the two forces charged each other across the steppe, and the Red cavalry retreated in disorder. Then Ulagai debouched onto the railway which formed the Bolsheviks' chief line of communication and destroyed the line. That night, some sixty miles from the scene of Ulagai's action, Wrangel moved up to the Manych and ordered his fences, now strengthened and weighted, to be sunk across the river bed. At dawn his troops began to ford the river on the causeway thus made – an endless file of soldiers now seemingly no bigger than flies in the vast expanse of level steppe and shallow salt lagoons. Cavalry followed, the horses splashing through the water one after another, and the artillery came last. Too late the Reds became aware of what had happened; General Chatilov, commanding the White vanguard, was on their positions before they could organise, forcing them to retreat.

That night the Whites bivouacked on the steppe. Everything was damp, and there was no fresh water. No one slept. The columns were on the move again before dawn.

Fighting on the second day was severe and protracted. White aircraft strafed the Red troops, but Soviet superiority in numbers told. Wrangel directed the battle from the top of a large haystack, which gave him a wide field of view, and only his prompt intervention prevented his men from being outflanked by Red cavalry. In his staff car, he drove to critical points on the field of battle – an apt term for once, since his haystack enabled him to survey miles of the level steppe grasslands.

The Reds brought up their reserves. Wrangel had none, and

his line of retreat was extremely vulnerable. On the morning of the 20th he summoned his troops, who had spent yet another night without shelter or food beyond their iron rations, to address them. Then he ordered their squadrons to be drawn up in order of battle, as though they were on St Petersburg's Champs de Mars, had the colours broken out, and commanded the bands to play. The wind flaunted the standards, sabres were presented, and the brigade charged – as though it had been a unit of the Imperial Army in 1914. The charge shattered the Reds who faced it, breaking their hold both on Velikoknyazheskaya and the Manych line. The Whites took 15,000 prisoners, fifty-five guns and a hundred and fifty machine guns. The way to the Volga was open.

In the Donets basin May-Maevsky had moved beyond the stage of railway operations. Cossacks had come in to him in great numbers and, using as a foundation a few units put at his disposal by Denikin, he soon had a cavalry force to rival Wrangel's. It was not as well disciplined but, for the moment, it was as effective. He rolled up the Red Eighth and Thirteenth Armies, which had attempted an abortive offensive in mid-May, and soon threatened to cut off the Red forces in the Crimea. In the north the entirely reorganised Don Cossack Army had made contact with the anti-Bolshevik Cossack rebels and defeated the Red Ninth Army. By 12 June Wrangel's men were facing Tsaritsyn.

On the same day Denikin, speaking at a farewell dinner given for General Briggs – Poole's successor as head of the British Military Mission, and now returning to England – announced that he intended to submit himself and his command to the 'authority of Admiral Kolchak, Supreme Ruler of the Russian State and Supreme Commander-in-Chief of the Russian Armies'. Denikin's statement, for which those present were not at all prepared, was made at that time in the hope that the Allies might extend formal recognition to the White régimes. It was an act that was entirely sincere, and made without reservation, but it was also a typical instance of Denikin's high-mindedness and total lack of political judgment. For, by acknowledging Kolchak's authority, he at once antagonised the governments of both the Don and the Kuban, as well as all those of his officers who disliked the political complexion of the Siberian régime. It was also a miscalculation from the military point of view: at just this time it was becoming apparent to Allied observers that Kolchak would never stand on the Volga again.

After the capture of Velikoknyazheskaya Denikin, who had done little more than to watch the battle being won for him by Wrangel and Ulagai, decided to reorganise his forces. Those under May-Maevsky became the Volunteer Army, the Don Cossacks retained their title of the Army of the Don, and Wrangel assumed command of the Caucasian Army on Denikin's right flank. The C-in-C's relations with Wrangel continued to deteriorate. When, after the battle at Velikoknyazheskaya, Denikin left the Manych front, he asked Wrangel how soon he intended to take Tsaritsyn. Wrangel replied that it was up to Denikin: the Caucasian Army could be at the gates of the town in three weeks, but a cavalry corps could not be expected to capture the town; for that he must have artillery and infantry, and these Denikin alone could provide.

As his train drew away from Velikoknyazheskaya station Denikin stood at the window of his carriage, beaming over his black moustache and white goatee, and holding up three fingers to Wrangel: he expected Wrangel to accomplish his very considerable task in the estimated three weeks. But, within a few days, he was grumbling that Wrangel was pushing on unnecessarily fast in order to satisfy his personal ambitions, and that he was a 'typically vainglorious Guards officer'. The remark was made in anger when Wrangel pestered the C-in-C's headquarters for the necessary infantry and artillery, but Wrangel inevitably came to hear of it. Nor were the promised reinforcements forthcoming, and this made Wrangel's chances of achieving his object in the agreed time very thin indeed. Wrangel, unable to extract a new car from headquarters – his previous one was being repaired – rode with his men over the desert steppe. As they drew nearer to Tsaritsyn opposition from the Reds became more determined. The wounded had to be sent back across two hundred miles of steppe in springless carts drawn by camels; there was no provision for shade.

Once again the extremities of the Russian climate were to prove as dangerous as any human enemy. The burning sun tortured men and horses through the day; the nights were cold and sharp. But still Wrangel kept his men going towards Tsaritsyn and the Volga. He had achieved his break-out; now he must exploit it.

For years advanced military thinkers had been saying that the cavalry was a wasteful anachronism; for years the military conservatives had kept it going. It was said that the Boer War was the last conflict in which cavalry played a serious part; this the experience of the World War had seemed to confirm. Yet in the Russian Civil War, the cavalry were of vital importance; not in the guise of mounted infantrymen – though we might imagine this from Trotsky's remark that the analogies were with the American Civil War – but in that form implied by their organisation and training within the Imperial Army. Wrangel had handled his Cossacks at Velikoknyazheskaya as though he had been on a parade ground, and the system had worked. His recruits had been the Tsar's horse levies, and, though they had fought hard in the Great War, they had not been decimated as had the infantry regiments. Their discipline and training gave them an advantage, despite the obsolescence of their weapons, over those who fought against them. On demoralised or bewildered troops, the effect of a cavalry charge, of naked steel, could be devastating.

Wrangel realised the importance of the psychological factor in the war, and behaved accordingly. What Krasnov had tried to do in the Don, Wrangel attempted in the Caucasian Army. He deliberately played up to the romantic image of the Cossack, dressing as one himself, and encouraging the traditional features of Cossack dress. His officers and men carried elaborate daggers; the horses were often splendidly accoutred; pennoncels flared on the wind. The significant thing is that this was successful; Wrangel was careful to keep within the bounds of Imperial Army tradition and not to perpetrate Krasnov's absurdities. In consequence he emerged as the commander of a remarkable force.

At the same time, there were bizarre contrasts. Hearing, through his intelligence service, that Trotsky was to attend a meeting of eighty commissars at Tsaritsyn in order to organise the defence of the town, Wrangel asked for the appropriate building to be bombed. A de Havilland bomber, complete with British pilot and a 112-lb. bomb was sent on the mission and scored a direct hit at the time that a meeting was known to be in progress. Unfortunately Trotsky was not in Tsaritsyn when the bomb fell; it nevertheless gave some satisfaction to the Whites that the building was almost totally destroyed and many of those inside killed. This contrast of the new and the old was a commonplace in the war. Cavalry units carried radios; sometimes aircraft worked in collaboration with horsemen; tanks attacked hastily occupied fortifications that dated from the eighteenth century.

It was just such an anachronism when, within the agreed three weeks, Wrangel arrived before the trenches and barbed-wire of Tsaritsyn with what was almost exclusively a cavalry army.

Whoever held Tsaritsyn commanded the entire eastern flank of Denikin's operations. Further than this, by capturing the town the Whites would put themselves in a position to disrupt communication between Moscow and the Red forces in Astrakhan. Most important of all, the capture of Tsaritsyn could lead, even now, to a connection with Kolchak's left flank.

When Wrangel's force arrived before Tsaritsyn their general was at once faced with a serious dilemma. He had none of the necessary equipment for an assault on the city, but his troops were already, after the rigours of the march from the Manych, anticipating their entry; delay threatened to undermine their morale. If Wrangel waited outside the fortifications, then it was a strong possibility that the Reds would come onto the offensive; he was realistic enough to see that, should this occur, the Whites had little hope of holding out on the barren steppe. Therefore he must attack. His senior commanders agreed.

On 13 June his cavalry broke through the Red picket line and did considerable damage. But the elaborate system of concentric defences with which the town was surrounded proved too much for them, as did the heavy and well-directed artillery fire. Wrangel continued his assault for two days until, knowing it to be hopeless, he withdrew to his old positions outside the Red trenches. He had lost nearly a quarter of his men, together with eight general officers and eleven regimental commanders. The latter figures are ample proof that, in Wrangel's army, the White commanders, far from shirking front-line fighting, led the attacks in person. At Tsaritsyn their efforts, however gallant, ended in failure. The Bolsheviks launched a counter-attack and Wrangel, mindful of the inadequacy of his positions on the steppe, withdrew his army a day's march from the city. He placed himself at just the wrong distance for the Red infantry to strike at him effectively, and enabled his cavalry to operate to best advantage.

Wrangel's next battle was with Denikin. He had to have the promised infantry and artillery. Eventually he sent a letter to the C-in-C, saying that he would resign as soon as the Tsaritsyn expedition was over, since it was clear to him that Denikin's behaviour was not likely to alter in the future. But he was persuaded by his Chief-of-Staff to stop the missive before it arrived at Denikin's H.Q. On the same day he heard that reinforcements were finally on their way. Denikin's attitude seems to have been that Tsaritsyn was subordinate to the northern front and the Donets basin, and he does not appear to have had the slightest understanding of Wrangel's needs. The railway line from Velikoknyazheskaya to Tsaritsyn remained in the damaged state in which the Reds had left it until the end of June. Yet it did not require military genius to see that it was the key to the Tsaritsyn situation. That Denikin, strongly influenced by Romanovsky, could continue to treat the Tsaritsyn offensive as little more than an elaborate side-show, is one of the most remarkable facets of the war.

The Reds were fully aware of the town's importance. Eleven regiments had been rushed into the town to reinforce the defence and bolster the Tenth Army, which had already suffered heavily on the Manych front. The Caucasian Army's first attempt on the town had demoralised the Reds more than Wrangel knew; the presence of his cavalry in the suburbs had convinced the faint-hearted that it was time for them to leave the town. The civilian population – those of them who were Bolshevik in sympathy or considered that they had been compromised by the Bolsheviks – were crowding onto trains and river steamers in their attempts to get to the north. Trains leaving Tsaritsyn station were full to the point where each carriage roof carried its contingent of refugees. When, late in the evening of 28 June, it was reported that Wrangel's reinforcements had arrived, the panic heightened.

Elsewhere in south Russia the Reds were in retreat. On 18 June the White troops in the Crimea began an offensive, and units from May-Maevsky's Volunteer Army took up positions across the isthmuses to block the Reds' withdrawal. The advance north from the Don continued, despite a determined Bolshevik attempt at reorganisation, directed by Voroshilov, Stalin's military protégé. Many of the former Tsaritsyn clique were now established in Kharkov and other south Russian towns; their predilection for the prosecution of personal feuds undoubtedly contributed to the disunity of the Red forces. Orders castigating the Red armies in the south poured forth from Moscow, but their effect was minimal. And, though Trotsky had now moved from the Urals front in an endeavour to stiffen resistance in the south, it was obviously going to take time before his actions could have any lasting effect.

It was at this juncture that the Reds lost the services of Nestor Makhno, the anarchist leader who had, until now, maintained a loose alliance with Bolshevik forces. Trotsky, who had no time for partisan forces, was determined that Makhno should be liquidated, but he does not seem to have realised how much popular support Makhno commanded, for the peasants of the Ukraine and south-west Russia rallied to his black standards. His base was the large village of Gulyay Pole: from there he set out with his men on forays against the enemy of the moment. Small, sallow, with an effeminate face hung round by long greasy hair, Makhno was seldom armed with less than a sabre, a dagger and two revolvers. His men wore whatever they pleased; headgear ranged from black-bowed boaters to guardsmen's shakoes, and their armament was correspondingly heterodox. They were, however, a formidable fighting force. Makhno developed techniques of fighting dependent on swift dispersal and assembly, together with rapid movement by carts and captured gun-carriages which were, when necessary, lifted onto flat-cars and moved by rail.

Early in June Shkuro had raided and captured Gulyay Pole: the right-wing brigand, in this instance, defeating his left-wing counterpart. The incident confirmed Makhno, who himself escaped, in his hatred of both Bolsheviks and Whites. Negotiations were opened between the Makhnovites and Grigoriev, the former Red commander in the south-west, who had mutinied after the French evacuation of Odessa and proclaimed himself Ataman of the territories he 'liberated'. The eventual outcome of this proposed alliance was bloody and final. Two messengers from the Whites were unwise enough, in late July, to visit Grigoriev at Makhno's headquarters. Their objective was to win Grigoriev and his partisan bands over to the White cause. It is possible that Grigoriev might have been persuaded; but we have no means of telling, for Makhno shot both the White envoys and, shortly afterwards, Grigoriev and his henchmen. After this Makhno began to translate his chief political doctrine, which can be loosely apostrophised as 'a plague on both your houses', into vigorous military action.

Denikin's main thrust to the north was made up the Donets valley in the direction of Kharkov. May-Maevsky dispatched a corps of his Volunteer Army, under the command of General Kutepov, against the town. Once secured, Kharkov would be the ideal base for operations both to the north against Orel and Moscow, and to the west, against Kiev and the Ukraine. Kutepov encountered opposition outside the town, was reinforced, and after five days of heavy fighting broke the Red defence. The cavalry at once advanced into the town as fast as they could, only to find themselves in danger of being cut off when hand-to-hand conflict broke out in the streets. Voroshilov may not have been much versed in higher strategy, but he was able to inspire a determined resistance by the Red units remaining in the town and groups of hastily organised workers. When the Whites finally suppressed the street fighting the workers, many of whom were not wearing so much as a red star or arm band, were dealt with even more ferociously than were the other prisoners – on the grounds that they had treacherously attacked the Volunteer forces. When the Reds launched an abortive counter-attack on Kharkov over a month later, they nailed the epaulettes of captured officers to their shoulders, whilst the wearers were still alive. The Whites did not generally practise this type of barbarity, though Shkuro's men were quite capable of torturing peasants to find out where they had hidden such meagre resources as they possessed.

On 27 June Kharkov fell to Kutepov; on 29 June Bolshevik resistance in the Crimean peninsula came to an end. The Reds in the Crimea fought well out of sheer desperation. They were cut off, they could expect no mercy, and many of the inhabitants of the Crimea were White sympathisers. But eventually they could hold out no longer. Most of the Reds who surrendered were given the option of joining the White Army or being shot.

Over to the east at Tsaritsyn, Wrangel had his long-awaited reinforcements march straight from the point at which they detrained into the front line. Wrangel himself supervised their move up to the start positions. On 29 June, at dawn, Wrangel resumed his attack on the Tsaritsyn perimeter. Tanks and armoured cars breached the barbed wire; infantry followed close behind them to mop up. The Reds could do nothing against the tanks: the British instructors, who were accustomed to remark that 'it was the only war they had', did their work well. So soon as the breach was made the cavalry moved in, trotting through the cleared area despite Red artillery fire, then peeling off from the main column at a canter before charging at the gallop into the rear of the Red defensive positions along the perimeter. Elements of the White armies were undisciplined – of that there has never been any doubt. But a British observer of Wrangel's attack on Tsaritsyn, an ex-cavalry man who had seen the light and gone into tanks, remarked that 'it was the kind of movement they dreamt up in the textbooks. I never imagined I would see it, because I did not believe it could be done. But I was wrong, and Wrangel was the man who did it.' By nightfall the Bolsheviks had been driven back to their final line of trenches.

The Whites returned to the attack the next morning. By this time they were certain of victory, and appraised of the straits in which the Bolsheviks now found themselves. For in the night the great stacks of wood that had been floated down the Volga from the forests of the north and now lay on Tsaritsyn docks were set alight. The city lay under a pall of drifting smoke. Soon the Whites had broken through the last Red defences, and were moving into the town. There was a certain amount of street fighting, and an attempt was made by the Reds to set on fire part of the suburbs, where the wood-built houses were dried to tinder by the sun. But there was insufficient wind for the flames to carry from building to building and before sunset the city was in Wrangel's hands, undamaged.

Some of the less orderly units attempted to loot, but the swift execution of four of their number together with the recollection of similar measures after the fall of Velikoknyazheskaya prevented any widespread pillage. Wrangel's motives were military rather than humanitarian, though he was very conscious of the need not to alienate the population of newly conquered territories. His first anxiety was to do as much damage to the retreating Bolsheviks as he possibly could. In this he was successful: his captures included two armoured cars, 131 locomotives, 10,000 lorries, of which 2,085 were loaded with munitions and ready for flight, plus the usual haul of guns, machine-guns and prisoners. If his men had run riot the defeat would have brought no such spoils.

On 1 July the Whites consolidated their hold on Tsaritsyn. On the 2nd Wrangel made his formal entry into the city and was greeted with enthusiasm by the population. When the Whites entered the town had been in a terrible condition; the Bolsheviks seemed to have made no attempt at imposing any measure of hygiene, and to put Tsaritsyn in order would clearly take some time. Wrangel's first action was to have the Cathedral, which had been used as a food-store, cleaned. At the same time the priests, most of whom had been imprisoned by the Bolsheviks, were liberated, and the Archbishop, who had been in hiding in the suburbs, returned to officiate at the victory *Te Deum* with which Wrangel was greeted.

These *Te Deums* were the first ceremonial event whenever the Whites took a town of any size. They stood for one of the very few positive things that the Whites claimed to represent. (The Whites would have said that law and justice came into this category, too, but they never gave them any convincing outward form.) When Cossacks captured a village the inhabitants would come out saying 'Christ is risen', and bearing ceremonial gifts of salt. It was quite apparent to everyone at Tsaritsyn that the crowds who attended the *Te Deum* were not doing so for fear of what might happen if they stayed away, but because one of the things that they most valued had been restored to them.

Denikin came up the newly repaired railway line to Tsaritsyn on the evening of 2 July. When Wrangel welcomed him at the station he took the opportunity to hand the C-in-C a report he had prepared. In this he recommended that the Whites construct defensive positions at Tsaritsyn, and also on the western flank of Denikin's salient in south Russia – which at this time was formed by the line of the Dnieper. Then, Wrangel argued, it would be possible to organise the territories already held by the Whites, prepare bases from which new advances could be made, and regroup the armies. Denikin's sole reaction to this report was to glance knowingly at Wrangel and remark that no doubt he 'wanted to be the first man in Moscow'.

On 3 July Denikin attended mass at Tsaritsyn Cathedral and afterwards reviewed the troops. Once the march-past was over he asked Wrangel and his Chief-of-Staff to call on him in his headquarters carriage, and there he read to them his general order to the White Armies. This document was of the foremost importance; having captured Tsaritsyn, Denikin's position was now immeasurably stronger than it had been hitherto, and he was in a position either to capitalise on his gains, or to throw away all that he had won.

His orders were not lacking in either simplicity or directness. They provided for a three-pronged advance on Moscow, to be made along the 'shortest lines converging on the centre'. The Volunteer Army under May-Maevsky was to advance on an axis through Orel and Tula; the Army of the Don was to proceed via Voronezh, and the Caucasian Army was routed through Saratov and Nizhny Novgorod. This plan, which came to be known as the Moscow Order, Wrangel called the 'death-sentence for the Armies of Southern Russia'.[1]

It is doubtful, however, whether Wrangel's opinion was shared by many of his brother officers – or, at least, those outside the Caucasian Army. To most of the Whites Tsaritsyn had been a triumph for anti-Bolshevik arms that presaged still greater victories in the future. They did not realise how hard-fought the battle had been, or how over-extended were their lines of communication. Nor, seemingly, did they reflect on the fate of Admiral Kolchak's three-pronged advance earlier in the year. 'To Moscow' carried more conviction than any slogan that the Whites devised before or after it. *Osvag*, the White propaganda organisation, blazoned the words across their posters. For many Whites, the belief that this goal would be attained became the first article of their faith.

But Denikin was drifting. He committed himself to the Moscow policy because it seemed to fulfil an emotional need, not because it was sound from a military point of view. When he

---

[1] Wrangel, *Memoirs*, p. 89.

tried to justify his actions his reasoning became confused and superficial. The nature of the process that now received his blessing was revealed by an incident that took place at the same time as the final assault on Tsaritsyn. General Shkuro, operating in the east, seized the Dnieper town of Ekaterinoslav without reference to Denikin. By doing so he was, in fact, contravening a caveat from the C-in-C, to the effect that commanders should not extend the White front without specific orders. But once Shkuro was in Ekaterinoslav there seemed no point in not taking advantage of his move, and the next step was a crossing of the Dnieper in order to protect the town against counter-attack.

Denikin had committed himself to a process of continual expansion. For this he produced some remarkable justifications, including an assertion that 'by expanding our front-line over hundreds of kilometres we became not weaker, but stronger'.[1] This defence he based on the assumption that by capturing more territory the Whites increased the size of their recruiting base. What he omitted to mention was the poor quality of recruits thus brought within the White fold; the very fact that they had not found their way south was evidence of their lack of interest in the conflict that played around them with the sliding and ephemeral fury of summer lightning. Once forced to the colours they would be adequate enough soldiers whilst the White successes lasted, but no faith could be placed in their behaviour in times of adversity or retreat.

Denikin was not oblivious of the need for internal organisation, and he ordered that the *zemstvo* administration should be set in motion once again. But it could not be recreated from nothing; the salaries offered to officials were tiny and, since corruption had always been an integral part of any Russian system of government, the sums offered served only as an incitement. The organisation of a police force was fraught with similar difficulties, and Denikin was unwilling to divert arms from the front in order to equip his gendarmerie.

The consequence, as can be imagined, was the complete disorganisation of the rear. Behind Denikin's sprawling front, now longer than Kolchak's had been in April, there was no

---

[1] Denikin, *Ocherki russkoy smuty*, V, p. 118.

consolidation. There was no civilian, no politician, to whom he could hand over responsibility for the land he controlled; nor had he advisers who understood what needed to be done. He might well have lamented, with the Emperor of Azania: 'If I had *one* man by me whom I could trust . . . a man of progress and culture'. So long as Denikin persisted in his general attitude to politics there was no chance of such an assistant coming to his aid. Consequently there was little certainty or security behind his lines. Several different forms of currency were in circulation; the exchange rates fluctuated with the news from the front. The appearance of a Military Mission, and the chance of obtaining foreign exchange, would produce an immediate and enormous rise in prices. Speculation thrived; the speculators were to be seen everywhere within White-held territory and 'wherever they went they sowed corruption and confusion. Thus, for example, when trucks were wanted to carry urgent military stores to the Front, they were never to be found; nevertheless, you heard of plenty of trucks going up the line full of speculators' wares.'[1] Many of the railway employees worked in close collaboration with these speculators, and all the railway officials took bribes as a matter of course. Meanwhile the townspeople in the White area were often close to starvation, dependent on the army for food and obliged, if they wished to survive, to take the utmost pains with every scrap they were given. One English journalist reflected, grimly, that 'if ever the extravagant English working classes find themselves in a similar position their sufferings will be dreadful'.[2]

The peasants were comparatively well-fed; not unnaturally, they persisted in hoarding grain, thus forcing prices still higher. Denikin hoped to align them with the Whites through the proclamation of a new land policy. But this was not a success. The Bolsheviks had promised so much on which they had later reneged that the peasants were distrustful of both parties. Denikin's policy was, on the whole, equitable – though it was hard to see how he was going to enforce it. But there was one clause in it that created uproar amongst the peasants, and totally obscured what good there was in his plan. This was a provision ensuring that a small amount of the land owned by the dispossessed land-

[1] Bechhofer, *In Denikin's Russia*, p. 79.
[2] Hodgson, *With Denikin's Armies*, p. 79.

owners was to be returned to them: this was to be sufficient to ensure them a living, no more. It satisfied neither peasants nor landowners. The former saw the clause as a loophole which would enable the landlords to reclaim all the acreage of their old estates; the latter saw the policy as a weak-kneed attempt to conciliate the peasants. Neither side was satisfied, and the peasants not only suspected White motives, but also made a point of staying on their land to ensure its safety. This did not make for easy recruiting. Eventually Denikin was forced to settle for an uneasy compromise: the matter was to be 'dealt with by the Constituent Assembly'; meanwhile, the peasants were regarded as leaseholders. This decision was still more disastrous.

Vodka was as much a scourge of the soldiery as it had been at any time in Russian history. Denikin had forbidden it, but it was everywhere available; during cold weather, if it was absent, soldiers had no hesitation in drinking the anti-freeze fluid intended for tank and lorry radiators. The Reds had the same problem, but solved it both by proceeding against offenders with more ruthlessness, and by making it a matter of communal responsibility. As one provincial Soviet had resolved the previous year: 'Commissars of temperance . . . are to be elected from those who completely abstain from drink. In case no teetotaler can be found, it is permissible to elect a drinking man.'[1]

But it was in their treatment of the Jews that the Whites were at their most inconsequentially brutal. The Jews were the traditional scapegoats; now they were widely believed to be directly responsible for the spread of Bolshevism. The combination of hallowed prejudice with the certain knowledge that several prominent members of the Bolshevik party were of Jewish origin was irresistible. It was widely asserted that Lenin was a Jew, that all commissars were Jews, and that all speculators were Jews. The first two propositions were demonstrably untrue, though they were widely believed by those who should have known better, including Englishmen.[2] The final proposition, though it was no doubt as statistically inaccurate as the preceding assertion, had rather more to it. In a country with a proportionally tiny middle

---

[1] Resolution of the Zargopodsky Soviet. Quoted in Bunyan, *Intervention, Civil War, and Communism in Russia*, p. 556.
[2] E.g., General Knox. See page 245.

class, where trade had been inhibited by both government monopolies and religious objections to usury, it was inevitable that many of the merchants and middlemen should be of Jewish stock. It was equally inevitable that many of these should make full use of the greatest opportunity for an untramelled pursuit of the profit motive that south Russia had ever offered.

The situation was complicated by guilt and fear. The inhabitants of south Russia knew what they had done to the Jews in the past; and they gathered that the Bolsheviks were, if not wholly Jewish, at least pro-Jewish. They therefore assumed that the Jews would support the Reds, and did not believe that they would attempt to come to terms with their former persecutors. So, if Jews remained in the south, they obviously did so from the most dubious of motives, and the whole cycle of pogroms and terror was repeated. There was no escape for either party. Denikin himself was not anti-Semitic, and he issued orders forbidding pogroms and threatening the most severe penalties for those who took part in them. But the terror went on, and the punishments were not enforced; Cossack units were particularly to blame.

Reaction in Allied countries, aroused by the reports of Jewish sympathisers, was distinctly unfavourable. Churchill adjured the C-in-C via the Military Mission, that 'it is of the very highest consequence that General Denikin should not only do everything in his power to prevent massacres of the Jews in the liberated districts, but should issue a proclamation against anti-Semitism'.[1] This had long since been done, but the tone of the document was prevaricatory, and there is no indication that many copies left headquarters. In the burning, dry summer of 1919 the vicious and merciless pogroms continued. They were not limited to the White territories: despite the pleas of Trotsky and other Soviet leaders, Jews and gentiles alike, a similar persecution was taking place in many areas which the Red Army occupied.

It was with full knowledge of all these matters that Wrangel opposed Denikin's plans for a late summer and autumn advance. He understood the fatuity of the C-in-C's talk about 'advancing on big lines now', and 'using large scale maps'. But he could not bring himself to resign, and it is dubious whether Denikin would

---

[1] Churchill to Denikin, 18 September 1919. Quoted Churchill, *Aftermath*, p. 255.

have accepted his resignation had he offered it. When the C-in-C left Tsaritsyn, Wrangel returned to work. The only thing to raise his spirits was that Chatilov had been appointed his Chief-of-Staff.

From this time on the Whites in the south were to be grouped in two factions: those who were for Wrangel and those who were for Denikin. Denikin came to believe that a systematic campaign was launched against him by his subordinate, and that Wrangel deliberately circulated letters which undermined his authority. This does not seem to be true, nor does Wrangel seem to have known of it; what appears to have happened is that junior officers, dissatisfied with Denikin's conduct of the war, exploited and distorted the disagreements between the two men. By now Denikin was running the staff on entirely authoritarian lines. There was no open discussion of the merits and demerits of his own plans, since the C-in-C would not brook criticism. Wrangel, convinced of Denikin's folly, circulated papers on the strategic situation to his own staff in the Caucasian Army – mainly because the army was affected, very closely, by Denikin's plans. It was these documents which were used to create dissent.

Tsarist Russia, as it has been pointed out at the beginning of this book, was in many ways close to a great military academy, and Russian military academies were close to schools. If we are to understand the intrigues that divided the Whites from this time on, we must think of the way in which gossip and scandal spread in an authoritarian educational establishment. So it happened in Denikin's armies, indirectly but insidiously. Matters were complicated by political, rather than military, disagreements. The extreme right was automatically anti-Denikin; finding that Wrangel had been established as an unofficial leader of the opposition, and imagining from the circumstances of his background – for he came from a family that was German in origin – that he would support their proposed appeal to Germany for aid, they gave him their unwanted allegiance. Yet Wrangel was far from sharing their political opinions, and himself looked to Britain for increased support. With members of the British Mission he got on well; this added to Denikin's suspicions, since the Mission made no secret of the fact that it adhered to Wrangel's strategic views in preference to the C-in-C's, and Denikin assumed that they were involved in the 'conspiracy' against him.

After the fall of Tsaritsyn Wrangel enjoyed only limited military success. He was beset by troubles in the Kuban, his main recruiting base, which was still agitating for autonomy. Denikin's decision to move headquarters to Taganrog, on the Don estuary, made Ekaterinodar a centre for factionalism and nationalist agitation. Trouble in the Kuban soon spread to the Caucasus, where the Muslim tribes rose; these were the first symptoms of the steady demoralisation of the rear.

At first Wrangel's troops advanced from Tsaritsyn with considerable speed. But they soon began to meet opposition, and Wrangel decided to do everything in his power to hasten the fortification of Tsaritsyn. The wisdom of this became apparent when his forces, over-extended and without the reinforcements that were so urgently needed, received the brunt of a Red counter-attack in mid-August. They retreated slowly on the town, which was soon suffering its second siege of the last three months. Wrangel attempted to evacuate the civilian population; but this effort was hampered by the profiteering of the railway employees – who sold train seats at enormous prices – and by the greed of wealthy individuals, who bought up space in order to remove their possessions. Trains that should have been carrying munitions were used instead to carry those who could afford the prices demanded by the railway staff. Wrangel's method of dealing with the problem was characteristic. Accompanied by Cossacks of his bodyguard he drove to the station and had pianos, mirrors and furniture thrown out of the carriages and destroyed. On discovering the basis on which the station-master and his employees were conducting the evacuation, Wrangel had the offending officials arrested, court-martialled, and hanged within the day.

The military situation continued to deteriorate. Soon the Reds were within artillery range of the town, and began to bombard the suburbs. A regiment made up of Red deserters decided to repeat its performance, and deserted back again; only the prompt action of a Kuban cavalry unit prevented a breakthrough. To many it looked as though the Whites could not hold out for long, and steps were taken to evacuate headquarters. Wrangel moved up to the front intending, if he had to retreat, to go with his men. On 5 September the position at Tsaritsyn was at its most acute; somehow the White troops managed to beat off the enemy assault; at the critical moment Wrangel launched an out-flanking move by the cavalry. There were three days of fierce fighting as the Reds were driven slowly back, and then the enemy temporarily broke off the battle. Wrangel had captured 18,000 prisoners and 31 guns, and he had cleared the immediate vicinity of the town. But the Reds, though defeated, were not broken; the town was saved, but the Soviets continued to exert pressure and to prevent Wrangel from making any convincing advance.

After he had visited Wrangel in the newly captured Tsaritsyn, Denikin moved to the northern front and inspected progress there. At Kharkov he was received by jubilant crowds and encouraging reports from the front line. All of this confirmed him in his optimism. He spent much time on the railways now; this became curiously symptomatic of his outlook. His staff set themselves up in railway carriages, often luxuriously appointed. Thus they were seldom in one place for long, despite the titular presence of H.Q. at Taganrog; they were not geographically tied down, with a territory to defend; they were always on the way somewhere. On a railway – even on a Russian railway – there is no standing still for long; you are either advancing or retreating. Denikin's travels helped to further the divide between his strategic aims and the reality of holding territory; moreover, when a crisis developed, it was frequently some time before he could be contacted, for he was often neither at the front nor at Headquarters but in between. The position of his coach on the railway was a thermometer of White success or failure.

Now he was committing himself to further fan-wise expansion. By this time the Polish situation had resolved itself, and the Poles were at war with Russia. The presence of the pianist Paderewski as Prime Minister lent, in the eyes of some Whites, a certain comic-opera atmosphere to the régime; but they were soon to discover that their assessment of its strength was wrong. Under the command of Pilsudski the Poles made considerable progress against Soviet troops, and their army was rapidly emerging as the most powerful single fighting force in the whole Russian cauldron. Pilsudski's aim was a confederation of east European states, dominated by Poland, directed at containing both the westward expansion of Russia, and the eastwards expansion of Germany. There was, he considered, a moral vacuum in east Europe which

Poland was destined to fill. This he proposed to do 'with a re-volver in my hand'.

His initial thrust was against Petlyura's forces – yet another complication in the Ukrainian tangle – but he also became involved with the Bolsheviks to the east. Reports of the fighting filtered through to Denikin, whose interest in a potential link was quickened when representatives of the Allied Missions expressed their hope that the Poles might be persuaded to co-operate with the Whites. Denikin was not to know that the expectations of the military were far more sanguine than those of their respective governments. Since Pilsudski was dependent on the Allies for his supplies of munitions, they were able to make him fall in with their suggestions to an extent that surprised those who remembered some of 'The Tiger's' more extrava-gantly anti-Russian pronouncements; but they did not achieve their primary aim. Pilsudski mistrusted Denikin and, perhaps more seriously, he mistrusted the Whites' military position. Had he been in the White camp he would probably have been regarded as one of Wrangel's fellow pessimists. For a moment he stalled the entreaties that reached him; Denikin, nevertheless, felt that if he could manage to link up with the Poles, then Pilsudski's doubts might be resolved. He therefore mounted an offensive on Kiev, thus committing his troops to an advance across territory which was dominated by Makhno's guerrilla bands.

In August Denikin's left wing pushed on up the Dnieper towards Kiev. It was captured on 30 August, just as one of Petlyura's units came on it from the south. The Allies, not content with their scheme to unite Pilsudski and Denikin, were also attempting to promote an alliance between Petlyura and Denikin. They were foolish to imagine that any of those who supported the idea of a Greater Russia would come to terms with the Ukrainian separatists, particularly those who shared Petlyura's political background and views. Petlyura's troops, the Gaydamaks, were notable for their extraordinary efforts to recreate a national dress: 'Meeting a Gaydamak in the street, people rubbed their eyes and stared – was it a soldier in uniform or an actor in disguise?'[1] But their fighting qualities were not remarkable,

---

[1] Paustovsky, *In That Dawn*, p. 132.

though they were to cause enough trouble when they operated as guerrillas. The Petlyurists, whom the Whites now found laying claim to the city, were no exception to the rule. As soon as they had sufficient troops in Kiev the Whites attacked Petlyura's men with a cavalry charge which continued right through the centre of the city. The Petlyurists fled; their sole act of retaliation, once they were safely away from the town, being to loose off a dozen shells 'in the general direction of Kiev. But there were no casualties, unless you count a wrecked ice-cream cart on Vladimir Hill, and one ear knocked by a shell-splinter off the plaster statue of either St Methodius or St Cyril.'[1]

Having made his drive on Kiev, it seemed to Denikin that it was incumbent on him to secure his rear. In order to do this he landed, with Allied assistance, a force of Whites at Odessa, and proceeded to attempt the recapture of the territory that had been occupied in the course of the French fiasco. The landing was accomplished successfully, Odessa pacified – not a difficult operation with Allied battleships standing off-shore – and expeditions sent out towards the main towns in the area. Superficially, it was a successful move. But it kept a large number of men tied down, and bands of Petlyurists, Bolsheviks, Makhnovites and guerrillas – who generally claimed to support one or other of upwards of twenty Atamans – roamed the countryside.

In August the results of the Red reorganisation became apparent. Kamenev, a former Imperial Army colonel and the new commander of the Red armies in the south, was a Stalin appointee. He had carried out the necessary regrouping with considerable skill and effectiveness, and he launched a general counter-offensive against the White front. The serious situation in which this put Wrangel we have already seen. But what was not clear to Wrangel at the time, nor to Denikin, was that this was the main thrust. The move against Tsaritsyn was the consequence of serious thought, on Kamenev's part, about Denikin's strategic position; if the Reds could retake the town, then the danger of a link with Kolchak or with the Urals Cossacks was over, and the lines of communication between the White armies and the Caucasus might be threatened once again. Trotsky,

---

[1] Paustovsky, *In That Dawn*, p. 174.

however, felt that the attack should have been directed at Denikin's northern front, the main target being the recapture of the Donets basin. This, Trotsky argued, though less attractive on paper than the Tsaritsyn plan, would be far more likely to succeed from the political point of view. The debate was the occasion of what threatened to become a serious split between Trotsky and the Politbureau. He proposed to resign as Commissar of War, and only Lenin's entreaties persuaded him to retain the post. But, after the attack on Tsaritsyn had failed, it became apparent that Trotsky had been right. Kamenev's troops attacked with vigour all along the line, but nowhere did they meet with success, for their main concentration had broken against Tsaritsyn. Suddenly, Denikin began to feel his opponent's weakness.

It was made apparent when, in late August, General Mamontov raided north to Tambov. He had under his command 8,000 picked Cossacks, mounted on the best horses that the Don could provide. They moved too fast for the enemy to be able to concentrate a force and bring them to battle, and they did havoc to the enemy lines of communication, cutting them anything between fifty and a hundred miles behind the front line. They destroyed enemy dumps of munitions and supplies in the rear areas, and finally occupied Tambov at a cost of only twenty men. Mamontov narrowly missed capturing Trotsky in the town; however, he compensated for this by sending to their homes or drafting into his own ranks 20,000 Red recruits whom he had found mustered at the depot there. He then raided Kozlov and the Red Army H.Q.: the staff escaped only at the very last moment. In September he returned to White territory, and was greeted with rapturous acclaim. Denikin now saw that if the adventure was repeated on a larger scale, even Moscow could be threatened. But Mamontov had inflicted no lasting damage on the Reds, mainly because his Cossacks preferred concentrating on bringing their loot home in safety to making the surprise attack on the rear of the Soviet Eighth and Ninth Armies that was the original intention behind their mission.

Not only had a major opportunity been thrown away, but a large number of good fighting men had been absent from the front line at a time when they would have been doing far better service there than by gallivanting around the countryside with Mamontov. Denikin knew this, but he could not stop it, and the wider possibilities of the expedition continued to fascinate him.

Summer ended in the south with the illusory triumph of Mamontov's raid and a temporary lull in the fighting. Men on both sides, but more particularly Cossacks fighting for the Whites, left the front line to get in their harvest, without which there would be no food for the winter. For a week it seemed as though both Reds and Whites were involved in a tactical Dutch auction, each side waiting for the other to be so weakened that they could successfully strike. But soon the recruits came or were herded back. Denikin, who had seen through his carriage windows the stubble-fields of some of the richest grain-producing provinces in Russia, now within his lines, began to issue orders for an autumn offensive.

To the north and east of Tsaritsyn Kolchak's forces were, by mid-May, in continuous retreat. The gap between the two armies had been little more than four hundred miles; if we include the activities of Dutov's Cossacks, then the distance was still less. But, after the fall of Ufa on 9 June, Kolchak's armies had lost any hope of recovering the lost ground. This was not at first obvious, and the Military Missions were divided on the issue. Whilst many of the Allied officers saw clearly what was happening, some persisted in the hope that reinforcements from the troops who had undergone the British training course might still stem the Soviet tide. Other plans were mooted, such as the formation of 'Anglo-Russian' regiments – officered by the British – and of shock detachments of Czech Volunteers. None of these units proved viable. But in May there could still be optimism about their outcome, and the overall picture was consequently misread. Another factor contributing to this error was that the chain reaction of retreats along the front, as commander after commander felt that his flank was exposed, took time to have its full effect; the position of Gajda, to the north, seemed misleadingly advantageous.

The Czechs were still a major problem. Their evacuation was no simple matter; it needed detailed planning and would require the co-operation of the other Allied nations. For various reasons the Allies were reluctant to take the step of shipping them home; something *might* happen in Siberia, they felt, to make them regret that the Czechs were no longer there. Churchill, whose tenacity was as marked in 1919 as at any other time in his life, tried to evolve ways of getting the Czechs out via either Archangel or Tsaritsyn, with a preference for the former route; but these schemes came to nothing. Meanwhile the Czechs were used to protect the Trans-Siberian Railway, and rapidly discovered that this put them in a position with considerable commercial poten-'ial. They did not, in general, attempt to emulate the methods of Semenov; but they nevertheless managed to exploit a position not dissimilar to his. Soon they were operating businesses, both of a legal and an illegal nature, and incurring the enmity of the native Siberians, who came to regard them much as the peasants of south Russia regarded the Jews. It was the behaviour of the Czechs, rather than any sense of political conviction, that accelerated the growth of anti-White partisan bands in Siberia. Throughout the summer these grew in number; trains on the Trans-Siberian carried armed men on the footplate and machine-guns on the carriage platforms. Behind the lines an atmosphere of tension became daily more marked. In the initial stages of his rule Kolchak had commanded, if not the heartfelt approbation of his subjects, at least the qualified assent of the greater part of them. Now he could no longer rely on that.

Yet there were great areas of Siberia which the war seemed hardly to have touched. In many self-sufficient peasant communities the conscription squads were only a distant rumour, and in small provincial towns life continued much as it had done in Tsarist times, the most significant feature of the war being the lack of one or two useful commodities and confusions about the currencies in vogue. Pasternak, in *Doctor Zhivago*, makes us aware of something which a concentration on the military conflict obscures – that for many Siberians, living in small and isolated communities away from the central artery of the railway, the war was peripheral.

In late May the Allied Supreme Council had telegraphed to Kolchak offering *de facto* recognition if he would give them certain assurances about his aims and intentions. Some of these points coincided with Kolchak's avowed policy, of which the

Allies must have been aware since November of the previous year; others showed the influence of Woodrow Wilson, and of Lloyd George's susceptibility to British public opinion, since they were designed to ensure that Kolchak gave a properly democratic tone to his régime. Kolchak's answer was carefully calculated to soothe liberal feelings; not for nothing had Churchill instructed General Knox to initiate the Admiral into the mysteries of Western political euphemisms. The Allies accepted his assurances, thus seeming to commit themselves to Kolchak's support at just the time when the Military Missions were beginning to take the opposite view.

The White retreat was accompanied by a wave of desertions; a British officer observed, apropos the fate of the equipment his country was dispensing: 'the uniforms walked over to the Reds, thousands at a time, with the Whites inside them'.[1] The fall of Ufa was precipitated by the mutiny of a Ukrainian regiment, who murdered their officers in the manner made traditional in 1917, and went over to the enemy. It was the shortest way home. Even amongst the British-trained troops led by General (formerly Colonel) Kappel there was a high incidence of desertions. Yet Kappel was one of the few able commanders whom Kolchak possessed; he directed the withdrawal of his troops himself, and refused the privileges that could have been his, saying that his place was with his men. But the example of even a hundred able officers would not have been enough whilst disunity prevailed amongst the high command at Omsk. Gajda remained as intractable as ever, recklessly optimistic despite the fact that the main Soviet thrust was now to the north-east, on Perm, and threatened to isolate his army completely. Whilst he was assuring the Allied representatives – with whom he liked to imagine that he had established a special relationship – that he could hold his front, his forces were already in undisciplined retreat.

It was widely hoped, with some justification, that Kolchak would be able to hold the line of the Urals. Once more the enthusiasts for an independent Siberia – which, they argued, could be as self-sufficient as the isolated peasant communities in its forests and tundras – began to urge their point of view.

---

[1] McCullagh, *A Prisoner of the Reds*, p. 67.

But, whilst they reckoned with the strategic strength of the mountains, they neglected to take into consideration the weakness of the men who were expected to hold them. I. I. Vatzetis, Trotsky's appointment as Soviet C-in-C, although he had daily reports on Kolchak's troops, found it impossible to believe that Kolchak would not hold the Urals in strength or, alternatively, mass his forces on the other side in order to trap the Reds as they emerged from the passes. Kamenev, who at this time was commanding on the eastern front, disagreed; he believed that he could inflict a crushing defeat on Kolchak if he followed him into Siberia, and refused to accept Vatzetis' argument. Being in closer touch with the front, he was the more easily able to feel Kolchak's weakness, and was determined not to be diverted from his objective. Trotsky, aware of the situation in the south, sided with Vatzetis, and dismissed Kamenev from the eastern command. The commissars on the eastern front, who supported Kamenev, enlisted Stalin's support, and through him persuaded Lenin to reinstate their commander.

In the event, Kamenev's arguments were proved correct. To the south a White division, cut off by Kamenev's thrust from Samara and now threatened by Bolshevik forces moving up from Astrakhan, where they had been driven by Wrangel, surrendered *en masse*. Dutov's Cossacks were forced to retreat from the Urals; the drive on Perm continued. Gajda, aware of his danger now, ceased sending his totally misleading situation reports, and began to clamour for help. Kolchak, who had believed Gajda when he said that he was holding the Reds and even advancing, now realised that he had been deceived, and refused him reinforcements.

The only move that Kolchak made to redeem the situation which could have had any hope of success was, at the same time, fundamentally unrealistic. On 23 June he telegraphed to Mannerheim, in a desperate effort to persuade the Regent of Finland to attack St Petersburg. The idea was attractive to Mannerheim, particularly as a Soviet defeat would enable the Finns to consolidate their position in eastern Karelia. But Kolchak's message, for all its urgency, was deliberately prevaricatory about the one basic issue – that of White willingness to recognise an independent Finland. So long as there was any uncertainty about this issue Mannerheim, for all his hatred of the Bolsheviks, could not and would not contemplate military action that might aid the White cause. In his reply he made this quite clear; and, though the Allies toyed with the scheme and its implications for another month or so, it had been doomed from the start.

Kamenev, who had now routed both Gajda and Khanzin, divided his forces and ordered them to advance along the two branches of the Trans-Siberian Railway that ran across the Urals – the northern branch being the St Petersburg line, and the southern branch coming from Moscow and the south. The two branches, it should be noted, join at Omsk.

The Whites, in their turn, attempted to establish positions on the railways. Fortifications should have been built to cover the areas long before, but despite an Allied plan providing for these, no work had been done. In late June and early July Tukhachevsky began to infiltrate his men across the Urals through the smaller and higher passes and, after regrouping, moved onto the White positions from the rear. The incident was to be highly coloured in subsequent Soviet accounts of the action, but there was little that was 'secret' about the paths that the Reds used to cross the mountains; the Whites had left many obvious routes uncovered and unwatched.

Tukhachevsky's appearance in the White rear increased the demoralisation, and on 13 July the town of Zlatoust, the key to the southern branch of the Trans-Siberian, fell to the Reds. Kolchak was desperate now; the day before he had dismissed General Gajda from his post both as commander of the Northern Army and as C-in-C of the Urals front. His dismissal must be regarded more as a consequence of Kolchak's inability to judge subordinates than as a reflection on his own lack of the qualities necessary for his post. After a long and vitriolic interview with the Admiral, which accounted for an ink bottle and several pens, Gajda left for Vladivostok, machine-guns prominently mounted on his train to guard against attack. He not only feared Semenov and partisans, but was fully prepared for treachery on the part of Kolchak.

Kolchak replaced him with General Dieterichs, a straight-forward and able officer who realised that the first priority was reorganisation of the rear, and suggested withdrawal behind one of the various rivers that flow north and south between the Urals and Omsk. Unfortunately for the Whites, he was overruled by Lebedev. Lebedev was fascinated by anything complex, whether in the field of intrigue or of warfare. Though quite unequipped for the realisation of his plans, he drew up a project for a voluntary withdrawal from Chelyabinsk, followed by an assault on the town from the flank and the rear as soon as the Reds had entered. The loss of Ekaterinburg on 14 July made Kolchak ready to try anything. On 27 July the first part of Lebedev's plan came off successfully; the Reds entered Chelyabinsk. The second part was a total failure; the Reds not only held onto the town, but decimated the White forces, including the last of Kolchak's reserves.

Lebedev was dismissed, and Dieterichs succeeded him. The constant changes amongst the senior officers added to the disarray of the Whites. Not that Lebedev should not have been dismissed – but, as in the case of Gajda, he should not have been appointed in the first place. The fall of Chelyabinsk meant that all hope of regaining the Urals had now to be abandoned. But its implications went further than this. In London Lord Curzon, the acting Foreign Secretary, received the news, whereupon 'he scrawled in blue pencil across the message: "A lost cause"'.[1]

This signified, for practical purposes, the end of British aid to Kolchak. It was a decision with which General Knox was in full accord. The General still retained considerable personal sympathy for Kolchak, but he had no patience with any of his staff. It was his opinion that they had 'learned nothing', and in this he echoed comments made by Ironside in Archangel, Holman in the south, and at least two of the British representatives in the north-west. And it is certainly true that in 1919 White officers appeared far more reactionary than they had done in the preceding year. Civil strife inevitably encourages extremist attitudes, and when this becomes armed conflict the possibility of conciliation and moderation is lost. But this, in itself, is not sufficient to explain White behaviour, which seems far more likely to have been a consequence of the despair born of defeat.

Dieterichs, his reserves squandered by Lebedev, drew back to

---

[1] Ullman, *Britain and the Russian Civil War*, p. 207.

the line of the Tobol river in order to regroup. He then discovered that he had only some 50,000 troops left to him. He
therefore retreated further, to the River Ishim, a more easily
defensible front, but only a bare hundred and fifty miles from
Omsk. There the Whites remained, their front line fluctuating
from time to time, but with the fighting staying more or less at
the level of skirmishes, until late September. Kamenev had been
called to face the far more impendent situation on the southern
front, where he proved that his strategy was not always better
than Trotsky's. The Reds had regained the Urals and the industrial plant that was so vital to them: by September trains loaded
with the products of these factories, in one of which Pasternak
had worked during the German war, were drawing away from
the mountains that he had described as 'pushing their hands
against the night'. Forced back half-way across the western
Siberian plain, the Whites continued their intrigues, whilst
Kolchak brooded and Dieterichs tried frantically to recruit
amongst a population whose sole desire was to keep out of the
war.

Though the Whites' position in Siberia was weak, they were
at least able to take comfort in the news from the Baltic. There
the Northern Corps had emerged as a serious threat to the Soviet
Seventh Army, responsible for the defence of St Petersburg and
the north-west. On 13 May the combined forces of the Northern
Corps and the Estonian Army began an offensive. The Northern
Corps was no more than 16,000 strong, and the Estonians numbered about 20,000; the Reds were at least 50,000 strong. But
the Whites were not excessively concerned; morale in the Red
Army was weak, and there was a steady flow of deserters.

The objectives of the advance were confused; the Estonians
were chiefly concerned to capture as much territory as would
enable them to bargain satisfactorily with the rulers of Russia –
Soviet or White – and ensure their independence. Some of the
Estonians, however, took the concept of independence to its
logical conclusion. Along the Baltic coast the order of the states,
from south to north, is: Lithuania, Latvia, Estonia. In 1914 all
three countries still maintained, despite centuries of Russian rule,
a tradition of national independence. But in the sixteenth century,

before the Russians had held the Baltic coast in feu, there had been a further territorial entity, known as Ingermanland.[1] Such was the force of Baltic nationalism that in 1919 there were those who seriously argued for the independence of Ingermanland, and were able to exercise a perceptible influence on Estonian counsels. That there was a regiment of Ingermanlanders in the Estonian Army gave point to their claims.

The Whites' motives were less involved. They needed territory, which would ease their humiliating dependence on the Estonians, and they cherished the more ambitious aim of an attack on St Petersburg. But the first move made by Rodzyanko's force was to the south and east, and its most spectacular consequence was the almost immediate capture of Pskov, which was firmly in White hands by 25 May. The movement was aided by British naval actions in the Baltic. Though these were not, as yet, co-ordinated with the army's movements, they did mean that the Whites could feel reasonably certain of the security of their Baltic flank. The Whites not only succeeded in capturing territory, but also found themselves aided by considerable reinforcements in the form of deserters; by mid-June they were 25,000 strong.

It was some little while before Rodzyanko realised just how poor in quality the Red Army troops opposing him actually were. He had no detailed knowledge of the extent to which, when the threat from the north-west had seemed negligible, the Soviet command had depleted the force with continual demands for drafts to act as cadres on the eastern or the southern fronts. Such intelligence as Rodzyanko did receive came via the White underground in St Petersburg. This continued to operate, despite an intensive campaign by the Cheka. But an intelligence organisation as hard pressed as the St Petersburg underground at that time is unlikely to be efficient; the information reaching Rodzyanko was generally fragmentary and often confused.

The same situation obtained in the Red camp. Having captured Pskov and Yamburg, Rodzyanko was content to restrict his forward operations and attempt to consolidate his gains – a policy with which his superior, Yudenich, was in favour. But the

---

[1] See map, p. 301.

Reds still imagined that he was conducting a full-scale advance on St Petersburg. This was not so; he was, as yet, entirely unprepared for such action, and he wished to establish new bases, clear of Estonia, before making his next move. Yet it was this assumption that conditioned the Soviet response, together with

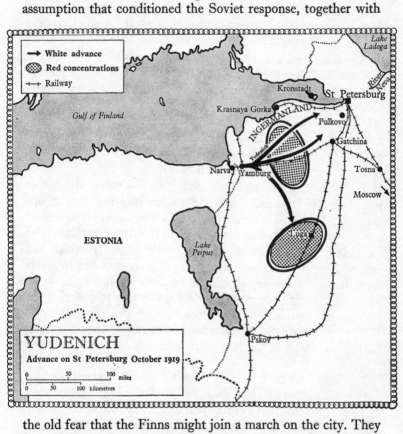

the old fear that the Finns might join a march on the city. They were confirmed in this latter suspicion by the frequency of Yudenich's visits to Helsingfors, though he was meeting with no co-operation there.

In order to redeem the 'threatened' city, Stalin was sent to St Petersburg. He sent out frantic demands for reinforcements, deliberately and unnecessarily short-circuiting the normal chain of command, and descended on Red Army units in the vicinity of the city demanding the instant court-martial of 'counter-revolutionary' elements. The immediate consequence of his behaviour was to convince many of the inhabitants of St Petersburg that the situation was far more serious than was the case, and to force those who had toyed with the idea of deserting to make their decision at once. On 13 June the garrisons of two forts guarding the western approaches to the city, Krasnaya Gorka and Seraya Loshad, went over to the Whites.

Krasnaya Gorka and Seraya Loshad were artillery forts built to command the southern entrance to the bay of St Petersburg. They mounted heavy guns with which, though they were not able to range the city itself, they could drop shells into Kronstadt, the great Baltic naval base where the Red fleet was now lying behind the protection of the chain of forts that guarded the entrance to the bay. The mutineers announced their new allegiance by opening up against Kronstadt.

The Red response was immediate, but their first attempt to recapture the forts failed when Estonian Ingermanland troops came up from the south-west. Stalin then decided upon an assault on the forts from the sea, and ordered that the two battleships *Petropavlovsky* and *Andrey Perovzvanny*, which had cleared Kronstadt harbour after being slightly damaged by shells from Krasnaya Gorka, should be used to bombard the forts. Meanwhile the Estonian commander was trying to prevail upon Rodzyanko to reinforce the units holding the forts, but the Whites, resenting the interference of the Ingermanlanders, and having no troops in the immediate vicinity, refused to come to their aid.

The forts were built to cover the entrance to St Petersburg bay, not to resist an attack from ships already in the bay. On the night of 15-16 June Krasnaya Gorka fell, and Seraya Loshad not long after. The fighting continued the next day and cost the Bolsheviks a cruiser – the *Oleg*, which had replaced the two battleships as a support vessel, and was sunk by a British torpedo-boat. It is instructive to note that there was no official state of war between Britain and the Soviet government, and that Lieutenant Agar who accomplished the feat was operating neither as an 'instructor' nor as a volunteer, but directly under the orders of Rear-Admiral Walter Cowan, British officer commanding in the Baltic.

This victory came too late; the Estonians, together with the survivors from the two garrisons, withdrew from the area of the forts. Stalin considered that he had won a major victory, which if it was not yet famous would certainly be made to appear so in the future, and on 18 June he executed 67 officers of the Kronstadt garrison in case the lesson of Krasnaya Gorka was insufficiently clear. He was already hard at work manufacturing that complex of lies and half-truths which, even today, mesmerises Soviet historians.

The 'conspiracy' was not so widespread an affair as Stalin imagined; the 67 Kronstadt officers had remained loyal when the base was shelled by Krasnaya Gorka, and for all that Stalin claimed to have documentary evidence of treachery, it had yet to be proven. He created the situation himself, and then had the satisfaction of clearing it up; in the process he made it appear as though the Whites seriously threatened St Petersburg in June. They did not; they were still finding themselves as a fighting force. But the lesson of Krasnaya Gorka was one that they were to bear in mind, for it exposed the weakness of the Reds.

Rodzyanko's refusal to aid the Ingermanlanders may not have been as foolish as it sounds: he had no forces to support such an attack. Its most serious effect was not that it left Krasnaya Gorka in the possession of the Reds, but that it intensified the quarrel between the Whites and the Estonians. One consequence of this was that when on 19 June von der Goltz attempted to further his policy for the eastern Baltic by leading his men against Estonian and Latvian troops quartered in the north of Latvia, the Estonians jumped to the conclusion that the Yudenich Whites – now known as the North-Western Army – were collaborating with him. They therefore refused all aid and assistance to Yudenich.

Pressure was put on him, through General Sir Hubert Gough, head of the Allied Military Mission to the Baltic States, to ensure that he would not negotiate with von der Goltz, and assistance was promised from Britain. Much to the anxiety of Gough, and the anger of the Russians, its arrival was delayed; though the North-Western Army was still increasing in numbers, it could undertake no further offensive action until it was properly equipped.

The interim period, whilst the Whites awaited the arrival of British aid, was occupied in political squabbling. Yudenich was an enigmatic figure; during the March Revolution, when he was commanding at Erzerum, he had played a waiting game, being careful not to commit himself to any particular party or faction. Yudenich must have seen just how precarious the revolution had made his position, for his brief accession of liberal sympathies was a façade. In 1919 he emerged as a decided reactionary. His capacity to drift, however, had not left him. Mannerheim, with whom he had abortive dealings about this time, recorded: 'To my surprise he struck me as physically slack and entirely lacking in those inspiring qualities which a political and military leader of his standing should possess.'[1] He had little control of his subordinates, and it was Rodzyanko who was the effective military leader. It was only with the greatest difficulty that Yudenich was persuaded to concede Estonian and Finnish national independence, without acknowledging which he could hardly expect to win St Petersburg. But Yudenich's word was not enough, particularly for the Estonians. The Estonians demanded a guarantee, and they wished it to come from a government, not an individual.

By now Gough was desperate; vital opportunities were being thrown away at a most critical time. Finally, in the words of a British official who was working closely with the head of the Allied Mission, 'General Gough decided to form a Russian Government'.[2] This he achieved on 8 August, by the simple expedient of summoning the members of Yudenich's Political Council to a meeting in the British Consulate at Reval, where they were addressed by his assistant, Brigadier-General Marsh. (Neither Gough nor Yudenich appeared at the meeting; it was probably as well from both their points of view.) The meeting opened at 6.15 p.m. Marsh informed the Political Council of the Estonian demands, pointed out that the Whites could achieve nothing without Estonian assistance, and then told them to 'stop talking and act'. The time, he remarked, was 6.20. If the Council had not formed a government by 7.00 p.m., he declared, they would be 'thrown aside'.[3]

---

[1] Mannerheim, *Memoirs*, p. 221.
[2] British Commissioner (Reval) to Curzon. *Documents on British Foreign Policy*, Series I, vol. III, no. 385.
[3] There is some dispute about Marsh's exact words. See Ullman, *Britain and the Russian Civil War*, p. 268.

Forty minutes of frenzied argument did not produce a government. But at least some of the groundwork was done, and on 14 August, after several more threats – the removal of Yudenich amongst them – agreement was reached. The White recognition of Estonia was grudging and qualified; but for the moment it had to serve. In the event it proved irrelevant; the Estonians became more interested in a peace with the Soviets, and Gough was severely reproved by his superiors for his high-handed behaviour. Yudenich was to return to the struggle alone. The episode had achieved nothing save the embitterment of the Whites, whose dealings with the British were largely restricted to complaints about the quantity of the war material of which they were now the ungrateful recipients.

They did the British scant justice. On the night of Sunday, 17 August, seven British torpedo-craft rendezvoused off the coast with another boat of the same class, commanded by Lieutenant Agar. Then the eight boats formed line and, piloted by Finnish smugglers, made their way through the chain of island forts that guarded the bay of St Petersburg. The sea was calm, the night cloudy, and there was the merest hint of a moon as they slipped by the black bulks of the forts. They did not pass undetected, for artillery opened up from two of the forts, but the guards cannot have understood what the boats were about, and no general alarm was raised. Once inside the bay the boats divided into two groups, and set course for their target – Kronstadt. Their aim was a direct assault on the Red fleet, which lay in the port. Kronstadt harbour was heavily defended, and had long been thought impregnable.

The attack went in under cover of an air raid; the R.A.F. were established on a secret airfield cleared in the Finnish forests, just as the torpedo-craft were based on the former St Petersburg Yacht Squadron, now in Finnish territory. The Red lookouts were totally distracted by the sensation of a night attack from the air, still a novelty in 1919. No such excuse exists for the Soviets' failure to put a boom across Kronstadt harbour, though the British were prepared to cope with one. Finding the way clear, they opened up their throttles and swept into the main harbour. Once inside their task was by no means easy; the harbour was only about half a square mile in area, and the turning circle of a

C.M.B. at full throttle was far too wide for a constant high speed to be maintained. Under heavy enemy fire the boats performed the manœuvres necessary if they were to get into position and loose their torpedoes. The outcome of their frenzied reversing and stopping of engines, with machine-guns as their only defence against the enemy in the meantime, was the sinking of the battle-ships *Petropavlovsky* and *Andrey Perovzvanny*, together with a destroyer and a submarine depot ship. British losses were three C.M.B.s with six officers and nine ratings killed, and three officers and six ratings captured. As Cowan put it in his speech to the survivors, the 'strongest naval fortress in the world' had been 'ravished and blasted' by a very small number of 'splendidly disciplined and dauntless Britons'.[1] The Red fleet had now practically ceased to exist, and there was no vessel with guns that might threaten any future Krasnaya Gorka or hinder an army marching along the coasts of the bay.

The Russians, White and Red, waited. The political squabbles went on, even though the time for a full-scale assault on St Petersburg was drawing near. The White officers were able enough, and the army that they were training promised well. But, to most observers, there seemed to be something lacking. Rodzyanko's Staff were described as 'dashing and brave and yet not quite serious . . . there was much heel-clicking and saluting, all done with a certain half-smiling air of detachment, like that of virtuosi playing a game they knew well'. These men, the commentator went on to say, behaved like the Russian officers who, at the beginning of the Great War, charged batteries on horse-back 'like knights in a tournament'; they were 'facing with the same amount of understanding the wild forces loose in their Russian world and the fanatic seriousness on the other side of the barricade. Most of them, or so it seemed, were still living in the Russia of 1914, and had learned and forgotten nothing.'[2] It was a comment that had often been made before.

---

[1] Bennett, *Cowan's War*, p. 157.
[2] Ruhl, *New Masters of the Baltic*, p. 92.

XV

Autumn and Winter

A peace-time traveller, making his way east on the Trans-Siberian Railway, might reflect on 'the hedgeless and forlorn plains' where 'man and his beasts were dwarfed to the merest microscopic toys, and each little group of figures seemed a pathetic, unavailing protest against the tyrant solitude'.[1] Few of the men who used the Trans-Siberian during the Civil War would have had the time or the inclination to express such feelings: yet the predominant impression, of the emptiness and the enormity of the Siberian plain, was one that almost everybody shared.

The railway was the ordering and unifying factor, giving dimension to the distances and, so long as the trains could get through from Vladivostok to Omsk, functioning as a lifeline for the armies entrenched on the Ishim line. At Omsk there was a certain amount of optimism amongst the officers at G.H.Q.; General Dieterichs was planning a counter-attack, and it was hoped to drive the Reds back to the River Tobol, if not to the Urals. But others were not so confident: on the *magistral*, the permanent way, trains travelling east were carrying the families of the wealthier White politicians and officers; on the *trakt*, the rough road running beside the line, peasants with their belongings loaded onto carts were also moving away from the direction of Omsk. The trains were heavily guarded, for the travellers went in fear of the partisan bands, some of which were five hundred strong: their desire for vengeance had been aroused by punitive expeditions sent from Omsk to those areas which had failed to produce the due quota of recruits.

In Omsk, as always, there were rumours: Dutov's Cossacks had broken out from the south and were coming to Dieterichs' aid; Red morale was weakening and their armies were inadequately

---

[1] Fleming, *One's Company*, p. 52.

supplied; Gajda was plotting to overthrow Kolchak from Vladivostok, all the Czechs were behind him, and he would institute a Social Revolutionary régime.

There was some truth in all of these rumours. The Orenburg Cossacks did break through to Petropavlovsk in September, a small and desperately tired army, worn out by their retreat across the steppes: they were of no military value. Dieterichs, who counter-attacked from Petropavlovsk at about the same time that the Cossacks arrived, did manage to drive the Reds back to the Tobol river, and found that his newly reorganised troops were possessed of better fighting qualities than those of the Reds. But the Reds had reserves, whilst Dieterichs was compelled to commit his whole strength, and he was unable to hold the line to which he advanced. The reduction of Allied aid meant that there were shortages in almost every field of supply, and the offensive had exhausted the Whites both physically and logistically. The Reds counter-attacked in their turn, and on 30 October they took Petropavlovsk. There seemed to be nothing that could stop them marching directly on Omsk.

Kolchak was determined to hold onto the town: in his opinion its fall would destroy what vestiges of credibility his régime retained. Dieterichs was in sharp disagreement: Omsk stood on the Urals bank of the River Irtysh, and hence was a poor defensive position; the obvious thing to do was to withdraw to the eastern bank and there to set up a new front line. When Kolchak refused to listen to Dieterichs' advice, the latter resigned and was replaced by Sakharov. Sakharov's chief boast was that he had led the Whites in their counter-attack to Tobol, but he omitted to remember that he also had a responsibility for their subsequent retreat. He was forced, too late, to decide that Dieterichs had been right; he could do nothing to hold back the Red advance. The situation was aggravated by the unusually warm weather; the Irtysh had not frozen as anticipated, and the railway bridge was inadequate as a means of getting the remnants of the Army across the river. There was the usual frantic activity; Kolchak's cabinet was still functioning loyally, devoting hours of debate and paper-work to projects of the most dubious utility. Meanwhile the firing squads were dispatching unwanted prisoners to the 'Republic of the Irtysh'. (The Bolsheviks used to send their officer prisoners to 'Dukhonin's H.Q.'; a touching reminder of the last days at Mogilev.) In Vladivostok Gajda was bringing his plans for a coup nearer to fruition, and the Allies were involved in a tangled diplomatic conflict – which continually promised to break out in open violence – with Semenov and his satellites.

On 12 November the Irtysh at last froze; by now Kolchak had come round to the opinion that retreat was the only course open to him. He had thoughts of defending the town to the last, but was dissuaded by those who argued that all was not yet lost. They were in a small minority; the Allied missions, save for a few British officers and men and two others, had left the town. The withdrawal continued under frenzied conditions. On the 14th Kolchak left his capital; later that day the Reds entered. They encountered no effective resistance, and succeeded in capturing

many of the trains that should have been evacuating the White Army's reserves of munitions.

Now the Siberian plain was one wide field of snow. The winds were ferocious, the cold intense. Frostbite began to take its toll of the troops who toiled eastwards along the *trakt*. Typhus began to spread rapidly amongst both the foot-soldiers and the fortunate individuals who had found places on the trains. The victims included women and children – the families of White officers and politicians, together with hundreds of other refugees – retreating with their menfolk. Kolchak was accompanied by his mistress, Madame Timireva. The *trakt* was blocked by unwieldy, solid-axled peasant carts; the *magistral* was congested by Czech trains moving ahead of those from Omsk, trains – as often as not – filled with property 'won' in the course of the Czechs' Siberian sojourn. Attempts to send trains westwards from Baikal with medicines and supplies were hampered by the fact that the official 'up' line was now in use as a priority 'down' line. At the water pumps along the line fighting broke out between Czechs and Russians – each claiming that the other group was monopolising the supply. The water was frozen hard and fires had to be lit before it could be pumped into the engines; if they lacked water, or if their fires went out, the pipes of the locomotives burst and they had to be abandoned; sidings were few and far between, and it was no easy task to lever an engine off the track.

On 17 November Gajda finally came out in open opposition to the Supreme Ruler; it was, strangely enough, the anniversary of the coup at Omsk. Gajda met with no success, for he was refused entry into Vladivostok town by the Japanese, and his troops were caught and trapped in the railway-yards on the outskirts of the town – from which they had attempted to launch their attack. After a fire-fight between his armoured train and some White naval craft in the harbour, Gajda was forced to surrender; he was severely beaten up by pro-Kolchak officers before being put on a ship that was leaving the port. Had it not been for the presence of the Allied Commissioners he might well have met with a more drastic fate.

Kolchak's cabinet established themselves in Irkutsk, but the Supreme Ruler himself proceeded more slowly down the line. Even on the former 'up' line, now kept clear of traffic where possible, the progress made by his seven trains was slow. In Kolchak's convoy were the Imperial gold reserves; behind him came Sakharov in his command train. But Sakharov had by now lost almost all control of his troops; it was left to General Kappel to cover the retreat.

The Czechs, aware that the Whites were defeated for good, were becoming increasingly strident in their demands. The National Council published an open letter declaring their distaste for Kolchak and all his works, and demanded to be evacuated. Kolchak responded by warning the Russians not to collaborate with the Czechs, and by asking Semenov to keep a close watch on the Baikal tunnels so that he could, if necessary, stop the Czech retreat. Unfortunately for Kolchak, the Czechs intercepted his embittered telegrams, and were confirmed in all their suspicions. Relationships with the other Allies had similarly deteriorated. General Janin was now of the opinion that Kolchak was a cocaine addict.

The slow retreat went on. The Whites still managed to have political disagreements; for some time there had been no Premier, and at this inauspicious moment the cabinet managed to appoint one. The new Prime Minister, Pepelyaev, and his brother, one of Kolchak's generals, decided that the Supreme Ruler must be made to assent to a programme of social reform. They met him on the station at Tayga on 7 December, and during their subsequent discussion Kolchak offered to resign. But this the Pepelyaevs did not want: there was the old difficulty occasioned by a total lack of anyone to replace him. But they did require a new C-in-C, and, when Kolchak hesitated to dismiss Sakharov, the brothers took matters into their own hands and arrested the General. Kolchak endeavoured to persuade Dieterichs to take up his old post once more, but Dieterichs declined. It was Kappel to whom he eventually turned, though this was an act of supererogation, since Kappel was the effective commander of the only organised body of troops left to Kolchak. But, it has been said, 'any such real authority as the Supreme Ruler still possessed had evaporated in the incident on Tayga station'.[1]

By now the Reds were capturing the rearmost trains on the

---

[1] Footman, *Civil War in Russia*, p. 224.

down line with wearisome regularity. The railway, from the point reached by Kolchak's convoy all the way to Vladivostok, was in the hands of the Czechs. On 13 December a Czech ensign ordered Kolchak's trains off the priority line and onto the 'slow' down line. The Whites were furious, but they could do nothing except to increase their consumption of vodka – by now the subject of censorious comment. Janin, who was technically in command of the Czechs, knew perfectly well that Kolchak's convoy had been delayed and did nothing about it.

The reasons for the Czech action are unclear to this day. It has been suggested,[1] and the argument carries conviction, that it was basically a political move designed to weaken Kolchak's position at Irkutsk so that the Czech political leaders and the Social Revolutionaries with whom they sympathised might take control. Czech obstructionism provoked uproar amongst the Whites, and Kappel challenged General Syrový, the Czech senior officer, to a duel. This gesture caused a great sensation: there is no doubt that it was seriously intended, but there is a strange pathos about it; the Whites were by now so impotent that this, in their own country, was the best they could do. It was in an attempt to remedy the situation that Kolchak decided to appoint Ataman Semenov as C-in-C of all the forces in the east – which meant, in effect, all the forces left to him save for Kappel's command.

On Christmas Eve revolt broke out in Irkutsk. A coalition of Social Revolutionaries and Mensheviks, aided by one of Kolchak's few intact regiments, headed the movement. Such fighting as took place was desultory in the extreme, the only determined supporters of the Supreme Ruler being the pupils of a cadet school. But interest was added to an otherwise monotonous display of indecision and hesitancy by the loyal commander's announcement that he intended to bombard the area of the railway station, which was the site of the mutineers' H.Q. It happened that the station also contained the remnants of the Allied Military Missions, and this prompted Janin, whose train was amongst those assembled there, to dissuade the Kolchakists from their proposed course of action. Instead the station, which was separated from the rest of the town by the swift-flowing

---

[1] Fleming, *The Fate of Admiral Kolchak*, p. 177.

river Angara, was declared neutral ground. The river was in full spate, having washed away the pontoon bridge across it, as always happened before it finally froze. It was obvious that when the ice began to bear, the insurgents, known as the 'Political Centre', would take over the town. The Kolchakists' hopes were raised when three of Semenov's armoured trains steamed up the line, but these were halted through the initiative of some railway workers, who expressed their approval of the Political Centre by sending an unmanned locomotive at full speed down the track. The Ataman's first train was derailed and after some haphazard fighting Semenov's men withdrew, their only gain being thirty-one hostages, whom the Kolchakists wanted 'sent east'.

No further direct conflict broke out between the Kolchakists and the Political Centre until 4 January, when the threat of street-fighting caused Kolchak's commander to flee, and left the Political Centre in control of the town.

Kolchak was still to the west of Irkutsk, his train immobile and guarded by Czechs, whose intentions and political sympathies were by no means clear. Towns both to the west and east of him were in revolt; news filtering through from Kappel's rearguard was uniformly bad, though the General was still succeeding in holding his men together. Kolchak kept to his carriage; there was little that he could do or say. On 1 January Janin had received from the Allied High Commissioners instructions that it was the duty of all Allied troops to 'make every effort to ensure the personal safety of Admiral Kolchak'. It was followed by another directive aimed at ensuring that the Imperial bullion remained in Allied hands. On 6 January Kolchak announced to Janin his intention to resign and to appoint General Denikin as his successor, both as Supreme C-in-C of the Russian forces, and as Supreme Ruler. Kolchak announced that he would sign the formal instrument at a station further down the track – a move calculated to ensure his own safety. For he was at the mercy of the Allies.

He had considered the possibility of attempting to escape into Mongolia, but eventually deemed that the Allied guarantee would serve him better. Thus it was that on 7 January 1920 he left the station where the Czechs had held his convoy, this time in a second-class carriage decorated with the Allied flags. In other carriages followed senior officers and members of the government, trusting that the Allies would protect them also. Their immediate destination was Irkutsk.

Behind them, independently, came Kappel's army. The retreat that they were supposed to be covering had long since disintegrated. They were now fighting for their own lives; they had no military objectives. No prisoners were taken on either side. Every time that they encountered a town the Whites had to decide whether to make a detour or to try to fight their way through. Sometimes they chose the latter course, more out of exhaustion than good sense. Yet they kept together; and, so long as they maintained discipline, they remained the most formidable force between the advancing Reds and the Czech forward posts. Those who straggled were left to the mercy of the partisans and already, in the towns they had passed, the Bolsheviks and their sympathisers were taking over.

If White emotions on the Siberian front were unrelievedly those of despair, the contrary is true of both the southern and the north-western fronts. The break with the Estonians, and subsequent British interference in White politics, had occasioned gloom in the North-Western Army; so too did the further news that the Estonians were trying to negotiate a peace with the Soviets, and that Mannerheim – of whom they still had hopes – now the Finnish Diet had decided for a republic rather than a monarchy, had proved unsuccessful in his candidature for the presidency. Mannerheim had been persuaded to run against his better judgment; he knew that the Finns, understandably turning away from the military tone of their recent past, did not want a 'man on horseback' to rule over them. Yet, despite these set-backs, the men of the North-Western Army were hopeful, and Yudenich was preparing a fresh campaign against St Petersburg.

Their optimism was not generated solely by the news from the south, though there can be no doubt that Denikin's successes encouraged them in their endeavour. A more local factor was the emergence of von der Goltz's Army of Western Russia. This, the Whites hoped, would be less an arm of German aggrandisement than a wing of the Northern Corps; Yudenich himself regarded the newcomers with scepticism, but it was not an attitude that he succeeded in communicating to his men.

There were various anomalistic aspects of the Army of Western Russia, the most remarkable of which was the personality of its commander, Colonel Prince Bermondt-Avalov. Dark in complexion, elegant in appearance, Bermondt-Avalov could be identified from afar by his white Circassian coat and the flamboyant manner in which he handled his horse. His fingers were lavishly bejewelled; his person perfumed. He proclaimed himself for the monarchy and for Germany, and despised those who disagreed with him. No one knew much about him, nor about the validity of his claims to either of his titles. The British representatives 'light-heartedly accepted alternative legends that he had been conductor of a Russian orchestra, or bandmaster of a Caucasian Regiment'.[1] It seems that he based his pretensions to princely rank on the fact that his maternal uncle, by whom he had been brought up, was Prince Avalov. But by what tortuous interpretation of Caucasian gavelkind he derived his succession remained unclear. For the British he had the profoundest contempt. He received visitors from the Military Mission lying in bed, languorously smoking and eating apples. When his callers had left he was wont, such was his suppressed anger, to empty his revolver into the ceiling.

The British were anxious to promote an alliance between the North-Western Army – now, after much fluctuation, about 17,000 strong – and the Army of Western Russia, which numbered 15,000. Since it was estimated that the Soviet Seventh Army stood at 24,000 men, the combined White forces would present a formidable challenge. But von der Goltz persuaded Bermondt not to march with Yudenich, but to devote his energies to an attack on Riga, now the capital of an independent Latvia – a political entity repellent, for rather different reasons, to both Germans and Russians. Yudenich, though he still maintained his full measure of Greater Russian prejudices, was opposed to this move; not only was it absurdly misjudged from the political viewpoint, but it also revealed that Bermondt was entirely lacking in a sense of military expediency. Despite the entreaties of

---

[1] Tallents, *Man and Boy*, p. 362.

Denikin and Kolchak, and the minatory warnings of Yudenich, Bermondt consistently refused to fall in with the plans of the North-Western Army, and when he finally made his independent choice of objective, Yudenich denounced him as a traitor.

As it was, after fighting through the whole of October and on into November, Bermondt failed to take Riga. Moreover, to the exasperation of Yudenich, the Estonian Army went to the aid of the beleaguered forces of their neighbour state, and any chance that the Estonians might think better of their negotiations with the Soviets and come to the assistance of Yudenich rapidly disappeared. A further consequence of Bermondt's move was that the Allies, who were deeply concerned by what they saw as an attempted revival of German expansionist policies, gave the Latvians their fullest support, and diverted to Riga vessels that might otherwise have been employed in aiding Yudenich.

The British General Staff tended to regard Yudenich's planned advance on St Petersburg as a doomed enterprise, and even advocated that his army be moved to the southern front. But British observers on the spot, impressed by the Bolshevik weaknesses, disagreed. It may be asked what the British had to do with it. The answer is to be found in the six tanks, six aeroplanes, numerous machine-guns, 3,000 rifles, and huge quantities of ammunition and equipment with which they had provided the North-Western Army. Yudenich himself was in favour of an immediate thrust on St Petersburg, before further desertions, which by now were plaguing him much as they had plagued the Soviets earlier, could diminish his fighting capacity. His offensive opened on 12 October with the recapture of Pskov – lost in the latter part of the summer – and Yamburg. Once established in Yamburg Yudenich was in a position to direct his main thrust down the Yamburg-St Petersburg railway. At the same time he planned to cut the lines of communication between St Petersburg and Moscow, thus isolating his objective.

In the south Denikin's troops threatened Moscow. Yudenich had nothing like the forces available to Denikin, and he was fully aware that any move on St Petersburg would have to be swift and decisive, since the North-Western Army had insufficient forces to protect the flanks of their main column. Once in the city they would have to face the problem of how to hold it. But if they could capture St Petersburg then the effect on Bolshevik morale would be devastating: the city where the revolution was made, the 'commune of the north', was a symbol of vital significance to the Soviets. Its fall would not necessarily shake the core of the party, but it would certainly convince waverers that the Bolsheviks had run their course. In a war waged by minorities the conviction of the indifferent might well lead to victory.

As the Whites advanced along the Yamburg railway, the Estonian-backed Ingermanlanders advanced towards Krasnaya Gorka once more. But Rodzyanko, commanding the northern-most White corps, studiously refused to co-operate with them. At the same time that Yudenich was protesting against Estonian inaction – which was, in any case, largely a consequence of the attack on Riga – he refused what help they were free to offer, and went out of his way to slight them. The White advance, spear-headed by the British tanks, was so fast that some of Yudenich's men were already convinced of victory. Guchkov, like a ghost from the past, had turned up in Yudenich's territory, and actually revisited Pskov where, it could be said, the whole war had started.

On 16 October Yudenich's advance guard entered Gatchina, thirty miles from St Petersburg. The Whites' optimism increased still further, though they would have done well to reflect that this was where both Krymov and Kornilov had stood before them. News from the south was good, and in Gatchina the White officers were in visible contact with the Russia that many had thought, not so long before, to have been irremediably lost. They could see the characteristic X-shaped pile fence round the former Imperial game reserve, though it was noted that no deer ran in the park – they had gone to feed the city long ago. In other respects, things had not changed to the extent that many of the insurgents had anticipated. A correspondent who followed the Whites into the town wrote:

In the pale sunlight of the early winter morning, down a long avenue strewn with yellow leaves, through air soaked not merely with the melancholy scent of autumn but with the crowding tragic memories of what had come between, the two strange trucks drummed into the almost deserted town. There was the great six-hundred room palace, just as it used to be, and the statue of Tsar Paul in front of it, outstretched hand resting proudly on his long cane, and here too, a dreary little queue of people waiting for food; and then a burned house, still smouldering; a couple of half-starved dogs shamefacedly tearing at the carcass of a dead horse, and a dead soldier lying face upward in the street.[1]

From Gatchina the Whites pushed on; their British tanks, still manned by British volunteers despite embarrassing questions at Westminster, totally demoralised the Red troops unfortunate enough to encounter them. Some of the British officers involved in the intervention embraced the White cause with more fervour than the Whites, hoping that their example of grit and pluck would see their allies through. For the moment, this is exactly what they were doing. By 20 October the Whites had captured the Pulkovo heights, on the outskirts of St Petersburg. From the positions taken up by Prince Lieven's brigade it was possible to watch the whole panorama of the city below: 'There was the dome of St Isaac's and the gilt spire of the Admiralty – one could even see trains pulling out of the Nicolai Station, and the white plumes of their steam trailing across the brown landscape as they hurried towards Moscow.'[2]

'Hurrying towards Moscow' was just what the trains should not have done. Yudenich had detailed units to raid to the south of St Petersburg and cut the roads and railways at Strelna and Tosna; this had not been carried out. There was no satisfactory reason for the omission; the Red Seventh Army had no forces to spare from the main battle before the city, and they had no troops with which to stop a determined move by cavalry. But the White commander responsible for the operation did not make any serious attempt to carry out Yudenich's orders, since he was privately of the opinion that there was nothing to stop the Whites entering St Petersburg at once, and that he would be much better employed in joining the assault on the city. The lines remained uncut because of this crass disobedience and, indirectly, because Yudenich carried insufficient authority. He could not control his lieutenants.

So long as the lines to Moscow remained open, the Reds were able to reinforce from the less threatened fronts, and with drafts

---

[1] Ruhl, *New Masters of the Baltic*, p. 104.
[2] *Ibid.*, p. 109.

of workers mobilised for the occasion. Lenin's original intention
had been to evacuate St Petersburg. It was Trotsky who had
dissuaded him from this course of action, arguing the effect on
Red morale of the city's fall. Even Stalin agreed with Trotsky's
sentiments. Whilst the battle against Denikin raged in the south,
Trotsky rallied the defenders of St Petersburg. The whole population was mobilised; sailors came into the city from Kronstadt;
the battleship *Sevastopol*, berthed in the Neva and officially 'out
of commission', trained her guns on the insurgent lines; for all
his distaste in normal circumstances for such forces, Trotsky
ordered that irregular units should be raised; the Red Guards
marched once more.

From Pulkovo the Whites could follow in detail the Soviet
movements. General Rodzyanko received the Soviet newspapers
daily, and was able to read all of Trotsky's decrees. In the
factories below the heights there was fierce fighting. An attempt was
made to counteract the effect of the British tanks by hastily con-
structing very heavily armoured cars. (The Soviets had planned
to copy Renault tanks, but this project was not yet under way.)
Elaborate road-blocks and barricades went up all over the city.
Trotsky was constantly in the front line, using a horse to ride
from sector to sector. It can be said that the St Petersburg
defence paralleled the Reds' whole defence of European Russia
for, once again, the fact that the Reds were centralised within the
city, that their communications were better, and that they were
capable of rapid and drastic reorganisation, worked in their
favour. It was apparent to the Reds that the defence had been
successful long before the Whites realised that their offensive
had failed.[1]

Yudenich tried for reinforcements to break the deadlock; he
made a last approach to Bermondt, and he attempted once more
to enlist the support of the Finns. His earlier experiences in
dealing with Finland had by now, a year too late, convinced
Yudenich that he must be prepared to accept Finnish independence, and the White Council in Paris – which had all the
doctrinal rigidity of Tsarism together with all the capacity for
prevarication and incompetence of the Provisional Government –

---

[1] Ample evidence that the Reds understood what had happened before
the Whites is provided by Lenin's letter in *Pravda* for 26 October 1919.

perforce agreed. Mannerheim was for action; he believed that a 'lasting Bolshevik régime – assuming that it were not stamped out now – would constitute a danger for practically the whole of the world, not least for Finland'.[1] But Mannerheim had been out of office since July 1919, and out of Finland as well. He did what he could, writing an open letter to Stählberg, the Finnish President, in which he asked him to 'lay foundations for a safe and happy future for our young realm'[2] by an attack on St Petersburg. But, though the letter was widely publicised in Finland, and though many of Mannerheim's former soldiers agreed with him, it met with short shrift in the Diet. One Social Democrat called the document 'stupid' and said that it put Mannerheim on a level with 'Mr' Yudenich. And, even if Stählberg had regrets later, there the matter stayed.

No help was forthcoming from the Poles either, and though the Ingermanlanders held their position before Krasnaya Gorka, where they were aided by the British fleet, so long as Rodzyanko refused to co-operate they had no hope of moving forward. On 23 October the Whites could no longer defend their positions in the suburbs, and were forced to fall back towards Gatchina. The essence of Yudenich's plan for an attack on St Petersburg had been speed: he had to capture the city before the Red Fifteenth Army, which was officially operating against the Poles to the south-west, but was in fact only skirmishing and could easily disengage, moved north to relieve the defence. If he had taken St Petersburg it was possible that the morale of the army might have broken; in any case he hoped that Cowan's squadron would provide artillery cover and so prevent any attempt to recapture the town. But now he had failed in his objective; the Fifteenth Army were coming up from the south and were already in contact with his cavalry. It was rapidly becoming apparent that it was Yudenich, not the Reds, who was trapped.

Yet, for the moment, he hung on. He persisted in the hope that the Finns might move down from the Karelian border, and he clung to a belief that there might be another mutiny within the city, such as that which had taken place at Fort Krasnaya in June. He was encouraged in this opinion by reports that there had been

[1] Mannerheim, *Memoirs*, p. 233.
[2] *Ibid.*, p. 234.

'treason' in the Seventh Army. But here he was under a mis-apprehension: after the events of June there had been a thorough purge in the St Petersburg command, and though there may have been one or two isolated instances of treachery in October – there always were, in a situation where officers were kept at their jobs by the unscrupulous use of threats – there was certainly no wide-spread conspiracy in the Red camp. By this stage of the war 'treason' had come to mean many things besides desertion, sabotage or espionage; it was a term that could be used to brand any mediocre performance in the military field, however well-intentioned. The fact that Trotsky was condemning 'treason' did not mean that there had been any direct move against the Soviets; rather, it signified that Trotsky felt that some of his officers were insufficiently motivated, and needed frightening into the more efficient performance of their duties.

By the 27th Yudenich was back at Gatchina, assailed from both east and south. He hung on grimly, demanding more help from the British, and castigating his staff who responded by giving full rein to a vicious series of feuds amongst themselves. Von der Goltz, now that the Riga enterprise had failed, was beginning to wonder whether Bermondt could not be used to aid the North-Western Army, thus replacing the Allies in the favours of the Whites – who he was sincerely convinced would win.[1] Predictably, all this came to nothing. The Whites were forced to retreat from Gatchina on 3 November, from Gdov on the 7th, and from Narva, the starting point, on the 14th. Their retreat resembled Kolchak's in that they were stricken by disease; the livid red typhoid spots made their appearance, and the epidemic swept through the army in a matter of days. Recriminations amongst the commanders were bitter: by now it was generally agreed that the British were responsible for the disaster. In particular, according to General Rodzyanko, they should have provided more tanks.

At Narva there was yet more bitterness; the Whites' only possible refuge was Estonia, and the Estonians now had no cause to take them in, particularly as it seemed that Trotsky might pursue them. The Whites – those of them who survived that

---

[1] Von der Goltz, Memorandum, 4 November 1919. Quoted in F. L. Carsten, *The Reichswehr and Politics*, p. 67.

long – were allowed across the frontier but were promptly disarmed and interned. A few broke away and crossed into Poland
instead; they were received with little more enthusiasm. Within
a month of having overlooked St Petersburg, the North-Western
Army had been defeated so decisively that not even a rump
formation remained. The North-Western Government, that had
with such unwillingness been brought to parturition, was given
a fortnight to leave the country, and the men who had complained
so vocally of the paucity of Allied aid were now forced – if they
wished to live – to partake of British and American bread.

Trotsky was undoubtedly right in his decision to defend St
Petersburg to the last. But Lenin was equally correct in asserting
that the greatest threat to the future of the Soviet régime came
from the south. For all the attendant dramatics of the White
presence in the suburbs of 'the cradle of the revolution', it was
Denikin's armies that constituted the real military problem.
Numerically they were weaker than the Reds – 78,000 against
about 140,000, by Denikin's reckoning – but they were still
continuing their advance from the south almost unchecked. The
Reds had, on paper, a considerable artillery superiority, but this
seemed of no avail against the Whites' British tanks and their
control of the air.

In September 'Denmiss' – the British Military Mission to
South Russia, now led by Major-General H. C. Holman –
seriously considered the possibility of bombing Moscow, but
the War Office refused to sanction this. Three British planes,
piloted by instructors from the 'Russian Flying School', played
a vital part in the defence of Tsaritsyn, carrying out a low-level
bombing raid against the heavily armed Bolshevik Volga flotilla.
Despite the fact that the Bolshevik craft mounted anti-aircraft
guns, the planes sank fifteen out of the forty vessels and so broke
the spirit of the crews that the flotilla never ventured forth again.
Eventually, under pressure from the War Office – which was
subjected to the usual criticisms about the 'misemployment of
British personnel' – many of the British instructors ceased temporarily to be members of the R.A.F. and volunteered for the
White Air Force. In this capacity they specialised in ground
strafes, and in co-operation with the White cavalry. They devas-

tated Red artillery units, machine-gunning the personnel, and played havoc with Red cavalry units in low-flying attacks. But they were limited by their small numbers. Two squadrons of aircraft were quite insufficient to counter-balance the Reds' superiority in numbers once the Red leaders had checked the general retreat.

By no means all British aid was so well employed. As in Siberia, British equipment seemed to get anywhere but to the front. 15,000 nurses' uniforms were sent to Denikin, and a British correspondent recorded that: 'I did not, during the whole of my service with the Army in Russia, ever see a nurse in a British uniform; but I have seen girls, who were emphatically not nurses, walking the streets of Novorossisk wearing regulation British hospital skirts and stockings.'[1] Staff officers commandeered the beds destined for military hospitals; medicines intended for military use were disposed of, at colossal prices, by private enterprise.

As the men of Denikin's armies came nearer to Moscow – which, as they were daily reminded by posters and broadsheets, was their goal – Red resistance stiffened. To a great extent this was attributable to the improvement and expansion of the Red cavalry and to Trotsky's understanding of the need for an effective Red mounted force, summed up in the slogan 'Proletarians, to horse!' Before Trotsky's campaign such cavalry as the Reds could muster tended to operate on a guerrilla basis, and to be of dubious loyalty. Trotsky realised that he was never going to get complete ideological conformity from units whose chief reason for fighting was that it was their traditional employment, and whose main object was an opportunity to loot. So he concentrated on building up Bolshevik cells within these units to act as a nucleus and an example to the remainder. In order to achieve this, he had to persuade members of the proletariat, who were likely to be loyal supporters of the Soviets, to master the art of riding so that they could join the cavalry at the front: 'the worker mobilised the peasant'.[2]

At the same time that Trotsky's reorganisations were beginning to have some effect, there emerged amongst the Reds a

---

[1] Hodgson, *With Denikin's Armies*, p. 181.
[2] Trotsky, *Stalin*, p. 275.

cavalry leader of major stature. Simeon Mikhailovich Budenny was a former Imperial Army N.C.O. who had declared for the Reds together with almost all the men-folk of his village of Platovskaya. A swarthy man with enormous moustaches, Budenny commanded the absolute loyalty of his men; Trotsky, who doubted the strength of Budenny's political convictions, was worried by the personal nature of his command. He pessimistically prophesied that 'where he leads his gang, there they will go; for the Reds today, tomorrow for the Whites'.[1] Nor had Trotsky much faith in Budenny's gifts as a strategist, though he acknowledged his abilities as a tactician.

These abilities were exaggerated, partly because it would have been embarrassing to the Reds to admit where Budenny's real strength lay. It was claimed, for instance, that Budenny had evolved an entirely new order of battle for the cavalry: experienced swordsmen, generally ex-Imperial Army troopers, rode in the front rank of a charging *sotnya*, whilst in the second rank rode men with revolvers or carbines. The idea was that the second rank covered the first with their fire, and that it was this piece of brilliant reorganisation which made Budenny invincible. A moment's reflection will reveal the transparency of the claim: handarms are ineffective at anything but the closest of quarters; the American Indian Wars revealed that the Indian practice of firing from horseback was as inaccurate as it was spectacular. What happened in the Red cavalry was that Budenny found he had insufficient time to train his new recruits in the testing business of handling a sabre on horseback. (In the hands of the uninitiated the weapon is more likely to strike the head of one's horse than the enemy.) Consequently he armed his more recent recruits with weapons which they would have a greater chance of using correctly, even if this did restrict them to dismounted action. Budenny's methods, in the end, were no different from those of Shkuro or Mamontov. He had his failures, as did any other general in the Civil War, but he did not allow them to be remembered. In the final months of 1919 he was to prove, again and again, that nothing succeeds like success.

But in the beginning of autumn the Whites had it all their own

---

[1] Quoted in Erickson, *The Soviet High Command*, p. 51.

way. The failure of Kamenev's August offensive was in itself sufficient to force a Red withdrawal. Pressure from May-Maevsky's Volunteer Army, combined with the advance of General Sidorin's Army of the Don, turned withdrawal into retreat. Only in the Tsaritsyn direction was there no note-worthy development (Wrangel was short of men, his cavalry urgently needed stocks of both saddles and swords – in September 1919 these had become essentials of war) and the Reds still faced the city in force. Such gains as the Caucasian Army made were strictly local.

May-Maevsky pushed northwards along the Moscow-Rostov railway and on 20 September he occupied Kursk. The importance of this city was obvious enough. Kursk is the junction of the four main railways in south Russia, and from Kursk runs the connecting line to Moscow. The occupation of Kursk enabled Denikin to concentrate his troops for the march on Moscow, as well as providing him with an effective line of support for a putative Volga front – assuming that Wrangel could break out of the Tsaritsyn box. What Denikin envisaged was an eastwards move by the Army of the Don which would result in the rupture of the communications between Moscow and the armies at present containing Wrangel. Then it would be possible for units of both White groups to move up the Volga and take Saratov, after which the way would be open for the capture of Samara and the key railway bridge over the river at Sezaran. If this could be denied to the Reds, the Soviets would be cut off from Turkestan, on which they had become increasingly reliant for materials essential to the war effort.

This grandiose plan was perfectly sound in the abstract. What it omitted to take into account was the state of the rear areas and of Denikin's force. The 'front' was, for long distances, nothing more than a strip of disputed territory up to a hundred miles in depth; where there was a perceptible front line, the trenches were shallow, with no communications system, and quite often no proper parados. It was nothing out of the ordinary for the defence of a mile of such trenches to be entrusted to ten men.

There were the usual diplomatic difficulties; dissident voices were raised both in the Kuban and on the Don. General Schilling was involved in a series of inconclusive battles with Petlyura.

A mission from Poland, received only in response to Allied entreaties, was subjected to long and complicated insults. Denikin persisted in being 'the foe of his own allies in the war against the Soviets'.[1] The Greens became increasingly troublesome, particularly in the Caucasus and in the neighbourhood of Odessa. The growing number of deserters swelled their ranks; many of the bands, so Denikin's staff discovered, were led by ex-regular officers. The Greens' habit of dividing their booty with the peasants of the area in which they were operating ensured them a virtual immunity from betrayal, despite the rewards offered for the capture of individual leaders.

The depredations of Makhno continued on an unprecedented scale. After being driven out of Gulyay Pole by Shkuro, he decided that he must reorganise his army before attempting further moves against the Whites. A consequence of this decision was the publication of his own Order No. 1 in which he laid down the methods and objectives of his force. The Order was issued at the beginning of August; by September he had a formidable army dedicated equally to the extermination of the 'rich bourgeoisie' and the Bolshevik commissars who 'use force to uphold a bourgeois social order'. Nevertheless, General Schilling, using picked troops, managed to drive Makhno's 'new model' back into the Ukraine, and to trap the Makhnovites between his own forces and Petlyura's. Makhno was equal to the occasion: he managed to contract an alliance with Petlyura, and was thus able to leave his wounded in the area of the Ukraine still clear of either White or Red troops. He then heard that Petlyura was simultaneously attempting to reach agreement with Schilling. He mounted a desperate attack on the Whites, who were entrenched at Peregonovka. Realising that if they did not break through they were doomed, his men fought with incredible ferocity; on 26 September he heavily defeated Schilling's forces, capturing twenty guns, 120 machine-guns and a great number of prisoners. Officers were executed on the spot; the remainder were given a choice between death and service in Makhno's army.

Having broken out from Peregonovka, Makhno moved east towards the Dnieper. Making forced marches he travelled five

---

[1] Churchill, *Aftermath*, p. 254.

hundred miles in eleven days, and wherever he went the black flags of revolt were raised. In the first week of October he appeared at Alexandrovsk on the Dnieper, where he blew up the vital railway bridge and cut the telegraph. At Alexandrovsk he dominated all the Taurida and the Crimea; a hostile force was menacing the heart of the White territory. He then moved over to the Sea of Azov, and from there he threatened Denikin's headquarters at Taganrog with an army of close on 15,000 men. At Berdiansk he blew up one of the Whites' most important munitions dumps, depriving them of most of their supplies of heavy artillery shells; it was a loss that Denikin could ill afford. At Taganrog there was near-panic, and forces had to be withdrawn from the front, where they were urgently needed, to defend G.H.Q. Special detachments of officers were formed to fight the Makhnovite menace, and the British Mission was put into a state of defence. This had the effect of creating still more alarm. When the Whites managed to assemble a sufficiently large force, they then found it impossible to bring Makhno to battle, since he employed his usual dispersal technique with devastating effect. Eventually troops under Colonel Sokolovsky, who understood the uses of railways, succeeded in clearing the immediate vicinity of Taganrog, and further operations against Makhno met with more success, though for several days he occupied Ekaterinoslav. By the end of November it could be said that he had been defeated. But his raid, whilst it lasted, had tied down large numbers of troops and preoccupied the White command at the one time when such a diversion could do the most harm.

Yet Denikin cannot escape the responsibilty for having allowed this state of affairs to come about. Something near to anarchy prevailed behind the White lines. There were the casual brutalities of the Cossacks, bringing in their prisoners half-running, half-hanging from lariats tied to their saddle-bows; the pogroms still took place with depressing regularity, particularly in the Ukraine.

Speculation and corruption grew greater as the autumn drew on. Huge sums of money were changing hands in gambles on stocks and on land. Estates which, it was presumed, a White victory would return to their original owners were bought and sold as the news from the north fluctuated. Great attention was paid to communiqués giving details of the position of the front line, but those issued from G.H.Q. at Taganrog were invariably misleading. Only the Bolshevik radio could be trusted, for the Bolsheviks preferred to err on the side of caution, representing their front line as being further back than it was until they were sure of an advance. In their ability to face facts lies one important reason for their ultimate victory.

On 6 October Sidorin and the Army of the Don took Voronezh. Soon afterwards May-Maevsky's left flank captured Chernigov in the northern Ukraine. May-Maevsky's main column pushed on from Kursk, cutting their way through what opposition the Reds could offer. On 13 October, just as Yudenich's North-Western Army was beginning its advance on St Petersburg, they took Orel, less than 250 miles due south from Moscow. It seemed to many as though Denikin's gamble was going to pay off.

Hopes were raised still further by rumours of an imminent rising against the Bolsheviks at Tula – the one major town between Orel and Moscow. Tula contained the Bolsheviks' most important munition factory, and it was widely believed that its fall would make the survival of the Soviet régime an impossibility. But those who were encouraged by these reports would have done well to reflect that anything that was general knowledge in south Russia was equally well known in Moscow. If the Reds had wind of such a conspiracy they were undoubtedly in a position to put it down. There was, in any case, a fundamental unlikelihood about the story, since an industrial centre such as Tula, with a large complement of commissars, was likely to be anti-White long after it had ceased to be pro-Red. Nobody, it seems, took note of this.

There had been unrest at Tula. Minor troubles in the factories were deliberately exaggerated by Soviet agents working in the south, with precisely the desired result. The Whites, optimistic as ever, raced for Tula, without pausing to consolidate or re-organise. But Tula, far from being aflame with revolt, was the holding depôt for the forces with which the Reds were planning to mount a crushing counter-offensive.

There was a desultoriness about the war that magnified the effect of any concentrated effort. In the front lines 'no one had taken the trouble to dig himself in, the opposing forces kept well away from each other, and neither side appeared to be courting an encounter. Yet patriotism appeared to stand high with all ranks, and on many an occasion physical bravery was carried to the point of fool-hardiness.'[1]

It was a situation in which one determined move by either side might well settle the future course of the war. The moment had come for such an effort on the part of the Reds. The Whites were hopelessly over-extended, and short of the trained recruits they so urgently needed. The Reds had been able to build up, as a result of their superior numbers, a large shock brigade which had been held in reserve for just such an emergency. Moreover, the Politbureau had now realised the folly of Kamenev's strategy for the south – by this time Kamenev had seen it as well, but argued that more was to be gained by persisting with it than by a change – and had agreed to a scheme very close to Trotsky's original plan. Their basic aim was to split the Volunteers and the Army of the Don, and to exploit the breach with a massive deployment of cavalry. Trotsky had supervised the basic dispositions for this counter-attack before leaving for St Petersburg: one thrust was to start north-west of Orel and move against the Kursk-Orel railway; the other, in the hands of Budenny and his cavalry, was to take place east of Voronezh. It was hoped that not only would the two armies be split, but that their advance units would be cut off and destroyed.

Nights on the steppe were cold; an autumn sharpness in the air reminded those Whites who thought about such things that they must capture Moscow before the winter set in. There could be no question of holding territory as far north as Orel; the White forces were totally insufficient. 'Christmas in Moscow' was no mere catch-phrase designed to hearten the waverers – it had become a strategic dogma that was the key to the survival of the White movement.

Emotion is only too easily distorted in retrospect. But it seems that White officers, and those who encountered them in these days, are remembering truthfully when they say that there were a good few of their number who did not understand how they had got as far as Orel and did not believe that they would get

---

[1] Hodgson, *With Denikin's Armies*, p. 111.

any further. Ilya Ehrenburg, who was in White territory at this time, has written of how they

> advanced as if across strange country, seeing enemies everywhere. In the night clubs, White officers wanted to hear a song then in fashion which went: 'You'll be the first. Don't get flustered. The stronger the nerves, the nearer the goal.' Drinking parties frequently ended in shooting at fellow customers, at mirrors, or in the air: the officers saw partisans, underground workers and Bolsheviks everywhere. The more they shouted about their strong nerves, the more clear it was that their nerves were giving way; and the goal was vanishing behind a fog of alcohol, hatred, fear and blood.[1]

It was at this time that it was being said outside Russia, notably by Winston Churchill, that Denikin had 'thirty millions of the people of European Russia and the third, fourth and fifth largest cities in the country' within his lines. (Denikin's estimate of the population was fifty million.) One had to be inside Russia to understand just how tenuously those lines were held.

On 20 October, the day that the North-Western Army looked down on St Petersburg from the Pulkovo heights, the Red counter-offensive in the south developed into something more serious than a series of cavalry skirmishes. The groups to the west of Orel and the east of Voronezh went over to the offensive, and another attack came in from between the two cities. The cavalry advance guards were followed by infantry in lorries and carts, together with light artillery and machine-guns. At Orel the Whites fought back with spirit and skill, but the Reds were able to throw against the town divisions withdrawn from the Siberian front – where, as we have seen, there was no need for them now. Other units came from the army group at Tsaritsyn; by this time it was as much as Wrangel could do to hold the city. The Red units operating against the Kursk-Orel railway were almost immediately successful; faced with the prospect of being cut off at Orel, May-Maevsky was forced to give the order to withdraw. Liaison with Sidorin, never easy, was becoming impossible owing to the operations of Red cavalry between the two armies. Sidorin, hard-pressed by Budenny, abandoned Voronezh on 24 October. Shkuro's cavalry, covering the town, were heavily defeated.

---

[1] Ehrenburg, *First Years of Revolution*, p. 94.

The Whites were able to fall back on Kursk, and Kursk remained the key point; so long as they held the town, Denikin considered, they might still advance on Moscow when the Red counter-offensive had blown itself out. Moreover, from Kursk it was relatively easy to protect the flanks of the White position, provided that communications continued to work. But the Whites had failed to reckon with Budenny's cavalry, and it was they who were to inflict the really severe damage.

In October 1919 the Whites were, more than ever before, dependent on the Cossacks. It was the Cossack cavalry that had made the great sweeping advances towards Moscow possible; it was the Cossacks who provided the only forces capable of guarding the White flanks. Most of the cavalry in the Orel salient were from the Don, and there were also a few units from the Kuban, though the majority of the Kuban cavalry were serving in the Army of the Caucasus under Wrangel. Almost every Cossack from the Don area who could bear arms was fighting on one side or the other, and the great majority had sided with the Whites. Nor were there only men in the Cossack *sotnyas*. 'Young girls were riding out with their brothers to the firing line in the proportion of five or six to every squadron.'[1] Dressed identically with the men, they were officially classified as nurses, but in fact they fought alongside their comrades, and several were to be decorated for their valour. By 1919 the Don Cossacks knew only too well the kind of war that the Bolsheviks were waging. At Novocherkassk the Don politicians continued as fatuously as before, but they had lost any real support amongst those who were fighting. The Cossacks in the front line were not concerned for Don autonomy or the legal niceties of a constitution for the Don, but for the survival of the Cossack way of life at the level of the *stanitsas*. They had realised that there was no place for the Cossack in the Soviet scheme of things. In the first weeks of November, within the triangle formed by the cities of Orel, Voronezh, and Kursk, the Don Cossacks were broken by Simeon Budenny, the outlander from Platovskaya, who had all of the anti-Cossack feelings of the *inogorodni*.

If any area in the Russian revolution corresponded to the

---

[1] Hodgson, *With Denikin's Armies*, p. 136.

Vendée, it was the Don territory. The Cossacks of the Don were concentrated in a small area which in early November, was enfiladed from both sides by numerically superior Red forces – forces that had the advantage of possessing short and effective lines of supply. The Cossacks were of necessity used to cover the White retreat, and also to guard lines of communication whilst the retreat took place. When Budenny attacked they were neither concentrated nor serving within an integrated frame of command. In the ensuing battles the flower of the Don Cossack cavalry was destroyed.

The commander of the Don cavalry was Mamontov, an energetic and able general who had proved himself adept in the handling of cavalry. But there was little that he could do against Budenny whilst the White troops remained strung out across miles of countryside. Budenny had no difficulty in breaking through the 'front line', and once he was behind the Whites he systematically destroyed their communications. Often the first indication received by White units that the enemy was in the area was provided by the thunder of hooves as Budenny's men swept in from the rear. In an effort to re-establish contact with their supporting units the forward troops fell back and were soon in full retreat towards Kursk. On the other side of Denikin's salient Red troops severed the Kursk-Kiev railway, cutting off the western column of the Volunteers.

At Kastornaya, on the Kursk-Voronezh railway, Mamontov attempted to rally his men. Only by bringing Budenny to battle with an equivalent force of cavalry could he check the Red counter-attack; by choosing Kastornaya as a rendezvous he hoped to cover the weak junction between the Army of the Don and the Volunteer Army.

But Budenny was reaping the fruits of victory. His successes in late October prompted the Red command to give him additional forces and to make of the troops he commanded an independent 'Cavalry Army'. On 11 November they began to take practical steps to implement their decision, and though it was some time before he could really be said to be commanding an 'army' the recognition implied by his promotion spurred him on. His main column arrived at Kastornaya before Mamontov had been able to regroup and before the Cossacks had assembled their full strength.

For the Whites the battle was catastrophic. Mamontov's men broke before the Red charge, and were never to recover their confidence. The *arme blanche* depended on shock effect, on the verve and co-ordination with which an attack was carried through. In the past the Cossacks had always followed the White guidons fearlessly, against infantry, cavalry, or artillery; now they could no longer be certain that at the shock of contact it would be the Reds who would break and flee.

A similar demoralisation afflicted the Volunteers, though the reasons were rather different. The Volunteer army fought well as it fell back on Kursk; there was no panic as yet, and no lack of discipline in individual units. Disintegration began at the top, when both the Commander-in-Chief and the army commander lost control of the situation. Denikin was unable to find reserves, despite the constant pleas of his embattled commanders. His only resort was to take them from one part of the front line and move them to another. But, instead of coming to the logical conclusion that his front line was too long, and resolving to sacrifice gains in one area in order to ensure that defeat was not turned into disaster, he compromised by bleeding the line of a regiment here and a brigade there, whilst still insisting that it be held in its entirety. May-Maevsky, commanding the Volunteers, went to pieces in a more obvious way. For the commander who had so brilliantly defeated superior forces in the Donets basin, and who had struck foreign observers as being both dynamic and efficient, now seemed incapable of issuing an effective order. His drinking, his repeated orgies, his preference for the brigand-elements amongst the White troops, and his concern for his train-load of booty and women had utterly sapped his powers of command; he was content to leave military matters to his staff. Since his staff had an innate preference for the rear, and were determined to remain there, the subordinate commanders found that they lacked even the most basic information. When an army of any size retreats without orders or direction, then it is unlikely to maintain its cohesion for long.

Kolchak evacuated Omsk on 14 November. The news of this had just become widespread in south Russia when on the 17th Kursk fell to the Reds. Denikin threw in all available forces. A heavy deployment of tanks took place to the east of the town;

they, it was hoped, could achieve what the Cossacks had not. The hope was in vain; the Reds were far too numerous to be turned by the few tanks that the Whites could put into the field. At the same time the performance of the tanks was restricted because of their condition and the lack of fuel. But, whilst the battle for the salient raged, ten British tanks lay idle on the dock at Novorossisk, their tarpaulins straining in the winds that tore down the mountains. The machines could only be moved up to the front on railway flat-cars; days and weeks passed but, despite the urgent entreaties of the British Mission, no transport arrived. Finally, in one of the late autumn Black Sea storms – the 'Nord-Ost' gales so feared by seafarers off the coasts of the Caucasus – a tank broke loose from its lashings, and all ten machines slipped from the dock into the harbour.

Inland from Novorossisk matters of greater moment were taking place, inflicting severer and more lasting damage to the White cause. Denikin had promised Wrangel a free hand in dealing with internal dissension in the Kuban, for it was the Caucasian Army that such disturbances most affected. In consequence Wrangel was greatly surprised when on 6 November, the day of the opening of the Kuban Rada, he received a telegram from Denikin informing him that in July the Kuban government had concluded a treasonable treaty with a Caucasian tribe, and ordering the arrest of several prominent Kuban politicians, including a member of the Rada. A copy of the telegram was also sent to the Kuban, thus forcing Wrangel's hand; he now had to take action. The Rada, believing their liberties to be threatened, began to raise a regiment with which to protect themselves, and in protest against Denikin's behaviour they elected Makarenko, a separatist, as President. In his address to the Rada, Makarenko deliberately insulted Wrangel, who had previously been invited to attend the sittings, but had not yet arrived in Ekaterinodar. When he heard about the speech, Wrangel publicly refused the Rada's invitation, and sent General Pokrovsky to arrest Kalabukhov, the offending Rada member.

Wrangel realised that he had one enormous advantage over the Rada in that he was in command of all the Kuban Cossacks of military age, of whose sympathies he was in little doubt. He assured himself of their support by parading the main body of his Caucasian Army at Tsaritsyn, outlining the situation, and observing the response. The Cossacks proved to be loyal supporters of their generals. Thus, when street-fighting broke out in Ekaterinodar on 12 November, he was not seriously worried about the outcome. On the 19th Pokrovsky surrounded the Rada with his Cossacks and demanded that ten of the chief separatists be handed over; the Rada had no choice but to comply. Kalabukhov was given a summary court-martial and hanged at dawn in front of Ekaterinodar Cathedral; a placard round his neck proclaimed him a traitor to Russia.

On the evening of the same day Wrangel arrived at Ekaterinodar, and was greeted at the station with an ostentatious display of military pomp, laid on for the occasion by General Pokrovsky. Wrangel, going straight from the station to the Rada, which was in session at the time, spoke to the assembly. Representing himself as 'only a soldier' he pointed out that the separatists were effectively betraying the men who were under arms and that only complete co-operation would ensure a victory over the Bolsheviks. Wrangel's Cromwellian methods, the display of military force in the city, and his possession of the persons of the dissident Rada members were factors of more significance than any eloquence. After some rather half-hearted negotiations – it would have been unseemly for the Rada to have thrown in its hand at once – the prisoners were spared and the constitution drastically revised; executive power passed from the Rada to the Ataman of the Kuban Cossacks, the former Ataman resigned, and an Imperial Army general was elected to succeed him. Wrangel could feel justifiably satisfied by the outcome of his mission.

But a local success in the Kuban, which amounted to no more than the rectification of a situation that should never have come about, was no consolation to Denikin. On 8 November, at the Lord Mayor's banquet in Guildhall, David Lloyd George gave it as his opinion that the only possible future for the anti-Bolshevik movement in Russia was one of 'prolonged and sanguinary struggle' and intimated that it was no longer either advisable or possible for Britain to continue her active support of the Whites.

The sentiments expressed by Lloyd George echoed doubts

expressed in Parliament, by the Cabinet, and by both the Foreign Office and the War Office. They came, however, as a complete surprise – at least in so far as they were intended for public consumption – to Winston Churchill. But there was nothing more that Denikin's chief supporter could do to sway the opinions of his cabinet colleagues or of the senior officials involved. He still had a few supporters in the War Office, but they were in no position to counter policy decisions such as that which Lloyd George had now made public.

Denikin, who had tended to disregard cautious and disapproving communications from the War Office – dispatched to him via the sorely tried Holman – now had no option but to take them seriously. He found himself faced by a rapid run-down of British aid, the total cessation of which was foreshadowed by a British request that he make an indent for enough munitions to cover his needs in the foreseeable future, and the warning that this must be the last such application. His situation was desperate, since he realised that he had no hope of winning in the time envisaged by the terms of this 'final demand'. As he asked an interviewer: 'Could your Cabinet have told General Haig in 1917 that he would be given so much and no more and that he must win the war on one indent? Bolshevism has destroyed nearly all our manufacturing resources, and we must, to a great extent, be dependent upon our friends abroad for material of all kinds until the final battle is fought.'[1] Prompted by Romanovsky, Denikin attempted to involve the French in the situation; and, largely influenced by an opportunity to score over Britain, that country showed a cautious interest in the possibilities. But it was clear that the French could never totally replace the British whose 'instructors', even now, were playing a vital part both in sustaining the front line and in keeping the railways operating in the rear.

Still more serious was the effect of the Guildhall speech on White morale.

'In a couple of days the whole atmosphere of South Russia was changed.'[2] The political position of the extremists was immediately strengthened, for the German connection now assumed a far

[1] Quoted in Hodgson, *With Denikin's Armies*, p. 174.
[2] Bechhofer, *In Denikin's Russia*, p. 121.

more attractive guise. Indeed, it required the direct intervention of Denikin to prevent Purishkevich, irrepressible even in adversity, from giving a public lecture in which he proposed to advocate an alliance with Berlin as the panacea for White ills.

After the fall of Kursk the measure of the White defeat became apparent. The question was no longer whether they could retain their base for an attack on Moscow, but whether they could hold onto south Russia at all. The strategic lynch-pin for the defence of the south was Kharkov; yet there were neither troops with which to defend the town nor officers willing to attempt such a defence. The station was blocked by trains laden with refugees from the north; railway traffic had virtually come to a halt. The Volunteer Army was entirely demoralised. Now the winter was upon them, and in its comparative mildness it was worse than any extremity of cold. Bitter frosts were succeeded by sudden thaws; the roads became impassable and the surface of the snow would not bear. Disease ravaged the armies: typhus was carried by lice, and in the crowded billets lice were common to soldiers and officers alike. The sick were shunned by the healthy; conditions on the railways made it almost impossible for hospital-trains to operate, and those who had caught the disease, or were immobilised by their wounds, were left behind as the Reds approached. By mid-December there were over 42,000 White troops unfit to fight. In these circumstances Denikin tried to organise some kind of defence, and finally summoned up the will to dismiss May-Maevsky, by now a drink-sodden wreck.

The only man with whom he could replace him was Wrangel. Wrangel was reluctant to take the post, despite the blandishments of Romanovsky who, as usual, acted as the C-in-C's go-between. In the end he was persuaded to accept it and moved up to the front, leaving units commanded by senior officers at the railway junctions. These details were to act as military police, returning able-bodied troops to their units, impounding booty, and shooting deserters and bandits. When Wrangel eventually arrived at his Headquarters on 9 December he found the situation even worse than he had been led to believe. Kharkov was abandoned, the railways at a halt, and the effective forces of the Volunteer Army reduced to 3,600 infantry and 4,700 cavalry, with 300 infantry in reserve. The infantry were at the end of their usefulness; the horses were unshod and lamed; batteries and armoured trains were being abandoned to the enemy along the length of the front.

When Wrangel, who was not interested in failure, dismissed Mamontov from command of the cavalry and replaced him with Ulagai, Denikin failed to back up the move. Mamontov, who much resented his dismissal, circularised the relevant telegram to all his regiments who took the substitution of a general from the Kuban for the Don leader as a national affront. Both Bogaevsky and Sidorin sided with Mamontov, and it seemed as though all the old separatist arguments were going to be raised again, at the very moment that the Don territories were over-run. Not surprisingly the cavalry striking force that both Denikin and Wrangel were agreed was a necessity if Budenny and his now fully established First Cavalry Army were to be stopped, was enfeebled from the start. Budenny found it far less formidable than the units that he had met with at Voronezh and Kastornaya, and after one brief encounter the 'striking force' ceased to exist.

This was a comparatively minor matter compared with the C-in-C's refusal to accept Wrangel's strategic analysis. At Taganrog Denikin, a man of scholarly mien, lived what had become virtually a scholar's life and it was entirely appropriate, in the circumstances, that his views should have ceased to be of anything but academic interest. It would not have mattered had he not come to believe in the infallibility of his cloistered judgment. Wrangel, in the field, could gauge the strength of the enemy and the morale of his men. He knew that the front line must be reduced to the minimum possible length, and that the only counter-attacks of any value were those made on the basis of a unified plan. In Wrangel's view the only possible course of action was a retreat into the Crimea and the Caucasus, followed by total reorganisation. But Denikin insisted that the Whites must not abandon the Don territories; if they were going to retreat, let them at least attempt to defend the Don, even if the attempt was doomed from the beginning.

When Wrangel presented his report on the state of the front and outlined his strategic plans, Denikin made no effort to disguise his dismay. It became quite obvious to Wrangel that the Commander-in-Chief had entirely lost touch with the situation.

He told Denikin that 'the Volunteer Army has dishonoured itself by acts of theft and violence. All is lost . . . We must emerge again under a different flag. But not a monarchist flag.'[1] Nevertheless, when he saw the extent to which Denikin was stricken by the gradual intrusion of reality, he felt compelled to write to him, pledging his moral support. Denikin replied that Wrangel's letter had 'touched him very deeply' and, in a postscript, informed him that some of his proposals had been carried out and that the rest were in hand.

It was the last communication between the generals to show any sign of cordiality. Wrangel was soon to discover that even the most basic precautions, such as the evacuation of Taganrog and Rostov, had not been implemented, and that Denikin was still convinced that he was conspiring against him. In an effort to bring about a concentration of the Volunteer Army and of the Army of the Don, as ordered by Denikin, Wrangel liaised directly with Sidorin. The consequence of this was a letter from G.H.Q. stating: 'The Commander-in-Chief cannot permit the generals of the Armies to treat directly with one another, and forbids them to leave their Armies in future without his express permission.'[2] When Wrangel taxed the C-in-C with his lack of trust, Denikin deliberately skirted the issue, cutting Wrangel short with the words 'Let us say no more about it.'[3] The evasion was entirely typical of Denikin's behaviour throughout those increasingly catastrophic December weeks.

On 16 December Kiev fell to the Reds. General Schilling, operating in south-west Russia, was driven back towards Odessa. Near Kharkov British officers volunteered to lead detachments against the Reds in threatened areas. General Holman, who had been touring the front line by aeroplane, in order to see that British equipment was used to the best advantage, was indefatigable in his efforts to aid the Whites. Wrangel and Sidorin did what they could to stem the tide from the north. Denikin occupied himself with a manifesto, the formation of a cabinet, and the incubation of suspicions about 'pretenders' to the post of Commander-in-Chief. Refugees poured south. In one town which

---

[1] Denikin, *Ocherki russkoy smuty*, V, p. 260.
[2] Wrangel, *Memoirs*, p. 117.
[3] *Ibid.*, p. 118.

was being evacuated, passengers on a train standing in the station saw what seemed to be several wolves coming along the platform in the half-light. As they moved nearer they were revealed as typhus-stricken officers, clad in grey dressing gowns, and crawling on all fours in an effort to avoid being left when the Bolsheviks moved in.

Red troops reached Ekaterinoslav on 30 December. The Whites were now falling back on Odessa, on the Perekop Isthmus and on a hastily constructed perimeter intended to defend Rostov. Taganrog was evacuated under conditions of total disorder – buildings were aflame as the last trains left the station. Denikin received information that his intelligence officers were plotting against him in collusion with General Lukomsky. After several arrests had been made it was discovered that the charges were baseless. But the informer retained his post, which was supposed to be of the greatest importance, and enjoyed the protection of General Romanovsky.

Thus, in an atmosphere of fear and suspicion, the year 1919 came to its end. It had brought no lasting military successes, and it had seen untold misery and bloodshed. Moreover, there were those amongst the Whites who were clear-sighted enough to realise that they had been defeated not by any deep-seated malaise of the Russian spirit – which is what Denikin appeared to believe – but by their own internal dissensions and by their failure to apply common sense to either the political situation or the prosecution of the war.

1920

Failure

Foe – Friend.
Thorn – Laurel.[1]
All – Dreams . . .
– He – Horse.

Horse – lame,
Sword – rusted.
Cloak – old.
Back – straight.

Marina Ivanovna Tsvetaeva
Return of the Leader

'Well, then, General,' May-Maevsky said, 'what is
the difference between the Bolsheviks and ourselves?'
He answered his own question without pausing . . .
'Is not the whole difference simply that the Bolsheviks
have not scrupled about their means, and have therefore gained the upper hand?'

As quoted by General Wrangel

---

[1] Laurel—*Lavr*—is a reference to General Kornilov.

XVI

Defeat

In January 1920 the Whites were everywhere in retreat. The North-Western Army had ceased to exist. Denikin, his headquarters once more in a railway coach, was attempting in vain to organise the defence of Rostov. Admiral Kolchak was a prisoner in a second-class carriage bedecked with the flags of the countries which were now widely regarded as having betrayed his cause. On 16 January the Allies lifted their blockade of Soviet Russia; trade meant more than flags.

On the afternoon of the previous day, 15 January, Kolchak's train had finally drawn into Glazkov – the station for Irkutsk. The three-hundred-mile journey from Nizhne Udinsk had lasted eight agonising days. It was with relief that the passengers noted, on Glazkov station, the presence of Japanese troops.

The train, which remained under Czech guard, waited in the station for over an hour. During that time Kolchak had discovered that, though there were Japanese outside the windows of his *coupé*, there was also a large contingent of Red Guards present in the station. The inmates of the train bought bread and water from Austrian prisoners, but their unease palpably increased.

Such security as Kolchak and his staff enjoyed was provided by the Czechs. The Japanese were no more likely to play a part at Irkutsk when the White downfall had been accomplished, than they had been earlier in the year when White victory had seemed almost certain. Their aims were local. And the Czechs too, though their rearguard was in action near Nizhne Udinsk, were concerned solely to cover their own retreat.

Yet the Political Centre was itself far from secure. The Red Army proper was no nearer than Nizhne Udinsk; Kappel's force menaced the town; there were Whites at liberty within Irkutsk, and there was sporadic street fighting.

What action was taken over Kolchak depended on two men –

General Janin, C-in-C of the Allied troops, and General Syrovy
C-in-C of the Czech Legion which was still subordinate to the
Allied command.

By this time Janin was at Verkhne Udinsk, east of Lake Baikal.
He was dependent, for news of events further to the west, on
Syrovy, who was still with his H.Q. at Irkutsk. On the day prior
to Kolchak's arrival in the town, Janin was in contact, by telephone, with Syrový. The Czech C-in-C gave it as his opinion
that 'it would be impossible to escort the Admiral further than
Irkutsk'. To this Janin replied that he was sure that Syrový
would do his best to preserve the honour of the Czech name.
Precisely what the General meant is unclear; but there is no
doubt as to what happened at Irkutsk.

After nightfall on 15 January two Czech officers passed the
sentries guarding Kolchak's *coupé* and talked to Colonel Rakitin,
one of Kolchak's staff. Rakitin at once went to the compartment
occupied by the Admiral and Mme Timireva, and then told
Kolchak that the Czechs could no longer accept responsibility
for the convoy of his person, and they were therefore going to
hand him over to the local authorities: that is to say, to the mercies
of the Political Centre.

Kolchak's immediate reaction was to demand that the officers
repeat this to him in person. The Czechs, disclaiming any
personal responsibility or liking for their orders, reiterated their
previous statement. The order, they told the Admiral, came from
General Janin. Kolchak received the news with the calm that he
had sustained throughout his confinement in the train. His comment, though interrogative, was a simple summary of the situation : 'In other words, the Allies are betraying me?'

There were a few minutes of chaos as members of his staff, by
now aware of what the Czechs had come to say, attempted to
escape. Some of them, abetted by the Czech sentries, evaded the
Red Guards and broke out of the station before they could be
stopped. Others preferred to share their leader's fate. A unit of
the Red Guards received the Admiral, Mme Timireva, and the
remaining staff officers from the Czechs. They gave a receipt for
the prisoners. Then they marched their acquiescent captives
across the river-ice to Irkutsk proper. They were driven to Irkutsk
prison.

On 16 January Janin received representatives of the Political Centre in his train at Verkhne Udinsk. After a long discussion about other matters he made an enquiry as to the whereabouts of the Admiral. When he heard what had happened he evinced no further interest in the matter.

The Admiral was not the only revenant of the Siberian régime to fall into the hands of the Political Centre. Together with his person they received the Imperial Gold Reserve. The Czechs, their passage now paid for, continued to move eastwards to Vladivostok.

In Irkutsk prison Kolchak's interrogation had begun. The examining body was a special commission made up of two Social Revolutionaries, a Menshevik, and a Bolshevik. There was no attempt at coercion. They were concerned with the Admiral as a man, and with the motives that caused him to become a leader of the counter-revolution. The Admiral's answers were truthful and concise; there were no histrionics, and his replies were consistently moderate in tone. The interrogations continued daily.

From the west, Kappel's Army drew nearer to Irkutsk. The Whites knew of the Admiral's imprisonment, and were determined to rescue him. On 23 January they marched out along the *trakt* from Nizhne Udinsk; on the railway itself were the last of the Czech trains. Kappel, travelling in a sleigh along the iced and rutted road, had been badly frost-bitten. The rugs under which he lay can have given him little respite from the freezing air.

He still continued to hold his army together. His staff became increasingly concerned about his well-being and endeavoured to persuade him to accept an offer from the Czechs and to ride in one of their trains. But Kappel refused. If he accepted Czech hospitality, he said, he would seem to be condoning the betrayal of Kolchak. The frost-bite moved up his body from the legs; he lost practically all sense of feeling. There was no longer anything that the doctors could do for him, except to give him morphia. He still refused to consider abandoning his men. On 27 January he died. Despite his attitude towards them, the Czechs received his body and took it east to Chita for interment: by Kappel's example, one of their officers said, they had been shown that not all Russian officers were typified by the staff at Omsk.

Shortly before he died, Kappel had handed over command to General Voytsekhovsky. Under this officer the Whites continued their march towards Irkutsk. On 2 February, through the agency of the Czechs, Voytsekhovsky announced certain conditions on which he would be prepared to call a truce at Irkutsk. These included unimpeded passage through the town, the handing over of Kolchak to the Allies, and the payment of an indemnity – which amounted to the return of the gold reserve.

The leaders of the Political Centre made no reply to these demands. On 5 February White troops attacked the Glazkov suburbs.

During this time Kolchak's interrogation continued. It was still keeping to the pattern of an unhurried and meticulous recapitulation of the Admiral's personal history and of his motives during the revolutionary period. The Admiral's behaviour, according to one of his interrogators, was 'that of the captive commander of a defeated army; and from this standpoint it was entirely dignified'.[1]

On 6 February the whole rhythm of the interrogation changed. The Admiral could have had no doubt as to the reason: he had already warned Mme Timireva in a note that if Voytsekhovsky attempted to take the town he would almost certainly be executed. The interrogators, who had intercepted the note, were aware that the Admiral realised this. Within the prison gunfire was audible. There was nothing exploratory about the questions that the prisoner had to answer now: he was taxed with all the gross barbarities of his régime.

The final decision on Kolchak was referred by the Political Centre to Smirnov, commander of the Red Fifth Army. Smirnov found that Moscow was anxious to stage a show-trial; it was what Trotsky had suggested in the case of the Tsar. But the Political Centre were worried about the speed of the White advance, and there were rumours of a White officers' underground within the city. Reluctantly, Smirnov approved that Kolchak should be executed at Irkutsk.

In the early hours of 7 February the Admiral was taken from

---

[1] K. Popov, Vice-Chairman of the Commission, in the foreword to the published transcript of the interrogation. Verneck and Fisher, *The Testimony of Kolchak*, p. 7.

his cell and, together with Pepelyaev (his Prime Minister), he was escorted down to a tributary of the Angara that ran close to the prison walls. The handcuffed prisoners were brought to the edge of the bank. Kolchak walked with calm and dignity, Pepelyaev had to be dragged. They were placed close together in the lights of a lorry; the firing squad stood at either side of the vehicle. The prisoners were ministered to by a priest; Pepelyaev was unable to control his fear. His panic emphasised Kolchak's calm. Then there were two badly synchronised volleys, and the bodies were pushed over the bank into a hole in the ice kept open for this purpose. Under the ice the Angara still flowed fast; in a moment the bodies were swept away.

The Whites had refrained from launching a full-scale attack on Irkutsk. But on the morning of 8 February the news of Kolchak's death was known, and there were those who were fervent for revenge. Voytsekhovsky was not of their party: the only object that the Whites could have for the present was survival. That night his troops by-passed the town and moved on, across the ice of Lake Baikal, to the east.

In the shadowy northern enclave of Archangel the events of Siberia and the South repeated themselves on a minor scale. In early February the Reds began a serious offensive against Miller's forces, and the C-in-C realised that there was no real hope of resistance. An elaborate evacuation plan was drawn up, but on 19 February the front disintegrated, and Archangel was beset by panic. Mutinies broke out on the ships earmarked as transports, and ice in the White Sea hindered navigation. Drunkenness and looting were additional hazards.

Miller, his staff, and some of the Archangel garrison left on an ice-breaker commanded by the troublesome but loyal Chaplin. The troops at Murmansk made their way over the border into Finland. But by far the greater number of those units serving at the front had no option but to capitulate to the Reds. The ease with which Archangel was captured amply demonstrated the truth of Lenin's assessment of the northern forces after the Allied withdrawal: 'An insignificant number of Whites of no importance.'[1]

---

[1] Lenin, *Sochineniya*, XXXV, p. 360.

347

In the south the retreat went on. Denikin continued to delude himself as to the strength of his position even arguing that: 'If chaos reigned in our rear, the Reds had no rear at all.'[1] It was left to the British Mission to endeavour to stiffen the attempted defence of Rostov. When General Holman's train had been attacked by a Red patrol he had himself opened up on them with a heavy machine-gun, treating it as a one-man weapon. Now he went into action once again, commandeering a tank and taking it through the front in an attempt to stem the retreat. English officers walked calmly through a Red artillery barrage, trying to steady the Volunteer regiments to which they had been attached. But it was to no avail. Tsaritsyn had fallen on 3 January, Taganrog two days later, then Novocherkassk and on 8 January Rostov. The rapidity with which these vital places collapsed is sufficiently indicative of the condition of Denikin's armies. In Rostov a Bolshevik rising hastened the end. At once spy-mania swept the rear, and suspects were brutally hanged from trees and lamp-posts. Disorders became general. There was a final spate of pogroms in the towns about to be evacuated. Meanwhile Denikin was telling journalists that the Volunteer Army could now be regarded as a 'solidly democratic force'.

White G.H.Q. was back at Ekaterinodar again. In mid-January there was a brief, illusory period of White victories. Denikin endeavoured to defend the line of the Don and the Manych with his cavalry; the Don Cossacks, in a last attempt to regain their homeland, defeated a large raiding column commanded by Budenny in person. The Cossacks seemed to recover something of their old *élan*, and the Reds continued to suffer reverses. The scale of these was magnified because of Red difficulties with the railways – which the Whites had destroyed as they retreated – and the severity of the typhus epidemic.

On 16 February General Pavlov, commanding 12,000 Don Cossacks, defeated Dumenko and a large body of Red cavalry on the Manych front. An attempt was made to take Torgovaya, but without success. Finally Budenny and Pavlov were left confronting each other across ten miles of snow-bound steppe, and neither Reds nor Whites were prepared to be first to advance.

---

[1] Denikin, *Ocherki russkoy smuty*, VI, p. 267.

On 25 February Pavlov finally brought himself to move across the steppe and attack Budenny; the Red response was immediate and overwhelming; the Whites, totally demoralised, dispersed and fled.

At the Ekaterinodar theatre the Moscow Arts Theatre company held the stage. They had deliberately arranged their summer tour so that they might play in the towns most likely to be over-run by the Whites. Now they too were acting out the last scenes of the Tsar's empire. Their repertoire included Turgenev's *A Month in the Country*, Chekhov's *Uncle Vanya* and *The Cherry Orchard*, together with an adaptation of *The Brothers Karamazov*. Chekhov's widow, Mme Knipper, was one of the company. Every night the theatre was full, and the players met with a reception that was often hysterical. One night, at the revolver shot in *Uncle Vanya*, a girl in the audience had to be forcibly carried from the auditorium in order to quiet her screams. It transpired that the Bolsheviks had shot her lover before her eyes only weeks earlier.

The hardships were endured in a manner characteristically Russian. In February 1920 a Novorossisk paper published 'A New French Course' – a parody of the conventional phrase book dialogues. It caused 'tears of laughter' amongst the Russians who read it. It ended:

Q. Is it true that your uncle is a remarkable man?
A. Yes, he is, indeed, a remarkable man. He has been ill once with ordinary typhus, twice with spotted typhus, and three times with recurrent typhus. He is impatiently waiting for the spring, in order to fall ill with cholera.
Q. Do you like walking in the cemetery?
A. Yes, I like walking in the cemetery, because all my friends and acquaintances are there. The day before yesterday my last friend in the town died. In order not to have to visit the cemetery every day, and so wear out my last pair of boots, I want to remove my residence to the sexton's quarters.[1]

On 7 February Odessa had fallen in disastrous circumstances. Faced with a Red advance that he could not contain, General Schilling abandoned his post and concentrated on organising his own personal evacuation. In the port there was chaos, as the

[1] Bechhofer, *In Denikin's Russia*, pp. 221-2.

Whites scrambled for places on Allied vessels. In the streets leading down to the docks the press of people was so great that windows and doors were shattered by the weight against them. The British involved in the evacuation enforced the principle of 'women and children first' – to the fury and dismay of many Russian officers. Most of these panicked with the crowd; it was left to two comparatively junior officers, Colonel Stessel and Captain Maximov, to attempt to control the evacuation.

The approaching Soviet forces were so astonished and terrified by the scenes in the port that they reined their horses on the edge of the steppes above the town and watched the ships sail out, some of them with people still hanging onto their unstowed gangplanks. As those who were left behind dispersed in search of shelter, Red cavalry moved in over the corpses of the men and women who had been crushed to death.

No better fortune favoured the Whites in the Kuban. Denikin worked eighteen hours a day to the end and achieved nothing. His quarrel with Wrangel came to a head, and the latter left for Constantinople feeling that there was no more than he could do whilst Denikin continued in command. Officially he was regarded as having been 'cashiered'. Disease ravaged the forces: 'smallpox and typhus epidemics made new alliances with sword and famine'.[1] The co-operation of the British Mission was soured by contradictory orders, White accusations of 'treachery', and an extraordinary minute from Holman to the effect that some British officers were 'windy'. It was surmised, correctly, that this imputation had originally emanated from White H.Q.

After Budenny's destruction of Pavlov's cavalry there was nothing to stop the Red advance. The Soviet armies moved forwards over the country traversed by the Whites in their Kuban campaigns, and they advanced with the confidence born of victory. An attempt was made by the Whites to hold the line of the Kuban river; despite the valour of isolated units it was a total failure. Once the Kuban was forced Denikin could no longer hope to hold on at Ekaterinodar.

It was obvious to him by now that the morale of the Whites was broken. The only hope was a period of recuperation in an area of

---

[1] Churchill, *Aftermath*, p. 261.

sufficient natural strength to allow the Whites to remain on the defensive. Denikin was inclined to favour Turkestan; for both political and strategic reasons the British were anxious to dissuade him from such a move, and in this they were finally successful. There then remained one such area in White hands – the Crimea. It was the solution that Wrangel had suggested in December; at that date a retirement into the peninsula could have been effected in an orderly manner. Now this was impossible. There were two possible routes to the Crimea from the Kuban. One involved a crossing of the narrow straits separating the Taman Peninsula from the mainland; the other depended on the availability of ships to transport the army from Novorossisk to the various Crimean ports. But Denikin disposed his troops in such a way that Kutepov, commanding in the western Kuban, was forced to decide between a defence of the approaches to the Taman route, or a defence of Novorossisk. He chose the latter course and, unwittingly, intensified the state of chaos that obtained in the port.

It was Odessa over again, only bloodier and more catastrophic. On 17 March the Soviets took Ekaterinodar, their primary objective in the Kuban. They then threw their whole weight against the White armies as they retreated to the coast.

The number of ships available for the evacuation was totally inadequate; the initial requisitions had been erroneously based on figures that presumed the Taman route was still viable. To evacuate his men Denikin was compelled to plead for British help; it was the Royal Navy that made the operation possible.

Freezing winds tore through the mountain passes, periods of thaw were terminated by appalling frosts, ice on the decks and rigging of the ships in Novorossisk had to be chipped off each day if the vessels were to remain stable.

The approach roads to the port were blocked for miles. It was not simply a case of evacuating the troops: there were thousands of families clamouring to be taken into safety. Many of these were relatives of White officers, and knew very well what treatment they might expect at the hands of the Reds. Amongst those who straggled through the mountain passes were some who had no idea where they were going, but were caught in the human tide and infected with the fear and panic which characterised the

whole retreat. There were Cossacks, nomad families with their
black tents, Caucasian tribesmen and families from the Caspian
shores. Their route was marked by bodies, stripped naked and
frozen; dead horses, mules, and camels; abandoned guns, field-
kitchens and vehicles, together with all the debris of an army in
flight.

Denikin's loss of control was complete. It had been precipitated by his discovery, made at the time his forces were falling
back from the Kuban, of another 'conspiracy' against him. It was
his contention that this had spread as far as the front line, and
that officers of the Wrangel faction were deliberately disobeying
his commands.

This was not so. If his orders were being ignored, it was because
the circumstances in which they could be carried out had ceased
to exist. Wrangel had been, all things considered, a loyal subordinate. The option was not open to front-line officers, who saw
daily that Wrangel was right and Denikin wrong. Had Denikin
been less convinced of his own infallibility he might yet have won
their loyalty once more. On 14 March as a result of heavy pressure
from all quarters, he dismissed Romanovsky and sent him to the
Crimea. But it was a move made a year too late.

On 25 March Kutepov, entrusted with the defence of Novorossisk, told Denikin that his troops could no longer hold the
Bolshevik advance. Denikin implored him to continue in his
efforts; and somehow the area of the port was defended for two
more days. Admiral Seymour, commanding the British squadron,
summoned as many ships as he could muster to aid him, and
loaded his vessels – which included H.M.S. *Emperor of India* – as
heavily as he possibly could. Contrary to Sidorin's expectations
almost the whole Don Cossack Army demanded to be evacuated;
he had expected that only the officers would wish to leave. At the
waterside the Cossacks shot their horses; starving refugees tore
the corpses to pieces for food.

It was not long before the Red artillery had begun to shell
Novorossisk from positions in the spurs of the mountains that
rose up behind the town. With the help of the British Mission
a rear-guard was organised while the last stages of the embarkation took place. The gangplanks had to be guarded by armed
marines and officers; at least one ship was attacked by those who

were turned away as it made ready to cast off. Denikin and his staff watched the evacuation from a destroyer anchored in the harbour; eventually it became apparent that a large number of those assembled in the port would have to be left behind. Only armed and organised bodies of men were allowed on board during the final hours, and, before the British squadron left, parties had started to make their way south along the coast. Families were separated, men attempting to board the destroyers that were the last to leave the port were clubbed with rifle butts. Several officers shot themselves on the quay; more drowned trying to swim out to the ships. On 27 March the Reds swept into the town, and the laden ships of the British fleet set sail for the Crimea. At Novorossisk the Reds captured 22,000 troops, besides those whom they slaughtered on the quays or as they fled the town. They also took close on a million pounds' worth of British stores. On board the Allied ships were some 50,000 Whites, many of them women, children, and wounded.

Denikin had endured his final defeat. There could no longer be any question that he was unfit to command. He continued to discuss his situation, endlessly arguing the rights and wrongs and obsessively returning to the theme of persecution, without perceiving its irrelevance. Leadership is something that either does or does not happen. In the case of Denikin it may have happened once, but it had long since ceased to be an operative principle. He continued to command the loyalty of some of his officers, but he no longer commanded their obedience or their respect. Xenophon's description of Proxenus can serve as well for Denikin – 'he was a good commander for people of a gentlemanly type'. The ideals he stood for remained valid, but his generalship was revealed as totally inept. At last he had to accept that this was so. His decision was precipitated by the news that officers of the Kornilov division were plotting to assassinate Romanovsky, whom they blamed for the catastrophe, and to depose Denikin. On his arrival in the Crimea he called a Council of War, to be presided over by General Dragomirov. The purpose of this Council was the 'election of a successor to the Commander-in-Chief of the Armed Forces of South Russia'.

The Council met on 3 April. On the 4th Dragomirov telegraphed to Denikin that no decision had been reached: would

Denikin continue? This was largely because the assembled officers were not prepared to establish the precedent of electing their C-in-C. Denikin replied that he would on no account change his mind. To this Dragomirov replied that the Council had elected General Baron P. N. Wrangel as his successor, but requested that the appointment should be made directly by Denikin. Denikin complied, thus acting as Dragomirov had hoped he would in the first instance. Honour was satisfied, and the general whom Denikin had accused of treason was safely established in his stead.

Denikin left the Crimea as quietly as possible; there were no formal farewells. The reason was simple: he was in fear of his life. Together with General Holman and Romanovsky he embarked on the *Emperor of India* at Theodosia. The two Russian officers' A.D.C.s, who were responsible for their protection, travelled on another, slower vessel. Once arrived at Constantinople Denikin and Romanovsky went to the former Russian Embassy. Denikin was reunited with his family at the Embassy. Romanovsky left the room to find some transport, and a moment later was seen, by those outside, to stagger and fall; he had been shot just beyond the door. His assassin was presumed to have been a man wearing a Russian officer's uniform and accompanied by a nurse; but he was never caught.

That night Denikin attended a requiem for his friend and comrade. To the intense irritation of the Russians present he came accompanied by a British guard, who took over the whole Embassy for the time he was present. The next day, accompanied by his wife and child, together with the two children of General Kornilov, he left for Malta on the battleship H.M.S. *Marlborough*; his ultimate destination being the United Kingdom.

Behind him, in the Crimea, what was left of his army fought on.

XVII

Wrangel and the Crimean Bastion

It had been General Wrangel's intention, while in exile at Constantinople, to move on to Serbia. The day before he intended to leave for Belgrade he was due to lunch with the British High Commissioner, Admiral Sir John de Robeck. As he set out to keep this appointment he received, in the form of a wireless message from General Holman, the first intimations of the course of events in the Crimea.

After luncheon, which was held on board H.M.S. *Ajax*, de Robeck invited Wrangel, together with the C-in-C of the Allied Army of Occupation in Constantinople, to discuss the matter with him in his cabin. He told Wrangel that there was no doubt that he would be chosen to succeed Denikin; he also gave it as his opinion that the situation in the Crimea was beyond redemption. He went on to say that he had just received a telegram from the British government, the effect of which was to make the situation still more desperate.

The telegram was addressed to Denikin but, since the opportunity had arisen, Admiral de Robeck considered it advisable to communicate its contents directly to Wrangel, whom the news would most drastically affect – it stated, in plain language, that if the Whites continued with the war, the British would no longer assist their endeavours in any way. Admiral de Robeck hoped that knowledge of the contents of this message would deter Wrangel from accepting the command of a doomed army. But the news had the opposite effect; until he knew of it he had still been in doubt as to whether he should accept the post. Now he had no doubts: 'If I am chosen, it is my duty to accept the command.'[1]

Chatilov, who had accompanied Wrangel to Constantinople, agreed with de Robeck that there was no hope of success; but

---

[1] Wrangel, *Memoirs*, p. 132.

when he realised that the General was not to be dissuaded from his resolve, he announced that he would go with him. Chatilov and Wrangel arrived in the Crimea on 4 April, shortly before the Council of War commenced its second sitting. Wrangel was soon to discover that the Council had reached deadlock on the issue of the new appointment. The questions which exercised them concerned the *method* of the appointment and the feasibility of a continuation of the war.

Wrangel at once established himself as the dominant personality of the Council. He began by reducing its size, maintaining that it was too big in its original form and that serious discussion of policy should be left to the senior commanders. He then told this inner circle that he did not think the new C-in-C could possibly succeed in crushing the Bolsheviks, but that it would be possible for the C-in-C to 'keep unstained the honour of the Russian flag'.[1] Having said this he left the conference, pleading tiredness; there seemed no more that he could say. While the Council continued to argue he walked the empty Sevastopol Boulevard, and finally decided to call on the Bishop of Sevastopol. He hoped to gain some peace of mind by telling the Bishop of the doubts which still made him uncertain as to whether he should accept the command if the Council finally offered it.

The Bishop was in no doubt that Wrangel had been right in his decision to return to the Crimea. Before the General left he blessed him with an icon, and Wrangel returned to the palace, where the Council was sitting, secure in the belief that he was equal to the task before him.

When he returned, the Council – as he had expected – communicated to him their wish that he should accept the post of C-in-C. His first act was characteristic: wanting no repetition of the ceaseless intrigue that had so seriously undermined the Denikin régime, he drew up a statement of policy, which at the same time defined the powers of the C-in-C, and requested that all those present should sign it. There were two dissidents who hesitated; but, after a discussion, all agreed.

In the course of this narrative we have already had some opportunity to observe Wrangel's main characteristics. After the death

---

[1] Wrangel, *Memoirs*, p. 142.

of Alekseev he was perhaps the most able strategist in the White armies; as a field commander he excelled, particularly in the handling of cavalry. In the pursuit of his military aims he was totally ruthless: he shot Red officers and hanged speculators and deserters without hesitation. When he took Tsaritsyn he had all

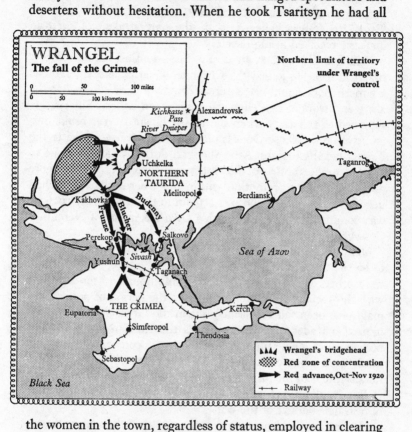

WRANGEL
The fall of the Crimea

0 — 50 — 100 miles
0 — 50 — 100 kilometres

Kichkasse ★ Alexandrovsk
Pass
River Dnieper

Uchkelka
NORTHERN
TAURIDA
Melitopol
Kakhovka
Budenny
Berdiansk
Frunze Blucher
Perekop Salkovo
Yushun Sivash
Taganach
Eupatoria THE CRIMEA Kerch
Simferopol
Theodosia
Sebastopol
Black Sea

Northern limit of territory
under Wrangel's
control

Taganrog

Sea of Azov

▲▲▲▲ Wrangel's bridgehead
Red zone of concentration
➤ Red advance, Oct–Nov 1920
+—+—+ Railway

the women in the town, regardless of status, employed in clearing up the chaos that the Bolsheviks had left; to be understood, this feat must be considered against the background of prevailing behaviour in the White-held areas. It was a remarkable achievement.

Perhaps some of his abilities can be attributed to the circumstances of his career. Born in 1878, he came from a family celebrated in German, Austrian and Scandinavian annals. But this cosmopolitan background did not detract either from his loyalty to the Russian Empire – which had been served by his branch of the family for a century – or his devotion to the Ortho-dox Church. His education had been unusual. He had attended a technical institute rather than one of the conventional high schools; his sobriquet in military circles henceforth became 'Stinker'. He was believed to be the only student of such an institute received in high society.

Wrangel did not, at first, put his scientific studies to any practical use. He joined the Chevalier Guards, and emerged as a superb horseman. Yet, after a few years' service, he left the army and worked as a chemical engineer in eastern Siberia. He returned to the army when the Russo-Japanese War broke out, and was one of those Guards officers who were seconded to the Trans-Baikal Cossacks. After the war, during which he came to the favourable notice of his superiors, there were many more opportunities for promotion within the Guards than there had been hitherto, and he chose to remain in the service. By 1916 he was commanding the Tsarevich's Own Regiment of Nerchinsk Cossacks.

Opinion about Wrangel was divided. Some considered him to be the most promising young officer of his generation; there were others who thought him over-ambitious and too involved with the social side of military life. In the period of peace these may have been fair criticisms, but in the Great War he proved himself a leader of cavalry such as the Russian army had not possessed for a long time. Politically he was conservative, and his ideals were monarchist, but these were private opinions. He did not, as leader of the forlorn hope of the anti-Bolshevik movement in Russia, allow sentimental or personal considerations to inhibit him in his conduct of the war.

His first act had been to ensure the loyalty of the senior officers. His second was to issue an order to his troops. In it he made no attempt to minimise the danger of the situation in the Crimea; it was never his practice to give grounds for false optimism – a respect in which he differed significantly from his predecessor.

Wrangel was, at heart, a believer in the integrity of the Russian Empire. But he differed from Denikin in realising that, unless he recognised the rights of nations within the Empire, he could not hope to win. His far less rigid line on the Greater Russian policy caused an immediate change in the attitude of many of the Cossacks. He extended this new flexibility to the field of foreign policy and began to exploit the differences of opinion between the Allies, in order to encourage the French to give him aid. At the same time he retained his independence of action, refusing to commit himself on the possible allegiances of a future Russian government, and making it quite apparent that he was not prepared to become a convenient tool for the shaping of French policy – or the policies of any other country, for that matter – in eastern Europe.

Wrangel faced a task of enormous difficulty. Of the White armies only a few scattered units retained their discipline. The total strength of his forces, disciplined and otherwise, was a mere 40,000. The Greens were established in the Crimean mountains, and disorder was prevalent throughout the rear. The isthmuses were held by cavalry only, and the Reds were known to be massing for an attack.

The new C-in-C at once initiated a period of military and civil reform. He regrouped the remaining reliable infantry units from the Volunteer Army and set them to support the cavalry in their watch on the Crimean approaches. Small-scale actions were carried out to clear the isthmuses at Perekop and Sivash, and to restore to the Whites the most important defensive areas. Serious attention was paid to the needs of the navy; the Crimea could not possibly be self-supporting, and an effective naval force was needed both to maintain the lines of communication with Constantinople, and to provide against the contingency of an evacuation. Steps were also taken to reconstruct the tiny air force, which had hitherto been entirely dependent on British personnel.

Having secured his front Wrangel set about organising the rear. He made it clear from the beginning that he was not interested in sweeping forward advances on the Denikin model. It was his object to establish law and order in one part of Russia, so that those who experienced this state of affairs might actively assist in the fight against Bolshevism. He did not subscribe to the assumption – typical of previous White leaders, however ostensibly liberal they might have been – that people would support the Whites because they had a 'duty' to do so; he saw that he had to create the conditions that might generate such support.

359

This he set about doing. He organised a cabinet, and he included men of apparently divergent political views who were, nevertheless, prepared to serve under him in the fight against the Soviets. His premier was A. V. Krivoshein, whom he selected not only on account of his known probity, but also because Krivoshein, though an experienced politician, was above party factionalism. The other members of the cabinet, amongst them P. B. Struve – a distinguished academic and political theorist – were all men who could be relied on to see the over-riding importance of loyalty to Wrangel. The cabinet was an advisory and executive organ, but there was never any suggestion that it was, in itself, the governing body. It was Wrangel himself who initiated the major reorganisations in the civil as well as the military sphere. He set up an effective counter-espionage organisation under General Klimovich, the former military governor of Moscow; he announced far-reaching reforms, including an agrarian policy that met with the active approval of the peasants.

His methods have been described as the furtherance of 'leftist policies by rightist hands'. This is accurate, except insofar as it suggests that Wrangel was insincere in his aims. He was not; he knew perfectly well that any suggestion that his reforms were temporary would destroy the credibility of his régime. When they were announced there were many who were reluctant to believe them; he made it his first duty to convince the inhabitants of the Crimea that they were genuine proposals.

In many ways Wrangel resembles Mannerheim. It is interesting, therefore, that when he decided that he should regularise his position with regard to civil power, he chose to adopt the style of Regent. It was not, as he hastened to point out, a monarchist move, but it did make clear the nature of his authority, and there seems little doubt that it was the example of Mannerheim that prompted him to select this title.

Conditions in the Crimea rapidly improved. The establishment of a police force, paid at rates based on army salaries, contributed to the enforcement of law and order. Klimovich rapidly succeeded in infiltrating the Bolshevik underground, and there was a perceptible change in the attitude of both the army and the native population. It became possible to hope once more.

This stiffening of morale, together with a dramatic turn of

events on the Soviets' western border, enabled Wrangel to move over to the attack.

On 25 April 1920 Pilsudski and the Poles mounted a major offensive against the Bolsheviks. Their immediate aim was the liberation of the Ukraine; their further ambition was the 'total defeat of Russian Imperialism'. Their advance into the Ukraine was rapid: on 7 May they occupied Kiev.

The consequent diversion of the Soviet armies to the Ukraine gave Wrangel an unrivalled opportunity to break out of the Crimea. Moreover, he was fully prepared to co-operate with the Poles, even to the extent of subordinating his armies to Polish command. This was in spite of the fact that, whilst he was quite prepared to recognise Poland, he was not so happy about the prospect of an independent Ukraine – at least, on the terms envisaged by the Poles. With considerable skill he avoided the issue: what mattered, he argued, was the defeat of the Bolsheviks; political arguments could come later.

There were various reasons why Wrangel held out hopes for an alliance with Poland. From the Crimea he could threaten the flank of any Soviet force operating against the Ukraine. The newly established relationship with France gave the Whites and the Poles a common ally. Wrangel himself had strong connections with Pilsudski's native Lithuania.

At the same time, he had motives relating more closely to the situation in the Crimea. He had built up a considerable force in the Crimea, but if he was to be able to support it he must acquire more territory. To remain on the defensive was bad for morale – his aims were not so narrowly restricted that he was content with the Crimea alone. At the same time they were limited: if he advanced too far he would suffer the fate of Denikin. His immediate aim was to capture the grain-producing northern Taurida. On 6 June, despite a British ultimatum which forbade him to advance beyond the isthmuses, Wrangel's forces debouched onto the Tauride plain. The Whites advanced on two fronts: one column came into the Taurida via Perekop, the other was sent by sea, and landed on the Azov coast, taking the Soviets in the flank. They inflicted heavy losses on the Red Thirteenth Army, and when the First Cavalry Corps – no longer commanded by Budenny – attempted a counter-attack, that, too, was defeated.

It was as well that Wrangel had not thrown in his lot with the Poles. Their forces were driven out of the Ukraine; Kiev was evacuated on 10 June. Thenceforward they continued to suffer reverses, which even the swarthy and dynamic Pilsudski could do nothing to check. It was not until the arrival of Allied missions in July that the Poles began to regain control of the situation, and they then found that their move against the Ukraine had provoked nothing less than a full-scale invasion of their country. Tukhachevsky, commanding the Soviet armies, had determined on a 'drive for Warsaw'.

Disagreements amongst the Red command about the conduct of the Warsaw campaign indirectly aided Wrangel's schemes; by the end of June all the northern Taurida was his. He began to contemplate his next offensive.

The French continued to prosecute their eastern European policy with vigour. Through Peter Struve, formerly a Marxist, now a whole-hearted adherent of Wrangel, they communicated their approval of the new régime and, unofficially, held out hopes of recognition. If this were achieved, it seemed to Wrangel, he need no longer regard the future with that studied pessimism which he had hitherto evinced. To the Poles the French sent substantial quantities of munitions, together with Weygand, one of their most distinguished generals.

Wrangel continued to maintain his personal ascendancy in the Crimea. It can be taken as an indication of the force of his personality that Red propaganda, which had never made wholly convincing villains of either Denikin or Kolchak, was eminently successful in the case of the Black Baron. This was not simply because he lent himself so easily to caricature; Wrangel posed a threat to the Reds which was far more serious than, at least in public, they were willing to admit. And it was part of his success that he was theatrical, that he did deliberately flaunt his Cossack dress and his personal courage.

In August Wrangel moved onto the offensive again. The success of his sea-borne assault on the Azov coast encouraged him to plan an invasion of the Kuban, flanked by an advance into the Don territories. The amphibious assault of the Kuban was carried out under the command of General Ulagai, with 6,000 infantry and 2,000 horse. The advance into the Don, conducted on a much smaller scale, was led by Colonel Nazarov.

Nazarov met with little success. He succeeded in raising the *stanitsas* on the lower Don, but provoked a massive response from Red forces which had been originally assembled to mount a counter-attack against the Taurida. The counter-attack failed, except in that it gave the Reds a bridgehead across the Dnieper – which was to cause Wrangel a great deal of trouble later on – but it did mean that troops were to hand to deal with the new threat. Trotsky himself moved to Taganrog to supervise operations, and Nazarov's small force was decisively defeated.

So, too, was Ulagai's expedition. Ulagai's objective was Ekaterinodar, and to gain it he mounted an operation closely resembling the second Kuban campaign. But, at the vital railway junction of Timashevskaya, Ulagai's advance faltered – it seems that the General himself lost confidence in the operation – and the Reds counter-attacked in overwhelming force. Ulagai, having been within forty miles of Ekaterinodar, was compelled to retreat; in the first days of September he re-embarked for the Crimea. His attempt to reconquer for the Whites the proving-ground of their movement had failed, but he came out with 20,000 men and 5,000 horses. Resistance to the Soviets was by no means dead.

For Wrangel this was a dubious consolation. Since his whole future depended on holding territory he was committed to organised armies; he could not revert to the guerrilla stage. The Soviets had at their disposal five million men. His own forces were, by comparison, minute. And, at some time, there must come an ending to the Polish war.

XVIII

The Last Stand

At Sevastopol Wrangel deliberately fostered an atmosphere of regularity. He himself rose at seven, saw his principal officers at eight, and worked round the clock, with brief breaks for meals, until eleven at night. When he had a spare moment he visited the hospitals and the refugees. In the evenings there were generally cabinet meetings; military reports might require his attention at all hours. But, outwardly, the impression created was one of calm and order.

There were the inevitable vicissitudes. The actions in the northern Taurida claimed an excessively heavy toll of officer casualties. The defeat in the Kuban damaged morale. In August Wrangel was forced to dismiss General Slachtov, who had become mentally unbalanced, no doubt partly as a result of his long dependence on drugs and alcohol.

The need for allies was urgent. French recognition of the South Russian Government, which had seemed to promise so much in June, now began to come into perspective. It could not solve the Baron's immediate need, which was for man-power with which to create an army reserve. In late June Wrangel sent envoys to Makhno, thinking that some agreement might be reached. The anarchist leader, after his raids into White territory during the previous November, had been greeted by the advancing Reds as a brother. Nevertheless, official Soviet distrust of his aims and methods continued unabated, and in January the Bolsheviks declared Makhno an outlaw. Soon the Red Army was operating against him.

It was the White experience that their enemy's enemy was seldom their friend. Makhno proved no exception. At a meeting of the Makhnovik Insurgency Council on 9 July 1920 the senior of Wrangel's representatives, a colonel, was shot. Shortly afterwards the other emissary, a captain, was hanged: a placard round his neck proclaimed that the same fate awaited any further suppliants from the Whites. In the event, Makhno's distaste for the Whites proved to eclipse even his ferocious hatred of the Bolsheviks. So much was this so, in fact, that a truce was patched up, and Makhnovite forces were offered to the Soviet High Command, to assist in the operations against Wrangel.

The turning point – and it is an irony typical of the whole war – was a Bolshevik defeat. On the banks of the Vistula, between 14 and 17 August 1920, the Polish army succeeded in checking Tukhachevsky's advance on Warsaw, and turned it into a bloody and disorganised retreat. Russian casualties were never fully known, but the Poles took over 70,000 prisoners and captured an immense quantity of *matériel*. Pilsudski's forces swept forwards, overrunning Brest-Litovsk and eastern Galicia, until they presently threatened the Ukraine. The Bolsheviks were spared further disasters because both Pilsudski and General Weygand knew that rapid unsupported advances, particularly by cavalry, could not continue indefinitely. The Polish Army was small and in danger of over-extending its lines of communication. There was no provision for political control of conquered territories, for – in the last analysis – the Poles were concerned simply to secure the most advantageous and defensible frontiers for their re-emergent state. Moreover, they were aware that if they annexed the Ukraine they could expect, in due course, a massive response from the Soviets; as famine threatened Russia, so the grain of the province would become increasingly important. After a consideration of these factors, the Polish made the first tentative proposals for peace.

Without Wrangel it is exceedingly dubious whether the Poles could have found themselves in so unexpectedly advantageous a position. His advance into the northern Taurida and the landings in the Kuban had tied down at least 35,000 Red Army troops – men who might well have helped avert the Soviet defeat on the Vistula. That defeat, however, had two consequences, both disastrous for Wrangel. Firstly, it meant that the support he had been receiving from the French abruptly ceased. As Millerand, the French President, later admitted: 'Help for the White Armies had no other object beyond the salvation of Poland' – in other words, to ensure their own security by establishing Poland as an ally against Germany. Secondly, the Politbureau in Moscow realised that they had seriously misjudged the Polish situation, that their hopes for a series of Communist risings within the country were ill-founded, and that they would be wise to concede defeat. The elimination of Wrangel, whose forces once again threatened the vital industrial areas of the Donets basin, must be their first priority.

Stalin and Trotsky were detailed to organise a fresh levy amongst party members to provide shock troops for the final assault on White territory; Budenny was ordered to move the major part of his cavalry from the Polish front southwards to the Taurida. Gradually the pressures on Wrangel's frontiers increased; patrols hesitated to go far beyond the lines, outposts were attacked and overwhelmed. There was a heightening of tension in the rear areas. The shortage of man-power in the White Army became even more acute.

Wrangel's diplomacy was flexible; he had neither the political naïveté of Denikin, nor the intransigence over matters of principle that always distinguished Kolchak's negotiations with foreign powers. He was fully aware of the prevaricatory nature of French policy, and of the difficulties that faced Pilsudski. He therefore commenced on two distinct and apparently contradictory courses of action: he opened negotiations with the Poles in an attempt to recruit Russians on Polish territory to help remedy his acute shortage of man-power; he also began to make contingency plans for an evacuation from the Crimea of the entire National Army, and with them all those civilians who wished to leave.

The sources of recruits in Poland included those remnants of Denikin's forces who had fled there and been interned, Red units who had gone over to the Poles, Bolshevik prisoners, and former Russian prisoners of the Germans who were still in Poland. It was Wrangel's original intention to create a Third Russian Army out of these men, an army to match the other two that were operating under his command, but he never managed to bring the force up to a sufficient strength. He was, however, able to incorporate 8,000 men, sent to the Crimea by the Poles, into his existing units.

It was this lack of man-power and of international support

that most concerned Wrangel when he set off on 12 September
for a tour of the front. He was accompanied by newspaper correspondents, and by the representatives of the French, Polish,
American, English, Japanese and Serbian military missions. It
was a propaganda exercise, with the object of demonstrating both
the soundness of the White position, and their urgent need for
munitions and stores. For the members of the Allied missions it
was a moving, but saddening experience. Given the poor quality
of their weapons, and their lack of sophisticated equipment, the
Whites had achieved a great deal. But, unless Wrangel had stood
at the gates of Moscow, the respective governments represented
by the missions had no intention of fulfilling his wishes. For this,
Wrangel blamed Lloyd George, 'playing the mentor of Europe',
and his 'shortsighted and egoistic policy'. To Lloyd George, this
policy was the recognition of a distasteful but unavoidable reality.
The missions to the Whites were a cipher, nothing more.

They went north by train. The railway line from Sevastopol
crosses to the mainland by a bridge at Taganach, then runs on
over the steppes, through Melitopol, until it comes parallel to the
Dnieper at Alexandrovsk. To the peninsula of the Crimea itself
there are two main points of entrance: the narrow Perekop
isthmus, and the bridge at Taganach, where the inlet of the Azov
sea that cuts off the Crimea from southern Russia is at its
narrowest. Both the Perekop Isthmus and Taganach, the military
representatives discovered, were in the process of transformation
into formidable defensive positions. What little heavy artillery
Wrangel had was well sited and dug in; trench and wire systems
were laid out with skill and cunning, but in some places there
were trenches only – the supply of wire had come to an end.

North of Taganach the railway was busy, for it was the chief
supply line for the White Armies in the northern Taurida.
Wrangel's party went up as far as Kronsfeld Kolon, where they
inspected the Kornilov division, which was based there whilst
being held in reserve. They watched one of the last formal
parades of the White Army. After the manner of the old Imperial
brigades, mass was sung at an altar in the middle of the vast open
square of soldiers. The richly embroidered red and golden vest-
ments of the priests were in sombre contrast to the drab and
ragged uniforms of the soldiers, who lacked tunics, shirts and

even trousers; one man, Wrangel noted, had nothing but a pair of woollen drawers. There was no trace of uniformity of dress; the men were wearing what they could strip from prisoners or killed comrades; they all had rifles, but differences of calibre created endless problems for the quartermasters handling the meagre ammunition reserves. Yet discipline was good and morale high.

On the evening of 13 September the correspondents and Allied representatives returned by train to Sevastopol, and Wrangel set out by car for another area of the front. His immediate military objective was to clear the whole of the Taurida of Soviet troops and to destroy the dangerous bridgehead so that the river Dnieper would become his left flank, the easily defensible Kichkasse Pass the northern extremity of his territories, and the watershed from Alexandrovsk to Berdiansk his right flank. Thus, northwards from the Crimea, he would be holding a triangular area of southern Russia, a triangle with its base on the Black and Azov seas and its apex at the Kichkasse Pass.

Wrangel was fully aware that to attempt to hold a front three hundred miles in extent, when he had at his disposal only 25,000 infantry and 6,000 cavalry, seemed close to military insanity. He was forced into this course of action because the Crimea was far too small an area to provide food for the two hundred and fifty thousand people whom he had to feed. Despite the small size of his effective fighting force, the total of wounded, prisoners, the personnel of the navy, security and the administrative tail of the army came to this considerable number. The Crimea was drastically overcrowded; at times it seemed more of a prison than a place of refuge. The finances of the South Russian Government were as insecure as ever: the budget for 1920 estimated a deficit of 250,000,000 roubles. The only possible export was grain, and the only possible source of this was the northern Taurida. Cavalry remounts, also, were in very short supply, and once again, the only source of horses was the Taurida. To these reasons Wrangel was inclined to add another; he was becoming increasingly convinced that it would be better to fight the Red Army on the steppes of the Taurida, in the open, where the superiority (in manœuvre) of the White cavalry might be utilised, rather than to attempt a battle of attrition hard against the Crimean defences. As the Polish situation became clearer, so did his recognition that enormous forces would shortly be in action against him. A rough calculation was enough to show that at least three hundred and fifty thousand men would be available to the Soviet High Command. Even with the entire National Army entrenched in the fortifications at Perekop and Taganach the traditional advantage of three to one in favour of the defence would not help them for long – and both Wrangel and Trotsky knew their Clausewitz. Sooner or later the Bolsheviks would break through; already a new slogan was circulating in the party meetings, and was being spread by the Commissars amongst the Red Army troops: 'Concentrate on Wrangel'. The Baron's censorship, however effective, could not prevent rumours of it reaching the Crimea.

Throughout September White troops were fighting in north Taurida to secure the frontiers. In the east Wrangel used his Don Cossack Cavalry to roll up the left flank of the Thirteenth Soviet Army; these Cossacks, under their very able commander Kutepov, were fighting on the borders of their own country. They knew the ground, they were well-mounted and well led; though greatly inferior in numbers to the Red Army they soon forced a Soviet withdrawal. Kutepov began operations with a rapid advance on Mariupol, the cavalry covering a hundred miles in twenty-four hours, sleeping in the open and taking no baggage train. Within days they had decisively out-flanked the Soviets who, menaced in the rear by a force that they could not pin down, began to retreat to the north. Kutepov turned away from the sea and harassed the withdrawal. By the end of September the threat from the east had disappeared and Wrangel was in a position to make the strategic move to which Kutepov's advance was a prelude.

Meanwhile, spurred on by the knowledge that Polish and Soviet delegates were already in conference at Riga, Wrangel mounted his major attack. It took the shape of an advance across the Dnieper and an attempt to reduce the Red bridgehead at Kahovka. This town he knew to be the concentration area of the Red army that the Politbureau had ordered against him. Once that army had assembled, his chances of defeating it were negligible. But if he could disperse its constituent units before they formed under one command, then there seemed to be some chance of averting disaster. In particular, Wrangel hoped to disrupt the existing units around Kahovka before Budenny's Cavalry Army arrived from Poland.

The consolidation of the areas behind the front continued. Through Krivoshein, the civil leader of the South Russian Government, Wrangel issued a series of edicts affecting land distribution, local elections, and municipal affairs. Unlike Denikin, he had no fear of dispossessing landowners; on estates where the owners were absentees, land automatically reverted to the peasants who worked it. The formation of district *zemstvos* and councils was encouraged, and in September the first elections were held. By no means all of Wrangel's changes were radical, but in every instance they were designed to rationalise existing institutions and to stamp out abuses and corruption.

In the base areas of the Crimea the administrative services had been pruned. Peculation continued – it seemed to be an inevitable corollary of White rear areas – but on a much reduced scale.

The air force, despite the enormous number of flying hours logged by its aged machines, was making regular sorties and provided air cover as far north as the Kichkasse Pass; their most pressing need was for spare parts, virtually unobtainable since the British mission had ceased to take an active rôle. The navy was at last in some kind of working order after the disasters of the winter; unfortunately Admiral Sablin, who had done the hard and thankless work of reorganisation, was dying slowly of cancer of the liver.

It was as well that in Admiral Kedrov Wrangel had found a successor of comparable ability. The flagship was the cruiser *General Kornilov*; she and her sister vessels were used to provide artillery support for coastal troop movements, including Kutepov's march eastwards, and the Whites retained supremacy in the Black Sea, thus obviating the danger of an amphibious assault.

General Klimovich kept his close control over the police and security forces.

In early October the operations across the Dnieper, intended to destroy the new Red army before it had time to group, were begun. A further impetus had been given to the plan by the arrival in Sevastopol of delegates of the National Ukrainian party, who opposed Petlyura's separatist movement and advocated a unified Russia with special provisions for Ukrainian autonomy. This prompted Wrangel to think in terms of a bridgehead over the Dnieper to act as a springboard for a possible advance into the Ukraine. The date for the start of operations was 8 October, and the first problem was the bridging of the river. Fortunately the Soviet troops had withdrawn and had not even maintained patrols along the river bank; the only contact with the enemy along the whole front was in the east, where they were sending out occasional cavalry units to reconnoitre for the entirely imaginary main body of the troops that had rolled up their flank earlier in the month.

The lower reaches of the Dnieper, where it widens as it flows into the Black Sea, are broad and shallow; a series of lagoons almost, stretching far back into the South Russian plains, but with a swift and powerful river running through them. Each spring the whole area floods, and the shape of the river changes. Wrangel had first to have the whole area re-surveyed, and then to commandeer boats the length of the river, in order to construct a pontoon bridge. The whole of this operation had to be carried out without attracting the attention of Soviet Intelligence. Much time was spent in deliberately hauling boats in the wrong direction, away from the spot near Uchkelka, which he had finally selected for the crossing.

Late in the night of the 8th, White infantry crossed the Dnieper by a ford near Alexandrovsk, upstream from the site of the bridge. It was an opposed crossing made under heavy artillery and machine-gun fire from the Reds; caught in the light of the greenish German flares used by the Soviets the White infantrymen, struggling in the deep water with their rifles held over their heads, made a perfect target. By dawn, however, they had taken the slopes leading up to the air ridge on the far side of the river, and were covering the crossing of other units who rapidly pushed back the Soviets all along the front.

At Uchkelka anxious engineers were supervising the last stages of the launching of the pontoons. The bridge, almost complete, was streamed from ropes controlled by winches on the Taurida side of the river. On the evening of the 9th, Cossacks of the Third National Army under Generals Babev and Dratsenko led their horses over into Soviet-held territory. The units that had crossed near Alexandrovsk swung south-west to join them.

By now Wrangel had received reliable information indicating that Budenny and his First Red Cavalry Army, who had been ordered by the Politbureau from the Polish front to Kahovka, would arrive on 29 October. Speed was imperative if the expedition across the Dneiper was to succeed in its object. At first all went well; on 11 October the White Cavalry captured 3,000 prisoners, eight guns, six armoured cars and an armoured train. Babev's cavalry outflanked Kahovka, and the movement seriously threatened the lines of communication between the Soviet Second Cavalry Army, in the west, and the elements of the Soviet Sixth and Thirteenth Armies that had drawn back from Wrangel's eastern flank. The Soviet response was an attempt to win back some of the ground lost to Kutepov when he made his raid to Mariupol, with the additional aim of forcing Wrangel's troops back across the Taurida so that they would be caught in a pincer movement when the advance over the Dneiper was checked. Though the Soviets achieved some initial successes, they were soon repulsed by Wrangel's First Army, which moved at them from its position in reserve at Melitopol.

The advance across and along the Dneiper, however, had slowed. Babev's cavalry were making significant progress, but the overall commander of the Second Army, Dratsenko, was failing to follow up the cavalry successes. Wrangel, back in Sevastopol, was becoming increasingly impatient; air reconnaissance had reported that Soviet evacuation of the heavily fortified position at Kahovka had commenced, and he at once ordered an attack to be launched. On the morning of 13 October troops under General Vitkovsky assaulted the town, only to be driven back by a fierce and well-directed artillery barrage. The tank regiment, earmarked by Wrangel for the assault, eventually succeeded in breaking through the defence system, only to be wiped out by point-blank fire. The information from the reconnaissance planes was false, and the Whites had made a frontal attack on a fully alerted and heavily defended position.

Dratsenko, paying the penalty of his earlier indecision, was now retreating. Wrangel was convinced that the situation was redeemable, but could not leave Sevastopol to take over command in the field, since by doing so he would lose his control over the situation as a whole – the fault that, in his view, had vitiated Denikin's generalship the previous year. On the morning of 13 October, just as Vitkovsky's troops were making their costly and fruitless attempt on Kahovka, he heard that General Babev had been killed by a shell. As always in White cavalry units, the leader was all important, and Babev's death at once demoralised his men. The process was completed when Naumenko, who succeeded him, was also wounded by a shell splinter. The consequent disruption of the cavalry soon began to demoralise the rest of the Second Army, and by the evening of 21 October they were in full flight through the forests that covered the approaches to the pontoons. Dratsenko made no real attempt to stop the rout, and eventually accelerated it by issuing an order for a retreat that made no provision for rearguards or phased withdrawal. That the movement was covered at all was mainly due to the independent action of a subordinate commander. As light faded on 13 October the pontoon bridge was dismantled, and on 14 October the forces still remaining over the Dnieper crossed by boat. The expedition had begun well and shown every sign of achieving its objective. The dispositions were sound and the strategy was faultless, but the death of Babev, the air force's mistake over Kahovka, and the incompetence of Dratsenko – who, however good he may have been as a defensive general, was quite unable to comprehend manœuvre in attack – had turned it into a disaster. Wrangel's last offensive, the last action in which he would be able to take the initiative, had failed.

The Soviets signed a provisional peace with Poland on 12 October; Wrangel's worst fears had been realised. In sixteen days' time he could anticipate the arrival of Budenny's army – perhaps before. Intelligence reported that Budenny was making forced marches and moving very fast indeed. Desperately, Wrangel had tried to establish contact with the Poles; he had acquaintances of influence in Polish administrative circles, who might at least have managed to protract the peace negotiations. But he had no way of communicating with them, and his requests to the Inter-Allied High Commissioners for permission to set up a wireless station on the site of the former Imperial Embassy near Constantinople were refused out of hand.

Wrangel's forces were by now outnumbered at least three to one, and the Red Army were receiving fresh reinforcements daily. The basic Soviet dispositions had been made by Frunze; but now that Budenny's First Cavalry Army was within striking distance of the Crimea, Trotsky moved south so as to be present at the final assault. In essence Trotsky's plan of attack was quite simple. The Second, Sixth and Thirteenth Red Armies would attempt an enveloping and encircling movement that would tie down and eventually wipe out the White troops in the Taurida, whilst Budenny and the First Army made a direct assault on the Taganach bridge in the White rear.

Wrangel's strategy may, at first sight, seem at fault. If he was determined to fight in the Taurida, then he left the Crimea wide open to precisely such a thrust as that which Trotsky intended. Wrangel realised this, but he also considered the course he adopted to be the only one possible. It was not simply a matter of his distrust of the efficacy of the Perekop and Taganach defences; he had also to gain time, and this he was more likely to achieve by a fighting retreat in the Taurida than by an im-mediate withdrawal to the fortifications of the isthmus. For in Sevastopol he was rapidly, but without panic, preparing an evacuation of the Crimea, an evacuation of the entire National Army, and of all those civilians who wished to accompany them. Since August he had been stockpiling fuel for the navy against precisely such an emergency. Wrangel had also arranged for a sufficient tonnage of shipping to be available in the various ports of the Crimea (Eupatoria, Yalta, Theodosia, Kerch) to take off the different units of his armies after they had covered the main evacuation, which he planned for Sevastopol. In the huge har-bour at Sevastopol itself, he kept what remained of the navy, ready to leave at short notice. In order to prevent disorder amongst civilians and panic in the army, he let the rumour circulate that the shipping was being held for raids on Odessa and the Kuban. He also arranged for the General Staff to 'leak' troop figures for these operations that would correspond with the tonnage available. The Crimea was calm and unsuspecting.

On 28 October the first Red attacks were delivered in shattering force. It was the coldest October in twenty-five years, and the scantily clad White soldiers lay shivering on the steppes awaiting the enemy's dawn assaults. Units of the Second National Army under Kutepov and Abramov bore the brunt of the fighting, and they were soon in retreat. Their shirts stuffed with straw and moss, their limbs bereft of feeling by frostbite, they marched painfully back through the Taurida. The morning of the 29th found the steppes enveloped in a thick fog, limiting visibility to a few yards; the temperature was fourteen degrees below zero. Red cavalry loomed out of the mist, subjected to an almost spectral magnification in the shadowy refracted light, and cut down the numbed defenceless infantrymen. The latter, out of visible contact with their officers, and often entirely unaware of their whereabouts, soon lost what vestiges of morale they still retained.

Wrangel himself went up to the front to attempt to stem the retreat. At once he realised that Budenny's cavalry were poised to cut off his army from the Crimea. The vital geographical feature was the isthmus at Salkovo, where the railway and road ran through a valley to make the crossing to Taganach. On the night of 29 October Wrangel ordered Abramov to entrain his infantry and send them down the line to guard the pass. He also sent a detachment of armoured cars to screen the railway from Budenny's advancing cavalry. But the railway was blocked; at the stations the water tanks for replenishing the boilers were frozen, and the movement proved impossible. Wrangel himself had managed to get back to the Crimea and sent the tiny number of troops he could scrape together – officer cadets of sixteen and seventeen, men from the Artillery School, his own escort, civilians – up to the pass. As darkness fell on the 30th, the first patrols of Red cavalry entered the pass and opened fire on the White positions. Their numbers increased, and as the last smudged gleams of light left the sky they came in at the White positions dismounted. For the time being the military cadets and Wrangel's escort managed to hold them off, helped by the well-directed fire of two two-inch field guns brought up from the Artillery School.

The night was bitterly cold; three times the Whites scrambled to the parapets of their positions, only to discover that they had been alerted by false alarms. In any case, those not on sentry duty found it almost impossible to sleep; they knew that they, and their comrades huddled in the rifle pits along the shallow crest of the pass, were the only troops between the Red Army and the Crimea. Not only did the safety of the civilian population depend on them, but also that of the White Army: for once the isthmus was taken there was no hope of retreat for Wrangel's forces.

Wrangel spent the night in a desperate attempt to get in touch with Kutepov; when he finally achieved wireless contact he ordered him to link up with Abramov's Second Army, which was still retreating slowly down the line of the railway, and to take over the command.

At dawn on 31 October the White commanders at Salkovo could see, as they searched the far end of the pass with their field-glasses, that the Reds had been reinforced during the night. But before the dismounted cavalry, advancing cautiously under cover of the heaps of shale along the sides of the pass, could seriously threaten the defenders, Abramov's advance guard, coming along the railway line, took them in the rear. Just before noon Kutepov's units moved across the line from a westerly direction towards Sivash – in time to break up a concentration of Budenny's cavalry, who were preparing for another attack on the pass. They caught them when they had stopped for their mid-day meal, horses unsaddled and, in some cases, weapons piled. In the confusion Kutepov succeeded in herding them southwards, to where the marshes of Sivash glittered with a crust of salt and frost, between the grey sea and overcast sky. In some places the crust broke, and the horses fell, throwing their riders. But Kutepov's units were too dispersed, and most of Budenny's cavalry managed to break through them and move out of danger to the north, or to retreat eastwards along the beaches until the Whites could no longer pursue them.

By 2 November the greater part of the White Army was through the pass. Wrangel tended to blame Kutepov for not following up his action on the Sivash marshes, but in fact there was little that could have been done. The spirit of the White Army was all but broken. Cut off from their base, desperately outnumbered, they were prepared to fight for survival, but their ability to take the offensive had gone. Their casualties were enormous; some forty per cent of their numbers. Most of the former Bolsheviks who had elected to serve in the White Army had deserted on the long retreat. The Army had lost five armoured trains, eighteen guns, ten million cartridges, twenty-five railway locomotives, and almost all the reserves of ammunition, provisions and grain. It would be impossible to feed the population in the Crimea for more than a month. The battle in the Taurida had been lost.

Both the civilian population and the army imagined the defences at Perekop to be impregnable. Wrangel was almost alone in realising that this was not so. The essential fortifications had been completed, but there were no billets for the defenders, and the intense cold of the unusually early winter had made these of vital importance. Though Red losses would be high if they attempted a direct assault, the chances were that such an assault would eventually succeed, for the Whites had spent all their reserves. Wrangel had no illusions about the Soviets' ruthless use of infantry in such circumstances. Moreover, one of the finest Red generals, Blücher, had been assigned to command the assault. Wrangel was much concerned that the gravity of the situation should not be communicated to either army or civilians; the result of panic would be another, bloodier, Novorossisk. He continued to make public appearances, and his ability to astonish and delight people by remembering their names and histories remained unimpaired. Only General Chatilov, his Chief-of-Staff, shared his knowledge of the true seriousness of the situation.

On 7 November, the third anniversary of the 1917 Revolution, the expected Soviet assault on Perekop began.[1] The fortifications on the isthmus consisted of three defensive lines. Across the north of the isthmus was a barbed-wire barrage, in places up to fifty feet in depth, shallower in others, because work had been hampered by lack of wire. Behind this was the Turkish Wall, a line based on a series of eighteenth-century works, and laid out

---

[1] It is almost impossible to reconcile Red and White accounts of the assault on Perekop. These differ over dates, times and geography. But that the assault opened on the 7th is certain.

on the fire base principle: a series of machine-gun nests with interlinked fields of fire dominating every sector. Further back again, across the south of the isthmus, a strong line of trenches and wire, anchored on the lakes that lie between the towns of Yushun and Armyansky Bazar, completed the defences. The whole area was covered by heavy artillery on railway mountings, which operated from a branch line ending at Yushun.

Wave after wave of infantry, headed by special shock units, and fired by the symbolic nature of this anniversary attempt to dislodge the last organised units of the counter-revolution on Russian soil, swept onto the wire. But they were easily held, and the cost in lives was prohibitive, even for the Red Army. The heightened mood of the troops was in danger of changing as swiftly into one of despair. Kutepov, commanding the White defenders, was confident that he had secured the gateway to the Crimea.

Reinforcements for the Soviet army were arriving continually. Even so, the Red command was not prepared to risk another frontal attack on the wire. They therefore decided to attempt an amphibious assault below the defences, covered by a diversionary attack on the wire. On the night of 9 November their artillery opened up on White positions behind the wire, and more infantry were sent in. Simultaneously, picked troops set across the head of the Sivash inlet, guided by local Bolshevik sympathisers.

They were aided by a freak of nature. Very infrequently in the past it had happened that a strong north-west wind would blow the shallow waters at the head of the inlet eastwards, leaving the mud flats exposed. In November 1920 such a wind coincided with the extreme cold; the sea-bed was laid bare and frozen hard. Across the path so formed Blücher's men picked their way. They landed on the frozen marches, out of sight of the White positions, which had been designed to protect the summer shoreline, and reached the beach unopposed. Most of the White forces were tied down by the attack to the north, unaware of the menace behind them. It was as well that the Red troops had not managed to circumvent the entire position, but had arrived between the Turkish Wall and the final line of defences, which had been left manned by a skeleton garrison, against such an emergency as this. It was also characteristic of Wrangel that he had personally insisted that this provision should be made.

On the morning of the 9th Kutepov discovered that he was virtually surrounded. The pressure on the wire had been maintained throughout the night, and prevented him realising precisely what had happened. He therefore ordered a general withdrawal to the Turkish Wall, only to find that Red troops were still threatening his rear. Had it not been for the fact that Wrangel had ordered the destruction of all boats over a certain size in the villages along the Sivash inlet, his position would have been even more drastic than it actually was. Throughout the 9th his troops fought on, holding the main Soviet attack at the Turkish Wall and temporarily tying down the infiltrators.

Late on 8 November Wrangel had heard the full extent of the White failure. He was in the chair at a council of the south Russian government when the news came. Chatilov was the first to read Kutepov's telegram; he passed it over to the Baron without comment. Remarking that he had to speak on the telephone to Kutepov, Wrangel handed over the meeting to M. Krivoshein and, followed by his Chief-of-Staff, left the room. They both agreed that the situation was hopeless, that the army's morale was on the verge of collapse, and that the Perekop defences would inevitably fall. It was at this moment that Wrangel finally conceded defeat. He sent an orderly to call Admiral Kedrov from the council chamber.

When Kedrov came Wrangel briefly outlined the situation to him. The Admiral's reaction was one of dismay: 'My God, why did I accept this burden?'[1]

But, impressed by the calm of Wrangel and Chatilov, he recovered himself, and the three men reviewed the situation. Thanks to Wrangel's precautionary measures, it was already possible for the navy to evacuate seventy-five thousand men. Wrangel further ordered Kedrov to commandeer every seaworthy boat in the Crimean ports, to get as many White ships as possible back from Constantinople, and to detain all foreign trading-vessels that could be used for the evacuation.

At this point the group was joined by an alarmed Krivoshein, suddenly conscious of impending disaster. It was with difficulty that he was persuaded that the situation was under control, and

---

[1] Wrangel, *Memoirs*, p. 314.

that he and his colleagues must do all they could to keep the civilian population from panic. Indeed, such a panic, rather than military collapse, was Wrangel's greatest fear.

The next day Wrangel left for the front. There he discovered that Kutepov had been forced to abandon the Turkish Wall and had fallen back on the last line of defences, between the lakes. Kutepov talked in terms of a counter-attack, but admitted that he had no faith in an ultimate success. Too many of the best commanders had been killed, and the speed with which Red losses were made good had demoralised the men. Attack after attack came in, and the enormous losses suffered by the Reds seemed to make no difference to the speed of their advance. Wrangel agreed with Kutepov's assessment of the situation; he had, nevertheless, to implore him to hold the line for five or six days more, in order to allow for the evacuation to get under way.

On the way back from the front Wrangel stopped at Simferopol, the central town of the Crimea, and put General Abramov in charge of the preliminaries for its evacuation. At 9 a.m. on 10 November he arrived at Sevastopol station and at once went to the palace, when he gave Chatilov, Kedrov, and Krivoshein their final instructions. These provided for a military take-over of all public services, the proclamation of martial law, and the precise arrangements for the evacuations and the priorities of the various groups involved.

At 10 a.m. he met the French High Commissioner and the representatives of the other Allied missions, and asked them for whatever help they could give towards the evacuation. The news had spread rapidly through the city, and had began to generate panic. The military policing of Sevastopol was in the hands of boys from the military schools: Wrangel had to hope that they would succeed in maintaining some kind of order.

Messages filtered through from the front that night. Kutepov's counter-attack had failed, and it was only the heavy artillery behind Yushun that was preventing the Reds from massing for their final attack on the defences between the lakes. The remaining few planes carrying the red, white and black colours of the White air force were flying continual sorties from the Taganach airfield, but the fading light had eventually grounded them. With fanatical bravery the Red troops came on; the area in front of the White trenches was devoid of cover, the artillery fire was laid on pre-sited markers, and machine-guns were operating on fixed lines, yet their advance continued. Late on the evening of the 10th the last defence line was breached. On the 11th Kutepov ordered a retreat and the Red Army began its deployment into the Crimea.

As Trotsky's forces moved forwards, a French cruiser, the *Waldeck-Rousseau*, anchored in Sevastopol harbour. On board was Admiral Dumesnil, acting C-in-C of the French Mediterranean Fleet. In the afternoon of the 11th the Admiral, together with the French High Commissioner, the Comte de Martel, called on Wrangel. The consequence of their interview was that the French promised to give all the help they could to complete the evacuation; in return Wrangel pledged the White Navy and the Mercantile Marine as security for the cost of the operation, and for the support of the refugees until such time as their future should be assured. Both de Martel and Dumesnil seemed satisfied with this arrangement; it should be noted, however, that they did not have time to consult their government about it; the agreement was subject to ratification.

Wrangel also took the opportunity to issue a formal proclamation announcing his intentions.

ORDER FROM THE REGENT OF SOUTH RUSSIA AND THE COMMANDER-IN-CHIEF OF THE RUSSIAN ARMY
Sevastopol, 29 October (11 November) 1920

People of Russia! Alone in its struggle against the oppressor, the Russian Army has been maintaining an uneven contest in its defence of the last strip of Russian Territory on which law and truth hold sway.

Conscious of my responsibility, I have tried to anticipate every possible contingency from the very beginning.

I now order the evacuation and embarkation at the Crimean ports of all those who are following the Russian Army on its road to Calvary; that is to say, the families of the soldiers, the officials of the Civil Administration and their families, and anyone else who would be in danger if they fell into the hands of the enemy.

The Army will cover the embarkation, knowing that the necessary ships for its own evacuation are ready and waiting in the ports according to a pre-arranged plan. I have done everything that human strength can do to fulfil my duty to the Army and the population.

We cannot foretell our future fate.

We have no other territory than the Crimea. We have no money. Frankly, as always, I warn you all of what awaits you.

May God grant us strength and wisdom to endure this period of Russian misery, and to survive it.

GENERAL WRANGEL[1]

To the troops the General sent more detailed orders. They were to disengage and move to their various ports of embarkation; heavy equipment was to be abandoned, the infantry were to travel in the wagons, a cavalry screen was to be thrown out to cover the retreat. The punishment that the Reds had received at Perekop made them cautious; they were advancing slowly, and were continually harassed by the White cavalry under Fostikov and Barbovich.

On the 12th Krivoshein left for Constantinople, with instructions from Wrangel to see what could be done to prepare for the influx of refugees. That night the Soviets sent by wireless an offer for surrender, guaranteeing an amnesty for the High Command and for all those who voluntarily laid down their arms. Wrangel at once ordered the wireless stations closed down, except that in the General Staff building, which was manned by officers.

On 13 November the French government at last ratified the terms under which their assistance was to be given in the evacuation; by then the operation was almost complete. Abramov's units had come in from Simferopol by train, and later in the day Kutepov and his staff arrived at the point of embarkation. The troops were still well disciplined, and the withdrawal to the ports was now almost finished. Sevastopol itself was virtually deserted; there was some minor looting and arson; this ceased when two or three of those responsible were captured and shot by Wrangel's bodyguard. The troops covering the approaches to the town were positioned in the line of fortifications originally constructed during the Crimean War.

At dawn on the 14th the last stages of the evacuation began. The rearguard came down from their positions on the hills surrounding the town and were ferried out to the waiting ships. General Wrangel, accompanied by an aide-de-camp, paced up

---

[1] Wrangel, *Memoirs*, p. 318.

and down the quay. From the ships the tall figure, wearing the distinctive Cossack *papakha*, was clearly visible. He had his hands in the pockets of his long greatcoat, against the cold, but he remained as commanding and as impassive as he had been at any moment of White triumph.

Shortly before mid-day the last outposts were drawn in. Wrangel had ample time for reflection as he walked up and down whilst the ship's boats took on their final complements of men; some of his feelings he expressed in the few words that he spoke to the military cadets before they embarked:

The Army, which has shed its blood in great torrents in fighting, not only for the Russian cause, but for the whole world, is now leaving its native shores, abandoned by everybody. We are going into exile; we are not going as beggars with outstretched hands, but with our heads held high, conscious of having done our duty to the end. We have the right to claim help from those who owe their continued freedom and even their continued existence to us; we have sacrificed much for their cause. . . .[1]

We may well disbelieve this statement, in an historical sense; we have every right to doubt that the White Russian Army did, in fact, perform such a function. But we must accept its subjective validity: this, for Wrangel, was the measure of his achievement, and his failure. We must also, if we are to understand this extraordinary man, realise that he had attained the other object which was in his mind when he accepted command from Denikin:

I could not promise the Army victory; all I could do was to promise it should come out of an almost hopeless position without loss of honour.

There can be no doubt that, for Wrangel, the honour he referred to was that of the Russian Imperial Army of 1914; there can be no doubt, either, that this honour he considered redeemed.

The General was the last man to leave the quay. At twenty past three his motor boat set off for the *General Kornilov*. After what seemed to be endless delays the fleet weighed anchor and set out eastwards round the coast of the Crimea. On the morning of 15 November it lay off Yalta, which the cavalry screening the retreat had reached by forced marches after breaking away

---

[1] Wrangel, *Memoirs*, p. 324.

from the vanguard of the Red Army. Many of the Cossacks shot their horses before they embarked; the corpses wallowed in the harbour.

Messages from Theodosia and Kerch indicated that the evacuation in those ports had not proceeded as smoothly as at Sevastopol: on the 16th the fleet anchored in the roads off Theodosia, but it was to discover that the operation had, by this time, been safely concluded. In the early afternoon a message to the same effect was received from Kerch. The fleet, numbering a hundred and twenty-six ships, and carrying 145,693 men, women and children in all, turned westwards for Constantinople.

EPILOGUE

The Reckoning

There are no casualty lists for the Russian Civil War. More men and women died through famine, disease, and reprisals than as a direct consequence of military action. The total number of deaths can only be approximately estimated: twenty-five million is a possible figure. Half a million died in the Siberian retreat, half a million were killed by the Cheka, and perhaps the same number by the White security forces – however estimated, the total mounts with horrifying speed. Three years of conflict, across all the Russian territories, have to be taken into account.

Of the combatants the Allies suffered least. Few of their troops were killed; the war had no direct effect on their home populations. Intervention was expensive in other ways. (It cost the British, who were most heavily committed, at least twenty-four million pounds.) Even so, it never became a central concern for any of the intervening nations. Nor, perhaps, was it as important to the Russians as we are prone to imagine.

The Russian Civil War can be understood only against the background of the World War and the circumstances of the German defeat. The Treaty of Brest-Litovsk, it has been pointed out, was Lenin's first major strategic decision in the struggle against the counter-revolution.[1] It was in anticipation of this treaty that the Allies began their intervention in the Civil War: a course of action that was to involve sixteen nations in the conflict. The result of this has been, in Britain and the United States at least, to focus a great deal of attention on an aspect of the war that is not of as great importance as has sometimes been suggested.

In many ways, intervention was to prove a hindrance rather than a help to the Whites; this was particularly so in the Siberian

[1] John Erikson, 'Lenin as Civil War Leader', in Leonard Shapiro and Peter Reddaway, *Lenin*, p. 181.

385

theatre, and where representatives of the United States or Japan were involved. It is also worth noting that the effects of intervention on subsequent Soviet foreign policy have often been confused with the effects of the purely internal crises. Certainly, intervention did help create a tradition of ill-will and fear that was to rebound, to the manifest disadvantage of the intervening countries, in the future. But the tradition had its roots in Marxist ideology, and was a corollary of the fundamental Marxist precepts about the nature of society. It cannot be attributed to the fact of intervention – it would have existed even had the Allies welcomed the Bolsheviks with 'fraternal greetings'.

Indeed, there was one important respect in which intervention actively helped the Soviets. In the hands of skilled propagandists, the Allied involvement could be used to make the Soviet cause appear to be patriotic rather than factional.

But it was the fact of civil war, rather than the fact of intervention, that was to be the real determinant in the Soviet outlook. It not only demonstrated, to those who wished to believe, the correctness of Marxist postulates about the nature of the class war, but also revealed that the forces of counter-revolution were stronger than either Marx, his disciples, or the events of November 1917 had indicated. The Civil War was the major pragmatic influence on the Soviet State; intervention was a side issue that reinforced the lessons learned. The closed structure of the state, the fear and suspicion that seem endemic, are far more products of internal than external events. Today the stigma of White Guardist ancestry can still be a debilitating factor in Soviet life;[1] in the purges of the 'thirties the White Guards were as significant a part of the phantom conspiracies as the Trotskyites, and to many people they seemed far more credible. Stalin returned to the topic again and again, and the 'White threat' received an important boost during the Second World War, when it became an all-purpose catch phrase for the activities of the Finns, the Ukrainian nationalists, the Roumanians and the Vlasov Army. And if today it is felt that the notion of a White Guard threat is a shade academic, then it has made it all the better a sneer to

---

[1] This was to become apparent from the circumstances of the defection of Oleg Penkovsky, who was investigated because it was discovered that his father had been a White officer.

direct at émigré writers who venture, from the crumbling West, to disturb the Soviet dream of history.

The Civil War removed from Russia, through death or exile, the greater part of the upper and middle classes. It polarised the political conflict and reinforced the monolithic structure of the emergent state. The decisive factor in the war was the existence and organisation of the Bolshevik Party, and opposition to the party became tantamount to treason. The devastation wrought by war meant that war-time conditions continued to prevail long after 1920. In these circumstances the implications of opposition remained the same. When Trotsky was finally expelled from the party the history of the Civil War had to be rewritten. He had become a traitor, and his actions in the Civil War had to be shown to be treasonable.

In 1917 nothing could have been further from the Bolshevik intentions than the creation of a standing army. Yet by 1920 they had five million men under arms. This, again, is an indication of the importance of the War on the Soviet outlook. The Soviet State as we know it was, in the phrase so often employed by Russian writers, 'forged' in the Civil War.

The war had no such unifying effect on the Whites. Only Wrangel learnt from it, and he came too late; the other White leaders merely demonstrated their failure to understand the situation and, lacking understanding, they proved unable to remedy it. Their failure is, to an extent, understandable: the business of revolutionaries is revolution, but the business of counter-revolutionaries is seldom counter-revolution. Revolutionaries are born to their condition. Counter-revolutionaries have it thrust upon them.

It does not follow from this that counter-revolution is doomed, or that the Russian counter-revolution, in particular, was doomed. To accept this is to accept a deterministic view of history for which there can be no warrant in any account of the events. The Whites failed as much as a result of their military mistakes as anything else, and these military mistakes were frequently the product of stupidity and carelessness. The Reds made mistakes also: in exclusively military matters they made far more than the Whites. Their greater degree of political organisation permitted them more latitude in this respect; in contrast, the Whites sacrificed political consolidation for the lure of immediate military gains, and then proceeded to throw away the advantages won in the field.

Given the White failure to organise politically, their achievements are all the more remarkable. It may be that the answer to their political problem was the one which Lenin gave them, by his insistence that the only alternative to the Communist dictatorship was the return of the Tsarist régime. It was a belief that he persisted in until the end of his life, and an argument that he used with great effect for the purposes of propaganda. After the Civil War, when the statement had come to be regarded as axiomatic, he used it with devastating results: the revolt at Kronstadt in 1921 – which was, in fact, a mutiny by men who could all be loosely classed as Communists – was against the party leadership. Therefore, Lenin argued, it must be a White Guardist plot and Tsarist in its aims. It was nothing of the sort, as Lenin knew full well, but what he had said served his purpose.

Had the Whites unilaterally declared themselves for a monarchist régime before it was too late for the declaration to be of use, they would probably have lost some of their adherents. Their gains would not, at first, have been tangible, but in the long run they could have been very considerable. The speculation is valueless except insofar as it leads us to consider why they did not make such a declaration. The answer is implicit in the Whites' refusal to pre-empt the expression of popular opinion through the Constituent Assembly. This decision did the Whites no good, but it reveals an aspect of the movement that the prejudices of fifty years have always served to obscure. It was this scrupulousness that made the open Greater Russian objectives of the Whites so severe a disability; the Soviets, pursuing the same aim covertly, did not allow the good repute of their cause to be sullied by the implication of such a policy. The practice continues.

After Wrangel's evacuation of the Crimea armed resistance to the Bolsheviks collapsed. Semenov, his Japanese support withdrawn, made a narrow escape by aeroplane from pro-Bolshevik forces. Savinkov made an abortive attempt to start an anti-Bolshevik rising in Western Russia; it came to nothing. For over a year Baron Ungern-Sternberg held out in Mongolia; in February 1921 he took Ulan Bator, where he set up court and ruled in barbaric splendour until the Red Army captured the town in July. His neurotic cruelty and his dreams of empire persisted until the end.

For a short time the Crimean refugees maintained their identity as an army. There was even talk of resuming the offensive – it remained talk. Gradually the refugees left their grim camps at Constantinople and Gallipoli to settle elsewhere: in western Europe, in the Americas, and in the Balkans. Wrangel was tireless in his efforts to provide for the destitute; he also endeavoured to maintain the cadre structure of the army, so that one day it might fight again. Thus he brought into being, together with the Grand Duke Nicholas, the World Organisation of Russian War Veterans, better known as R.O.V.S.

His health broke down under the strain. In April 1928 he died in Brussels. It seems probable that Wrangel died a natural death – of an illness brought on by overwork – but there can be no doubt that the Cheka (now the O.G.P.U.) dealt with his successor to the leadership of the White Russian forces, General Kutepov.

On the morning of 26 January 1930 Kutepov set off from his Paris flat to attend mass at an Orthodox church established by veterans of the Civil War. When he had walked a few hundred yards, he was approached by two gendarmes who forced him into a waiting car and drove off with him at high speed. Later that day a group of men, including a gendarme and a young woman, were seen transporting a long package wrapped in sacking down the sea-cliffs near Villers-sur-Mer. On the beach they loaded it onto a motor launch, which set out for a cargo-ship hove-to off the coast. The ship was almost certainly the Soviet *Spartak*. Beyond that, nothing more is known of the fate of General Kutepov, the 'hero of Perekop'.

Kutepov was succeeded as chairman of R.O.V.S. by General Miller, the former White C-in-C at Archangel, now resident in Paris. On 22 September 1937 Miller left his office in the Rue du Colisée to attend a rendezvous with two Germans; the object was allegedly to investigate the possibilities of collaboration between Nazi Germany and the White Movement. The meeting had been arranged by General Skoblin, former commander of the Kornilov division and now a prominent member of R.O.V.S. Before going out Miller left a note, detailing the place and circumstances of the rendezvous. It ended: 'the meeting was arranged at Skoblin's initiative. This is perhaps a trap, which is why I am leaving this note.'[1]

It was a trap – so well arranged that it is not known how Miller was carried off. But it is certain that later that day a large wooden packing-case was off-loaded from a Ford van owned by the Soviet Embassy onto the Soviet freighter *Mariya Ulyanova*, which was lying in Le Havre.

The next day General Skoblin, by now aware that Miller had left a note, also chose to disappear. He had been working for the O.G.P.U. for some years. He might well have been caught, had not the Daladier government – dependent on left-wing votes and signatory to several agreements with the U.S.S.R. – evinced a remarkable sensitivity to Soviet feelings and failed to pursue the case. Nothing more was heard of either general.

Miller's disappearance was an indirect consequence of the death of another Civil War general, but this time a Red. In 1937 Tukhachevsky, now a Marshal, had been executed for his part in a conspiracy against Stalin. In the intricacies of this conspiracy both Miller and Skoblin had been involved – with the important distinction that Skoblin was in communication with the O.G.P.U. The removal of Miller would have the effect both of silencing a man who knew too much and of enabling Skoblin to take over his position. Had Miller not left a note the scheme would have almost certainly succeeded.

Miller did not throw in his lot with the Nazis. But General Krasnov, Ataman of the Don, saw in the Führer 'the hope of the Cossacks': and in 1944 was engaged in establishing a Cossack State in the Italian Alps. It was populated mainly by those Don Cossacks who, when south-western Russia was overrun by the Panzer Armies, sided with the Germans. Stalin's systematic destruction of all traces of Cossack national identity had made the survivors more than willing to enlist in the various corps formed by the Germans to fight against the Communists. When

---

[1] Quoted in Bailey, *The Conspirators*, p. 239.

the German Armies retreated from Russia the Cossacks went with them.

In the spring of 1945 the British advance through northern Italy forced the Cossacks, some 35,000 strong, to move into Austria. There, at Linz, they surrendered to the British. Before the news that the Allies had agreed to return them to the Soviet Government was broken, the Cossack generals and officers were tricked into leaving their men; only then were they informed of their fate. A few managed – or were allowed – to escape; the greater number were sent back to the U.S.S.R. In January 1947 *Pravda* reported the execution, by hanging, of four generals: the two most important were Krasnov and Shkuro. They were old men; since the Civil War Krasnov had written novels and Shkuro had ridden in a circus. They were also guilty: Krasnov had broken his parole to Trotsky, Shkuro had committed appalling acts of barbarism. But the rulers who condemned them were equally treacherous and equally brutal: it was the Whites' crime to have lost.

Shortly before, Ataman Semenov suffered the same penalty from the same rulers. In the final weeks of the war the Soviets had over-run Japanese-held Manchuria. There they captured the former ruler of Trans-Baikal; he had spent the intervening twenty-five years as a petty warlord in Japanese employ. But he had none of Krasnov's enthusiasm for the Nazis. One of the few admirable things he ever did was to condemn 'the extreme enthusiasm of our [White Russian] young people for fascism and for Hitler's national-socialism'.[1]

Nestor Makhno, surprisingly, died in his bed. In 1921 his band had finally been hunted down by the Reds and surrounded. Makhno attempted to break out towards the Roumanian frontier and eventually managed to cross the Dnieper into safety with 250 men. After imprisonment in Roumania and Poland Makhno established himself in Paris, where he lived out his last years in poverty and squalor, until his death in 1935.

General Denikin died peacefully at Ann Arbor, Michigan, in 1947. General Mannerheim, now Marshal of Finland, died in

---

[1] Quoted by Erwin Oberländer, 'The All-Russian Fascist Party', *Journal of Contemporary History*, Vol. 1 (1966), p. 166.

Switzerland in 1951. His victory of 1918 had earned him no repose. When Finland was subjected to savage and unprovoked Russian aggression in 1939, it was Mannerheim who conducted a brilliant defensive war which forced the Russians to come to terms. Finland suffered, but in the process she inflicted grave losses on the U.S.S.R. The truce that followed did not last.

During the subsequent 'Continuation War' the Finns accepted German aid in an attempt to recover their lost lands. But Britain and Russia were now allies, and Winston Churchill's government declared war on Finland – a reprehensible and unprincipled move. In 1944 it became apparent that Germany would be conquered. Mannerheim, who had saved his country from military failures in his capacity as C-in-C, was now largely responsible for the negotiation of an armistice with the Allies. By so doing he preserved for Finland her national integrity. It was his unique achievement to demonstrate that those qualities which gave him the victory in 1918 would stand his country in as good stead in her hour of defeat.

Select Bibliography

ADAMS, ARTHUR E. *Bolsheviks in the Ukraine: The Second Campaign.* New Haven, 1963.

AGAR, CAPTAIN AUGUSTUS, R.N. *Baltic Episode.* London, 1963.

ALEKSEEV, GENERAL M. V. *Iz dnevnika M. V. Alekseeva.* Ed. J. Slavik. Prague, 1949.

ANTONOV-OVSEENKO, *Zapiski o grazdanskoi voine.* Mosscow, 1924-1933.

ATEN, CAPTAIN MARRIOT, WITH ARTHUR ORRMONT. *Last Train over Rostov Bridge.* London, 1962.

BAILEY, GEOFFREY. *The Conspirators.* London, 1961.

BARCLAY, BRIGADIER C. N. *Armistice 1918.* London and New York, 1968.

BAYLEY, JOHN. *Tolstoy and the Novel.* London and New York, 1966.

BECHHOFER, C. E. *In Denikin's Russia.* London, 1921.

BECVAR, GUSTAV. *The Lost Legion.* London and New York, 1939.

BENEŠ, E. *Souvenirs de Guerre et de Révolution 1914-1918.* Paris, 1928-29.

BENNETT, GEOFFREY. *Cowan's War: The Story of British Naval Operations in the Baltic 1918-1920.* London, 1964.

BERMONDT-AVALOV, COLONEL PRINCE P. M. *Im Kampf gegen den Bolschewismus.* Hamburg, 1925.

BONCH-BRUEVICH, GENERAL M. D. *Vsya vlast sovetam.* Moscow, 1957.

BORENIUS, TANCRED. *Field-Marshal Mannerheim.* London, 1940.

BRADLEY, JOHN. *Allied Intervention in Russia 1919-1920.* London and New York, 1968.

BRINKLEY, GEORGE A. *The Volunteer Army and Allied Intervention in South Russia 1917-1921.* Notre Dame, 1966.

BROWDER, R. P. AND KERENSKY, A. F. (ed.) *The Russian Provisional Government 1917. Documents.* Stanford, 1961.

BRUNOVSKY, V. *The Methods of the O.G.P.U.* London and New York, 1931.

BRUSSILOV, GENERAL, A. A. *A Soldier's Note-Book 1914-1918.* London, 1930. New York, 1931.

BUCHAN, JOHN (ed.) *The Baltic States.* London, 1923.

BUCHANAN, SIR GEORGE. *My Mission to Russia.* London and Boston, 1923.

BUDBERG, ALEKSEY. *Dnevnik belogvardeitsa.* Leningrad, 1929.

BUKHARIN, N. AND PREOBRAZHENSKY, E. *The A.B.C. of Communism.* Trans. E. and C. Paul. London, 1922.

BUNYAN, JAMES. *Intervention, Civil War, and Communism in Russia. April-December 1918. Documents and Materials.* Baltimore, 1936.

CALWELL, MAJOR-GENERAL SIR C. E. *Field Marshal Sir Henry Wilson. Bart. His Life and Diaries.* London, 1927.

CARR, E. H. *The Russian Revolution 1917-1923.* London and New York, 1950-52.

CARSTEN, F. L. *The Reichswehr and Politics 1917-1933.* Oxford and New York, 1966.

CHAMBERLIN, W. H. *The Russian Revolution 1917-1921.* New York, 1935.

CHARQUES, RICHARD. *The Twilight of Imperial Russia.* Oxford, 1938.

CHILDERS, ERSKINE. *War and the Arme Blanche.* London, 1910.

CHURCHILL, THE RT. HON. WINSTON S. *The World Crisis; The Aftermath.* London and New York, 1929.

—— *Great Contemporaries.* London and New York, 1937.

COATES, W. P. AND ZELDA K. *Armed Intervention in Russia 1918-1922.* London and New York, 1935.

CMD. 8 (Russia No. I). *A Collection of Reports on Bolshevism in Russia.* London, 1919.

CMD. 772 (Army). *A Statement of Expenditure on Naval and Military Operations in Russia.* London, 1920.

CMD. 818 (Army). *The Evacuation of North Russia.* London, 1920.

CONNELL, JOHN. *Wavell, Scholar and Soldier.* London, 1964. New York, 1965.

DANILOV, GENERAL Y. *La Russie dans la Guerre Mondiale.* Paris, 1927.

DEGRAS, JANE (ed.). *Soviet Documents on Foreign Policy 1917-1924.* London, 1951.

DENIKIN, GENERAL A. I. *Ocherki russkoy smuty.* Paris-Berlin, 1921-26.

—— *The Russian Turmoil.* London and New York, n.d. (An abridged translation of vol. I. of the above.)

—— *The White Army.* Trans. Catherine Zvegintsov. London, 1930. (A drastically shortened version of the remainder.)

DENISOV, GENERAL S. V. *Zapiski: grazhdanskaya voyna na yuge Rossii.* Constantinople, 1922.

DEUTSCHER, ISAAC. *The Prophet Armed: Trotsky, 1879-1921.* New York, 1954.

—— *Stalin: A Political Biography.* 2nd edn. London and New York, 1967.

DUKES, SIR PAUL. *The Story of S.T.25.* London, 1938.

DURANTY, WALTER. *I Write as I Please.* New York, 1935. Revised Edn. London, 1937.

EFREMOFF, I. N. *The Cossacks of the Don*. Paris, 1919.

EHRENBURG, ILYA. *First Years of Revolution*. Trans. Bostock and Kapp. London, 1962.

ELLIS, C. H. *The Trans-Caspian Episode 1918-1919*. London, 1963, *British Intervention in Trans-Caspia* (American edition of the above). Stanford, Calif., 1963.

ERICKSON, JOHN. *The Soviet High Command*. London and New York, 1962.

FAINSOD, MERLE. *How Russia is Ruled*. Cambridge, Mass., 1955.

FEDOTOFF-WHITE, DMITRI. *The Growth of the Red Army*. Princeton, 1944.

FEDOTOFF-WHITE, G. *Survival through War and Revolution*. London and Philadelphia, 1939.

FISCHER, FRITZ. *Germany's Aims in the First World War*. London, 1967.

FISCHER, LOUIS. *The Soviets in World Affairs*. London and New York, 1930.

FLEMING, PETER. *The Fate of Admiral Kolchak*. London and New York, 1963.

—— *One's Company*. London and New York, 1934.

FLORINSKY, MICHAEL T. *The End of the Russian Empire*. New Haven, 1931.

FOOTMAN, DAVID. *Civil War in Russia*. London, 1961. New York, 1962.

—— (ed.). *St Anthony's Papers. Soviet Affairs*, VI. London and New York, 1959.

FRANCIS, D. R. *Russia from the American Embassy*. New York, 1922.

FRUNZE, M. V. *Izbrannye proizvedeniya*. Ed. Dolgi and Shiryakin. Moscow, 1957.

GERMANOV, L. *K istorii chekhoslovatskovo nastupleniya v Sibiri*. Moscow, 1922.

GESSEN, I. V. (ed.). *Arkhiv russkoy revolyutsii*. Berlin, 1921-27.

GOLOVIN, GENERAL N. N. *The Russian Army in the World War*. New Haven, 1931.

—— *Voenne usiliya Rossii v mirovoy voyne*. Paris, 1939. (Russian version of the above with expansions.)

GOLTZ, GENERAL GRAF RÜDIGER VON DER. *Meine Sendung in Finnland und im Baltikum*. Leipzig, 1920.

GOLUBEV, A. (ed.) *Shturm Perekopa*. Moscow, 1938.

GORKY, M., MOLOTOV. V., VOROSHILOV, K., STALIN, J., etc. (ed). *Istoriya grazhdanskoy voyny v S.S.S.R.* Moscow, 1936.

GOUGH, GENERAL SIR HERBERT. *Soldiering On*. London, 1954.

GOURKO, GENERAL VASSILY. *Russia in 1914-1917*. London, 1918.

GRAVES, MAJOR-GENERAL WILLIAM S. *America's Siberian Adventure 1918-1920*. New York, 1931.

GRONDIJS, L. H. *La Guerre en Russie et en Sibérie*. Paris, 1926.

GUINS, G. K. *Sibir, soyuzniki i Kolchak*. Peking, 1921.

HALLIDAY, E. M. *The Ignorant Armies*. London, 1961.

HANBURY-WILLIAMS, MAJOR-GENERAL SIR JOHN. *The Emperor Nicholas II as I Knew Him*. London, 1922.

HANNULA, LT.-COLONEL J. O. *Finland's War of Independence*. London, 1939.

HERZEN, ALEXANDER. *Sobrannye sochineniya*. Moscow, 1954-66.

—— *My Past and My Thoughts*. Trans. Constance Garnett; revised Humphrey Higgins. London, 1968.

Hetman Skoropadsky. (Ukrainian Press Bureau.) Kiev, 1918.

HINDENBURG, FIELD-MARSHAL VON. *Out of My Life*. London, 1920.

HINDUS, MAURICE. *The Cossacks*. London, 1946.

HODGES, PHELPS. *Britmis*. London, 1931.

HODGSON, J. E. *With Denikin's Armies*. London, 1932.

HOFFMAN, MAJOR-GENERAL MAX. *War Diaries and Other Papers*. London, 1929.

IGNATEV, GENERAL A. A. *Pyatdesyat let v stroyu*. Moscow, 1955.

IRONSIDE, FIELD-MARSHAL LORD EDMUND. *Archangel 1918-1919*. London, 1953.

JACKSON, J. HAMPDEN. *Finland*. London and New York, 1938.

—— *Estonia*. London, 1941.

JANIN, GENERAL MAURICE. *Ma Mission en Sibérie 1918-1920*. Paris, 1933.

JEANNERET, P. *En Campagne contre les Bolshéviques*. Lausanne, 1919.

KALEDIN, VICTOR. *K. 14-O.M.66. Adventures of a Double Spy*. London, 1934.

—— *High Treason: Four Major Cases of the St Petersburg Personal Court Branch*. London, 1936.

KALININ, I. M. *Pod znamenem Vrangelya*. Leningrad, 1925.

—— *Russkaya Vandeya*. Moscow, 1926.

KAMYSHANSKI, B. *I Am a Cossack*. London, 1934.

KARAEV, G. N. *V boyakh za Petrograd*. Moscow, 1951.

KARAMZIN, NICHOLAS. *Memoir on Ancient and Modern Russia*. Trans. Richard Pipes. Cambridge, Mass., 1959.

KATKOV, GEORGE. *Russia 1917: The February Revolution*. London and New York, 1967.

KENNAN, GEORGE F. *Soviet American Relations 1917-1920*. I. *Russia Leaves the War*. London and New York, 1956. II. *The Decision to Intervene*. London and Princeton, 1958.

—— *Russia and the West under Lenin and Stalin*. New York, 1961.

KERENSKY, A. F. *The Prelude to Bolshevism: The Kornilov Rebellion*. London and New York, 1919.

—— *The Catastrophe*. London and New York, 1927.

—— WITH CAPTAIN BULYGIN. *The Murder of the Romanovs*. London and New York, 1935.

—— *Memoirs: Russia at History's Turning Point*. New York, 1965. London, 1966.

KNOX, MAJOR-GENERAL SIR ALFRED. *With the Russian Army 1914-1917*. London, 1921.

KOKOVTSOV, V. N. *Out of My Past*. Stanford, 1935.

KORF, BARON SERGEY. *The Constitution of the Cossacks*. Paris, 1919.

KOROSTOVETZ, V. K. *Lenin im Hause der Väter*. Berlin, 1928.

—— *The Rebirth of Poland*. London, 1928.

KOURNAKOFF, SERGEY. *Savage Squadrons*. London and Boston, 1936.

KRACHTOVIL, J. *Česta Revoluče*. Prague, 1928.

KUTEPOV, GENERAL A. P., *Sbornik statey*. Paris, 1934.

LA CHESNAIS, P. G. *The Defence of the Cossacks against Bolshevism*. Paris, 1919.

—— *La Guerre Civile en Finlande*. Paris, 1919.

LAMPE, A. A. VON (ed). *Beloe delo*. Berlin, 1926-28.

LENIN, V. I. *Sochineniya*. 4th edn. Moscow, 1940-51.

LIDDELL-HART, CAPTAIN B. H. (ed.) *The Soviet Army*. London, 1956.

LITTAUER, VLADIMIR. *Russian Hussar*. London, 1965.

LLOYD GEORGE, DAVID. *War Memoirs*. London and Boston, 1933-36.

LOCKHART, R. H. BRUCE. *Memoirs of a British Agent*. London, 1932.

LUDENDORFF, GENERAL ERICH. *My War Memoirs 1914-1918*. London, 1919.

LUKOMSKY, GENERAL A. *Vospominaniya*. Berlin, 1922.

—— *Memoirs of the Russian Revolution*. Trans. Mrs Vitali. London, 1922. (An abridged version of the above.)

MANNERHEIM, FIELD-MARSHAL BARON GUSTAV. *Memoirs*. Trans. Count Eric Lewenhaupt. London, 1953.

MANNING, CLARENCE A. *The Siberian Fiasco*. New York, 1952.

MASARYK, T. G. *Svetova Revoluče*. Prague, 1926.

MAYNARD, SIR C. *The Murmansk Venture*. London, 1928.

MCCULLAGH, CAPTAIN FRANCIS. *A Prisoner of the Reds*. London, 1921.

MELGUNOV, S. P. *Tragediya Admirala Kolchaka*. Belgrade, 1931.

NAIDA, S. F. (ed.) *Istoriya grazhdanskoy voyny v S.S.S.R.* Moscow, 1959.

NEMIROVICH-DANCHENKO, G. *V Krymu pri Vrangele*. Berlin, 1922.

NEMIROVICH-DANCHENKO, V. I. *Personal Reminiscences of General Skobeleff*. Trans. E. A. Brayley Hodgetts. London, 1884.

NEWBOLT, SIR HENRY. *History of the Great War: Naval Operations*, vol. V. London and New York, 1931.

OBERLÄNDER, ERWIN. 'The All-Russian Fascist Party', *Journal of Contemporary History*, vol. 1, no. 1. London, 1966.

PALÉOLOGUE, MAURICE. *La Russie des Tsars pendant la Grande Guerre*. Paris, 1921-22.

Papers Relating to the Foreign Relations of the United States: Russia 1918-1920. Washington, 1931-34.

PARES, SIR BERNARD. *My Russian Memoirs*. London, 1931.

—— *The Fall of the Russian Monarchy*. London and New York, 1939.

PAUSTOVSKY, KONSTANTIN. *In That Dawn*. Trans. Harari and Duncan. London, 1967.

PILSUDSKI, MARSHAL JOSEPH. *Joseph Pilsudski: The Memoirs of a Polish Revolutionary and Soldier*. London, 1931.

—— *Rok 1920*. London, 1941.

PIPES, RICHARD. *The Formation of the Soviet Union: Communism and Nationalism 1917-1923*. Cambridge, Mass., 1964.

—— (ed.). *Revolutionary Russia*. Cambridge, Mass., 1968.

PRICE, MORGAN PHILLIPS. *War and Revolution*. London, 1918.

PRIDHAM, VICE-ADMIRAL SIR FRANCIS. *Close of a Dynasty*. London, 1956.

Puty revolyutsii. Berlin, 1923.

RANSOME, ARTHUR. *Six Weeks in Russia in 1919*. London, 1919.

REED, JOHN. *Ten Days that Shook the World*. London and New York, 1961.

RESHETAR, J. S. *The Ukrainian Revolution 1917-1920*. Princeton, 1952.

RINTALA, MARVIN. *Three Generations: The Extreme Right in Finnish Politics*. Bloomington, Indiana, 1962.

RODZYANKO, GENERAL ALEXANDER. *Vospominaniya o Severo-Zapadnoy Armii*. Berlin, 1920.

RODZYANKO, COLONEL PAUL. *Tattered Banners*. London and New York, 1938.

—— *Mannerheim*. London, 1940.

ROSENBERG, WILLIAM G. *A. I. Denikin and the Anti-Bolshevik Movement in South Russia*. Amherst, 1961.

RUHL, ARTHUR. *New Masters of the Baltic*. New York, 1921.

SALOMON, E. VON. *The Outlaws*. London, 1931.

SAVCHENKO, E. *Les Insurgés du Kouban*. Paris, 1929.

SAVINKOV, BORIS. *K delu Kornilova*. Paris, 1919.

—— *Memoirs of a Terrorist*. New York, 1921.

SAZONOV, S. D. *Fateful Years 1909-1926*. London and New York, 1928.

SCHAPIRO, LEONARD. *The Origins of the Communist Autocracy*. London, 1955. New York, 1956.

—— AND REDDAWAY, P. (ed.) *Lenin: The Man, the Theorist, the Leader. A Reappraisal*. London and New York, 1967.

SERGE, VICTOR. *Memoirs of a Revolutionary 1901-1940*. London and New York, 1967.

SETON-WATSON, G. H. N. *The Decline of Imperial Russia*. London and New York, 1952.

SIKORSKI, GENERAL W. *La Campagne Polono-Russe de 1920*. Trad. M. Larcher. Pref. Maréchal Foch. Paris, 1928.

SMITH, C. JAY. *Finland and the Russian Revolution 1917-1922*. Athens, Georgia, 1958.

SOKOLOV, NICHOLAS. *Enquête Judiciare sur l'Assassinat de la Famille Impériale Russe*. Paris, 1924.

SOKOLOVSKY, VASILY O. (ed.) *Military Strategy: Soviet Doctrine and Concepts*. London, 1965.

SOLDOVNIKOV, BORIS. *Sibirskiya avantyury i General Gajda*. Prague, n.d.

SOROKIN, PITIRIM. *Leaves from a Russian Diary*. London, 1925.

—— *Leaves from a Russian Diary—And Forty Years After*. Boston, 1950.

SOUTAR, ANDREW. *With Ironside in North Russia*. London, 1940.

STALIN, J. *Sochineniya*. Moscow, 1949-52.

STANKEVICH, V. B. *Vospominaniya 1914-1919*. Berlin, 1920.

STEWART, GEORGE. *The White Armies of Russia*. New York, 1933.

STRAKHOVSKY, LEONID I. *Intervention at Archangel*. Princeton, 1940.

—— 'Was there a Kornilov Revolt?—A Reappraisal of the Evidence', *Slavonic and E. European Review*, vol. XXXIII, No. 81, 1955.

STRUVE, P. B. *Razmyshleniya o russkoy revolyutsii*. Sofia, 1921.

SUKHANOV, N. N. *The Russian Revolution 1917.* Ed. and trans. Joel Carmichael. London and New York, 1955.

SUVORIN, A. *Pokhod Kornilova.* Rostov, 1919.

SWETTENHAM, JOHN. *Allied Intervention in Russia 1918-1919.* London, 1967.

TALLENTS, SIR STEPHEN. *Man and Boy.* London, 1943.

TROTSKY, LEON. *Kak vooruzhalas revolyutsiya.* Moscow, 1923-25.

—— *My Life: The Rise and Fall of a Dictator.* London and New York, 1930.

—— *A History of the Russian Revolution.* Trans. Max Eastman, London, 1965.

—— *Leon Trotsky's Diary in Exile. 1935.* Cambridge, Mass., 1958. London, 1959.

—— *Stalin.* Ed. and trans. Charles Malamuth. New edn. New York, 1967. London, 1968.

—— *The Trotsky Papers.* Ed. Jan J. Meijer. The Hague, 1964.

TUKHACHEVSKY, MARSHAL M. *Voyna klassov.* Moscow, 1921.

ULLMAN, RICHARD H. *Anglo-Soviet Relations 1917-1921.* I. *Intervention and the War.* Princeton, 1961. II. *Britain and the Russian Civil War.* Princeton, 1968.

VARNECK, ELENA AND FISHER, H. H. (ed.) *The Testimony of Kolchak and other Siberian Materials.* Stanford, 1935.

VINING, MAJOR L. E. *Held by the Bolsheviks.* London, 1924.

VOLINE, V. M. *La Révolution Inconnue 1917-1924. Documentation inédite sur la Révolution Russe.* Paris, 1947.

VOLKONSKY, PRINCE PETER. *The Volunteer Army of Alexeev and Denikin.* London, 1919.

VOLKONSKY, PRINCESS SONIA. *The Way of Bitterness: Soviet Russia 1920.* London, 1931.

VOROSHILOV, K. E. *Stalin and the Armed Forces of the U.S.S.R.* Eng. edn. Moscow, 1951.

VULLIAMY, C. E. (ed.) *The Red Archives: Russian State Papers and other Documents 1915-1918.* London, 1929.

WALSH, DR EDMUND, S.J. *The Fall of the Russian Empire.* Boston, 1928. London, 1929.

WASHBURN, STANLEY. *Field Notes from the Russian Front.* London, 1915.

—— *Victory in Defeat.* London, 1916.

—— *The Russian Advance.* London, 1917.

WARD, COLONEL JOHN. *With the 'Die-Hards' in Siberia*. London, 1920.

WARNER, OLIVER. *Marshal Mannerheim and the Finns*. London, 1967.

WHEELER-BENNETT, J. W. *The Forgotten Peace: Brest Litovsk, March 1918*. London, 1938. New York, 1939.

WOLLENBERG, E. *The Red Army*. London, 1942.

WOODWARD, E. L. AND BUTLER, R. (ed.) *Documents on British Foreign Policy 1919-1939*. First Series. London, 1947-49.

WRANGEL, COUNT GUSTAV. *The Cavalry in the Russo-Japanese War*. Trans. Lieut. J. Montgomery. London, 1907. New York 1930.

WRANGEL, GENERAL BARON P. N. *Memoirs*. Trans. Sophie Goulston. London. (This is a shortened version of Wrangel's *Zapiski* to be found in von Lampe (*q.v.*), vols V and VI.) *Always with Honour*. (American edition of the above.) New York, n.d.

XDIAS, J. *L'Intervention Française en Russie 1918-1919*. Paris, 1927.

YAROSLAVSKY, E. *Krasnaya Armiya*. Moscow, 1919.

ZEMAN, Z. A. B. *Germany and the Revolution in Russia*. Oxford and New York, 1958.
—— *The Break-Up of the Hapsburg Empire 1914-1918*. London and New York, 1961.

Index

Kultuk, 167
Kursk, 328, 329, 331, 332-3, 337
Kutepov, Gen. A. P., 31, 109, 279, 352, 369, 373, 375-6, 378-83; fate of, 389

Lagutin, 106
Land reforms, 158-9, 249-50, 284-5, 370
Lapps, 126
Latvia, 231, 299, 303, 316
Laurila, Matti, 137
Lebedev, Col. V. I., 48, 72, 75, 263, 298
Lenin, V. I., fears failure of revolution, xvii, xviii; 5, 39, 48-50, 58, 91, 94, 141, 161, 183, 260, 292, 296, 319, 322, 385; & Kornilov 'revolt', 77; & murder of Romanovs, 165-7; & Murmansk, 198; & military affairs, 233-4
Lettish riflemen, 108, 166
Leuchtenberg, Duke of, 160
Liberals, 35, 37, 47, 67, 72
Lieven, Prince, 318
Lithuania, 231, 299
Lloyd George, David, 205, 295, 335-6, 367
Lockhart, R. H. Bruce, 232
Löfström, Maj.-Gen. E. B., 148
Lomonsov, Maj.-Gen. Y. V., 32
Ludendorff, Field-Marshal E. von, 143
Luga, 81-2
Lukomsky, Gen. A. S., 88, 95, 110, 186, 249, 340; & Kornilov 'revolt', 79, 85-6
Lvov, Prince G. E., 20, 27, 41; resigns as premier, 59
Lvov, V. N. (Procurator of the Holy Synod), 73-9

Makarenko, 334
Makhno, Nestor, 254, 278-9, 291, 326-327, 364-5; death, 391
Maklakov, V. A., 28
Mamontov, Gen. K. K., 157, 292-3, 332, 338
Manchuli, 210
Manchuria, 209-13
Manner, K. A., 147, 149

Mannerheim, Count Carl Eric, 127
Mannerheim, General Baron Carl Gustav Emil (1867-1951), xvii, 48, 96, 124, 125-53, 173; origins, 125-8; career, 127-30; & revolution, 129-30; return to Finland, 129-30; & White movement in, 131-4; C-in-C, 135; & finance, 135; establishes base, 136-40; character, 137-8; strategy, 139; & Jaegers, 142; mounts offensive, 143; opposes intervention, 143; divides forces, 148; attacks Wiborg, 149; victory, 151-3; threat to Soviets, 231; as Regent, 269-70, 296; & Yudenich, 304, 314, 320; death, 391-2
Manych, river, 251-2, 258-60, 271-3, 348
Markov, Gen. S. L., 84, 115, 121-2; death, 178-9
Marsh, Brig.-Gen. G. F., 304
Martel, Comte de, 381
Marushevsky, Gen. V. V., 203
Marx, Karl, xviii, 386
Masaryk, T. G., 160-1
Maximov, Capt., 350
May-Maevsky, Gen. V. Z., 251, 254, 255-6, 273, 277, 279, 282, 325, 328, 330; collapse of, 333, 337
Melin, Capt., 146
Mensheviks, 40-1, 313, 345
Michael Alexandrovich, Grand Duke, 24, 31, 35, 41, 66, 129; refuses throne, 36
Middlesex reg., 171, 219, 221
Mikhailovsky artillery school, 62
Mikkeli (St Michel), 148
Military Revolutionary Committee (Bolshevik), 81, 90
Military Soviet, Supreme, 117-18, 161
Miller, General E. K., 203-4, 207-8, 262, 347; fate of, 389-90
Milner Mission (1916), 47
Milyukov, P. N., 99, 194
Ministry of War, 8, 14, 44, 59, 64, 67, 175
Mironov, 195
Mogilev, 19, 24, 28-35, 42, 48-9, 57, 60, 66-7, 74, 76, 78, 82-5, 87-9, 94, 109
Mogilev Conference (Officers' Congress), 49, 51-5